Heresy and Obedience in Tridentine Italy:
Cardinal Pole and the Counter Reformation

HERESY AND OBEDIENCE IN TRIDENTINE ITALY : CARDINAL POLE AND THE COUNTER REFORMATION

DERMOT FENLON , *Fellow and Tutor of Gonville and Caius College, Cambridge, and University Assistant Lecturer in History*

CAMBRIDGE *at the University Press* 1972

Published by the Syndics of the Cambridge University Press
Bentley House, 200 Euston Road, London NW1 2DB
American Branch: 32 East 57th Street, New York, N.Y. 10022

Library of Congress Catalogue Card Number: 72–87177

ISBN: 0 521 20005 9

Printed in Great Britain by Alden & Mowbray Ltd
at the Alden Press, Oxford

TO MY MOTHER AND FATHER

Contents

Preface

Reginald Pole is a figure who slips into two overlapping historical perspectives. The first opens upon the history of Tudor England, the second upon that of the European Counter Reformation. In England, Henry VIII initiated two conflicting movements in the religious history of his country. The first began with his book on the sacraments and his attack on the Reformation, in the service of which he enlisted More and Fisher. The second began with his repudiation of papal jurisdiction, in the course of which he executed, among others, More and Fisher. The protagonists of the first movement became the victims of the second: they found a hagiographer in Reginald Pole.

Pole's *Defence of the Unity of the Church*, composed in Italy, marks the transition from the English involvement with the Counter Reformation to what eventually became the English recusant tradition.[1] Nearly twenty years after it was written Pole returned to England, a Cardinal of the Church of Rome, to reconnect the Counter Reformation with the Tudor monarchy and link it with the European Catholic revival. Time and the succession of the Tudor dynasty were against him. His proposals for the reform of the English Church (partly inspired by the example of Verona in the 1530s), were adapted posthumously in the Milan of Borromeo, and from there transmitted to the dioceses of Northern Europe.

This is one perspective to which Pole belongs. The other, upon which it depends for its completion, opens upon Pole's introduction to certain Italian religious circles in the years immediately preceding the Council of Trent: it concludes with the collapse of the eventful, but neglected movement in the Catholic Church to avert the Counter Reformation. The object of this movement was to establish reunion with the Protestants

[1] *Pro ecclesiasticae unitatis defensione, libri quatuor* (Rome, *c.* 1537). B. H. G. Wormald, 'The Historiography of the English Reformation', *Historical Studies: Papers read to the first conference of Irish historians*, ed. T. W. Moody and T. D. Williams, I (London, 1958), 50–8, remarks acutely on the place of Pole.

of Northern Europe, thereby preserving for the Church the growing number of their adherents in the Italian cities. This book examines Pole's emergence as the figurehead of that movement, culminating in his experience of defeat at the Council of Trent, and concluding in the resultant recriminations from Italian Protestants and Catholics, which surrounded his return to England as Papal Legate. The realisation that reunion was intrinsically unattainable marked the moment of deliverance for the Counter Reformation: a process crystallised and reflected in Pole's individual experience. His return to England coincided with the aftermath of his eirenic hopes; he did not live to see the eventual translation of the Counter Reformation into the pastoral revival in the Catholic Church to which his own efforts had in fact contributed.

But this is not a biography of Pole. It is a study of the influence of the Reformation on the Catholic Church, in so far as that influence can be discerned in the history of Pole and the Italian circles among which he moved, encompassing the world of Valdés and Vergerio, Carnesecchi, Flaminio and Contarini: a world divided between the claims of heresy and obedience. Protestantism, historically, was a revolt against the Church of Rome. It refused obedience; it called for separation. For that separation, the Catholic Church of the Renaissance bears her burden of responsibility, as Pole so forcefully reminded the assembled fathers at the Council of Trent. It was at Trent that the Catholic revival unequivocally assumed the form of Counter Reformation, issuing in a period which saw the completion of a long movement of renewal. But a caesura occurred between the completion of that movement and one of its most important antecedents. The call for a laity conversant with Scripture was the common point of departure historically obscured in the contested issues of Reformation and Counter Reformation. Luther, in the course of revolt, gave the vernacular Bible to the laity. The Church of the Counter Reformation refused that step, and refused to recognise the spirituality which her enemies derived from it. The profoundly Christian content of Protestant spirituality is among the most moving aspects of that tragedy which caused, and continues to underly, the separation of Christians. It is part of a heritage indispensable to the Christian tradition.

To have finished a book is to be aware of debts and a certain measure of defeat. The debts are easier to recount. The origins of this book lie with my friends and teachers in University College Dublin and in Cambridge. To Peterhouse I owe a debt of special gratitude for admitting me as a research student and enabling me to pursue my studies without financial hardship. To the Master and Fellows of Gonville and Caius College I wish to express my signal thanks for conferring upon me the privilege of admission to their own number, initially as a research fellow; an honour for which this book can be no more than a most imperfect expression of gratitude. My cordial thanks are due to Mgr Hubert Jedin, Professor Heinrich Lutz, Professor J. J. Scarisbrick, Professor J. I. Tellechea Idigoras, Professor George Parks and Fr Joseph Crehan, S.J., for assistance in the early stages of the work; to the late Mr Alfred Ehrman and his wife for permission to examine an unpublished inventory of Pole's books, now in the possession of New College Oxford; to Dr R. H. Pogson for kindly allowing me to consult his forthcoming work on Pole's administration of the Church in England; to Fr Bernard Franck, for permission to consult an unpublished essay which set me thinking afresh about problems which were still obscure; to Dr Christiane Thomas, of the Austrian State Archives, Vienna, for unstinting and generous assistance; to Dr Dominic Baker-Smith, for allowing me to draw upon his extensive knowledge of questions which have preoccupied us both; to Mr Nicholas Reed and Dr Alan Griffin, who wrestled with the obscurities of medieval latin; to Mr G. C. Morris, a generous benefactor and friend; to Dr J. K. McConica, Fr Martin Trimpe, Rev. Breifne Walker and Mrs Judith Neri, who provided valuable criticism of an earlier draft of this work, in its original form of a Ph.D. dissertation; to Professor A. G. Dickens and Dr Philip McNair, who examined it gently and let it pass; to Professor Charles Brink, who came to my rescue at a difficult moment; to Mr Michael Hendy and Mr Robert Williams for indispensable assistance; to Dr Denis O'Brien, for helpfully allowing me to waste his time; to Mr and Mrs Owen Grazebrook, for expansive hospitality; to my typists, Mrs Bass, Mrs Pledger and Mrs Barrett, for their painstaking achievements in deciphering an often cryptic text and combating a daunting timetable.

My particular thanks are due also to the personnel of the University Library, Cambridge; the British Museum; the Public Record Office; the Bodleian Library; the Austrian State Archives; the Vatican Library; the Vatican Archives; the Biblioteca Nazionale, Naples; the Biblioteca Comunale, Viterbo; the Biblioteca Palatina, Parma; and the other libraries and archives into which I found my way during the course of my research and where I repeatedly benefited from the special generosity and resourcefulness, not to say friendliness, which seems to be a universal characteristic of librarians and archivists.

Finally, there are friends whom I can never adequately thank: my supervisor, Professor G. R. Elton, whose encouragement and guidance, cautions, queries and corrections, combined with monumental patience and humour, supported me, against the odds, through an education in research, and much more than research; his wife Sheila Lambert, who generally took my side when it counted; Patrick and Ruth Cosgrave, Neasa McErlaine, James McGuire, and Hans and Hildegard Modlmayr, who helped and sustained me, through good and bad times, more than they will ever realise; to my brother Frank and his wife Alice; and (first and last) my parents, who stood by tactfully reminding me that I kept talking about a book, and to whom at last it is now gratefully dedicated.

One's defeats, like one's debts, are entirely personal. The emotions which went into this book, and the mistakes in it, are all my own. I might have written a better book; but as my mother remarked when I explained the problem, Pole was a man who encountered many disappointments in his own lifetime, and he is unlikely to be much bothered by anything that can happen now.

Gonville and Caius College, Cambridge   D.F.
24 March 1972, Eve of the Annunciation
and Dedication Day of the College

Abbreviations

Carteggio	E. Ferrero and G. Muller, *Carteggio di Vittoria Colonna*
'Compendio'	C. Corviersi, 'Compendio di processi del Santo Uffizio di Roma'
Council	H. Jedin, *A History of the Council of Trent*, vols. I, II
C.S.P.S.	*Calendar of State Papers, Spanish*
C.S.P.V.	*Calendar of State Papers, Venetian*
C.T.	*Concilium Tridentinum: Diariorum, Actorum, Epistolarum, Tractatuum Nova Collectio*
Epistolae	*Epistolae Reginaldi Poli S.R.E. Cardinalis et Aliorum ad Ipsum*
L.P.	*Letters and Papers, Foreign and Domestic, of the Reign of Henry VIII*
N.C.M.H.	*New Cambridge Modern History*
O.S.V.	Österreichisches Staatsarchiv, Vienna
'Processo'	G. Manzoni (ed.), 'Estratto del processo di Mons. Pietro Carnesecchi'

NOTE: I have retained the original spelling, punctuation and accentation in all citation from original sources. This sometimes makes for eccentricity, but so do the originals.

CHAPTER ONE

The movement 'ad fontes'
and the
outbreak of Reformation

At the close of the middle ages the condition of the Church was nowhere considered to be healthy. A papacy preoccupied with politics and taxation, magnificent in everything except religion; an absentee episcopate; an ignorant clergy; an uninstructed laity; a widespread indifference to the spirit of Christianity beneath the forms of established, though sometimes irregular observance: everything had combined to reduce the spiritual life of Christendom to a state not far removed from bankruptcy.[1]

But to those who looked upon her with minds still informed by faith, the Church had not lost the imprint of her divine founder. The quest for and discovery of His presence within her, and its mediation to her members in the world at large, became increasingly a theme of fervent spiritual endeavour, in proportion to the very obstacles which emerged to oppose it. In Northern Europe, the mystical piety of the later middle ages brought a perceptible quickening of spiritual life: in Germany, issuing from the school of Tauler and his followers; in the Low Countries, from the monastery of Windesheim which, through its foundations, helped to spread abroad the spirituality of the *devotio moderna*.[2] In Italy too, the humanism of the late Quattrocento

[1] Bankruptcy is not always the same as intent to defraud. The prevailing state was one of mediocrity, not of wholesale iniquity. On the pre-reformation Church the following may be consulted: J. Toussaert, *Le sentiment religieux en Flandre à la fin du Moyen Age* (Paris, 1963); H. Lortz, *The Reformation in Germany* (2 vols., London, 1968), I, 54–77; D. Knowles, *The Religious Orders in England*, III, *The Tudor Age* (Cambridge, 1959); P. Heath, *The English Parish Clergy on the Eve of the Reformation* (London and Toronto, 1969); M. Bowker, *The Secular Clergy in the Diocese of Lincoln* (Cambridge, 1968).

[2] R. R. Post, *The Modern Devotion: confrontation with Reformation and Humanism* (Leiden, 1968).

turned in a direction favourable to renewal. The idea arose that Christianity might yet be revived by a return 'ad fontes' – to the Bible and the Fathers of the Church. The critical achievement of Lorenzo Valla, in approaching the text of Scripture with a new philological precision, moved the imagination of other humanists – in particular, of Marsilio Ficino and Pico della Mirandola – to attempt a new kind of synthesis between Christianity and classical antiquity. Plato was introduced as the gateway to St Paul: Christianity became the crown of human dignity, the source and culmination of inner tranquillity.[1]

But the influence of these movements was restricted. Christianity, if it were to be again effective, demanded an expression at once more vigorous and universal. The spirituality of the *devotio moderna* could never aspire to be a substitute for pastoral renewal. The scriptural humanism of Ficino was for scholars. In the end, Pico himself seems to have recognised that it was such; he turned from the Florentine Academy to Savonarola. But Savonarola foundered on the reef of politics.[2] In Florence – a microcosm, almost, of the world beyond – mind and action were turned back helplessly upon themselves. If the key to renewal were indeed to be found in the return 'ad fontes' and the recovery of the Word in its original integrity, the manner in which that recovery could be transmitted to a wider audience remained a mystery. Philology in itself could not lead to the regeneration of the Christian people. Philology therefore went in search of a new mode of exegesis.

At the end of the fifteenth century the schools of Oxford and Paris began to develop an approach to the epistles of St Paul which was to achieve considerable influence. At Oxford especially, the efforts of John Colet were devoted to a direct textual examination of St Paul; and in this task he was assisted by the philological expertise which he had acquired in Italy.[3] In the Pauline epistles, with their stark contrast between the wisdom of the intellect and

[1] R. Cessi, 'Paolinismo preluterano', *Rendiconti dell' Academia nazionale dei Lincei* (Cl. di sc. mor. Sto. e filol.) ser. VIII, vol. XII (1957), 3–30, traces important links between Italian humanism and the revival of interest in St Paul.

[2] R. de Maio, *Savonarola e la Curia Romana* (Rome, 1969).

[3] Cessi, 'Paolinismo preluterano', pp. 19ff. Cf. also F. Seebohm, *The Oxford*

the communication of the Spirit, with their emphasis upon the personal encounter of the soul with Christ and the liberation of mankind from formalism, Colet found the antidote to the cerebral configurations of nominalist theology and of Platonic humanism. Colet's influence, perpetuated at Magdalen in the teaching of William Latimer and Thomas Linacre, was extended throughout Europe by a writer of outstanding quality: in the person of Erasmus, the new approach to Scripture found a propagandist reared in the spirit of the *devotio moderna* and nourished upon the humanism of antiquity. Henceforth, the epistles of St Paul became the texts which, more than any other, released the religious energies of the new century.

In 1503 Erasmus published his *Enchiridion Militis Christiani*, the first of a series of works outlining the programme of the new theology. Firmly based upon the inspiration of Scripture, and in particular, upon the teaching of St Paul, his writings were designed to provide a simple instrument of interior regeneration, no less than a means of collective renewal in the life of Christianity. Erasmus, however, was not Colet: at his hands St Paul lost some of his more drastic qualities, his immediacy and uncompromising fervour. The wisdom of Christ, revealed in the pages of the Bible, was to be accessible to every Christian: the unlettered woman would attend to Scripture, and be familar with the epistles of St Paul; the ploughman in his tasks, the weaver, the traveller – all alike would meditate upon the gospels, and be enriched with the philosophy of Christ.[1] It is this expression, *philosophia Christi*, 'a phrase rich with patristic overtones, signifying a life of wisdom entirely consecrated to God',[2] which contains the essence of Erasmus: a phrase too, which suggests the limitations of an approach never likely to arouse much popular response. To espouse in all things restraint and moderation, to cultivate an unimpassioned equipoise – these were his most cherished mental

Reformers (3rd edition, London, 1887), and S. Jayne, *John Colet and Marsilio Ficino* (Oxford, 1963).
   [1] Cessi, 'Paolinismo preluterano', p. 28.
   [2] J. K. McConica, *English Humanists and Reformation Politics* (Oxford, 1965), p. 15. An excellent account of Erasmianism appears in pp. 13–43.

habits: they had their origin in the study, and their appeal, inevitably, was to the educated.

Nevertheless, his influence was immense. It is probably not an exaggeration to state that in the first two decades of the sixteenth century Erasmus gradually captured the intellectual élite of Europe. The originality of his approach – that which constituted its appeal – lay in a conception of the Christian life which depended, not on a series of external observances, but a sustained meditation on the gospels in a manner available to every Christian.[1] The direct reading of Scripture was to be the key to a personal experience of Chrisitanity, which would in turn result in a renewal of the Church at large.

The theology advanced by Erasmus was a matter of the heart and of the emotions, rather than of argument:[2] a spiritual eloquence which drew its warmth from the living breath of Scripture, and its powers of expression from the literature of classical antiquity and the Fathers. It is not surprising that the humanists of Europe, contemptuous of scholastic thought and impatient with the decadence of ecclesiastical life, should have turned enthusiastically to the new critique of Christianity and society which he provided. Nor is it any less surprising that the theologians of the Sorbonne should have taken profound umbrage. Not only did Erasmus prove himself to be a gifted satirist at their expense: there was also in his thought an aversion to definition and conceptual exactitude, which seemed to threaten the intellectual stability of theology, and hence of orthodoxy itself. It was indeed, this intellectual delicacy, coupled with his own fastidious detachment from popular involvement, which in the long run sapped the Erasmian ideal of its content.

At the same time that Erasmus was embarking on his elaboration of the *philosophia Christi*, Lefèvre d'Etaples was devoting

[1] Cessi, 'Paolinismo preluterano', p. 23. The standard account of the influence of Erasmus is still M. Bataillon, *Erasme et l'Espagne* (Paris, 1937). Cf. also M. Mann, *Erasme et les debuts de la réforme francaise, 1517–1536* (Paris, 1933).

[2] 'At praecipuus Theologorum scopus est, sapienter enarrare Divinas litteras: de fide, non de frivolis questionibus rationem reddere: de pietate graviter atque efficaciter disserere: lacrymas excutere, ad coalestia inflammare animos.' *Opera*, v, Leyden, 1704, 83F–84A.

4

himself at Paris to a task which, similar in purpose, differed nonetheless in spirit from that of Erasmus. Lefèvre was no less concerned with the recovery of Scripture: but he looked to it for a hidden, spiritual meaning, accessible only to the mystically enlightened mind. His spirituality, moreover, was marked by an ascetical rigour and intensity of a kind alien to Erasmus. But even less was he a figure of commanding popular appeal. His examination of St Paul remained pre-eminently contemplative: it did not, despite his purpose, engage the field of action. Lefèvre's reflections on the Pauline texts led him to place more reliance upon grace, and to put greater emphasis on faith, than was common in the accepted view of Christianity. But it did not result in any widespread pastoral renewal.[1] The will to reform was unmistakeably present in Lefèvre: the means, all too evidently, were not.

Only in Spain did the reform of the Church receive the support of those in power. Under the direction of Cardinal Cisneros the religious orders, and especially the Franciscans, were recalled to fervour; the clergy were reminded of the true character of their vocation; the university of Alcalá was brought into existence for their education, and for the study and dissemination, through its printing press, of sacred literature. In 1517 there appeared at Alcalá the text of the Complutensian Bible, in Hebrew, Greek and Latin.[2] During these years of the Cisnerian reform there also developed, independently, a movement based on little reading groups in private homes, where the Bible was extolled as the foundation of interior life. Its adherents were known as the *alumbrados* or 'enlightened'; their spirituality, far from being internally consistent, was marked by differentiations which led some of them into ever closer relationship with the Church, while others moved quietly into the paths of private inspiration.[3] At the castle of Escalona, where the Marqués de Villena was patron to a little circle of *alumbrados*, the young Juan de Valdés, whose spiritual influence was to be so deeply felt in the

---

[1] Despite the intention of the Meaux reform group. Cf. Mann, *Erasme*, *passim* and Cessi, 'Paolinismo preluterano', pp. 26–7.

[2] For the Cisnerian reform, see Bataillon, *Erasme et l'Espagne*, and J. C. Nieto, *Juan de Valdés and the Origins of the Spanish and Italian Reformation* (Geneva, 1970).

[3] Nieto, *Juan de Valdés*, pp. 51–97.

religious history of the sixteenth century, first became familiar with the methods of Scriptural exegesis which, in a developed form, he was later to transmit throughout the whole of Europe.[1] We shall return to Valdés in a later chapter; for the moment, it is sufficient to note that by 1527, as a student at the University of Alcalá, he had acquired proficiency in Hebrew and Greek, and was known as a 'iuvenis divi Pauli studiosissimus'.[2] In Spain, as elsewhere in Europe, the study of St Paul was by now paramount among the younger humanists.

In Italy, too, where the influence of Valdés was eventually to be most keenly marked, the early years of the century witnessed a new flowering of religious foundations[3] and, in certain circles, a return to the spirit of St Paul. The most remarkable instance of this latter development occurred at Venice, where a group of young noblemen intent on personal sanctity dedicated themselves over a period of years to an exploration of the means available to their ambition. All were humanists; all had been educated at the University of Padua; all were dissatisfied with the sustenance provided by Platonic humanism. At length, in 1510 the leader of this group, Paolo Giustiniani, entered the hermitage of Camaldoli, near Arezzo. He had resolved upon contemplative life as the most effective form of spiritual action.[4] Shortly afterwards, he was followed into the monastery by almost all the members of his group. There was, however, one notable exception: Gasparo Contarini, at this time a young man of twenty-seven. Contarini's experiences in these months, his internal conflict, its resolution, and its ultimate consequences are vividly portrayed in a series of letters which he wrote to Giustiniani and his friends.[5]

[1] Nieto, *Juan de Valdés*, pp. 99–101. For the posthumous influence of Valdés, see D. Ricart, *Juan de Valdés y el pensamiento religioso europeo de los siglos XVI-XVII* (Mexico, 1958).

[2] J. N. Bakhuizen van den Brink, *Juan de Valdés réformateur en Espagne et en Italie* (Geneva, 1969), p. 16.

[3] A. Cistellini, *Figure della Riforma Pretridentina* (Brescia, 1948).

[4] J. Leclercq, *Un humaniste érémite: le bienheureux P. Giustiniani, 1476–1528* (Rome, 1951); also J. Leclercq, *Alone with God* (London, 1962) gives substantial extracts from Giustiniani's writings. Cf. also, F. Gilbert, 'Cristianesimo, Umanesimo e la Bolla "Apostolici Regiminis" ', *Rivista Storica Italiana*, 79 (1967), 976–990.

[5] H. Jedin (ed.), 'Contarini und Camaldoli', *Archivio italiano per la storia della pietà*, II (1959), 51–117. Contarini's difficulties at this time are examined by Jedin

6

Contarini's letters reveal beyond doubt that he was preoccupied at this time with problems very similar to those which Luther was experiencing in Germany: and that. after an early crisis, he resolved them in a manner not dissimilar to that which Luther independently adopted. Contarini's crisis, like that of Luther, revolved around the problem of salvation, and the necessary means to its attainment. In contrast to Luther's experience, however, it was precipitated by the decision of his friend Giustiniani to retire into monastic life. Contarini could not feel it in himself to follow, but his failure to do so made him feel profoundly miserable. On 1 February 1511 he wrote to Giustiniani:

> I shall not say, lest I deceive you, that I am coming to keep you company. Such good thoughts are not in me. I only grieve...that I see my friends every day going from what is good to what is better, while my so obstinate mind and hardened heart go from bad to worse.[1]

He felt himself like a rudderless ship in the middle of the sea; his mind was troubled, more so than he could express.[2]

Easter approached, and Contarini retired for recollection to San Giorgio Maggiore. He thought there of Giustiniani who, even yet, feared that his remaining time would be inadequate to atone for his past sins; he thought of his own life, and his failure so much as to approach the standard which Giustiniani set. Reflecting on the contrast, he 'remained very ill-content and almost in despair'.[3] On Holy Saturday he made his way in this frame of mind to San Sebastiano, where he confessed his sins. There he fell into conversation with a priest whom he had never before met. This man, 'as if he knew my trouble, began to reason with me that the way of salvation was much broader than

in two further articles: 'Ein Turmerlebnis des jungen Contarini', in *Kirche des Glaubens Kirche der Geschichte* (2 vols. Freiburg im B., 1966), 1, 167–80 and 'Gasparo Contarini e il Contributo Veneziano alla Riforma Cattolica' in *La Civilta Veneziana del Rinascimento* (Florence, 1958), pp. 103–24. Cf. also H. Mackensen, 'Contarini's Theological Role at Ratisbon in 1541', in *Archiv für Reformationsgeschichte*, LI (1960), 36–49; F. Gilbert, 'Religion and Politics in the Thought of Gasparo Contarini', *Action and Conviction in Early Modern Europe: Essays in Memory of E. H. Harbison*, ed. T. K. Rabb and J. E. Seigel (Princeton, 1969), pp. 90–116; and Cessi, 'Paolinismo preluterano', *passim*.

[1] 'Contarini und Camoldoli', p. 62.   [2] Ibid. pp. 61–2.   [3] Ibid. p. 63.

7

many persuaded themselves'.[1] The result of their conversation was that Contarini began to ponder in a new way upon the problem of salvation. It became apparent that he was himself incapable of satisfying for his sins:

After I had left him I began to think over for myself what that salvation ('felicita') is, and what our condition is. And I understood truly that if I did all the penances possible, and even many more, they would not be enough at one great stroke, I shall not say to merit that salvation, but to atone for my past sins.[2]

Yet it was not necessary for him to attempt so much; for he now saw that God had permitted His Son to suffer atonement 'for all those...wish to be members of that body of which Christ is the head'.[3] Thus satisfaction had already been accomplished. Hence the members of Christ's body could 'with little effort, hope to atone for their sins through the influx of the atonement which our head has made'.[4] The rest of Contarini's description must be given in full:

We must attempt merely to unite ourselves with this, our head, with faith, with hope, and with such little love as we are capable of. As regards the satisfaction for the sins committed, and into which human weakness falls, His passion is sufficient and more than sufficient.

Through this thought I was changed from great fear and suffering to happiness. I began with my whole spirit to turn to this greatest good which I saw, for love of me, on the cross, with his arms open, and his breast opened right up to his heart. Thus I, the wretch who had not had enough courage for the atonement of my iniquities to leave the world and do penance, turned to him; and since I asked him to let me share in the satisfaction which he, without any sins of his own, had made for us, he was quick to accept me and to cause his Father completely to cancel the debt I had contracted, which I by myself was incapable of satisfying.

Now shall I not sleep securely although in the midst of the city, although I have not paid off ('satisfaci') the debt I had contracted, since I have such a payer of my debt? Truly I shall sleep and wake as securely as if I had spent all my life in the hermitage with the intention of never tiring of such a task.[5]

[1] 'Contarini und Camoldoli', p. 64. [2] Ibid. [3] Ibid.
[4] Ibid. [5] Ibid.

In this episode, as recounted by Contarini, we may observe the same advance from fear to confidence, from helplessness to absolute assurance, which characterised the experience of Luther. It is enough to justify Jedin's description of the matter as a *Turmerlebnis*. Contarini himself spoke of it as 'an experience brighter than the sun'.[1] Like Luther, Contarini found in the contemplation of Christ's sacrifice the solvent of his fears, and the resolution of his anxious strivings for perfection. His own works were powerless to assist him: confidence in Christ was everything.

But in certain important aspects, and in its consequences, Contarini's experience was not identical with that of Luther. Contarini did not altogether dismiss the role of human effort in salvation: men, he believed, were justified by faith, but not by faith alone. In addition, there was hope, and 'such little love as we are capable of'. Luther would not allow that any effort, however 'little', could be availing to salvation; nor did he believe that man, in himself, was capable of love. To suppose that works were meritorious in any sense, seemed to him to place a blasphemous limitation on the absolute efficacy of Christ's sufferings. Contarini, unlike Luther, made no negations: he sought merely to remove the props of self-reliance which prevented men from trusting themselves utterly to Christ. He replaced an emphasis; he did not distrust, as Luther did, the idea of cooperation between grace and nature.

Thus he was not prompted to assume the task of prophecy, declaiming against the corruption of a Church which placed obstacles between mankind and God. On the contrary, his experience of renewal had occurred within the bosom of the Church, and was closely linked with the sacrament of penance. He remained convinced that the means to reform lay within the Church herself: despite every humanly-contrived deformity, the Church retained the Spirit of grace and truth. Hence reform must be initiated from within.[2]

---

[1] 'experientia più chiara che il sole'. (Cf. A. Stella, 'La Lettera del Cardinale Contarini sulla Predestinazione', p. 418, *Rivista di Storia della Chiesa in Italia*, xv (1961), 411–41.)

[2] Jedin, 'Gasparo Contarini e il Contributo Veneziano alla Riforma Cattolica', p. 116.

As yet, Contarini was in no position to reform the Church.[1] He was not a priest; he held no ecclesiastical office. Instead, he served the Venetian government for a further fifteen years, until the time came when he was finally enabled to influence the course of Catholic reform. During the intervening period, the fruits of his experience began to ripen and, 'in the midst of the city', its consequences became ever more apparent. He continued to correspond with his friends in the hermitage of Camaldoli, visiting them occasionally and conversing with them on spiritual matters. He strenuously defended the validity of a Christian life lived in the world, at one time even arguing its superiority to contemplative life.[2] He read continuously in Scripture and the early Fathers, especially St Augustine and St Gregory, whom he considered to excel 'in interpretatione mystice de la Scriptura'.[3] Most significantly, he found in the writings of St Paul the confirmation of his innermost experience. On 20 April 1513 he wrote to Giustiniani: 'I know fully that in ourselves we are insufficient, as St Paul says, to think, let alone do, anything good, and that all praise must be directed to him alone who is the source and origin of all things good.'[4]

The last of Contarini's surviving letters to Giustiniani was written on 7 February 1523. In it, he speaks of 'various emotions' which still trouble his 'scarcely confirmed, or rather my unstable heart'; and he continues with a renewed affirmation of his confidence in Christ, in support of which he again appeals to the testimony of St Paul:

Wherefore I have truly come to the firm conclusion (which, however, I had first read and experienced for myself) that no one can at any time justify himself through his works or purge his mind of its inclinations. One must turn to the divine grace obtained through faith in Jesus Christ, as St. Paul says, and repeat with him: 'Beatus, cui non imputavit Dominus peccatum, sine operibus.' Now I see both in myself and in others that whenever a man thinks to have acquired

---

[1] Only to write about it. In 1517 he published *De Officio episcopi*, discussed in Gilbert, 'Religion and Politics,' pp. 105–10.

[2] Contarini to Giustiniani, 22 September 1511. ('Contarini und Camaldoli', p. 69.)

[3] Ibid. pp. 75, 77.

[4] Ibid. p. 89.

some virtue, he falls at that instant all the more easily. Whence I conclude that every living man is a thing of utter vanity, and that we must justify ourselves through the righteousness of another, that is, of Christ: and when we join ourselves to him, his righteousness is made ours, nor must we then depend upon ourselves in the slightest degree, but we must say: 'A nobis retulimus responsum mortis'.[1]

This is a significant modification of Contarini's earlier position. Works have been eliminated; faith in the righteousness of Christ, imputed to the believer, has become the one thing necessary. The Pauline antithesis between the law, with its burden of guilt, and faith in the security of Christ, seems firmly lodged in Contarini's thought. The question must therefore arise, whether this is St Paul as understood by Contarini in the sole light of his personal experience; or whether, as seems likely, the influence of Luther has been brought to bear upon his reading of the Pauline texts. The first sub-clause in the above passage strongly suggests something of the sort.[2] One is prompted to wonder too, about the 'various emotions' which afflicted his 'unstable heart', and concerning which, as he wrote to Giustiniani, 'I cannot write in particular' – but remained confident, nevertheless, that they would be comprehensible to 'a prudent man such as you are, and one experienced in the world's affairs'.[3] Certainly, by 1523 Luther had become a figure of inescapable importance: his influence was already beginning to be manifest in Italy at this time.[4] Contarini, moreover, had only recently witnessed the growth of Lutheranism in Spain;[5] and it seems impossible that he, who had been present at Worms in 1521 when Luther was condemned, should have remained impervious to his influence.[6]

[1] Ibid. p. 117.
[2] So perhaps, may the following interesting remark: 'In questa materia io ben desidereria vedere qualche cosa del vostro, perchè, a dirvi il vero, facta experientia di me et vedendo quel che io posso, mi ho reduto a questo solo, parendomi tuto il resto nulla.' (Ibid.)   [3] Ibid.
[4] D. Cantimori, *Eretici italiani del Cinquecento* (Florence, 1939), p. 24. E. G. Gleason, 'Sixteenth Century Italian Interpretations of Luther', *Archiv für Reformationgeschichte*, 60 (1969), 160–73.
[5] Mackensen, 'Contarini's Theological Role', p. 39.
[6] He took great care, however, neither to see nor speak with Luther at Worms, 'for he has the sharpest foes and the greatest friends and his affair is accompanied by such great strife as you would not easily believe'. (Ibid. p. 38.)

Luther's spiritual crisis had differed both in force and depth from that of any of his contemporaries.[1] Hence his interpretation of the epistle to the Romans, where he at last found the answer to his difficulties, possessed an immediacy which was overwhelming. In his hands, the Pauline doctrine of justification became imbued with a meaning which revolutionised the life of Christianity. In the epistle to the Romans he found the key to release him from the burden of his sins and the terror of a vengeful God. His continual penances had not relieved him of his anguish: they had seemed, rather, to mock the inadequacy of his efforts at perfection. But the discovery that the just man was saved by faith – that Christ had already merited salvation for those who would believe in Him – cut through his fears, and provided him with an instrument of direct action.

This was especially important: for he had approached St Paul with a mind convinced of the futility of human action. This conviction, indeed, never left him. At no time did he cease to stress the depravity of human nature, and its absolute incapacity for good. What altered was his belief in the nature and efficacy of divine activity: the righteousness of Christ, gratuitously bestowed, would render a man just before the scrutiny of God. Sin remained: but it was not imputed to those who, through faith, were vested with the righteousness of Christ. Man was not just; but he was accounted so because of faith: *semper peccator, semper iustus*.

Luther, moreover, followed his convictions to certain inescapable conclusions. If man were saved by faith alone, and not by works, then he could contribute nothing to his own salvation: faith itself was a gift, unmerited by sinful man. Hence the teaching and worship of contemporary Christianity was in great measure based on idolatrous delusion: by encouraging mankind to offer sacrifice and to merit a reward by works, it presumed to add something further to the sacrifice and works of Christ Himself. Hence the Catholic priesthood, and in particular, the papacy, was no more than a device to replace Christ's labours with the machinery of human effort. So too, were doctrines such as purgatory,

[1] G. Rupp, *The Righteousness of God* (London, 2nd impression, 1963). G. Ebeling, *Luther* (Tübingen, 1964, Eng. trans., London and Philadelphia, 1970).

which supposed that human suffering could be enriched with a redemptive content.

The root of Luther's doctrine may be found in the conviction that grace and nature were forever, and implacably, opposed.[1] His identification of concupiscence with sin and his conception of imputed righteousness, which together seem to constitute his primary originality, are each of them a response to this primary conviction, colouring every subsequent conclusion. His mind worked in antitheses: grace and nature, faith and works, the Bible and the Church of Rome, were irrevocably separate and hostile in his mind. In practice, he never ceased to recommend good works; he was not offering a rule of licence. But he insisted that works be preached as a thing subordinate to faith: the consequence, and not the cause of justification. Salvation was by faith alone, and the Bible was the repository from which faith derived its principal support. It was the supreme instrument whereby Christianity would be restored to its original condition.

In this conviction Luther undertook the task of purifying Christendom. The simplicity of his message, and its fervour, acted as a clarion call to all who were discontented in their faith, or were opposed to Rome. Politics determined the geographical boundaries of its reception: but its driving force lay in the passionate simplicity of its utterance. Faith alone, the Bible alone: these were the twin pillars of the Christian life; and it was this doctrine which, in the second quarter of the century, began to dominate the climate of religious argument.

Thus, in the early years of the sixteenth century the Scriptures, and in particular the writings of St Paul, were generally, and in a variety of ways, presented as the source for a renewal of religious life. Christianity became predominantly evangelical: a widespread preoccupation with the problem of salvation, and a desire for personal religious experience, led men to consult the Bible, as the uncorrupted expression of the Word of God. Hence the term

[1] This is not to suggest that he always spoke as though they were. His ideas cannot satisfactorily be abridged in a manner that will do him justice: his pastoral interests were always more important to him than his theoretical consistency.

'Evangelism' may be applied without intrinsic inaccuracy to the various manifestations of this impulse in the first decades of the century.

In the scholarship of the past fifty years, the term Evangelism has in fact acquired a distinct and specialised significance among historians. In 1914 it was adopted by Pierre Imbart de la Tour to describe the religious attitudes of certain French reform circles: attitudes which he distinguished both from Protestantism and from the Catholicism of the Counter Reformation.[1] Later the term was taken up by Hubert Jedin and Delio Cantimori to describe the same phenomenon in Italy;[2] and since then it has become an integral part of the vocabulary of Reformation historians. In 1953 Evangelism in Italy was made the subject of an influential article by Dr E. M. Jung, whose conclusions, however, have recently been criticised by Dr Philip McNair in an important study of the Italian reformer Peter Martyr Vermigli.[3]

According to Dr Jung, the essential characteristics of Evangelism (as expounded principally by Contarini and Juan de Valdés) were threefold: it was undogmatic; it was aristocratic; it was transitory. It absorbed the elements of reform which existed in Italy before 1517. Like Protestantism, it was a reaction against the intellectualism and optimism of the preceding age. It was Pauline rather than Erasmian, in its pessimism about human nature, and its concern with the problem of justification; but it remained independent of the Pauline and Augustinian strains in Protestantism. Unlike Protestantism, it did not protest: it was intent on privacy, and sought to preserve the existing ecclesiastical order. It was essentially a religious attitude, not a theological system; a spontaneous development, not the creation of a single leader. But

[1] Cf. E. M. Jung, 'On the Nature of Evangelism in Sixteenth-Century Italy', in *Journal of the History of Ideas*, XIV (1953), 511–27, and P. Imbart de la Tour, *Les Origines de la Réforme*, III, *L'Évangélisme* (Paris, 1914). French Evangelism has been examined in a series of recent works by Professor Michael Screech: *The Rabelaisian Marriage* (London, 1958); *L'Évangélisme de Rabelais* (Geneva, 1959); *Marot Évangélique* (Geneva, 1967).

[2] H. Jedin, *Girolamo Seripando*, II (Würzburg, 1937), 135; D. Cantimori, 'La riforma in Italia' in *Problemi Storici e orientamentic storiografii*, ed. Rota (Como, 1942). Cited by Jung, pp. 511–12.

[3] P. McNair, *Peter Martyr in Italy* (Oxford, 1967).

in its preoccupation with the question of salvation, its distrust of
human works, and its emphasis on the supremacy of faith, it
assumed positions which were in essence Lutheran; so that the
condemnation of these positions by the Council of Trent put an
end to its effective life. Even before that, however, it had received
a death-blow at the colloquy of Regensburg: the failure of
Contarini's eirenic policy in 1541 was, according to Dr Jung, the
failure of Evangelism as a whole.

In its general lines, Dr Jung's account seems to me to be a just
description of Evangelism. In certain details, it is no doubt
misleading.[1] Dr McNair has criticised the argument (common to
the other historians mentioned above) that Italian Evangelism was
an indigenous development, an aspect of Catholic reform which
remained independent of Protestantism.[2] His stress on the innate
character of Italian Protestantism is a valuable corrective; but we
should not forget the importance, in their turn, of Contarini's
early letters, which undoubtedly reveal an attitude of spirit
strikingly similar to that of Luther: one which developed in the
milieu of Italian Catholic reform, and which was, in its origins,
not only independent of, but precedent to the growth of Lutheranism. Whether it remained so, however, is another matter: and
Dr McNair is thoroughly convincing in his argument that
Protestantism, during the 1530s, exerted a considerable influence
on the Italian adherents of Evangelism.[3] His case is established by
the recent discovery that the work which, more than any other,
has been regarded as the most typical expression of Italian
Evangelism, was indubitably influenced by religious developments beyond the Alps.[4] To suppose that such an influence was

[1] In its assertion, for example, that Sadoleto's theological views were akin to
those of Contarini. R. M. Douglas indicates the substantial opposition of their
views (*Jacopo Sadoleto*, Cambridge, Mass., 1959, pp. 145ff.). Again it is incorrect
to assert, as Dr Jung does, that the common denominator of Evangelism was the
doctrine of 'twofold justice'. (See below, p. 145.) Finally, Evangelism was not
exclusively aristocratic. E. Pommier, 'La societé vénitienne et la réforme protestante au XVIᵉ siecle', *Bolletino dell' Istituto di Storia della Società e dello Stato
Veneziano*, I (1959), 3–26. O. M. T. Logan, 'Grace and Justification: Some Italian
Views of the Sixteenth and Early Seventeenth Centuries', *The Journal of Ecclesiastical History*, 20 (1969), 67–78.
[2] *Peter Martyr in Italy*, pp. 5ff.
[3] Ibid. pp. 8ff. [4] See below, pp. 74ff.

unlikely to be felt would therefore obviously be unwise. On the whole, other historians have been intent simply on arguing that the Italian preoccupation with the problem of salvation – a preoccupation by no means academic, but immediate and pressing – was one which had spontaneously arisen in Italy, independently of Protestant developments. Dr McNair, however, has helpfully drawn the argument to a finer point of definition, in describing Evangelism as 'the positive reaction of certain spiritually minded Catholics to the challenge of Protestantism, and in particular to the crucial doctrine of Justification by Faith.'[1] The challenge of Protestantism, indeed, was the essence of the matter. It had not been so at first; but it became so.

The emergence of Luther inevitably altered everything. The circumstances in which men pursued the question of salvation, their consciousness of a new immediacy in the problem, and their awareness of the possibly dangerous consequences which attended their conclusions, could not but have been affected by the situation which existed after 1520. For a time, it seemed that Luther and Erasmus might find common ground in their denunciation of ecclesiastical abuses; but it soon became apparent that there were between them differences so fundamental as to preclude any likelihood of friendship. In 1524 Erasmus published *De Libero Arbitrio*. The reply, when it came, so overwhelmed him that he wrote to the young Reginald Pole, then studying at Padua: 'Luther has written against me in a way which no one would use against the Turk.'[2] It was a fateful moment, and it signified the repudiation of a more hesitant spirit than the age was to experience again.

Luther, indeed, was overwhelming: his words carried an appeal which aroused multitudes, and accomplished revolution. He spoke simply and effectively: not only in learned commentaries but in manifestos; not to little groups but to whole peoples; and he spoke directly to the troubled conscience.

[1] *Peter Martyr in Italy*, pp. 8ff.

[2] Erasmus to Pole, Basle, 8 March 1526. *Opus Epistolarum Desiderii Erasmi Roterodami*, VI, ed. P. S. Allen and H. M. Allen (Oxford, 1926), 283. Also printed in *Epistolae*, I, 395.

In 1523, as we have seen, Contarini's conscience was still troubled by 'various emotions' which afflicted his 'unstable heart'. It has already been suggested that he was at this time influenced to some extent by Luther;[1] it must now be emphasised that his attitude to Luther was determined, in the last analysis, by his concern for the unity of the Church. To Contarini it seemed that Luther had betrayed the most fundamental of considerations in disrupting Christendom. During the 1520s, as a member of Charles V's suite, he had witnessed at first hand the spread of Lutheranism in Spain. Afterwards, during his retirement at Venice, he wrote a refutation of Lutheranism. The work displays a thorough understanding of the issues in question, and, as Mackensen remarks, a mildness of tone, which has impressed subsequent students of the composition.[2] Contarini was by this time emerging as one of the leading figures in the Italian movement of Catholic reform which was developing at Venice during the early 1530s.[3] The rest of his life was devoted to assimilating what he believed to be the orthodox elements of Lutheranism into the traditional framework of Catholic belief and practice.

In this task he was impelled by an attitude towards justification which was deeply sympathetic to, though not in every respect identical with that of Luther. His doctrine of justification was distinguished by certain differences of emphasis and detail; but the fundamental difference lay in the use he was prepared to make of it. He refused to employ it as an instrument of schism. Instead, it remained for him the internal principle which found its outward expression in the movement to reform the Church. But the difficulty of publicly declaring his belief on the question was

[1] Cessi too, makes the interesting suggestion that Contarini felt himself involuntarily attracted to the Lutheran rebellion, 'alle cui ispirazione l'animo suo ... si sentì affine'. ('Paolinismo preluterano', p. 12.)

[2] 'Contarini's Theological Role', p. 39. F. Hünermann, ed., *Confutatio articulorum seu quaestionem Lutheranorum*, in *Gasparo Contarini. Gegen reformatorische Schriften, 1530–42.* (*Corpus Catholicorum*, VII, Münster in Westfallen, 1923, 1–22.) For a further account of Contarini's theological position cf. A. Stella, 'La lettera del Cardinale Contarini sulla predestinazione'.

[3] Jedin, 'Gasparo Contarini e il Contributo Veneziano alla Riforma Cattolica'.

considerable. The distinction between his views and those of Luther was detectable only to the most discerning theologian, and even then with difficulty: for Contarini's theological position, unlike his ecclesiastical affiliation, never ceased to be unstable. It underwent a continual process of refinement and redefinition as he advanced his efforts to maintain the difficult equilibrium between the implications of his doctrine on the one hand, and on the other, his loyalty to the belief of Rome.[1]

Hence he was obliged to conduct his examination of the matter out of hearing, discussing the question privately with friends. Publicly to express his views would have been tantamount to encouraging schism. Instead, he chose to remain silent, until the time should come when a General Council would throw the question open to discussion. Thus from the outset there existed between his private and his public roles a discontinuity which characterised the movement of Evangelism as a whole, introducing an element of equivocation which proved fatal, not only to its own self-confidence, but ultimately, to its very existence.

During the 1530s, however, there grew up at Venice and Padua a circle of men who, sharing his spirit, dedicated themselves to the task of purifying the Church of its abuses. Quietly they anticipated the advent of a day when the unity of the Church might be restored by the recognition, on the part of a General Council, of the orthodox element in Luther's teaching. In certain respects they inherited the spirit of Erasmus. All were humanists: and they shared his view that the differences between Christians were not so great as to warrant their continued separation.[2] They were impatient, as he was, with abstruse theological distinctions: their theology was predominantly Scriptural; it was addressed to the affections, not the intellect; and it was expressed in the language of persuasion rather than analysis. But in their pessimism about human nature, their preoccupation with the helplessness of man, and their insistence on the supremacy of faith, they were more

---

[1] He attempted the balance with an intellectual impressiveness which, because of his philosophical and theological acumen, placed him in a different category from other members of his group.

[2] Erasmus, *De Amabili Ecclesiae Concordia* (1533), *Opera*, v, 470–506.

akin to Luther than Erasmus.[1] Their most cherished ambition was to reform the Church and put an end to schism.

These, then, were the characteristics of what is generally known as Italian Evangelism; and in the persons of Gasparo Contarini, Gregorio Cortese, Reginald Pole, and later, Giovanni Morone, we may discern the most notable exponents of this movement in the realm of action at the Roman Curia. They were not its only exponents. It so happened that in other parts of Europe – especially in France and Spain – a similar spirit was at work; but in Italy the movement known as Evangelism was connected, through these men, with the higher reaches of the Roman Church.[2] Its adherents were in a position to advise the papacy.[3] Hence from this point of view alone, it is possible to treat of Italian Evangelism as a distinct phenomenon.

Its debts to European spitituality and humanism should not be underestimated; one of its most significant theoreticians was the Spanish humanist Juan de Valdés, who took up residence at Naples in the 1530s. But it is important to stress the indigenous origins and inspirations of the movement: not because they should be themselves considered as entirely self-contained, and impervious to external influence; but because they existed in Italy before the Reformation. Evangelism was not created by the Reformation: it was most certainly re-directed by it.

Thus Dr McNair's helpful definition might be extended marginally in one direction. Italian Evangelism *was* 'the reaction of certain spiritually minded Catholics to the challenge of Protestantism'; its adherents were intensely preoccupied with the question of justification by faith alone; but we must beware of asserting

[1] Bataillon misleadingly refers to the promotion of Contarini, Pole and Morone to the college of Cardinals as 'la promotion érasmienne'. In general, it seems to me that his description of 'erasmians' is illuminating in almost everything but nomenclature. (*Érasme et l'Espagne*, p. 534 and *passim*.)

[2] For Spain, cf. Bataillon, *Érasme et l'Espagne*, with the reservation introduced above, n. 1, for France, above, n. 1, p. 5.

[3] O. Ortolani, 'The hopes of the Italian reformers in Roman action'. *Italian Reformation Studies in Honor of Laelius Socinus*, ed. John A. Tedeschi (Florence, 1965), pp. 11–20. D. Cantimori, 'L'influence du manifeste de Charles Quint contre Clement VII (1526) et de quelques documents similaires de la litterature philo-protestante et anticuriale d'Italie', *Charles Quint et son Temps* (Paris, 1959), pp. 133–41.

that the preoccupation was born exclusively of the Reformation. The epistles of St Paul as we have seen, had provided food for meditation before Luther. In particular, the spirituality of the religious orders is of distinct significance. Not enough is known of the Benedictine order in the years before the Reformation to permit confident assertions about the traditions which encouraged so many of its Italian members to respond with sympathy to Luther's doctrine: but it is surely remarkable that Contarini's experience should have occurred in Venice, while residing at San Giorgio Maggiore, the Benedictine monastery of which Cortese was later to be Abbot; that the Benedictine house at Padua should have nursed the man who, more than anyone, induced in Pole a sympathy with the psychological disposition animating Luther; that the same order should have produced the writer first associated with the *Beneficio di Cristo*, the most radical manifesto of the nascent Italian Reformation; and that the author's friend and fellow-Benedictine, Giorgio Siculo, should have emerged, after the early sessions of the Council of Trent, as the principal exponent of what Calvin contemptuously designated 'Nicodemism' – the principle of secretly adhering to a doctrine outlawed by the visible Church.[1] These developments, with the significant exception of Contarini's *Turmerlebnis*, took place after the Reformation; they represented a response, certainly, to the religious revolution; but it was a response so variable and fissiparous, and so distinct in expression from the intransigence of Geneva and Tridentine Rome, that one is forced to consider it in relation to its traditions and its concrete setting, in Italian monasteries and private households from Venice to Palermo, and in the academies and pulpits of Naples, Venice, Modena, Bologna, Ferrara, Lucca and Viterbo.[2]

Hence it is necessary to think of Italian Evangelism as a phenomenon which, drawing upon spiritual currents already existing not only in Italy, but in Europe as a whole, sought to adapt the

---

[1] Calvin's contempt, of course, was directed against the secrecy, not the doctrine.

[2] Unfortunately there is no adequate study of the subject as a whole. A. Rotondò promises a study of Bologna and Modena, 'Per la Storia dell' eresia a Bologna nel secolo XVI', *Rinascimento*, 13 (1962), 125 n. 1.

insights of Luther, and later (in its more radical exponents) of Calvin, to the practice of a Christianity not externally different from that of Rome. Its spiritual axis was the doctrine of justification by faith alone. Such a movement, by its very nature, eludes more concrete definition. Most of its adherents expected their views to be ratified by a General Council. Some, no doubt, were consciously heretical or, like Ochino, Vermigli and Vergerio, became so. When it was made finally apparent that there was no hope of Conciliar ratification, those who persisted in their views earned, for the first time (since it was only now fully certain that there was no visible Church to welcome them), the title 'Nicodemists'. Their spokesman was Siculo, and he was put to death for it.[1]

Hence the word heresy in the title of this book. Its consequences in the sixteenth century were fearful, and known to be so. Some modern writers, notably Hans Küng, have supposed that there is no real contradiction between the Protestant doctrine of justification and the teaching of the Church of Rome.[2] An historian cannot help wondering whether the process of Küng's argument is not a little historically insensitive. Luther did not suppose that what he was saying was compatible with fidelity to the Church of Rome. Neither did Vergerio, nor poor Siculo. In this at least, both Newman and Barth would have been in agreement with Luther, Vergerio, Siculo and as it turned out, Pole.

The following pages will be concerned with Pole and his associates. The terminology of Evangelism, appropriate perhaps in languages like French or German, but confusing to minds familiar with Anglo-American usage, where it recalls a style of worship more recent and less equivocal, will be abandoned, in favour of the term employed by contemporaries themselves. In Italy, the term *spirituali* was applied to the conventicles meeting in the towns and cities, nourishing a devotion to the doctrine of justification *ex sola fide*, and hoping to see a *rapprochement* between the Church of Rome and the reformers of the north. Through their preachers these little circles seemed at one time likely to

[1] See below, pp. 265ff.
[2] H. Küng, *Justification* (4th edn, Einsiedeln, 1957, Eng. trans., London, 1964).

capture a substantial basis of popular support. Between 1530 and 1550, they probably did achieve as much, in places like Naples, Ferrara, Bologna, Lucca, Modena and Venice.[1] It was no doubt for this reason, and because of the related sense that influential posts were falling to their adherents, that they aroused the fear and determined opposition of those who saw in their gatherings a series of fronts for the advancement of Italian Protestantism. It was perhaps with a freshly apprehended sense of this particular conclusion that the bishop of Verona, Gian Matteo Giberti (himself for many years a patron of the *spirituali*) observed in 1542, following the death of Contarini, and the apostasy and flight to Switzerland of the preachers most conspicuously associated with their cause, that the fortunes of the *spirituali* had suffered decisive reversal, and that it would be necessary, henceforward, to withdraw support from them.[2] Giberti's sense of historical reality was in this moment more acute than that of Pole and his company of Viterbo, who still expected in these years to see their aspirations to reunion vindicated by the course of events. Devoted supporters of the Church of Rome, they sought to express her teaching in a manner acceptable to moderate Protestants. Their policy, however, was vulnerable from the outset: theologically, it was rife with contradictions which events, and a rigorous scholasticism, would expose; practically, the Roman connection put paid to any hope of reunion with the Lutherans. Their misfortune was to be conciliators without enjoying the conditions favourable to conciliation. The spirit of the Reformation belonged perhaps more to Luther than Melanchthon; to Calvin rather than Servetus. At Rome, the spirit which, after twenty-five years of disarray emerged triumphant, owed little to Erasmus or to Contarini:

[1] For Naples, Nieto, *Juan de Valdés*, p. 147, and the text of Carnesecchi's deposition, 'Estratto del processo di Mons. Pietro Carnesecchi' ed. G. Manzoni, *Miscellanea di Storia Italiana*, x (1870), 196 for the connection between the thought of Valdés and the pulpit; for Bologna and Modena, Rotondò, 'Per la Storia dell' eresia' and his forthcoming work; for Venice, Pommier, 'La societé vénitienne'; for Ferrara and Lucca, Cantimori, 'Italy and the Papacy', *N.C.M.H.* II, 261–4. The Spiera case (below, p. 221), and the case of Padua (below, p. 32) are also instructive.

[2] 'Poiché questi nostri spirituali ne dan sì poca consolazione parte col morire parte con andar profughi, credo che sara bene lasciar la loro compagnia'. (A. Prosperi, *Tra Evangelismo e Controriforma: G. M. Giberti* (Rome, 1969), p. 314.)

it was the spirit of militant authority, of a revived scholasticism, of Loyola and the Council of Trent. The hopes of the *spirituali* belonged to the years of beneficent illusion. They yielded eventually to the reality of the Reformation and the Counter-Reformation. The *spirituali* lived to witness the rejection of their programme, and to align themselves, for the most part, along new fronts. The plans of Contarini, who died in 1542, were repudiated in the last year of his life by Catholic and Protestant alike. As Dr Jung observes, his failure was the failure of all the *spirituali*. But many of his collaborators were not persuaded that the repudiation had been absolute: and they did not become so, until the Council of Trent finally disabused them of their expectations. After the death of Contarini, his role devolved upon his closest friend and collaborator, Reginald Pole. Supported by Cardinal Morone, Pole assumed the dominant position among those *spirituali* who still looked to the approaching Council for an official confirmation of their views. We must now examine the course which led him to this equivocal, and ultimately unhappy position within the movement of Catholic reform.

CHAPTER TWO

Pole in Italy

Pole was born at Stourton Castle, Worcestershire, in March 1500, the third son of Sir Richard Pole and Margaret (later Countess of Salisbury), daughter of the ill-starred Clarence. He was educated at the grammar school attached to the Carthusian monastery at Sheen, a 'devout and pleasant place' according to his first biographer.[1] In 1513 he went to Oxford, where he entered Magdalen, and spent the next eight years.[2] At Magdalen, his principal tutor was William Latimer, formerly a student at the University of Padua, a friend of Colet, and an enthusiast of the New Learning. During this period Pole made the acquaintance of numerous humanists and scholars, the most notable of whom was Thomas More; in a letter to her father, Margaret More wrote of Pole as a young man 'noble as he is learned in all branches of Letters, nor less conspicuous for his virtue than for his learning'.[3]

Pole's formative years, therefore, were spent in the ambience of that devout humanism, basing itself on Scripture and Patristics, which exercised so powerful an effect upon his generation: an ambience in which his own family played a formative role, as sponsors of scholarship and devotional literature.[4] It would be surprising if his outlook had not already been fashioned under its influence by early manhood.

In 1521 he was sent by Henry VIII to complete his studies at the University of Padua, thereby following the course adopted

[1] Ludovico Beccadelli, *Vita del Cardinale Reginaldo Polo*, in G. Morandi (ed.), *Monumenti di Varia Letteratura* (2 vols. in 3 parts, Bologna, 1797–1804), I, ii, p. 281.

[2] Schenk, *Reginald Pole, Cardinal of England* (London, 1950), p. 2.

[3] Ibid. p. 5.   [4] McConica, *English Humanists*, pp. 60, 61, 62, 68.

earlier by Latimer and Linacre. Padua was at this time recovering its former brilliance, after the interval of the Venetian wars. Its geographical position, moreover, made it susceptible to influences from beyond the Alps. As Dr McNair has written, 'there was scarecely an Italian prominent in his country's frustrated Reformation who was not connected with the University of Padua'.[1] Among Pole's contemporaries at the university were Pier Paolo Vergerio the Younger, who in 1522 was appointed to a lectureship in jurisprudence;[2] Vittore Soranzo and Tommaso Sanfelice who, like Vergerio, were to become bishops;[3] Alvise Priuli, a young Venetian of patrician family, who became Pole's most devoted follower;[4] the Latin poet Marcantonio Flaminio;[5] Peter Martyr Vermigli, whose name was indelibly to be associated with the Reformation in two countries; and the young Giovanni Morone, who was to preside brilliantly over the final stages of the Council of Trent.[6] All of these men were to be centrally involved in the religious history of their country during the next half century.

But if the impact of the Reformation was shortly to be felt at Padua, the school of theology remained impervious to it. Scholasticism made little appeal to a generation devoted to elegance and learned wit, and which, when it turned to the affairs of God, thought only of embracing the theology of the pure Gospel. At Padua, as at the other European universities, an aspiring humanist was virtually obliged by his profession to deem scholastic philosophy a thing incorrigibly obscure and abstract: 'Darke, intangled, difficult and beastlie', as Vermigli was to recollect it (from an admittedly prejudiced perspective) in his later years.[7] By con-

[1] *Peter Martyr in Italy*, p. 86.

[2] P. Paschini, *Pier Paolo Vergerio il giovane e la sua apostasia* (Rome, 1925). Cf. also, F. Church, *The Italian Reformers* (New York, 1932), *passim*.

[3] An account of Soranzo appears in P. Paschini, *Tre ricerche sulla storia della chiesa nel cinquecento* (Rome, 1945), pp. 89–151; and notices of Sanfelice in G. Alberigo, *I vescovi italiani al concilio di Trento* (Florence, 1959), pp. 224–5 and 365–7.

[4] P. Paschini, *Un Amico del Cardinale Polo: Alvise Priuli* (Rome, 1921).

[5] C. Maddison, *Marcantonio Flaminio: Poet, Humanist and Reformer* (London, 1965).

[6] Paschini, *Tre Ricerche*, p. 91. Cf. McNair, *Peter Martyr in Italy*, pp. 86ff. for an account of Padua in the years 1518–26.

[7] McNair, *Peter Martyr in Italy*, p. 101.

trast, Pole's interests at this time were predominantly literary. At the end of 1521, accompanied by a large suite of retainers, he was installed in a luxuriously furnished house at Padua, where he 'began', as his biographer expressed it, 'to consort with the clever men of that University, by whom he was often visited and esteemed for the fine wit and breeding they beheld in him'.[1]

Among Pole's English familiars at the university was Thomas Lupset, an outstanding scholar, who until recently had been one of Bishop Fox's classical lecturers at Corpus Christi. Lupset, who was Pole's senior by five years, had been educated as a boy in Colet's household. Later, he had assisted Erasmus in his preparation of the New Testament and the letters of St Jerome. He died young, in 1530, but he left behind him a number of works which, as Schenk remarks, clearly indicate the real centre of his interests: *A Treatise of Charitie; An Exhortation to yonge men, perswading them to walke in the pathe that leadeth to honeste and goodness: A Compendious and a very Fruteful Treatyse, teachynge the ways of Dyenge well.*[2] In addition to Lupset's company, Pole enjoyed frequent visits from the English ambassador to Venice, Richard Pace, whose accomplishments included a translation of St Chrysostom.[3]

Pole, therefore, continued to be rooted in an ambience of devout and learned humanism. His studies, it should be observed, remained noticeably secular. Under the guidance of his tutor Leonico he read extensively in Plato and Aristotle; he collaborated in a plan to produce a critical edition of the works of Cicero; and he undertook a similar enterprise in respect to Galen.[4] Shortly after his arrival he was introduced to Bembo's literary circle, and there he became friendly with the Flemish Ciceronian, Christophe de Longueil (Longolius). The latter was a close friend of Marcantonio Flaminio, and it is probable that Flaminio first became

[1] Beccadelli, *Vita*, in *Monumenti*, i, ii, p. 282.
[2] Cf. J. A. Gee, *Life and Works of Thomas Lupset* (New Haven, 1928), and Schenk, *Reginald Pole*, p. 6.
[3] F. A. Gasquet, *Cardinal Pole and his Early Friends* (London, 1927), pp. 37, 41, 54. Cited by McNair, p. 100. Cf. also Gasquet, pp. 84–5.
[4] Ibid. pp. 35, 91; Zeeveld, *The Foundations of Tudor Policy* (Cambridge, Mass., 1948), pp. 54–7.

acquainted with Pole during the year which Longueil spent in Pole's household, before his early death in 1522.[1] Pole payed tribute to his memory in an anonymous *Life* which he published together with Longueil's letters in 1524, couching it in elegant Ciceronian Latin; a style which he never afterwards adopted.[2] Pole's Ciceronian phase was coming to an end.

Nevertheless, his five years at Padua had given him a thorough grounding in classical philosophy and letters, and he had become fully conversant with Italian intellectual life. Bembo described him at this time as 'possibly the most virtuous, learned and grave young man in the whole of Italy today'.[3] It is a sober enough description, and the epithet 'grave' suggests a strain of austerity which is reminiscent more of Colet than of Bembo. Longueil, too, considered Pole to be 'prodigiously taciturn':[4] a description worthy of attention, for Pole's reticence was a characteristic which, in future years, was to mislead a variety of people into supposing that he was favourable to their interests – until circumstances, to their abrupt discomfiture, proved otherwise. Behind a passive exterior, Pole's mind pondered things carefully, often taking years to reach a decision; when his mind was made up, it tended to be absolute.

The first occasion for the exercise of reticence was provided by the King's Great Matter. Pole, having travelled home in 1526, took up residence with the Carthusians in the house which Colet had built for himself at Sheen.[5] The following year saw him drawn reluctantly into discussion of the King's divorce.[6] From 1528 to 1530 he found himself, probably against his will, pressed into service on the King's behalf. He travelled to Paris a number of times, accompanied by Lupset and Thomas Starkey, and in 1530 he cooperated with Edward Fox in eliciting from the Sorbonne a favourable opinion on the royal divorce. His temperamental

[1] Gasquet, *Cardinal Pole*, p. 31.
[2] C. Longolius, *Orationes duae . . . Longolii vita* (Florence, 1524; facsimile reprint by Gregg Press, 1967).
[3] Bembo to Cardinal Cibo, 17 July 1526. Cited by McNair, *Peter Martyr in Italy*, p. 100.
[4] Gasquet, *Cardinal Pole*, pp. 29–30.
[5] Schenk, *Reginald Pole*, p. 19.
[6] Zeeveld, *The Foundations of Tudor Policy*, pp. 66–71.

distaste for the whole business is not difficult to envisage; his family connections inclined him sympathetically to the Queen; but as Zeeveld remarks, it may be that he had not achieved complete conviction about the merits or demerits of the King's case, and was therefore willing to accommodate himself, however uneasily, to the demands of the moment.[1] But in 1530 he greatly angered the King by blurting out his opposition to the divorce proceedings: with the result that he was shortly afterwards permitted to leave England, fortified by a royal pension, and a commission to resume his studies.[2] Clearly, he intended to stay away for no more than a few years, until the matter had blown over; in the event, another twenty-three years elapsed before he again set foot in England.

For a while, he stayed at Avignon, occasionally calling upon the humanist bishop of Carpentras, Jacopo Sadoleto. Eventually, he moved on to Padua, where he settled at the end of 1532; from there he took the opportunity of paying frequent visits to Venice. Meanwhile he kept up a sporadic correspondence with Sadoleto, and it is interesting to observe in these letters his newly emphatic concern with the study of theology as the crown of knowledge and the necessary completion of a classical education.[3] It may be that for Pole, as earlier for More, the influence of the Carthusians had begun to prove enduring. At this time too, he began to renew many of his earlier Italian friendships, and to associate with the members of the Oratory of Divine Love who, after the Sack of Rome, had reassembled at Venice under the auspices of Contarini.[4] His household at Padua also included a number of his English friends: Starkey, Richard Morison, Thomas Goldwell, Henry Cole, George Lily and others, who

[1] In this view, 'his conduct in Paris need not be interpreted as a purely prudential policy adopted in self defence so much as an attempt at putting learning to use in a cause concerning which he had not achieved conviction. Hence, although he continued to be reticent on the great question, and indeed, on all questions of state, he meanwhile found the company of the moderate reformers [i.e., Starkey and Fox] in all other respects wholly congenial. Such conduct would be characteristic of Pole; he acted in 1535–6 with the same deliberation.' (Ibid. p. 71.)

[2] Schenk, *Reginald Pole*, pp. 25–30.

[3] *Epistolae*, I, 397–422. Schenk, *Reginald Pole*, pp. 32ff.

[4] L. von Pastor, *History of the Popes* (London, 1910–24), X, pp. 415ff.

had come to extend their acquaintance with Renaissance learning.[1]

But it was with the Oratory of Divine Love that Pole's future lay; and it was at Venice and Padua that developments now occurred which were permanently to affect his future. Shortly after Pole's arrival in Venice, he was introduced to the remarkable Gian Pietro Carafa, a founder member of the Theatines, as well as of the Oratory of Divine Love; a man some twenty-four years Pole's senior, single-minded, austere, and unremittingly dedicated to the task of purging the Church of its abuses. Pole had been recommended to Carafa by the bishop of Verona, Gian Matteo Giberti, himself a leading figure in the movement for reform, whose diocesan legislation was to establish a precedent for the Tridentine regulations on Church government.[2] At the end of 1532 Carafa wrote to Giberti, thanking him for his introduction to 'quel gentil spirito inglese'; and, following an interview with Pole on New Year's Eve, he wrote to Giberti again on 1 January 1533, expressing his gratitude for the 'bona et particular informatione' which Giberti had supplied concerning Pole.[3] Carafa's first impressions remained carefully qualified: he did not yet understand Pole, for Pole would not allow himself to be understood. He appeared to be a man whose intentions were admirable; but his devotion to literature implied, perhaps, a certain levity of spirit. He was not sure that Pole distinguished sharply enough between secular and sacred literature; nevertheless, he had shown 'great affection' towards the Theatines, and had expressed a wish to lodge in their vicinity, so as more easily to hold converse with them. Carafa added dryly that he hoped Pole would find more to avail of in their converse than he was prepared to find in their austerity.[4]

Carafa, clearly, was not unconditionally impressed. In view of the subsequent relations between the two men, the circumstance

[1] Zeeveld, *Foundations*, pp. 83–5.
[2] Prosperi, *Tra Evangelismo e Controriforma*. A notice of Giberti appears also in Schenk, *Reginald Pole*, pp. 54ff. Cf. also, M. A. Tucker, 'Gian Matteo Giberti, Papal Politician and Catholic Reformer', *English Historical Review*, 18 (1903), 24–51, 266–86, 439–69.
[3] G. M. Monti, *Ricerche su Papa Paolo IV Carafa* (Benevento, 1923), pp. 143–54.
[4] Ibid. p. 154.

is not entirely without interest. Carafa was later to find sufficient ground for his distrust of the reserved and ambiguous element in Pole's deportment: what is remarkable is that it should have been the first thing about Pole that he noticed. Nevertheless, his immediate qualms turned out to be devoid of substance: during the next four years Pole's dedication to sacred literature became increasingly wholehearted. In this direction, his interests were sustained and developed by his close association with the members of the Oratory of Divine Love and their supporters: Marcantonio Flaminio, who had been associated with the movement from the first;[1] Gregorio Cortese, the regenerator of the Benedictine Order, in the garden of whose monastery at S. Giorgio Maggiore the members of the circle met to discuss the projects closest to their hearts;[2] Alvise Priuli, with whom Pole grew rapidly in friendship; and above all, Gasparo Contarini.[3] In October 1534, Pole wrote to Sadoleto that he was on his way to Venice to join Carafa (whom he described as 'vir sanctissimus') and Contarini, with whom he had by now formed the closest bonds of friendship.[4]

At Venice, in the Benedictine setting of S. Giorgio Maggiore, and at Padua, in that of S. Justina, Pole now came into contact with the new Biblical scholarship, and with a style of exegesis which began profoundly to influence his whole cast of mind. He attended lectures on Isaiah given by the Hebrew scholar Jan van Kempen (Iohannes Campensis) whom Contarini had summoned to S. Justina; there too, he became familiar with the Scriptures as expounded by the Benedictine scholar Isodorus Clarius.[5] From this time forward, we find in his writings a pervasive consciousness of

[1] Maddison, *Marcantonio Flaminio*, p. 42. It is not without interest that Flaminio had half-heartedly applied for membership of the Theatines, and had been rejected on grounds of insufficient commitment. (Cf. Carafa to Francesco Capello, 17 February 1533 in Monti, *Ricerche*, pp. 274–6).

[2] Pastor, *Popes*, x, 416ff.

[3] The standard study of Contarini is still F. Dittrich, *Gasparo Contarini* (Braunsberg, 1885). Orestes Ferrara, *Gasparo Contarini et Ses Missions* (translated from the Spanish by Francis de Miomandre, Paris, 1956) is a semi-popular work, not without interest. Jedin's articles (cited above, n. 5, p. 6) are of decisive importance.

[4] *Epistolae*, 1, 417; and Dittrich, *Gasparo Contarini*, pp. 210 and 835–6.

[5] Dittrich, *Gasparo Contarini*, p. 210; Schenk, *Reginald Pole*, p. 45.

God's continuous dealings with mankind in history. Pole's thought becomes from this date permeated by the Bible. The effect may be described as follows. He learnt to apply the Bible as an interpretative key to history, including the events of his own time. Time became for him the movement of Providential history; he began to read events in the light of what the Scriptures yielded. Henceforward, his response to experience invariably took the form, almost instinctively, of a meditation on the Bible; his problems were resolved in Scriptural commentary; his conception of the Church (which we shall see reflected in the pages ahead) was from this time forward intimately formed and coloured by the text of Scripture. And at the same time, his attention began to turn to the question of justification by faith.

No doubt Contarini's preoccupation with the problem was a stimulus to Pole's developing concern with what had by now become the most momentous issue of the day; no doubt it was a recurrent theme of discussion among the *spirituali* of S. Justina and S. Giorgio Maggiore, and in the *milieux* in which they moved. But of all the influences brought to bear upon Pole at this crucial period, none seems to have been of greater single importance than that exercised by a certain Benedictine monk named 'Marco'. The latter has been conjecturally identified as Mariani or Mario Armellini of Cremona, a monk of S. Justina of Padua, and a commentator on the Pauline epistles whose discourses are known to have drawn large attendances.[1] Pole himself considered that this man had 'nurtured him in Christ'.[2] There can be no question that he exerted a tremendous, and probably decisive, influence on Pole in introducing him to the 'pretiosa Christi dona' which were the constant theme of Luther's, and of Contarini's meditations.[3]

[1] *Epistolae*, I, 298. A further notice concerning Marco appears in Stella, 'La Lettera', p. 412.

[2] Cf. Pole's reference to 'Marcum meum, qui me in Christo genuit'. This occurs in a letter to Bembo, written from Rome on 22 January, *s.a.*, but probably 1537, since it refers to Pole's unexpected detention at Rome, seemingly on the commission to reform the Church. (See below, p. 42). A transcript of the letter, marked 'ex Cod. Vat. 6416, pag. 254', may be seen in the Cambridge University Library, Add. MS 4876, fols. 189r–190v. The reference to Marco is on fol. 190r.

[3] *Epistolae*, II, p. 139.

Marco of Cremona's lectures at Padua attracted great attention; not all of it favourable. On 12 June 1537, Contarini wrote to Giberti, praising Marco, and complaining of his denigrators:

who, because Luther has said various things *de gratia Dei et libero arbitrio*, have opposed everything he preaches and teaches concerning the greatness of grace and concerning human weakness; and who, believing that they thus contradict Luther, actually contradict St Augustine, Ambrose, Bernard, St Thomas; and in short, under the impulse of fine zeal, but with some vehemence and mental heat, in these contradictions they deviate unawares from catholic truth and approach the pelagian heresy, and create tumults among the people.[1]

Here we can catch a glimpse of the theme animating Marco's public discourses: the weakness of man, the saving gift of grace. We can sense too, the atmosphere in which such questions could scarcely, in these years, be touched upon without a consciousness of Luther's overshadowing presence in the background. We can see, therefore, the difficulty which faced men like Contarini and the *spirituali* of S. Justina, in distinguishing their position from that of Luther, however emphatically they might point to the doctrine, in the first place, of Augustine, and then of Ambrose, Bernard and Aquinas: always, there were hostile observers – 'under the impulse of fine zeal', but with what vehemence – to raise a tumult with the people, by the cry of heresy. 'Salvation by works', the instinctive utterance of the *zelanti* in these years, was for Contarini and his friends nothing other than the 'pelagian heresy'. And between the *spirituali* and the *zelanti* there stood the 'popolo': as yet unclaimed by either side, contended for by both, and now beginning to throng to the pulpits, as the struggle for their religious destiny intensified.

Years later, a hostile witness recollected 'un domino Marco, monaco in Padova' who lectured publicly at the monastery of S. Justina, a man 'much favoured' by Contarini, Pole and Giberti.[2]

[1] Cited by Stella, 'La Lettera Del Cardinale Contarini', p. 412. Stella points out that Dittrich leaves the name of the recipient anonymous. (F. Dittrich, *Regesten und Briefe des Kardinals Gasparo Contarini*, Braunsberg, 1881, p. 270.)

[2] Cited by Stella, 'La Lettera Del Cardinal Contarini', p. 412, who cites in turn from G. Buschbell, *Reformation und Inquisition in Italien um die Mitte des XVI. Jahrhunderts* (Paderborn, 1910, p. 262).

The witness in question was the notoriously vigilant Dionisio Zanettini, later prominent at Trent, who from the outset kept a close watch on the *spirituali*, losing no opportunity to denounce them as an heretical fifth column occupying places of high influence within the Church.[1] Zanettini's fears, like those of Carafa and the *zelanti* who later staffed the Roman Inquisition, were based on the conviction that there were needed only a few men in influential posts to manoeuvre the Italian states into a position of religious alignment with the Protestant territories beyond the Alps;[2] that the people would in the end be won by such preachers as might be employed by those who held authority (the history of the Catholic revival after Trent bears out the accuracy of such sentiments); and that the essential task was therefore to ensure the orthodoxy of those who held positions of command in Church and State, as the first requisite for the preservation of the faith in Italy. It was this policy which, being finally adopted in 1542, with the establishment of the Roman Inquisition, rendered so tragically vulnerable the position of surviving *spirituali* such as Pole (whose devotion to the Church was never in question) together with Nicodemists such as Siculo and Carnesecchi who had at one time looked to Pole as their last hope, but who, after the Council of Trent had clarified the character of Catholic belief, chose to dissimulate rather than publicise their disaffection. Their history forms one of the enduringly tragic episodes of the period. The Nicodemists paid for their dissimulation with their lives.

These developments reached a climax only in the middle and later years of the century. They were far from being apprehended by the *spirituali* of Padua in 1536. In the summer of that year, Pole and his director, Marco, accompanied by Cortese, retired from Padua to the cooler heights of the surrounding mountains. There they addressed themselves to prayer and spiritual discourse; Pole, writing to Contarini and Giberti, related his initiation to heavenly

---

[1] Jedin, *Council*, I, 341n, 482, 570n, and below, p. 209.

[2] 'Forty persons at the key posts of the nation could have been more dangerous than a popular reformation.' (Nieto, *Juan de Valdés*, p. 147.) In fact they could probably have arranged one. Only the power of the Habsburgs could have stopped them; and that had proved notoriously weak in Germany.

mysteries.[1] Afterwards, when Pole was living at Rome, he kept up a correspondence with Marco, and his letters convey some idea of the kind of influence which the latter was continuing to exercise on his spiritual development. In one of these letters, written on 25 February 1538, Pole refers to the 'release from bondage' which he had formerly experienced through Marco's help: and he begs him to expand upon a certain phrase which the latter had evidently employed, attributing everything to God: 'Dominus opus habet.'[2]

'Dominus opus habet': is it too improbable to discern in this phrase a suggestion that only divine works, and not human ones, were availing to salvation? There is no way of knowing what the answer to Pole's query may have been. But on 9 November 1538, Pole, hearing that Marco was ill, wrote to him again, expressing his concern, and reiterating his indebtedness to him in terms which are altogether remarkable. Marco's teaching has 'planted and irrigated' the channels of grace in Pole; 'separating human works from divine, and reducing everything to its one source'.[3]

These last two phrases contain the key to Marco's influence, and reveal it to be similar in kind to the disposition which we have already observed in Contarini: to diminish or deny the specifically human element in salvation, and to emphasise instead the unique otherness of God's activity.

It is further apparent from this same letter that Marco was regarded as a spiritual father by a number of Pole's closest friends now living at Rome: notably by Priuli, and a certain 'Federicus' – possibly Federigo Fregoso, with whom Pole was by now associated as one of the principal advocates of radical reform.[4] If it be remembered that Contarini had long been persuaded of the dominant, if not exclusive, role of faith in man's salvation; that Fregoso and Giberti were reputed to have held the same opinion;[5] and that Pole had held continual discourse with these men over a

[1] Cf. the references in Pole's letters, to Contarini, 4 August 1536, and Giberti, 10 August 1536. (*Epistolae*, I, 475, 479.)
[2] *Epistolae*, II, 135.   [3] Ibid. p. 138.   [4] Ibid. p. 139.
[5] By Ochino, in 1546. (McNair, *Peter Martyr in Italy*, p. 222, n. 2.)

period of years, it must seem that his letter to Marco indicates that he was by this time already sympathetic to the central doctrinal axiom of the Reformation.

In reality, the only question is the extent of his sympathy at its point of origin: for by 1546 Pole had come to accept a doctrine of justification almost indistinguishable from that of Luther.[1] The process of development, it would seem, was gradual. In 1541, Pole told Contarini that he had for some time favoured an attitude towards salvation similar to that which had been just agreed upon between the Lutheran and Catholic delegates at Regensburg; but he had hitherto been vague as to its details.[2] The evidence, as we have seen, suggests that it was Marco who, above all, initiated him into 'things hidden from the wise and prudent',[3] and that this had occurred in the years 1535–8. It is not, therefore, altogether surprising that, on reading Melanchthon, Pole should write to Contarini on 10 June 1537, assuring him that he had now 'the greatest hope' that if only the Pope would persevere in reform there would not be in the future great controversy about 'other matters', and all parties would 'easily agree in the profession of one faith in charity'.[4]

This is a new note in Pole's correspondence: the belief that reunion might, after all, be feasible. Only a year earlier he had noticed with despair that Cranmer now referred to the Pope as 'antichrist', to the Lutherans as 'Fratres in Evangelio', and that there was talk in England of 'abolishing' purgatory. 'With matters thus', he had written, 'how can there be hope of reconciliation in the Church?'[5]

But his hope of reconciliation grew, as the year advanced, along with his interest in the theme of justification. In this letter to Contarini of 10 June 1537 we find a statement of the means which Pole now believed likely to issue in reunion: an immediate reform of the Church's abuses, and a deepening of that 'fides' and 'charitas' in which all parties might yet find it possible to be at one.

1 See below, pp. 174–208.   2 Below, p. 60.
3 Pole to Marco, 25 February 1538. (*Epistolae*, II, 135.)
4 Pole to Contarini, 10 June 1537. (Ibid. p. 68.)
5 Pole to Priuli, Venice, 24 March 1536. (*Epistolae*, I, 444.)

It is highly instructive to observe how, from the year 1537, these hopes began to deepen and take root in Pole's mind. They did so in proportion to his understanding of the entirely gratuitously bestowed gift of faith. Just as Pole had discovered in this theme the ground and content of his own conversion, so did he begin to discover it at the heart of the Lutheran Reformation. Simultaneously, he found himself appointed to a papal commission to reform the Church.[1] Thenceforward, his hopes of reunion grew apace. Let the Pope but persevere, and the Lutherans would find it possible to return to 'the profession of one faith in charity'. The importance in Pole's thought of this expression, 'fides in charitate', which we first find in his letter of 1537, was to strengthen and develop in the years ahead, until it provided the very substance and principle of his hopes for the ultimate reunion of separated Christians in the one fold of the Church founded and preserved by Christ.[2] The ground of reunion would be discovered in the conviction of God's freely bestowed gift of mercy.

The seeds of that conviction had been established in Pole's mind for some time. In December 1535, John Friar, a member of Pole's English circle, wrote from Padua to Starkey: 'Pole is studying divinity and *meteorologizei*, despising things merely human and terrestrial. He is undergoing a great change, exchanging man for God.'[3] As Zeeveld shows, others in Pole's household were similarly affected: George Lily wrote to Starkey telling him that he was seriously contemplating membership of 'this new school of Chieti'.[4]

By this time, however, Pole's English household was on the verge of dissolution. Starkey had returned to England in December 1534. For a while, he acted as chaplain to Pole's mother in her home at Howgate; shortly afterwards, he became chaplain to the king.[5] During his two years at Padua he had undertaken the composition and partial revision of a work concerning the affairs of Church and State. Couched in the form of a discussion between

---

[1] Below, p. 42.   [2] Below, pp. 110ff.
[3] *L.P.*, IX, no. 917. (Cited by Zeeveld, *The Foundations of Tudor Policy*, p. 117.) In Greek, to 'meteorologize' is 'to think or talk about the heavenly bodies'.
[4] The Theatines. (*L.P.*, IX, no. 292; cited by Zeeveld, p. 97.)
[5] Zeeveld, *Foundations*, pp. 91–2.

Pole and Lupset, the manuscript, which was first published in
1878, has become known as *A Dialogue between Reginald Pole and
Thomas Lupset.*[1] The contents of the *Dialogue* have long been
familiar, although it had been recently re-examined in a novel
and illuminating way.[2] An examination of its argument is not,
therefore, immediately relevant to our purposes. But there is one
very striking passage which calls for attention. It follows a suggestion by Pole that divine service might reasonably be conducted
in the vernacular. Lupset replies sharply, horrified that Pole should
favour 'by your communycatyon, the Lutheranys maner, whome
I understond to haue chaungyd thys fascyon long usyd in the
Church', and concludes, 'I wold not that we shold folow theyr
steppys. They are yl masturys to be folowyd in gud pollycy.'[3]
To these remarks Pole replies humorously (and with a certain
appositeness, in view of Lupset's rather yielding role throughout
the *Dialogue*): 'Master Lupset, I se wel in thys you wyl not be so
sone persuaydyd as in other thyngs before you were'; and he
continues:

I wyl not folow the steppys of Luther, whose jugement I estyme veray
lytyl; and yet he and hys dyscypullys be not so wykyd and folysch
that in al thyngys they erre. Heretykys be not in al thyngys heretykys.
Wherfor I wyl not so abhorre theyr heresye that for the hate thereof I
wyl fly from the truth.[4]

Leaving aside the general question of how faithful Starkey was
to Pole's opinions in writing the *Dialogue*, it is nevertheless
remarkable that this passage should so accurately reflect the
attitude which Pole unquestionably adopted between 1541 and
1546.[5] At the Council of Trent he recommended an identical
approach to the assembled fathers almost word for word.[6]
Starkey, better than most people, knew the bent and disposition
of Pole's mind. It seems at least probable that he here recorded a

---

[1] Ed. J. M. Cowper, in Herrtage (ed.), *England in the reign of Henry VIII*
(London, E.E.T.S., 1878). A new edition appeared in 1948 edited by K. M.
Burton.
[2] G. R. Elton, 'Reform by Statute: Thomas Starkey's Dialogue and Thomas
Cromwell's Policy', *Proceedings of the British Academy*, 54 (1968), 165–88.
[3] *Dialogue*, p. 134.   [4] Ibid. p. 135.
[5] Below, pp. 62ff.   [6] Below, p. 134.

sentiment which he had actually heard Pole express. This is not to argue that Pole had accepted Luther's view of justification in the period during which Starkey knew him. Such sentiments might reasonably have been uttered by any humanist who considered that Luther was protesting against much that stood in need of reform. It is simply that Pole's later career reveals his willingness to endow such sympathies with more substance than was altogether safe.

Starkey, therefore, may be credited with having justly represented Pole's opinion on this question: but he was thoroughly mistaken in assessing his reaction to another question which, at the time of the composition, was more directly relevant to Pole's immediate career. In 1535 Starkey was commissioned to elicit Pole's support for the King's assumption of the title 'Supreme head of the Church of England'. He was confident of winning Pole, for he considered that his friend regarded the primacy of Rome as no more than a conventional arrangement. He may have been right: faith in the spiritual primacy of the Pope had noticeably weakened during the period of the Conciliar movement and the Renaissance papacy. On the other hand, it seems more likely that Pole had been simply unsure about the question; or merely circumspect. But in the same year that Starkey wrote to ask for Pole's opinion, More and Fisher were executed for their adherence to papal primacy, and their deaths put paid to any indecision which Pole may formerly have entertained.[1] With tears in his eyes – tears which literally made the ink run on the manuscript before him – he retired to draw up a defence of the papacy which irrevocably separated him from the developments of Henry's

[1] Cf. Starkey's assurance to Cromwell 'that in thys mater of the prymacy, I could neuer perceyue hym to abhorre from my Iugement & sentence, whereby I dyd euer affyrme hyt to haue only the consent & constytution of chrystn men, & not to be rootyd in goddys word expressly. In the wych sentence also he stoode, at the fyrst motyon of the mater to hym by the kyngys hyghnes, whereof I haue honest wytnes in england the same to testyfye. but aftur when he saw More & Rochester defende the cause wyth the shedyng of theyr bloode, ponderyng wythal a consent of doctorys agreyng to the same, wyth the practyse of the church so ma (ny) yerys, then he leynyd & formyd hys Iudgement therby, as in hys book he wrytythe playnly, whych was long aftur my departure from hy(m).' (*S.P.*, I/105, fol. 47r; *L.P.*, XI, no. 73.)

reign, and set his feet upon the path which led, within a period of months, to his appointment as a Cardinal.[1]

Pole's treatise, usually referred to as *De Unitate*, is an emotionally charged attack upon the King; it is a patently sincere attempt to induce him to repent; and it impressively argues the case for papal primacy in the Church. A recent French edition of the work provides an admirable introduction and commentary on the text.[2] We may note the predominantly Scriptural and Patristic basis of Pole's thought about the Church, and the place of the papacy within it; his deeply Augustinian outlook;[3] the centrality of penance in his conception of Christian life;[4] and his organic sense of connection between faith and reason.[5] Faith, Penance, the Church: these are the recurring constituent features of Pole's spiritual outlook, drawn always from Scriptural foundations, already fully matured by 1536, and applied from this time forward to the pressing problems of renewal in the Church and reunion among Christians: problems which for Pole, as for the other *spirituali*, awaited imminent solution in a General Council.

There is one further aspect of the work which will repay attention: a feature of Pole's thought which is reflected in one brief passage of the work. The section in question refers to the attitude of Peter and Paul to the ceremonial laws of the Jews. In the early days of the Church, explains Pole, 'even as now, there were Jews (should we wish to look around us; one may test the thing for oneself) who placed all hope of their salvation in observing the

[1] The full title of Pole's treatise, as printed at Rome *c.* 1537, without Pole's consent, is: *Reginaldi Poli Cardinalis Britanni pro ecclesiasticae unitatis defensione, libri quatuor*, Romae: Apud Antonium Bladum. A facsimile reprint by Gregg Press appeared in 1965. The work has recently been translated by J. G. Dwyer, *Pole's Defense of the Unity of the Church* (Westminster, Maryland, 1965). G. M. Marc'-hadour notes some important inaccuracies in this edition, *Moreana* (May 1967), pp. 101–2. Cf. Pole's admission of grief concerning the death of More: 'inuito lachrimae oboriebantur, ut scriptionem maxime impedirent, & ipsas saepe literas delerent, ut uix ultra progredi possem'. (*De Unitate*, p. xciv v).

[2] *Défénse de l'Unité de l'Église* ed. N. M. Égretier, (Paris, 1967). Hereafter, 'Egretier'. Rev. Breifne Walker has also written illuminatingly about the *De Unitate* in his unpublished M.A. dissertation of University College Dublin.

[3] Egretier, pp. 32, 36, 40, 62n, 75n, 116, 121, 122, 143n, 168n, 169n, 174–6, 182, 199, 201, 324n.

[4] Egretier, 34–5, 306–11, 326–8.

[5] Egretier, 35, 311–26.

law, and in external and shadowy ceremonies'.[1] Both Peter and Paul knew that the ceremonial laws had been superseded by the law of Christ: but 'they did not in the beginning greatly attempt to abrogate the ceremonies of the law'. Instead, as 'prudent dispensers of the word', they accepted this condition of affairs with a charitable dissimulation of their inner views, so as to protect the Jewish Christians from offence:

But all the while they were concealing their own true opinion of these ceremonies from the people, to whom an open profession of faith would have profited nothing. In fact, this very concealing profited them all the more. They, nevertheless, never passed an opportunity, if they saw that their disciples were apt to perceive the truth, of explaining their own true judgement of the law and the ceremonies.[2]

At length, Paul, 'instructed by the Holy Spirit, thought the time had come for revealing the truth more freely', and began, accordingly, to disseminate it.[3]

The interest of this passage lies in Pole's readiness to support a policy of concealment until the opportunity for clarification should arise. It is further interesting that he should advert to this procedure in a passage which deals with the efficacy of ceremonial observances: and that he should consider that there were still 'Jews...who placed all hope of their salvation in observing the law, and in external and shadowy ceremonies'. Did he mean Christians, whose dependence on 'works' he considered to be reminiscent of Jewish dependence on the Law? Whatever the truth, it is by no means certain that he had yet embarked upon the policy, for which he was in later years denounced, of secretly advocating the doctrine of justification by faith alone. Towards the end of his life, he was accused of having persuaded men to content themselves with their own secret convictions, and not to preoccupy themselves unduly with the errors and abuses of the Church, which God, in His own time, would correct.[4] This

[1] *De Unitate*, p. lxix v. [2] Ibid.
[3] Ibid. p. lxx r; *Acts* 13, 38, and 15, *passim*.
[4] *Giudicio soprà le lettere di tredici huomini illustri*, published anonymously in 1555. Quoted also in J. G. Schelhorn, *Amoenitates Historiae Ecclesiasticae* (Frankfurt and Leipzig, 2 vol. 1737–8), II, 9. Schelhorn (pp. 7–8) suggests that the author was

description of his attitude refers to the period 1541–6 when Pole, as another observer put it, sheltered in his household 'a platoon of heretics.'[1] In 1536, his views were perhaps already basically formed, but a number of years were to pass before he would assume the role of a 'prudent dispenser of the word', concealing his inner convictions until the opportune moment, and shielding his opinions from the inquisitive scrutiny of enemies.

As yet, Pole's only enemies were in England. The years 1534–6, so vital for his own spiritual formation, were in certain other ways also decisive for the Christian humanist community throughout Europe: confessional and political attachments now took over. It was in these years that Calvin completed the first draft of the *Institutes* and left France on the path that took him to Geneva. The implications of the Reformation for Christian humanists were now becoming clear; but the primacy of confessional considerations had been latent from the first. As early as 1516, the publication of *Utopia* had signalised the political insolvency of Erasmian ideals.[2] In 1523 More's *Responsio ad Lutherum* had recognised the inescapably confessional character of the Reformation heralded by Luther.[3] In 1535 his execution revealed the character and priority of the confessional divide cutting across the links which the humanist community had once supposed immutable. Melanchthon mourned his execution, but his lament was for the author of *Utopia*, rather than of the *Responsio ad Lutherum*. The circumstances which had produced the first book had long since disappeared and given way to those which had prompted More to write the second.[4] By 1535 it was becoming evident to even the most dedicated advocates of reunion that a fundamental

Vergerio, and his judgement is confirmed, not merely by a reference to Vergerio's patron Duke Christoph (p. 9), but more decisively, by the evidence concerning Vergerio's campaign against Pole during the years 1554–5. (Below, pp. 258–69.)

[1] See below, p. 230.

[2] A view which I have argued more fully in a paper entitled 'The Counter Reformation and the Realisation of *Utopia*', in *Historical Studies: Papers Read at the Ninth Conference of Irish Historians*, ed. J. Barry, 9 (Dublin, 1973).

[3] J. Headley, 'Thomas More and Luther's Revolt', *Archiv für Reformationgeschichte*, 60 (1969), 145–59. Fenlon, 'The Counter Reformation'.

[4] Fenlon, 'The Counter Reformation'.

choice had been dictated to them on the ground of conflict opened earlier by Luther's revolt: the choice concerning the ultimate location of authority within the Church. As Pole was later to express the matter, from the far side of his own disappointed expectations of reunion:

> thatt the same [Evanngell] is the doctrine of peace, herein is no controuersie att all, in thys both the catholike and the heretike wyll agree, but when itt cometh to this poynct of whome this doctrine shuld be learned...here nowe begynneth the greater trouble and dissention in religion.[1]

But it was many years before these words came to be written; years of frustrated expectation. In the summer of 1536, Pole was summoned to Rome, where Contarini, now a Cardinal,[2] was preparing a papal commission to reform the Church. In December, Pole reluctantly accepted nomination to the College of Cardinals. He was appointed along with Carafa, Sadoleto and Aleander; and with these men, together with Contarini, Giberti, Fregoso, Cortese and Tommaso Badia, the Master of the Sacred Palace, he collaborated on a report which, produced in the following year, recommended a wide-ranging and drastic series of proposals to reform the Church.[3]

The proposals, however, made no mention of doctrine: the elucidation of doctrinal issues was to be the business of a General Council. When, in 1538, a pirated edition of the text was published in Germany, the Lutheran pastor, Johann Sturm, severely criticised it for its neglect of the essential issues of the Reformation.[4]

---

[1] Vat. Lat. 5968 (Bodleian MS Film 33), fol. 256v.

[2] But still a layman. He was appointed, to his surprise, in 1535. The Pope's decision inspired the remark, widely repeated at Rome: 'This Venetian wishes to reform the Sacred College without knowing the names of the cardinals.' (Mackensen, 'The Diplomatic Role of Gasparo Cardinal Contarini at the Colloquy of Ratisbon of 1541', in *Church History*, XXVII (1958), 312–37.

[3] *Consilium delectorum Cardinalium...de emendenda ecclesia* (C.T., XII 131–45). The December nominations, and the proposals of the commission, are discussed by Jedin, *Council*, I, 423–8. Pole's reluctance to become a Cardinal was related to his (justifiable) fear of reprisals against his family in England. (Schenk, *Reginald Pole*, p. 74.)

[4] Friedensburg, 'Das Consilium de emendenda ecclesia, Kardinal Sadolet und Johann Sturm von Strassburg', in *Archiv für Reformationgeschichte*, XXXIII (1936), 1–69.

Yet it was only because of its omission of doctrinal questions that the *Consilium de emendenda ecclesia* was presentable as the last unified expression of the Catholic reform movement in the period before the Council. There existed within that movement differences so fundamental as to divide it utterly, before the Council itself assembled; and these differences revolved around the attitude of its participants to the Lutheran Reformation.

As early as 1532, Carafa had written that 'a heretic must be treated as such; the Pope lowers himself if he writes to him and flatters him or even allows graces to be procured for him; it is, indeed, possible that in this or that instance some good result may follow, but as a rule the recipients of such favours are only made more obdurate and gain fresh adherents'.[1] Against this attitude, there was the conviction of Pole and Contarini: 'Heretykys be not in al thyngys heretyks.' Four years after the *Consilium de emendenda ecclesia*, these two attitudes came into sudden conflict, when a religious conference between Lutherans and Catholics briefly established agreement on the fundamental doctrine of the Reformation.

But in the interval, it was still possible for *spirituali* and *zelanti* to work together, and to hope. At Rome, Pole and Carafa were collaborators in the task of initiating reform within the Church, Pole, indeed, passionately arguing with the Pope for the advancement of Carafa to the Sacred College. The two men agreed about the primacy of holiness as the precondition and conclusion of all their labours; they probably studied the same spiritual authors; and where they differed, they did so in their attitude not to schism but to schismatics. Throughout these years, we find Pole and his associates continuously seeking to ponder the words of Scripture 'nel suo interiore senso',[2] avidly attending to the

---

[1] Carafa to Pope Clement VII, 4 October 1532. (Cited by Pastor, *Popes*, x, 311.)

[2] Priuli to Beccadelli, 10 August 1537. Priuli remarks on Pole's insistence that Scripture must be assimilated in an interior sense: 'et ci concluse infine S. Sria che chi non facea cusi dei libri sacri non poteva ricever molto frutto da essi né sentir la dolceza che è in quelli nascoste' (Bodleian MS Italiano C 25, fol. 24v). These manuscripts, Italiano C 24 and C 25, are an important source for the history of the Italian *spirituali*. They are fully described by C. Dionisotti, 'Monumenti Beccadelli', in *Miscellanea Pio Paschini* (2 vols, Rome, 1948–9, ed. A. Casamassa *et al.*), II, 251–68. Dionisotti prints the above letter in full, pp. 264–5.

Imitation of Christ (a favoured document also of the English Carthusians),[1] and together meditating upon the epistles of St Paul. In the summer of 1537 Pole, together with Priuli and Giberti, found himself temporarily halted on a diplomatic mission in the see of Liège.[2] A letter of Priuli evokes the atmosphere of their activities and conversations.[3]

Each member of the company would spend the morning in his room, before assembling in the private chapel at a given hour to recite matins, 'more theatinico senza canto'. Following this, they would hear Mass, and a little later they would eat. During the meal there would be readings from St Bernard. Afterwards, there would be a reading from some edifying work – usually a chapter from Eusebius's *De Demonstratione Evangelica* – and there would then follow 'qualche honesto et grato ragionamento' for an hour or two. Vespers and compline were sung before the evening meal; and on alternate days Pole would read from the epistles of St Paul, 'to the great satisfaction of the Bishop and the rest of us'.[4] Sometimes they would spend an hour or two on the river, or strolling in the garden, discussing business, and lamenting only the absence of Contarini and his secretary, Beccadelli, from 'questo nostro honesto et bel tempo'.[5]

These, indeed, were the best years for the *spirituali*; the time of confidence and hope, when it seemed that the schism might be healed. But such times were not to last. In 1541 the negotiations at Regensburg achieved a short-lived reconciliation between Lutherans and Catholics; and the more fundamental grounds of their division became apparent. We must now examine the reaction of Pole and his associates to the events which signalised the apparent triumph of the *spirituali* – only to issue in the long years of reversal and defeat.

[1] R. Lovatt, 'The *Imitation of Christ* in late Medieval England', *Transactions of the Royal Historical Society*, 5th ser., 18 (1968), 97–121.
[2] Jedin, *Council*, I, 352.
[3] MS Italiano C 25, fols. 157r–159v, Priuli to Beccadelli, 20 July 1537. The letter is cited in *Epistolae*, II, civ–v, but mistakenly dated 28 July.
[4] Bodleian MS Italiano C 25, fol. 158v.
[5] Ibid. fol. 159r.

CHAPTER THREE

The collapse of Regensburg

Between 1541 and 1542 the concerns of the Italian *spirituali* became historically dominated by the fact of the Reformation. The convergence of interest in the theme of justification by faith, so marked in the Italian cities throughout the fifteen thirties, was bound at some point to pass from the stage of affinity and implicit preoccupation with the major thrust of northern Protestantism, to that of explicit interaction and exchange. When it did so, the question would necessarily arise: was there to be reconciliation and reunion between the parties, or conversely, the discovery of irreconcilable contradictions – a conflict, soluble only by the conversion of one side to the other? The breakdown, in 1541, of a reunion conference at Regensburg, in which the Catholic delegates were led by Contarini; the apostasy and flight to Switzerland, a year later, of the two preachers recurrently commissioned by Contarini and his friends to prevent the spread of heresy in the Italian cities; the reorganisation by Carafa and his supporters, of the Roman Inquisition in the summer of 1542; these three events provided an answer to that question, and marked the stages by which there began to be realised in the Italian cities the irreconcilable character of the conflict between Reformation and Counter Reformation. The first movement of the emerging conflict turned upon a struggle for control of the Italian pulpit. Its first casualties were the eirenic ambitions of the *spirituali*. The decade witnessed the eclipse of their hopes in the face of obstinately fundamental contradictions; it opened with the passing of their principal representatives. The death at Naples of Juan de Valdés in the summer of 1541, followed by that of Contarini a year later, introduced the last phase in the history of the *spirituali* before the Council of Trent: an interlude in which their internal disintegration was only marginally offset by the patronage and encouragement still discreetly afforded to their aspirations by Cardinal Pole and his circle of adherents at Viterbo.

In August 1541, Pole was appointed Papal governor of the *Patrimonium Petri*, the largest of the Papal states, with Viterbo as its seat of government.[1] A month later, when he took up residence, Viterbo became a final locus of reference for the Italian *spirituali*, following the collapse of the Regensburg talks and the dispersion of the Valdés group: a place where the deliberations of the former could in some sense be continued, and the members of the latter welcomed, as in a second home; a surviving centre for the discussion of questions which, soon to be banished from the Italian pulpit, might yet privately be considered, until the impending and as Pole believed, opportune moment for their renewed ventilation at a General Council. Since the public occasion of these questions had been the conference of Regensburg, it seems best to begin with the reunion talks and Pole's reaction to them, in the light of the situation developing in the Italian cities, before considering the role of Valdés, and the posthumous legacy which the conversations of Regensburg and of the Valdés group imparted to the deliberations at Viterbo.

Throughout the 1530s, in the Benedictine circles of Padua and Venice, men like Cortese and Contarini had incurred the disapproval of Carafa in availing of Papal permission to study the works of the Protestant reformers.[2] They found in these works the reflection of their innermost concerns: the centrality of Scripture, justification by faith, the exaltation of Christ's merits. They found too, to their intense sorrow, that these very concerns were made to serve as ground for the repudiation of the Church. They sought, therefore, to refute the contention that the Church

[1] Vat. Arch.; Arch. Consist. Acta Miscell. t. 18, fol. 344v: 12 August 1541.
[2] Cortese to Contarini, 22 June 1536, *Gregorius Cortesius Card. Omnia quae huc usque colligi potuerunt, sive ab eo scripta, sive ad illum spectantia* ed. A. Cominus (2 pts in 1 vol., Padua, 1774), I, 107–8.

was the enemy of Scripture: to separate the Scriptural premise from its anti-papal application, and to reestablish the interdependence of Church and Scripture.[1] At the same time, they worked for the renewal of the Church; from 1535 they did so with the support of Paul III.[2] To their fellow Catholics they spoke of justification by faith. To Protestants they stressed the merits of the Church. As time advanced, they found allies in Germany. The eirenic theology of Catholics like Johann Gropper helped to reinforce their conviction that reunion was not an impossible objective.[3] All that was needful was goodwill and charity;[4] that, and the continuance of Catholic reform.[5] All that was wanting was an opportunity for the opposing sides to meet.

In 1541, the opportunity arose. Charles V needed a united empire and the support of the Schmalkalden League against the Turks. A majority among the German Electors favoured religious reunion as the best counterpoise to Imperial preponderance. The Pope was reluctantly persuaded to cooperate. He therefore suspended his plan for the convocation of a General Council (which the Protestants would never acknowledge as authoritative) in favour of a reunion conference on German soil.[6] As an earnest of his sincerity he sent as his representative Gasparo Contarini, one of the four members of the Sacred College recognised in Germany as favouring an agreement with the Protestants. The others (who remained at Rome) were Pole, Sadoleto and Fregoso.[7] From Regensburg, Contarini relied above all on Pole to advocate his position at the Roman Curia.

In this, as in everything else connected with his mission, Contarini suffered disappointment. The conference at Regensburg

[1] This might be described as the basic purpose of the Curial *spirituali.*
[2] Above, p. 142n. 2.   [3] Jedin, *Council,* I, 368.
[4] 'Non est opus concilio, non disputantationibus et syllogismis, non locis ex sacra scriptura excerptis ad sedandos hos Lutheranorum motus; opus est tantum bona voluntate, charitate erga Deum et proximum'. Contarini, *Confutatio* (*Corp. Cath.* VII, 22).
[5] Above, p. 36.
[6] Jedin, *Council,* I, 355.
[7] 'ne ha nominati 4, in quali loro haveriano confidentia...et sono li Rev[mi] Contareno, Sadoleto, Polo et Salerno.' Campeggio's report from Germany, 23 December 1540, *Nuntiaturberichte aus Deutschland,* Abt. I, 1534–59 (12 vols., Gotha, 1892ff.), VI, 90.

achieved two things: agreement between the delegates concerning the doctrine of justification – followed by a complete impasse and breakdown of communication concerning the sacramental and juridical structure of the Church. Such limited agreement as the delegates did achieve was discountenanced both at Wittenberg and at the Roman Curia; their own internal disagreements explain why. As Jedin has shown the breakdown of agreement between the delegates at Regensburg itself is more significant than the external repudiation of what little they did achieve.[1] It illustrates that the dream of an understanding was no more than that; that the institutional differences which intervened between the delegates at the conference table were already irreconcilable. No sooner had each party reached agreement on the question of justification than they found themselves ranged against each other on the question of the sacraments and jurisdiction of the Church. Contarini, in the face of considerable pressure, refused to yield on the doctrine of transubstantiation. To do so would have been to reject the teaching of the Fourth Lateran Council, to deny a doctrine clearly defined by the Church, to achieve, as he expressed it, nothing but an empty agreement, *concordia palliata*.[2] The talks broke down. Goodwill, as it turned out, was not enough. Each side blamed the other. But the real cause of their differences was impersonal and institutional. Two irreconcilable communities were in existence, reflecting utterly contradictory conceptions of the means of salvation.[3]

The failure of Regensburg reflected the ineradicable character of the opposition between the religious parties. It led to the resumption of the papal plan for a General Council, and it explains why that Council could never have been a Council of reunion. Historically, Regensburg was more significant as a

---

[1] A judgement found 'unduly harsh' by B. Hall, 'The Colloquies between Catholics and Protestants 1539–41', *Studies in Church History*, VII, ed. G. J. Cuming and D. Baker (Cambridge, 1971), 266. But it is unfortunately difficult to see that any other judgement meets the reality. P. Matheson argues that 'the dialogue between Protestantism and Catholicism at the Diet of Regensburg in 1541 did not fail. It never took place.' *Cardinal Contarini at Regensburg* (Oxford, 1972), p. 181. This seems to me to be closer to the truth.

[2] Jedin, *Council*, I, 385.

[3] Ibid., pp. 359, 391, 409.

failure than as a success. What it revealed was the tragic reality of
the division between Protestantism and Catholicism. What it
proved to Catholic churchmen was the necessity of firmly
mastering the prevailing confusion of theology and belief with a
lucid presentation of Catholic teaching. What it purported was
the need for a General Council to achieve this end. It signified the
reality of the Reformation and the necessity of the Counter
Reformation.

From the vantage point of the *spirituali* the events at Regensburg
conferred an ambiguous inheritance: the memory of reunion, and
the experience of its loss. The former impressed them no less
profoundly than the latter: they clung to it in the hope that it
might yet bear fruit. In doing so, they sought to keep open a
question which had in fact been closed. The price of their commitment was that they were now more than ever open to the suspicion of heresy, by association.

Contarini returned home in the autumn of 1541 to find that
alarm had now broken out at the Curia about the advance of
heresy in the Italian cities. At Rome, he was himself under suspicion in certain quarters. But Paul III stood by him. In January
1542, Contarini was appointed to the Legation of Bologna, the
second city of the Papal state.[1] From there, he was entrusted with
the task of supervising the campaign against heresy in the cities
of the north. His allies were the leading prelates in the northern
dioceses and at the Curia: Morone at Modena, Gonzaga at
Mantua, Giberti at Verona, Pole and his supporters at Viterbo
giving encouragement and advice: Cortese and Badia at the
Curia.[2] The *spirituali* were therefore now in command of the
campaign against heresy in the Italian cities. Their policy was to
achieve their end by gentle discourse and without coercion. They
aimed to win their audiences by persuasion. They therefore set
out to man the pulpits of the north with preachers renowned for
eloquence and spirituality. They wrote manuals on preaching to

[1] F. Dittrich, *Gasparo Contarini* (Braunsberg, 1885), pp. 798–9.
[2] A. Casadei, 'Lettere del cardinale Gasparo Contarini durante la sua legazione di
Bologna (1532)', *Archivio storico italiano*, cxviii (1960), 77–130, 220–85, especially
p. 93, n. 37.

establish the strategy of the enterprise[1] and they turned for recruits to the *spirituali* from other centres – notably to those of the Valdés circle now beginning to disperse from Naples. At Bologna, Contarini employed Filippo Valentini to advise him 'alle cose di Modena'; Morone's diocese was the immediate focus of alarm.[2] He invited the General of the Capuchins, Bernardino Ochino, to preach at Modena as he had done at Bologna with such notable success in 1541.[3] Ochino, indeed, was in demand everywhere. At Naples, he had been among the most devoted admirers of Valdés, and had received from the master the themes of his sermons on the night before he preached.[4] The death of Valdés, in July 1541, marked the climax of Ochino's public career as a preacher everywhere sought after throughout the peninsula. Contarini at Bologna, Giberti at Verona, at Rome the Pope, competed for his services.[5] Competition was scarcely less rife for the Augustinian preacher, Peter Martyr Vermigli, also a disciple of Valdés, whose name now became a household word in the Italian cities at the same time as Ochino's and for the same reasons.[6] From Ferrara the Duchess Renée wrote to Contarini to request the dispatch of Vermigli as preacher; but his services had already been commissioned at Modena by Cardinal Morone.[7] Not since Savonarola had the Italian cities turned so enthusiastically to preachers.[8]

The control by the *spirituali* of the Counter Reformation in the Italian cities was not a policy which appealed to everyone. Preachers and town governments were an explosive combination, as the experience of Germany had proved. Why should the same

---

[1] Below, p. 62.

[2] Pastor, *Popes*, XII, 501. Casadei, 'Lettere', p. 93, n. 36, for Valenti.

[3] Casadei, 'Lettere', p. 93.   [4] 'Processo' p. 196.

[5] R. Bainton, 'Four Reviews', *Italian Reformation Studies in Honor of Laelius Socinus*, ed. Tedeschi, p. 5, in a notice of B. Nicolini, *Aspetti della vita religiosa, politica e letteraria del Cinquento* (Bologna, 1963), a copy of which, unfortunately, I have not been able to see.

[6] Especially in Lucca. McNair, *Peter Martyr*, pp. 206–38.

[7] Casadei, 'Lettere', p. 258.

[8] The limits of this study and the present condition of research preclude a full investigation of the relations between the *spirituali* and the forces making for Reformation and Counter Reformation in the cities. The religious history of the Cinquecento in its urban setting remains to be written. Rotondò's work on Bologna and Modena (above, n. 2, p. 20) promises to constitute an important point of departure. But a study of cities like Naples, Lucca and Ferrara is badly needed.

experience not be repeated in the city states of Italy? The Habsburgs had not prevented Reformation in the Empire; why should
they be any more successful within Italy? The irony of the situation as it now developed was that the *spirituali* were employing
as custodians of the faith, preachers – the Augustinian, Vermigli,
the Capuchin, Ochino – who were in fact moving inexorably
under the logic of their doctrine and the encouragement of their
congregations (or at least some members of them) into the very
position they were being asked to reverse: the position of overt
hostility to the Church's teaching. At Bologna, Contarini's
auditor, Valenti, was already gravitating towards the beliefs
which eventually led to his citation on a charge of heresy, and his
exodus over the Alps to Switzerland.[1] At Modena, the Jesuits
protested against Morone's unwitting patronage of doctrines
which advanced the very process he was endeavouring to control.
They sought to preach the doctrine of merit; Morone forbade
them; Loyola's protest went unheeded at the Curia.[2] But at
Rome, Carafa and his supporters were shortly to find cause for
grievance in the patronage extended to Ochino and Vermigli by
Pole, Giberti, Contarini and Cortese.

Carafa's hour was approaching. In the summer of 1542 Modena
and Lucca were thought to be in imminent danger of collapsing
before the advance of heresy. In response to this situation the
Roman Inquisition was reestablished in July 1542, and Carafa
was placed in charge of its operations. His task was to secure the
preservation of the faith throughout the whole of Italy.[3] From
this point onwards the control of the Italian pulpit began to move
away from the *spirituali* to the *zelanti*. And it was at precisely this
point that the magnetic attraction of the Reformation intervened
to dramatise, in the apostasy of Ochino and Vermigli, the exact
character of the situation which the *spirituali* had so signally
allowed to develop beyond their own control.

In July 1542, Ochino was summoned to Rome – not, as was

---

[1] Casadei, 'Lettere', p. 93, n. 36.
[2] P. Tacchi Venturi, *Storia della Compagnia di Gesù in Italia* (3rd edition, 2 vols.,
Rome, 1950–1), I, ii, pp. 154–8, 160–71; II, ii, pp. 221–35.
[3] Pastor, *Popes*, XII, 503ff.

once believed, to appear before the Inquisition, but to accept the responsibility of taking in hand the reform of his own order.[1] It may be that the invitation itself served to bring home to Ochino the contradiction between what he had by now come to regard as mandatory in conscience, and what he would be obliged to require of the Capuchins. At any rate, he hesitated. He conferred with Vermigli. Together, the two men recognised that the logic of their religious standpoints led inescapably in the direction of the Protestant Reformation. In August 1542 they took flight for Switzerland, Ochino pausing only to make a final despairing call upon the dying Contarini.[2] After that, he made his way out of the country.

Nothing could have been more catastrophic to the cause espoused by the Curial *spirituali* than the departure of Ochino and Vermigli. Their decision to make for Switzerland signalled a new and unlooked for coalescence between the concerns of the *spirituali* and those of the Protestant reformers. What it amounted to was the conversion of one side to the other – in the wrong direction. Affinity had passed over into subscription. Reunion was one thing; apostasy was another. But the enemies of the *spirituali* could draw only the opposite conclusion. Giberti was not mistaken when he recognised in the death of Contarini and the defection of Ochino and Vermigli, the passing of an epoch in the fortunes of the *spirituali*.[3] Henceforward, Carafa and the Inquisition were in the ascendancy at Rome.

With the death of Contarini in August 1542, Viterbo took over from Bologna as the directing centre for the examination of the issues raised at Regensburg, pressed to their logical conclusion in the Italian cities, and now depending upon Pole and his supporters among the *spirituali* for their eventual ventilation at a General Council. We must therefore devote some attention to the formula of reunion established at Regensburg, which became the occasion of a sustained exchange of views between Bologna and Viterbo,

[1] Bainton, 'Four Reviews', p. 5. Text of Ochino's summons to Rome published by P. Piccolomini, 'Documenti Vaticani sull'eresia in Siena durante il secolo XVI', *Bulletino Senese di storia patria*, xv (1908), 299.
[2] McNair, *Peter Martyr*, p. 280.
[3] Above, n. 2, p. 22.

in the last year of Contarini's life: an exchange prompted by and directed to the solution of the problems posed to the *spirituali* by the issues agitating the Italian cities in the months leading up to Contarini's death. To examine the reaction of the *spirituali* to the Regensburg formula is to recognise the discrepancies of outlook which existed among them – discrepancies which served only to heighten the dilemma imposed upon them by the contradiction between their own absolute allegiance to the authority of the Church, and the demands, both in logic and in practice, from the urban reformers of their own dioceses whom they sought to moderate, for the conversion of the cherished tenets of the *spirituali* into an instrument of attack upon the Church.

The basic contention between the Lutherans and Catholics at Regensburg, when they came to discuss the problem of justification, revolved around the question of 'works' and 'merit'. The importance of this question was that it entailed in logic (if not necessarily in the subjective intention of those who talked about it) a whole way of thinking about the Church. It implied a judgement upon the economy of salvation itself, and in particular upon the sacraments – their number and significance in the scheme of redemption. Luther's identification of the inclination to sin (concupiscence) with sin itself,[1] had led him to deny redemptive significance to anything attributable to the human will. Salvation was through the imputed righteousness of Christ. The inner man remained in sin. The Catholic conception of salvation, on the other hand, entailed the transformation of the inner man through the grace which reached him in the sacraments. Once justified in the faith which came to him in baptism, man, according to Catholic belief, was further sanctified through the operation of the other sacraments. His concupisence remained; but his sins were forgiven in the sacrament of penance. His sinful condition was continually transformed through the grace which reached him in the reception of the eucharist. Cooperating sacramentally with the merits of Christ, his works performed in grace therefore merited salvation. Hence the question of merit stood at the centre

[1] Jedin, *Council*, I, 408.

of the dispute between the Catholics and Protestants. Its discussion was a way of talking about the Church's sacramental system: it was a way of coming to judgement on the Church.

The formula of agreement between the parties at Regensburg was devised to reconcile two conflicting demands: the Protestant insistence that the sufficiency of Christ's merits precluded the attribution of merit to any works performed by man; the Catholic belief that man was made inherently just, with the reception of the gift of grace. The relation between faith and works was the hinge upon which all else turned. It was in order to meet these requirements that a formula had been worked out from an idea provided by the German theologian Johann Gropper.[1] It was this formula which received the assent of both parties on 2 May 1541.

The formula rested on the assertion that man was justified by 'illa fides, quae est efficax per charitatem',[2] faith rendering itself efficacious in love (that is good works). To be justified was to be the recipient of the justice of Christ Himself, imputed by faith; justice was inherent also in man ('etiam inhaerentem').[3] The two forms of justice were only tacitly distinguished in the formula itself, but they provide the germ of that theory of 'twofold justice' with which Contarini sought to recommend the agreement to the Curia.[4] According to the agreement, man was justified by faith in Christ, not by his own works.[5] Since his works were the expression of the justice inherent within him,[6] it followed logically that good works and inherent justice did

---

[1] Cf. Jedin, *Council*, I, 381; and P. Pas, 'La doctrine de la double justice au Concile de Trente', in *Ephemerides Theol. Lovanienses*, XXX (1954), 8–9. The formula is printed in *Corpus Reformatorum*, IV, 198–201, ed. C. Gottlieb Bretschneider (Halle, 1837); also in, Le Plat. J. *Monumentorum ad historiam Concilii Tridentini Potissimum illustrandam spectantium amplissima collectio*, III, 15–17 (Louvain, 1783).

[2] *Corpus Reformatorum*, IV, 199–200.   [3] Ibid.

[4] Below, p. 57.

[5] 'tamen anima fidelis huic non innititur, sed soli iustitiae Christi nobis donatae, sine qua omnino nulla est nec potest iustitia. Et sic fide in Christe iustificamur seu reputamur iusti, id est accepti, propter ipsius merita, non propter nostram dignitatem aut opera.' (*Corpus Reformatorum*, IV, 200.)

[6] 'Et propter inhaerentem iustitiam eo iusti dicimur, quia, quae iusta sunt, operamur' (ibid.).

not contribute to salvation. Man was therefore edged out as a cooperating agent in his own salvation. But the logic of this position was not rendered explicit. Good works were held to be rewarded by God – not because they were intrinsically meritorious but because being performed in faith, they served to augment faith and charity.[1] Therefore those who preached (here man was allowed back by necessity, and theology passed over into action) salvation by faith alone – should simultaneously insist upon penance, fear of God, good works.[2] Apart from its concession to an (ineffectual) inherent justice, the orientation of the formula was Protestant.

The Venetian ambassador reported that agreement appeared to have been reached among the learned men of Regensburg: man was justified by a 'lively and efficacious faith working through charity'; they ought not to preach 'faith alone' unless 'love, the fear of God, penance and good works' were also added.[3]

His account was accurate, and it caught the scissors and paste element in the agreement. 'Faith working through charity' threw everything, in reality, on faith; the injunction not to preach 'faith alone' meant precisely the reverse of what it said; the additional 'unless' tells the whole story. The Regensburg agreement was designed to legitimate the proclamation of salvation 'de sola fide': the 'addition' of good works in reality conceded the Protestant case.

Contarini was well aware of the need to defend so major a concession at the Roman Curia. He therefore dispatched a concisely worded brief to Pole and Gonzaga, designed to assist them in presenting the case.[4] The agreement, he stressed, had excluded the conception of 'merit'.[5] Even Aquinas and Scotus had understood 'merit' to be that which God in His mercy attributed to human works; merit was not, therefore, intrinsically attributable to works considered in themselves.[6] Pole and Gonzaga must

---

[1] Ibid. p. 201.   [2] Ibid.
[3] F. Dittrich, *Regesten und Briefe des Kardinals Gasparo Contarini* (Braunsberg, 1881), p. 178.
[4] Text in T. Brieger, 'Aus italienischen Archiven und Bibliotheken', *Zeitschrift für Kirchengeschichte*, v (1882), 593–5.
[5] Ibid. p. 595.   [6] Ibid.

stress the necessity in practice for the Christian to rely, not on his own works, but on the imputed righteousness of Christ.[1]

This was not an easy case to argue at the Roman Curia: it amounted to the Protestant theory of salvation. Neither Pole nor Gonzaga undertook to defend it. Gonzaga's theological adviser flatly opposed the formula.[2] Pole, by the time he received Contarini's letter, had left Rome to spend the summer at Capranica.[3] He dispatched Priuli to defend the agreement at Rome.[4] Writing to Contarini he remarked on the regrettable necessity for his own absence from Rome, his delight at the agreement, and his intention to comply with Contarini's cautions about the secrecy of the matter.[5] His absence, however, provoked Contarini to remark that it could scarcely have occurred at a worse time;[6] on consideration it seems difficult to resist the suspicion that Pole was taking the easy way out and that he was afraid to defend the formula at Rome. In fairness it must be said that he himself had reservations about the formula; they arose (like Luther's) from his inability to find its origins in Scripture.[7]

Priuli's reception at Rome revealed to the *spirituali* the extent of the opposition to the formula in the College of Cardinals. In a letter to Beccadelli (now acting as Contarini's secretary at Regensburg) Priuli graphically described the response of Carafa and Aleander.[8] He had met Carafa twice. Carafa had been kind but firm: the formula was unacceptable. It was a traditional gambit of heretics to confuse the faithful with cleverly spun phrases: the formula might be capable of a Catholic interpretation; but the Protestants would interpret it in their own sense, and claim that the Catholics had been won over.[9] Priuli found an equally formid-

---

[1] Ibid. p. 594.

[2] H. Jedin, 'Il cardinal Pole e Vittoria Colonna', *Italia Francescana*, XXII (1947), 20. A German text of this article appears in Jedin, *Kirche des Glaubens Kirche der Geschichte*, I, 181–94.

[3] Ibid. p. 595.   [4] *Epistolae*, III, 25.   [5] Ibid.

[6] 'in vero non poteva essere absente a tempo più incomodo' (Dittrich, *Regesten*, p. 341).

[7] Below, p. 60.

[8] Bodleian MS Italiano C 25, fols. 169r–173v, Priuli to Beccadelli, Rome, 20 May 1541. Fully printed in Dionisotti, 'Monumenti Beccadelli', pp. 266–8; and excerpts in *Epistolae*, III, xlv-ix, but with some mistranscriptions.

[9] MS Italiano C 25, fols. 169v–170v.

able opponent in Aleander, who maintained that the German
question would not be settled by a meeting of learned gentlemen.
He was particularly curious to know what Pole thought of the
agreement. Priuli replied that Pole understood it to reflect the
standpoint adopted by Melanchthon in his defence of the *Confessio
Augustana*.[1] His reply indicates that the *spirituali* were by now
avowedly committed to defending the Protestant doctrine of
salvation.

They found themselves obliged to do so, not only against
their Curial antagonists, but also against the opposition of some
of their own erstwhile supporters, like Gonzaga, who drew the
line well in advance of the Regensburg agreement.[2] Against their
strictures, Contarini felt himself pressed further to explain and
clarify the character of the agreement. Accordingly, on 21 May
1541, he drew up a defence of the agreement, designed to illustrate and amplify its principles.[3] His defence turned upon the
thesis of twofold justice, already implicit in the agreement.
According to Contarini, the Christian, once justified through the
assistance of the Holy Spirit, found himself the recipient of a twofold justice (*duplex iustitia*) – that inherently his own, which
remained full of imperfection, and that of Christ himself, on
which the Christian must rely for salvation.[4] Progress in sanctifi-

[1] 'mi rispose che esso non credea chel Melanton fusse mai per voler partirsi
ponto da quello che l'ha detto nella sua apologia et che quanto a questi doi
articuli de peccato originali et de iustificatione convenero etiandi nel convento di
Augusta' (MS Italiano C 25, fol. 173r; Dionisotti, p. 268). – Melanchthon, although not one of the primary negotiators, had been associated with the Regensburg agreement by his presence there. Pole's opinion was broadly speaking
correct: Melanchthon's view, both in the *Confessio Augustana*, and the *Apologia*
had been: 'sola igitur fides iustificat, ac bona opera propter fidem placent'. (*Confessio Fidei exhibita invictiss. imp. Carolo Caesari Aug. in Comiciis Augustae Anno
M.D.XXX. Addita est Apologia confessionis*, Augsburg, 1535, p. 43b.) The principle of twofold justice was however, peculiar to the Regensburg agreement.
Aleander, in common with other Catholics, had been impressed by the *Confessio
Augustana* and the *Apologia* in 1532 (Jedin, *Council*, I, 274 n. 1.)

[2] Above, p. 56.

[3] Printed by F. Hünermann, *Gasparo Contarini, Gegenreformatorische Schriften*,
in *Corpus Catholicorum*, VII, 23–34. Bembo sent a copy of this treatise to Pole.
(Bembo to Contarini, 11 June 1541, Morandi, *Monumenti*, I, ii, p. 177.)

[4] 'Attingimus autem ad duplicem iustitiam, alteram nobis inhaerentem, qua
incipimus esse iusti et efficimur "consortes divinae naturae" (2 Petr, 1.4) et
habemus charitatem diffusam in cordibus nostris, alteram vero non inhaerentem,

cation was then achieved by works performed in the spirit of charity.[1] By virtue of introducing the notion of progress in sanctification, Contarini was enabled to conclude that man was justified by faith, and also by works.[2]

But the status of the 'and also' remained obscure. In distinguishing between two kinds of justice, Contarini unwittingly exposed a major weakness in the Regensburg agreement. For if, as he had argued, inherent justice did not render man acceptable to God, it might reasonably be asked what value it possessed at all? It was, he had declared (in the same terms at the Regensburg decree), the ground from which good works were bred and flourished so as to augment the store of grace within the soul and render it more justified. But if its value in the sight of God was inadequate to render man acceptable, it was difficult to see precisely how this could be so. Contarini's purpose was clearly to deflect the charge of Pelagianism directed against Catholics, and to prevent the Christian from relying, in a self-righteous way, upon his own inherent justice. In doing so, he had acknowledged the necessity for good works, and the reality of inherent justice – but he had denied to them any inherent merit in the sight of God. This left the imputed justice of Christ as the sole and exclusive agent of salvation. The old antithesis which Luther had proclaimed unbridged: man could do nothing to please God until he accepted, in faith, the justice of Christ, imputed to him freely. But neither Contarini, nor the Regensburg decree which had inspired his treatise, made the deduction which Luther had drawn: that man remained inherently unjust, and was, rather *accounted* just, by the righteousness of Christ, imputed to him.[3] By endeavouring to maintain the reality of inherent justice, while at the same time denying it the power to render man acceptable to God, the Regensburg agreement incurred the rejection both of Luther and

sed nobis donato cum Christo, iustitiam inquam Christi et omne eius meritum. Simul tempore utraque nobis donatur et utramque attingimus per fidem.' (*Corpus Catholicorum*, VII, 28.)

[1] Ibid. pp. 30–3.   [2] Ibid. p. 33.

[3] Contarini's commentary was nevertheless, more explicit than the Regensburg decree, which had declared: 'Et sic fide in Christum iustificamur, seu reputamur iusti...' (see above, n. 5, p. 54).

the papacy.[1] Perhaps the most notable feature of Contarini's commentary is his confidence that the issues at stake were exclusively a matter of emphasis. It was a heroic, and creditable confidence; but logic and the course of events were to reveal it as delusory. The Regensburg distinction of a twofold justice was based on an insecure foundation, which subsequent developments increasingly betrayed.

As yet, however, its advocates remained convinced of its unassailable character. Contarini, as we have seen, sent copies of his treatise to Gonzaga and to Pole; but before they reached their destinations, opposition to the formula had solidified at Rome. On 27 May, Bembo wrote to Contarini, informing him of the hostility to the agreement in Rome; only Fregoso had defended it among the Cardinals.[2]

Fregoso's indeed, was the only voice raised at Rome in defence of the agreement. On 29 May 1541, Farnese's secretary, Niccolo Ardinghello, wrote to Contarini, telling him that those who had seen the formula felt that while its sense might be Catholic, it could have been more clearly phrased.[3]

Effectively, the question had been closed. By the end of June, Contarini had learned from Farnese that the opinion, even of the most learned, was that the Regensburg agreement denied the merit of good works performed in the state of grace.[4] Contarini was broken-hearted. He wrote to Bembo on 28 June, explaining that he had already been over this ground in his communication with Pole.[5] He had made it clear that Protestants did not deny the efficacy of good works performed after justification. They merely avoided the use of the word 'merit', because they interpreted it in its strictest sense, whereas Catholics employed it in an altogether wider sense. He expressed his regret that Pole should have been absent from Rome at such a time, and with such important business in hand.[6]

Pole was evidently quite conscious of Contarini's displeasure.

[1] Luther dismissed it as 'a thing of vagaries and patches'. (E. Bizer, 'The German Reformation to 1555', *N.C.M.H.*, II, 179.)

[2] Morandi, *Monumenti*, I, ii, pp. 167–9.   [3] *Epistolae*, III, ccxxxi-xl.

[4] Dittrich, *Regesten*, p. 341.   [5] Ibid.   [6] Ibid.

He wrote to him from Capranica on 16 July, apologising once again for his absence from Rome, and expressing his confidence that, although the matter had been abandoned, it could be raised again on Contarini's return.[1] He went on to thank Contarini for his treatise: not only was it well argued, and admirably clear, but it had passed into general circulation a truth which Pole, under the guidance of Contarini, had hitherto recognised, but never adequately explored.[2] It was like a jewel which the Church had always held, partly hidden and partly revealed: Contarini had enabled it to pass into the hands of many.

Pole's remarks have usually been taken to signify his acquiescence in the Regensburg formula.[3] By his own admission, this would amount to accepting Melanchthon's theory of salvation.[4] It must be recognised, however, that his reservations about the formula were no less significant than his delight about the fact of agreement: and his reservations emerged from a perspective distinguishable (at least in his own mind) from Melanchthon's. His one regret, as he explained, was that Contarini had not been forced by even stronger opposition, to demonstrate the Scriptural foundation of the doctrine.[5] (By 'opposition' he understood the Catholic opponents of the formula.)[6] His criticism signifies a

[1] *Epistolae*, III, 26–30.

[2] 'De hoc vero tibi plus certe nunc gratulor, quam olim, cum te primum vocatum cognovi ad hunc honoris gradum, quem nunc in Ecclesia geris, de quo scis me non parum gavisum, sed tunc non ita exploratum habebam...' (ibid. p. 29).

[3] Schenk, *Reginald Pole*, p. 102.

[4] Above, p. 57.

[5] 'Hoc tantum desiderabam, ut acriorem adversarium habuisses, qui tibi occasionem dedisset ad ea respondendi, quae ex Scripturis contra istam, quam tueris, sententiam afferi solent, quae quidem plura esse videntur, ac talia quae explicatione, ac te explanatore indigeant.' (*Epistolae*, III, 27.)

[6] Jedin, 'Pole e Vittoria Colonna', p. 21. There were also other kinds of opposition to the agreement. On 16 September 1541, Flavio Crisolino, a familiar of Bembo, had written to Beccadelli, who was making his way home with Contarini: 'ragionaremo di mille et migliara di cose quanto vedo che havete da dire; di tutto il resto vi ascoltaremo voluntieri, escetto che del Lutheranesmo; di questo non accasarà che parliate con noi, perchè siamo stati quelli chi sempre vi habbiamo difesi apparechiatevi pure a dire delle miracoli del mondo, et delli errori di ulisse, et delle prove di Hercule, et di quelle fole che si sogliono dire intorno al foco l'inverno, et noi apparechiaremo l'orrechie ad ascoltarvi' (Bodleain MS Italiano C 24, fol. 266).

fundamental, if politely expressed, detachment from the scholastic mode of thinking reflected both in Contarini's defence and in the formula itself. In Pole's opinion, the Regensburg agreement was insufficiently Scriptural. We must shortly return to the implications of his criticism, which seem to place him closer than Contarini to the issues associated with the indigenous advance of the Reformation within Italy.

CHAPTER FOUR

The aftermath of Regensburg

In the months which followed the collapse of Regensburg, the exchange of views between Pole and Contarini came to be dominated by the pastoral situation confronting them in the Italian cities. Faced with the growing impatience of the urban reformers within their dioceses, they chose preachers to conciliate the proponents of Reformation: preachers who knew how to expound the Scriptures (and in particular, St Paul) without advancing further upon the ground occupied by the Protestant reformers. The effect of their policy was merely to accentuate the contradictions which it concealed. Under the pressure of the demands imposed upon them from below, they became aware of the need to resolve a dilemma which became every day more acute: how to hold the line against spontaneous reformation. Having commissioned preachers, they wrote manuals of instructions for them. Pole compiled a treatise on preaching, which is unfortunately lost.[1] They exchanged letters with each other, seeking opinions and offering advice. The theme of their exchanges was the theme agitating Morone's diocese of Modena: the theme of justification and its consequences. What Pole and Contarini were now looking for was a hermeneutical framework for the doctrine of salvation *ex sola fide* which would not undermine the Church they sought to renew: a means of enabling preachers to convey the essence of the matter without encouraging their congregations to abandon the Church. In the course of doing so,

---

[1] *De Modo Concionandi*, no copy of which I have been able to discover. Quirini mistakenly attributes Contarini's work of the same title to Pole. (*Epistolae*, III, 75–82.) Pole completed the work about Christmas 1541. (Pole to Contarini, 23 December 1541, ibid. pp. 43–6.)

they found themselves having to acknowledge the inherent difficulties of the enterprise, and the disparity of outlook which they brought to bear on its resolution.

The context of the discussion between Contarini and Pole, by the summer of 1542, was the difficulty of reconciling the Catholic system of atonement with the doctrine of justification by faith alone. The one necessitated a theology of meritorious action or suffering, such as that implied, for example, in the doctrine of the sacrament of penance, or of purgatory; the other evacuated the meritorious content from salvation. To believe that salvation was, once and for all, by faith alone, through the imputed merits of Christ, was to be left with the question – what need was there for further expiation; for purgatory, for the sacrament of penance?

These were not academic questions. They were precisely the questions being posed to Morone from the reformers in his diocese of Modena.[1] Contarini composed a handbook to assist Morone. He sent a copy to Pole who annotated it.[2] Pole's annotations are unfortunately lost, but their sense can be regained from Contarini's reply. The exchange of views reflects the quandaries opened up at the centre of their own convictions by the demands for further reformation. On one side the implications of 'sola fides' were being pressed in a direction which neither Pole nor Contarini could allow – one which led to the dismantling of the Catholic economy of salvation. How were demands of this kind to be resisted, and the authority of the Church upheld? How, on the other side, were the Curial opponents of 'sola fides' to be brought to an awareness of its integral connection with the life of the Church? On the one hand there was the Protestant objection to the Church; on the other, the Curial objection to 'sola fides'. How was the connection to be demonstrated to the conflicting parties?

These were the questions which stood at the heart of the correspondence between the leading *spirituali* in the summer of 1542.

1 'circa il Purgatorio; circa il sacrificio della Messa, & la Verità del Corpo, & Sangue nel Sacramento; circa l'Adoratione di esso; circa la Confessione auriculare; circa l'Authorità della Chiesa in far le Costitutioni; circa l'Intercessione, & Invocatione de' Santi; & circa alcuni altri, come della Gloria de' Beati, quali dicono non essere ancora con Christo'. Morone to Contarini, 21 May 1542, *Epistolae*, III, cclxx.
2 *Epistolae*, III, 31–2.

Contarini thought he perceived the way to a possible solution in Pole's annotations to his little handbook. That he could do so betrays his fatal confidence that the matters in dispute could be resolved by a scholastic brainwave.

One of Pole's annotations was to the effect that the sinner, being perfectly reconciled with Christ, could add nothing further to his own redemption.[1] Salvation by faith alone left no room for human cooperation with the merits of Christ. But what were the sacramental implications of such a view? What need was there for purgatory or the sacrament of penance? Pole's attempt to grapple with this question remained, as we learn from Contarini, unresolved;[2] but he happened in passing to make another observation which suggested to Contarini a means of harmonising the problem. Pole had remarked upon the triple satisfaction which the sinner had to make: to God, to the Church and to his neighbour.[3] Could it not be that here was a means for establishing a theology of atonement which would respect the Catholic economy of salvation while securing the Protestant theory of its attainment? At some length, and with considerable ingenuity, Contarini went on to propose a theory of human reparation for sin in its aspect as an offence against natural, ecclesiastical and positive law: thereby opening the door for purgatory and the sacrament of penance, while closing it on the doctrine of salvation by meritorious works. His theory, he was careful to explain, was not designed to detract from the fundamental tenet of Lutheranism, which was Catholic.[4] But the terms of his solution were less impressive than his graphic depiction of the difficulties. The problem, from both ends of the dilemma, was acute. For the Lutherans, observed Contarini (and here we must remember that the term 'Lutheran' was

[1] 'perche vedo, ch'ella dice, che il peccatore per Christo e perfectamente reconciliato cum dio, ne vi bisogna che vi pongamo del nostro, poi dice che ha offeso la chiesa et se stesso' (Dittrich, *Regesten*, p. 360.)

[2] 'In questo punto volendomi io sforzare di explicare ad ambi dui noi lo istesso senso, il quale V.S.Rma. tocca nelli sui scritti, ma non lo explica, sicome non lo ho explicato io nelli miei'. (Ibid.)

[3] 'Hora veggio, che V.S.Rma. desidera da me maggiore explicatione, il che io similmente desiderei da lei circa quello che dice della satisfactione verso di dio, et verso della chiesia et del proximo.' (Ibid. p. 354.)

[4] 'et pero il fundamento dello aedificio de Lutherani e verissimo, ne per alcun modo devemo dirli contra, ma accetarlo come vero et catholico, immo come fundamento della religione Christiana'. (Ibid. p. 358.)

applied in Italy indiscriminately to all Protestants, and that Contarini is talking about Modena as well as Wittenberg), purgatory was a chimera, designed to extract money from the people; so too, with indulgences and monastic penances.[1] Some people, seeing the consequences of Lutheranism as abhorrent to the Church, argued that men were justified by works, and not by Christ alone. They thereby impugned the foundations of faith, and greatly enhanced the reputation of the Lutherans.[2] Others, however, realising that the foundations of Lutheranism were genuine, followed the consequences, thereby presumptuously abandoning the Church.[3]

Here, with vivid economy of phrase, Contarini innocently depicts the central weakness of the *spirituali:* their ability to suppose that the connection between a premise and its consequence could be 'presumptuous', whereas the creation of a disjunction between them was devout. Despite the ingenuity of his attempt to settle the question, Contarini was in reality stranded intellectually: his theology could not bridge the gap between two doctrines which led in contrary directions. What kept him secure in the faith to which he adhered was his confidence that, beyond theology, and the resources of human ingenuity, there lay the indefectibly established authority of the Church. Some might assert the doctrine of salvation by works alone, others presumptuously abandon the Church: Pole and he must submit to the Church's doctrine. Let them steer securely through Scylla and Charybdis, 'not abandoning the doctrine of the Church, but believing in it more than in our wits'.[4]

But how were they to convey the same spirit of obedience to those in Modena whom they sought to moderate? And how were they to reconcile the authority of the Church with the implications of 'sola fides'? Was it to be by distinctions of the kind so tortuously devised by Contarini? Pole's reply, on 8 August 1542, was written in haste and under pressure. He thanked Contarini for his 'most learned' writings of the previous month. He promised to reply in full later on; he was busy at present and could not, like Contarini, play the parts of Martha and Mary

[1] Ibid. pp. 354–5.   [2] Ibid. p. 355.   [3] Ibid.   [4] Ibid.

simultaneously.[1] But on 14 August 1542 he wrote again, this time to the effect that the matter required 'non piccola considera-tione'; it would be best to discuss it by word of mouth, when the opportunity arose.[2] The opportunity, however, never arose; within a fortnight Contarini was dead.[3]

Pole's precise views on the question of justification in the months that followed Regensburg remain something of a mystery; it seems that in certain aspects even Contarini found them so. Towards the end of his last letter to Pole he expressed the hope that Pole, together with his 'sancta et docta compagnia' at Viterbo, would devote their leisure to scrutinising everything he had said, correcting whatever they believed to be erroneous.[4] Contarini's final letter, indeed, indicates the way in which his thought developed after Regensburg. It was, for all its weakness, a more intellectually impressive piece of work than his earlier defence of twofold justice, and it crystallises the issues which, increasingly, were gaining currency in Italy. Preoccupied with the question of how man was liberated from his sins he had dis-closed his mind to Pole: together they had recognised each other's quandary. Each felt obliged to acknowledge the truth of Luther's contention that man could add nothing to the merits of Christ; that his works could do nothing to redeem him. Yet they could not accept the necessary conclusion that doctrines such as purga-tory, or the intercession of the saints, could be dispensed with. In rejecting these, and other articles of Catholic belief and practice, the Protestants had, in their view, been guilty of rejecting the word of God, and of disobeying the divinely instituted authority of the Church. They had thereby disrupted the unity of Christen-dom. Their problem was that the Protestants were now threaten-ing to disrupt their dioceses.

Faith alone, then, justified, as Scripture taught, and Luther recognised; but Scripture must be interpreted and amplified by

[1] *Epistolae*, III, 60. Pole's plea was legitimate: he was busily negotiating for a reduction of the salt tax recently imposed by the Curia. In the long run he secured the desired reduction. Biblioteca Comunale, Viterbo, Cod. 331 II C VII 8, *Riforme*, 41, fols. 47–112; also mentioned by G. Signorelli, *Viterbo nella storia della Chiesa*, III, ii (Viterbo, 1940), p. 154.

[2] *Epistolae*, III, 61.

[3] He died on 24 August 1542. (Dittrich, *Gasparo Contarini*, p. 848.)

[4] Dittrich, *Regesten*, p. 361.

the teaching authority of the Church. Here we can discern the common denominator in the outlook both of Pole and Contarini, and the reflection, also, of their pastoral dilemma: how to dissuade people from separating the two tenets and pitting each against the other. They were equally attached to the authority of the Church and the doctrine of 'sola fides' which they sought to wrest from those who opposed her. But they were not united in their attempts to resolve the difficulties presented on all sides by this already sufficiently difficult objective. Pole, as we have seen, found the Regensburg agreement insufficiently Scriptural. He found the theology of its Curial antagonists no less so. He found the only solution of the question in the unity of Scripture and experience ('Le Scritture sancte, le quali nel suo interiore senso non predicano altro che questa justitia').[1] The Roman 'adversaria' of 'questa verita' opposed the doctrine precisely because they were ignorant of Scripture. Their refusal to examine the question in the light of Scripture and experience ('per queste doi regole, delle Scritture, con la experientia') was at the root of the whole issue. If only they would realise it there would be an end to controversy.[2]

Here we may discern the terms which, by the summer of 1542, had emerged in Pole's mind as the dominant criteria for the evaluation of the controversy: 'the two rules of Scripture and experience'. They were not likely to recommend themselves as sufficiently precise criteria to the custodians of orthodoxy who manned the Inquisition – who subsequently found his treatise on preaching, for example, positively dangerous in its aversion to scholastic theology, its attachment to 'sola fides', and its emphasis on the 'pure and simple gospel' as the basis of preaching.[3] The strictures of the Inquisitors on Pole's treatise on preaching enable us to gain a crucial insight into his strategic directives to Contarini

---

[1] *Epistolae*, III, 53.

[2] 'Et per questa via se li altri adversarii di questa verità si mettesero a examinare, come la sta, cioè per queste doi regole, delle Scritture, con la experientia, cesseriano senza dubbio tutte le controversie. Nunc enim ideo errant, quia nesciunt scripturas'. (Ibid.)

[3] 'Conscripsit librum de modo et arte concionandi...Idem Polus defendit et nititur probare doctrinam Lutheranam de Justificatione esse veram, et improbat Theologiam Scholasticam, et persuadet purum et simplex evangelium esse praedicandum'. C. Corviersi, 'Compendio di processi del Santo Uffizio', *Archivio della Società Romana di Storia Patria*, III (1880), 261–91, and 449–73. The above reference appears on p. 284.

in the summer of 1542: his strategy for the control of heresy was to recommend to preachers the exposition of 'sola fides', the elimination of scholastic language, the elevation of the simple gospel – and, we may be sure, submission in everything to what the Church believed. At the same time, we find the likeliest ground of his detachment from Contarini's outlook: his indifference to the scholastic basis of his friend's attempts to resolve their shared predicament.

He was, moreover, becoming increasingly reluctant to express himself on paper. By 1542 he was becoming more aware of the pressures and suspicions mounting at home against the little groups dispersed all over Italy, which so actively concerned themselves with the pressing religious problems of the day. Viterbo was not the least prominent of these; and it was there that his own views were crystallising more precisely, under the influence of ideas brought to bear not so much from Regensburg, but from the Naples of Valdés. To understand the questions which preoccupied him and his friends, it is necessary, therefore, briefly to consider the circle which had gathered around Valdés at Naples; some of whose members were to provide the nucleus of Pole's company of Viterbo, and to relay to him (as seems probable) one of the more interesting formulations of the Valdés group: that the business of Christians lay in the acquisition not of knowledge, but of experience ('che il negocio Cristiano non consiste in scienza, ma in esperienza').[1]

[1] *A Second Tract upon Justification by Faith without Works*, in *XVII Opuscules by Juan de Valdés*, translated and edited from the Spanish and Italian by John T. Betts (London, 1882), p. 158. Nieto, *Juan de Valdés*, p. 9, cites the expression in its original Spanish from Eduard Boehmer (ed.), *Sul principio della dottrina cristiana. Cinque trattatelli evangelici di Giovanni Valdesso, ristampate dall' edizione romana del 1545* (Halle sulla Sala, G. Schwabe, 1870), p. 44. Nieto ascribes to Valdés himself the tract from which this expression comes. Fray de Sta Teresa thinks it more likely to have been compiled by a member of the Valdés circle, possibly by Flaminio or Benedetto da Mantova (*Juan de Valdés*, p. 421). They are agreed in regarding the sentiment itself as quintessentially Valdesian. For the role of 'esperienza' in the thought of Valdés, cf. Fray de Sta Teresa, *Juan de Valdés* (Rome, 1957), pp. 159–60, and below n. 2, p. 70. For Flaminio's influence on Pole, *Epistolae*, III, 42, examined below, p. 90.

CHAPTER FIVE

Valdés, Viterbo,
and the
'Beneficio di Cristo'

In Italy, the Scripturally informed piety of the reforming humanists received a vital impetus from Spain, where the influence of the
alumbrados lent, in both its orthodox and heterodox expressions,
a strong contemplative foundation to the religious revival. Valdés,
Loyola and Servetus were born in Spain: their initial influence
was most keenly felt in Italy.[1] Loyola and Servetus stood at
clearly distinguishable points of the religious spectrum; but the
teaching of Valdés was marked by the ambiguities generally
characteristic of the Italian *spirituali* among whom he emerged
as so important a formative influence. The ambiguities, indeed,
continue to be reflected in the subsequent attempts of scholars to
relate his work to the dominant religious currents of the age.[2]

The spirituality of Valdés was derived from Scripture. His
teaching, like that of Luther (which must surely have influenced
his outlook) turned upon the question of justification. According
to Valdés, justification was imparted to man as a gratuitous gift,
whereby he enjoyed the benefit accruing from Christ's death –
the *beneficio di Cristo*, as he called it.[3] The Christian's chief responsibility was to appropriate this gift, mediated to him through

[1] F. C. Church, *The Italian Reformers*, p. 8.

[2] Bakhuizen Van Den Brink, *Juan de Valdés*, pp. 51–62, gives a balanced survey.
Nieto, *Juan de Valdés*, sees the religious meetings of Valdés at Naples as 'an attempt
to found a "Christian Church" apart from the Pope and the Roman Catholic
tradition' (p. 166). His book is full of valuable insights, and usefully relates the
thought of Valdés to its Spanish origins, but in at least one instance his reading of
evidence is seriously at fault, leading him to discover (p. 317) 'a polemic against
the doctrine of "twofold justice"' in a letter by Valdés which makes no reference to the subject. (*XVII Opuscules*, pp. 146–53.)

[3] *The Hundred and Ten Considerations of Juan de Valdés*, translated and edited

Scripture under the inspiration of the Holy Spirit, and manifested in good works which were not, however, meritorious.[1] The appropriation of the *beneficio di Cristo* was ratified in 'esperienza' which brought home to man the awareness of his justification and redemption.[2]

The principal concern of Valdés was to lead people to the point at which they would recognise the *beneficio di Cristo*. Carnesecchi conveys the impression that he made no 'deductions' beyond this point.[3] He is not known to have concerned himself with the visible features of the Church, with questions of structure, authority or ministry. It may be that he was indifferent to such questions. His confessional standpoint has always been difficult to determine. In effect (whatever his intentions) the orientation of his theology was Protestant.[4] He addressed himself to the interior conversion of his audience: his instrument at Naples was Ochino's pulpit. The effect of his teaching, given its proximity to Protestantism in all but its external form, was tacitly to undermine the Church. In 1532 he had left Spain, having incurred the disfavour of the Inquisition. He died, an inspector of Castles at Naples, a year before the establishment of the Inquisition at Rome. His followers dispersed, most of them into positions of detachment from, and eventual (though sometimes private) opposition to the Church.

His personal friends and followers included a number of figures scarcely of lesser interest than the master himself, many of them better known historically: Ochino and Vermigli, who made so outstanding an impact on the development of the Reformation outside Italy; Vergerio, who left his diocese of Capo d'Istria to follow them into exile seven years later; Giulia Gonzaga, who stayed in Italy, and escaped the Inquisition only by virtue of her social station and a timely death; Vittoria Colonna, familiar to

from the Italian by John T. Betts, in Benjamin B. Wiffen, *Life and Writings of Juan de Valdés* (London, 1885), pp. 296–8, 431–4 (*Cons.* 34, 75). Fray de Sta Teresa, *Juan de Valdés*, pp. 167–71.
[1] *The Hundred and Ten Considerations*, pp. 325–7, 472–5, 517–20, 521–6 (*Cons.* 43, 86, 97, 98).
[2] Ibid. pp. 536–9 (*Cons.* 102).   [3] 'Processo', pp. 335–6, 533–4.
[4] Nieto, *Juan de Valdés*, pp. 333–7.

readers of Michelangelo's sonnets, the patroness of the Capuchins and supporter of Ochino until his flight across the Alps; Flaminio, whose contribution to the literature of the Italian Reformation deserves to be better known; Carnesecchi, whose deposition before the Roman Inquisition furnishes us with a compass to the development of the Valdés circle after 1541. But when Valdés himself died in July of that year, a number of his followers felt themselves bereft of immediate direction. One of them wrote to Carnesecchi from Lake Garda: where could they go, now that Valdés was dead?[1] Carnesecchi's answer, and Flaminio's, was to accept the invitation extended to them by Reginald Pole who, on 14 September 1541 had made his official entry to Viterbo, as Papal Governor.[2] In November, the two men took up residence in Pole's household.[3]

In composition the Viterbo circle which now came into existence was similar to other such groups in Europe; a small number of devout enthusiasts bent on personal sanctity, and nourishing fervent hopes of ecclesiastical reform. Together with these was a larger number of friends, guests and servants who participated to a greater or lesser degree in the discussions.[4] The inner group consisted of those who, mostly by virtue of longstanding acquaintance with Pole, were closest to him: Alvise Priuli and Flaminio; Vittoria Colonna – herself, like Flaminio, a writer of poetry, and like him, possessing a disposition at once sensitive and nervous. She stayed at the convent of S. Caterina, and placed herself under Pole's spiritual guidance. Pole, still labouring under the grief caused by the execution of his mother,[5] came to regard her as a second mother; and their friendship deepened as they sought to turn their suffering to spiritual advantage in prayer and medita-

---

[1] Iacopo Bonfadio to Pietro Carnesecchi, *s.a.* (but 1541), in *Opuscoli e Lettere di Riformatori Italiani del Cinquecento*, ed. G. Paladino (Bari, 1913), p. 96.
[2] Bib. Com. Viterbo, Cod. 331 II C VII 7, fol. 104v; also Signorelli, *Viterbo*, II, ii, p. 143.
[3] 'Processo', p. 198.
[4] Carnesecchi recalled nineteen names, together with a number of others, 'maestro di stalla, credenzieri, parafrenieri et altri officiali' whom he could not remember. ('Processo', pp. 254–5.)
[5] On 27 May 1541 (*C.S.P.S.*, VI, i, p. 351). She was a victim of the King's hostility to the Pole family, her death was a way of hurting Pole.

tion.[1] Another member of the circle was Pole's chaplain, Appolonio Merenda, who in later years fled Italy, to escape the Inquisition;[2] and the group also included a wealthy Venetian merchant named Donato Rullo, who later apologised to the Inquisition for associating with Pole.[3] Rullo was a close friend of Carnesecchi, and he had left Naples together with Flaminio and Carnesecchi in 1541.[4] Another associate of the group was Vittore Soranzo, who spent some time at Viterbo from 1541, and kept up a close contact with the circle until in 1544 he was appointed coadjutor to Bembo in his diocese of Bergamo.[5] Soranzo's friend, Tommaso Sanfelice, whom the former had introduced to the circle of Valdés at Naples, also maintained some contact with the Viterbo group.[6]

In many ways, therefore, the Valdés circle was transplanted to Viterbo at the end of 1541: Flaminio, Vittoria Colonna, Carnesecchi, Rullo, with Soranzo and Vergerio as occasional visitors or aquaintances. Ochino and Vermigli were commissioned as preachers by Pole, Contarini and Morone, and reciprocated their good regard. Vermigli in particular was recommended for advancement by Pole and Contarini alike, in the year 1541–2, as a man of outstanding ability, in need of further recognition at Rome.[7] Hence the death of Contarini in August 1542, coinciding with the sensational defection of both Ochino and Vermigli, came as a shattering setback to the Viterbo *spirituali*.[8] From this moment onwards the Viterbo circle was a focus of intense sus-

[1] Vittoria Colonna had left Rome in 1541, in order to avoid the embarrassment which followed the unsuccessful revolt of her brother against the papacy, and the consequent ruin of her family's wealth. (Pastor, *Popes*, XI, 336–44; cf. also Jedin, 'Pole e Vittoria Colonna'.) B. Nicolini, *Ideali e passioni nell' Italia religiosa del Cinquecento* (Bologna, 1962) provides a further notice concerning Vittoria Colonna (pp. 25–44, 147–50) together with a study of Giulia Gonzaga (pp. 79–102).

[2] Below, p. 236.

[3] Stella, 'La Lettera', p. 416, n. 19. C. de Fred, *La Restaurazione cattolica in Inghilterra sotto Maria Tudor* (Naples, 1971).

[4] L. Amabile, *Il Santo Officio della Inquisizione in Napoli* (Citta di Castello, 1892), p. 142. Cf. also 'Processo', p. 198.

[5] G. Alberigo, *I vescovi italiani al concilio di Trento, 1545–7*, p. 78.

[6] Ibid. pp. 213 and 224–5.

[7] McNair, *Peter Martyr in Italy*, pp. 133, 166, 167–8, 171, 191, 197–8, 255 and 284.

[8] Ibid. pp. 238–93. Vermigli's apostasy was followed shortly afterwards by that of Emanuele Tremelli, a Jewish scholar who had been converted by Pole in 1540

picion.[1] At Rome, the commissioners of the newly established Inquisition, Carafa, Toledo, and Cervini conferred together not only about 'le cose de Napoli', but also about 'li rumore che si fecero della cose di Ratisbon'.[2] Naples and Regensburg were henceforward suspect: the implications for Viterbo were already clear. At Viterbo itself, the effect of Ochino and Vermigli's flight may be seen in Pole's reaction to Ochino's desperate letter, written to Vittoria Colonna on the eve of his departure, requesting her judgement, and that of Pole, on his decision.[3] Pole's response was to inform her that she must send any further such communications to Cardinal Cervini at Rome.[4] It was a response based on his belief that the Pope was the Vicar of Christ, and that to abjure him was to abjure the truth; but his reaction did nothing to allay the rumours which were circulating at Rome against the supporters and encouragers of heresy.

It was in the atmosphere of fear and suspicion generated by these events that a little book appeared anonymously at Venice, in a second edition, towards the end of 1543. It was a work which Morone liked to circulate in his diocese at Modena. It was entitled the *Beneficio di Cristo*.[5] Its republication was received 'not without

(Ibid. pp. 223–4, and W. Becker, *Immanuel Tremellius*, 2nd edn Leipzig, 1890).

[1] Cf. the report of Cardinal Gonzaga's agent, Nino Sernini, on 2 September 1542, that a close watch was being kept on the Viterbo group. A. Luzio, 'Vittoria Colonna', in *Rivista storica mantovana*, I (1885), 39.

[2] Priuli to Beccadelli, 20 June 1541 (MS Ital, C 25. fols. 208r–210r).

[3] *Carteggio di Vittoria Colonna* (Florence and Rome, 1889), pp. 247–9. Vermigli too, wrote a last letter to Pole, explaining his apostasy; no doubt it met with the same response. (McNair, *Peter Martyr in Italy*, p. 284.)

[4] She wrote to Cervini on 4 December 1542, expressing her distress at Ochino's efforts to excuse his apostasy. The more he sought to excuse himself, the more he accused himself; and the more he believed himself immune from shipwreck, the more he risked the torrent, being outside the security of the ark. (*Carteggio*, pp. 256–7.)

[5] *Trattato Utilissimo del Beneficio di Iesu Cristo Crocifisso*, Venice, 1543. A copy exists in the library of St John's College, Cambridge. A facsimile version of this copy was published by C. Babington, *The Benefit of Christ's Death* (Cambridge and London, 1855). Another edition was published by G. Paladino, *Opuscoli e Lettere*, pp. 3–60. I have used Babington's edition (having compared it with the original at St John's) since it retains the original spelling. An excellent and valuably annotated translation of the work has recently been published: *The Beneficio di Cristo*, translated, with an introduction by Ruth Prelowski, in *Italian Reformation Studies* (ed. Tedeschi), pp. 21–102. A critical edition by S. Caponetto is to appear as vol. II of the series *Corpus Reformatorum Italicorum*.

a certain uproar and suspicion of novelty': a circumstance not altogether surprising; for it was the most revolutionary product of Italy's unaccomplished Reformation.[1] We must now turn aside to consider its significance, and the circumstances of its composition; for they throw considerable light on the function and significance of the Viterbo circle.

The *Beneficio di Cristo* was among the most popular of those works of spiritual devotion which in the sixteenth century exercised a peculiar attraction for the European mind. The second edition, as we have seen, was published at Venice in 1543 ('apud Bernardinum de Bindonis'); six years later, according to one witness, it had sold 40,000 copies in the city alone.[2] It was later translated into French, Croat, English and Castilian.[3] Its authorship, for long surmised but never determined, was unequivocally divulged for the first time on 21 August 1566, when Carnesecchi revealed that it had been written by two men.[4] 'Il primo autore' was a Benedictine monk named Benedetto da Mantova. He had composed it in a Sicilian monastery near Mount Etna. He had then given it to his friend Flaminio, 'begging him to polish and illustrate it with his fine style, so as to make it more readable and delightful'. Flaminio had agreed. Keeping the subject intact, he had rewritten it in the light of his own judgement ('serbando integro il subgietto, lo reformò secondo che parse a lui'). Carnesecchi had been the first to see the finished product, and since he approved of it, he passed on a copy to 'qualche amico'.[5]

[1] 'Ho ritrovato il Beneficio di Christo stampata già la seconda volta, ma non senza qualche rumore e suspicione di novità: ve ne mando uno.' Scipione Bianchini to Ludovico Beccadelli, 28 October 1543, from Venice. (Biblioteca Palatina, Parma, Cod. Pal. 1022, fasic XI, unfoliated. Cited by Bozza, *Introduzione al Beneficio di Cristo* (Rome, 1963), p. 9, but without source. In 1965 the MS was in Bozza's keeping at the Biblioteca Nazionale, Rome.)

[2] P. P. Vergerio, *Il catalogo de libri, li quali nuovamente nele mese di Maggio nel anno presente 1549 sono stati condonnati...e aggiunto...un indicio e discorso del Vergerio* (s.l., 1549).

[3] Babington, *Benefit*, Introduction, pp. lii–iii. Cf. also V. Vinay, 'La Riforma in Croazia e in Slovenia e il "Beneficio di Cristo"', in *Boll. della Soc. di Studi Valdesi*, CXVI, 1964 (Dec.), 19–32.

[4] 'Processo', pp. 202–3.

[5] 'dal quale io prima che da nissun altro l'hebbi, et come io l'approvai et tenni per buono, così ne detti anco copia a qualche amico.' (Ibid.)

After the appearance of the second edition the work was rapidly suppressed by the Inquisition in Italy, although it clearly continued to enjoy a massive underground readership. With the recovery of certain copies in the nineteenth century scholarly investigation began to accumulate. There is a vast historiography on the subject, admirably surveyed in a recent article;[1] we shall be concerned here only with the views of two distinguished scholars, Tommaso Bozza, and Salvatore Caponetto.

Caponetto, advancing the researches of another writer[2] has recently confirmed the hypothesis that Carnesecchi's 'Benedetto da Mantova' was a Benedictine monk named Benedetto Fontanino who was professed at Mantua in 1511.[3] In 1534 he was residing in Venice, at Cortese's monastery of S. Giorgio Maggiore. (He was therefore conversant with Pole's circle.) In 1537 he was transferred to the Catanian monastery of S. Nicolo de Arenis di Nicolosi, not far from Mount Etna.[4] He remained there until 1542, after which his movements, though occasionally discernible, are somewhat obscure. He does not seem to have known Valdés personally, although this, of course, does not preclude the possibility of his acquaintance with the works of Valdés, which circulated in manuscript form.[5] Carnesecchi, it should be remembered, described him as 'amico di M. Marcantonio Flaminio': a friendship that had doubtless developed during their joint sojourn at Venice.

In a recent study, Bozza has demonstrated beyond question that the *Beneficio di Cristo* was heavily indebted to the 1539 edition of Calvin's *Institutes*, from which it translated or abridged whole passages.[6] Arguing from this Bozza concludes in a further

[1] V. Vinay, 'Die Schrift "Il Beneficio di Giesu Christo" und ihre Verbreitung in Europa nach der neuen Forschung', *Archiv für Reformationgeschichte*, LVIII (1967), Heft I, pp. 29–72.
[2] C. Ginzburg, 'Due note sul profetismo Cinquecentesco', *Rivista storica italiana*, LXXVIII (1966), pp. 184–227.
[3] Caponetto, 'Benedetto da Mantova', *Dizionario*, VIII, 437–9.
[4] Ibid. p. 437.
[5] Caponetto, 'Benedetto da Mantova', *Dizionario*, VIII, 439.
[6] He gave notice of his discovery in a privately printed paper entitled *Il Beneficio di Cristo e la Istituzione della religione cristiana di Calvino* (Rome, 3 February 1961; cf. Vinay, 'Die Schrift "Il Beneficio di Giesu Christo" ').

paper that the work was begun in the second half of 1540.[1] His basis for this conclusion is that Cortese is known to have acquired a copy at Venice in August 1540. Cortese described the little book as 'another work by the Lutheran John Calvin'.[2] Bozza does not suppose that Benedetto came to know the work through Cortese, since the latter was unlikely to propagate works which were, in his own phrase, 'liable to have a corrupting effect on minds'; he supposes, rather, that Benedetto had himself acquired a copy of the *Institutes* at about the same time, that is in the summer of 1540. Admitting that 'it is a very weak argument', Bozza nevertheless claims that the *Institutes* came to be known in Sicily at the same time that it first reached Venice.[3]

Bozza, then, argues that Benedetto composed the work in Sicily, not earlier than the second half of 1540, and before the end of 1541. Early in 1542 Benedetto travelled to Viterbo. There he gave the manuscript to Flaminio for revision. He then moved on to Padua and Venice to publish the work, the first edition of which appeared at Venice either late in 1542 or early in 1543.[4] Bozza's evidence for this hypothetical reconstruction of events rests on a letter which Priuli wrote from Viterbo to Beccadelli at Bologna, on 18 July 1542 – a letter which refers to Benedetto's journey.[5]

Since Bozza neglects to append the sources of his most intriguing citations, the value of this hypothesis which he builds on mysteriously produced evidence has been called in question by Caponetto.[6] But the survival of Priuli's letter among the Italian

---

[1] *Introduzione al Beneficio di Cristo* (privately printed at Rome, 1963).

[2] He wrote at this time to Contarini: 'Mi è poi capitato alle mani un' altra opera fatta per un Giovine Calvino Luterno, intitolate: *Instituto Religionis Christiana* di molta, e mala erudizione... al giudicio mio sino al presente non è fatta Opera alcuna Luterana più atta ad infettare le menti; tanto il buono è mescolato con quel suo velono' (Cortese, *Opera*, i, 236, 29 August 1540).

[3] *Introduzione al Beneficio di Cristo*, p. 28.   [4] Ibid. p. 16.

[5] 'Per le ultime vostre al S. Vicelegato ho inteso che D. Placido era costì col P. don Benedetto per ritornar tosto insieme a Padova; non essendo per ventura ancor partiti, potrete dir a padre D. Benedetto per che ho ricevuto le sue in risposta delle mie ultime et che al ritorno di Messer Donato [Rullo] vi scrivero poi a Padoa, raccomandandomi in questo mezzo alle sue orationi.' (*Introduzione al Beneficio di Cristo*, cited p. 16.)

[6] 'Benedetto da Mantova', *Dizionario*, VIII, 438.

manuscripts at Oxford establishes beyond question Benedetto's connection with Viterbo, and his presence at Bologna and Padua in the summer of 1542.[1] It does not, however, as we shall see, establish that Flaminio revised the *Beneficio di Cristo*.

Allowing for the significant elements in the work which can be traced directly to the thought of Valdés – not only the title, but certain other characteristically Valdesian phrases which recur – Bozza concludes that these elements were contributed by Flaminio, stressing the importance of Carnesecchi's statement that Flaminio keeping the subject intact, rewrote it in the light of his own judgement ('serbando integro il subgietto, lo reformò secondo che parse a lui').[2] But he does not consider that the Valdesian element in the work is very important, and towards the conclusion of his paper he allows himself to be carried away into asserting that the work 'has nothing in common' with the doctrine and spirituality of Valdés; that it is, in essence, a summary, and often a translation of Calvin's *Institutes*.[3] It is at this point that Caponetto comes in to the attack. Employing close textual analysis he demonstrates decisively that the 'anthropological pessimism' of the first chapter is quite different in character from Calvin's appraisal of the natural capacity of man, and that it is, on the other hand, entirely in keeping with the views of Valdés; that Valdesian phrases and images recur throughout the work; while the treatment of the eucharist, in chapter six, is taken directly, not from Calvin, but from St Augustine.[4] Thus he concludes that Calvin is not the model, but the 'precious instrument' of a work in which the doctrine of Valdés 'constitutes the heart'.[5]

The value of Caponetto's contribution is that it reaffirms the inspirational and structural unity of the *Beneficio di Cristo*. The book itself is characterised by exceptional tightness of control. Each of its six chapters is briskly driven forward with an economy of argument that wastes no time. A careful reading of the work,

[1] MS Italiano C 25, fols. 213r–214r. The passage cited above appears on fols. 213v–214r. Bozza has modernised the spelling and omitted the word 'sante' before 'orationi'.

[2] *Introduzione al Beneficio di Cristo*, p. 17.

[3] Ibid. p. 25.

[4] 'Benedetto da Montova', *Dizionario*, VIII, 440.   [5] Ibid.

indeed, conveys the dominant impression of a mind possessed with the urgency of what it has to say, and assisted by an imagination which lends grace and striking illustration to the argument.

It is this feature in particular which leads one to re-examine Bozza's argument. The most serious weakness in his chain of thought lies in the difficulty of supposing that the 1539 edition of the *Institutes* should have reached Sicily at the same time that it reached Venice. The next most serious is his supposition that the 'Valdesian' and 'Calvinist' elements in the work are the product of two separate minds. If, on the other hand, we pay closer attention to Carnesecchi's testimony, these weaknesses become irrelevant, and a rather different picture begins to form.

In the first place, we must give full weight to the statement that Flaminio, 'serbando integro il subgietto, lo reformò secondo che parse a lui'. This must be allowed to mean what it says: that Flaminio, given a manuscript which dealt with the subject of justification, rewrote it in the light of his own judgement. A substantial part of that judgement, of course, derived from his acquaintance with the person and doctrine of Valdés; not a little of it derived from his absorbtion in Scripture and the early fathers; but a good deal of it derived from his acquaintance with Calvin's *Institutes*, which (as we find from Carnesecchi's testimony) he had been reading during the year 1541.

In May of that year, some two months before the death of Valdés, Flaminio left Naples with Carnesecchi, intending to take up residence at Verona, with Giberti.[1] They travelled together with Donato Rullo, and a certain Marc'Antonio Villamarini, described as 'an abbot'. Flaminio, then, was leaving Naples for good. By the time he left there is reason to suspect, as we shall see, that he was carrying Benedetto's manuscript. The four men stopped at Rome on their journey, and Rullo remained there, joining Pole's household.[2] Carnesecchi and Flaminio travelled north; Villamarini stayed behind, entering Morone's service.[3] Flaminio, however, instead of going on to Verona, stayed at

[1] Ortolani, *Pietro Carnesecchi* (Florence, 1963), p. 31, and 'Processo', pp. 198, 210–11.
[2] 'Processo', p. 198. [3] Ibid. pp. 210–11.

Florence for 'some months' in Carnesecchi's house.[1] While they were together at Florence, Flaminio gave Carnesecchi a copy of Calvin's *Institutes* to read. The effect of the book was to instil in Carnesecchi's mind doubts about the existence of purgatory, and the sacramental status of confession: doubts which Flaminio had first expressed to him at Naples in 1540.[2] Now Flaminio had been reading the works of the reformers for years;[3] he had been, during the late 1530s, especially preoccupied with the question of pre-destination;[4] and he was therefore likely to be well-disposed to the doctrine of the *Institutes*. We cannot know when he first read the work; but it must have been available in Florence by 1541.

It is at this point that we must revert to another statement in Carnesecchi's testimony: namely that he was the first person to see the revised version of the *Beneficio di Cristo* ('io prima che da nissun altro l'hebbi'); and that having read it, and approved it, he gave a copy to a friend of his ('a qualche amico').[5] Why should Carnesecchi have been the first person to see the revised manu-script, unless he also happened to be the most obvious person to give it to? The only time that the two men were in each other's company, without being members of another group, was in the months between the spring and winter of 1541. At some time during this period Carnesecchi therefore read the work and gave a copy of the manuscript to a friend; it was probably this copy which later became the first printed text of the *Beneficio di Cristo*.

What is certain, is that Beccadelli read the revised *Beneficio di Cristo* in 1541. In that year he was in Regensburg with Contarini, and travelled back to Italy in the summer. Three years later, he was at Reggio, as Vicar-General to Cardinal Cervini. On 19 January 1544, he received from Cervini 'a learned discourse on that book

[1] Ibid. p. 198.
[2] 'credo che cominciassi sino a Napoli nel 1540 a dubitare del purgatorio et della confessione, et di questo principio fu autore il Flaminio, allegandomi, quanto al purgatorio, un loco di S. Augustino sopra Salmi...Ma inanzi che andassimo a Viterbo, essendo il Flaminio alloggiato meco in Fiorenza, mi haveva imbuta la mente di simili opinioni' (ibid. pp. 194–5).
[3] Maddison, *Flaminio*, p. 84.
[4] Jedin, *Girolamo Seripando*, pp. 112–16 (German edn; pp. 85–7, Eng. edn).
[5] Above, n. 5, p. 74.

of which the Inquisitor spoke', warning him that he must prevent
the book in question from circulating at Reggio. Beccadelli
replied on 29 January.[1] He told Cervini that he had known the
work for something like three years, and had been profoundly
impressed by it; that he had been moved by the 'autorità' of the
'person who abbreviated it', and that he held him indeed to be
'learned and good'; but if the book were heretical, he would
certainly withdraw his good opinion of it, and defer to the
judgement of Cervini 'and other learned and good people'.[2]

This letter makes it clear that Beccadelli had read a copy of the
'abbreviated' *Beneficio di Cristo* (presumably in manuscript form)
in the summer or autumn of 1541. It is noticeable that he refers
to the 'authority' of the 'abbreviator' rather than to that of the
original writer (whom he also knew, as we have seen from Priuli's
letter of July 1542); a fact which suggests that Flaminio, not
Benedetto, was credited with the essential authorship of the work.
The same implication seems to appear in a letter which Scipio
Bianchini wrote to Beccadelli on 15 September 1543, 'il libro del
Flaminio'.[3] This was a month before Bianchini sent Beccadelli
the second edition of the *Beneficio di Cristo*. There can be little
doubt that 'il libro del Flaminio' was in each case the same book,
as Morone was at this time enthusiastically circulating the work at
Modena.[4]

Thus there is the reason to believe that Flaminio re-wrote the

---

[1] Beccadelli to Cervini, 29 January 1544. (Biblioteca Palatina, Parma, Cod.
Pal. 1009, fols. 17r–18v. In 1965 the MS was in the keeping of Professor Bozza
at the Biblioteca Nazionale Rome.)

[2] 'Et per questo a me piacque il libretto detto di sopra, lo qual mihi gia tre anni
sono parendomi che andasse a questa via di farci conoscer il beneficio di Iesi
Christo et infiammarci di lui, si come douressimo fare, movendomi ancho l'auth-
orita della persona che lo abbrevio, la quale ho per dotta et da bene'. (Cod. Pal.
1009, fol. 17r.) Beccadelli further explains that if the book contains 'o per
l'ignoranza o per malitia cose ambigue et scandalose' he (Beccadelli) wishes to
submit to the judgement of others better informed: 'voglio vivere et morire bon
figliolo di Sta Chiesa'. Any doubt that the work referred to is the *Beneficio di
Cristo* is dispelled by Beccadelli's report in the same Codex, encompassing the
years 1543–4, which notes the Inquisitor's proceedings 'del libro de beneficio
Christi' (ibid. fol. 26v; and 27v, reference to 'il libretto de beneficio').

[3] Cod. Pal. 1022, fasic. XI (unfoliated).

[4] Cf. Morone's *Difesa* before the Inquisition printed in C. Cantù, *Gli eretici
d'Italia* (Turin, 1865–6), vol. II, pp. 176–90, especially p. 180.

manuscript of the *Beneficio di Cristo* at Florence in 1541. The book could have been first published in any north Italian city, at any time between the autumn of 1541 and that of 1543. All we can say with certainty is that the second edition appeared in Venice in the autumn of 1543. But of Flaminio's responsibility for the main lines of the work (not just its form) there can scarcely be any doubt. We know that he was familiar with the thought both of Valdés and of Calvin; we cannot be sure that Benedetto was familiar with either (although the probability is that he had read Valdés). If in addition to this we note that Benedetto da Mantova was described in 1564 as a 'disciple of Marc'Antonio Flaminio'[1] we may reasonably conclude that the real originality of the work derives from Flaminio, who drew upon his knowledge of Calvin, Luther, Valdés, Scripture and the early fathers to compose the most impressive document of the Italian Reformation. If this interpretation is correct, then Benedetto's visit to Viterbo and Bologna in 1542 was simply a courtesy visit to Flaminio and Pole, and later to Contarini and Beccadelli – visits which he paid, as we have seen, on his way to Padua, to which city he was probably transferred from Sicily in 1542. Certainly there is no record of his presence at Catania after 1542;[2] and the *Beneficio di Cristo* had been in circulation for some months by that time. His contribution to the final product is historically indeterminable; Flaminio's is not. Thus there is no need to posit a separable or disjointed presence in the work, of 'Valdés' and 'Calvin': both were equally present in Flaminio's mind, and the same preoccupations, arguments and linguistic constructions which characterise the *Beneficio di Cristo* may be found also in his letters; but before turning to them we must briefly devote some attention to the work itself.

The first four chapters systematically expound the doctrine of salvation by faith alone. Once justified by faith, man is enabled to perform good works; but they are not intrinsically meritorious. Justifying faith is compared to a flame which burns a piece of

---

[1] On 10 March 1564 one 'I.F.A.' testified to the Inquisition that the *Beneficio di Cristo* 'fu composto da un monaco di S. Severino Mantuano, discepolo di Marc' Antonio Flaminio'; an account less exhaustive than that of Carnesecchi two years later, but highly revealing nonetheless. ('Compendio', p. 468.)

[2] Caponetto, 'Benedetto da Mantova', *Dizionario*, VIII, 438.

wood while simultaneously emitting light: so faith extinguishes and burns away men's sins, while incidentally yielding an effect in works. Absence of works, therefore, indicates absence of the true faith which God gives His elect in order to justify and glorify them.[1] All this is pure Valdés.

Towards the end of chapter four a change occurs, as the tone becomes more militant: attention is directed to the differences existing between those who accept the doctrine there outlined, and those who believe in salvation by both faith and works. The difference lies in that the latter, elevating human pride, cannot bear to be justified through the free gift of Jesus Christ: whereas the other party ('noi') displays true humility and gratitude.[2]

With this argument, and the sustained use of the first person plural which it introduces, the boundaries have been drawn. It is quite clear that the book is intended for a definite group of people who are in possession of the truth, and determined to stand by it – however anonymously – in the face of every opposition. Thus the doctrine of Valdés has been grafted into a tree of considerably tougher growth; while the attempt of Contarini and the Curial *spirituali* to mediate between conflicting attitudes has been decisively rejected. And, as the work becomes more combative, it is impossible not to feel the spirit of Calvin asserting itself with vigorous assurance.

The argument resumes with a further broadside against the belief that good works can assist man to attain salvation, and continues with a meditation (which forms the theme of the fifth chapter) on the need for every Christian to rejoice in suffering the ignominy and persecution lavished by false Christians upon those who wish to live devoutly in Christ.[3] This leads directly to the considerations which underlie the sixth, and final chapter, entitled 'alcuni remedii contra la diffidentia'.[4] The Christian, it argues, continually beset by the temptations posed by Satan and by human

---

[1] *Beneficio*, pp. 2r–35v (Babington facsimile).

[2] 'In questo siamo differenti, che noi diciamo, che la fede senza lo aiuto delle opere giustifica, & la ragione e in pronto, perche noi...non possiamo esser tanto ingrati, ciechi, & impij, che crediamo, che ella senza le nostre opere non sia bastante a farci grati, & giusti nel cospetto di Dio.' (*Beneficio*, p. 36r.)

[3] *Beneficio*, pp. 36v–45r.   [4] Ibid. pp. 45r–70v.

prudence both, must arm himself for spiritual combat. The most powerful spiritual armoury consists of prayer, frequent communion, the recollection of baptism and the awareness of predestination. Baptism makes the Christian a partaker of Christ's righteousness, so that his sins are hidden, and are not imputed to him. The eucharist is his perpetual remedy for doubts concerning the remission of his sins: the blood of Christ, shed for his sins upon the altar of the cross is distributed again beneath the veil of the most holy sacrament, and renders visible once more his reconciliation with almighty God. The eucharist, as sign and seal of man's redemption, imparts to his soul the assurance of salvation, and to his body the assurance of immortality.[1]

Confronted with his own sins, the Christian knows himself worthy of damnation: but his assurance of salvation is recovered when he considers the promises which God has made; for God has shed His blood in remission for the sins of men. Hence the soul may take confidence in the love which God has shown it. Thereby is fear dismissed, charity augmented, faith confirmed and conscience liberated. The eucharist lies at the centre of the Mass, enabling the Christian to consider in his mind's eye the passion of Christ. There he may contemplate, on the one hand Christ, suffering upon the cross the weight of all men's sins, and on the other God, chastising and scourging His son in place of all sinners. The effects of the eucharist, moreover, are not merely to reassure the Christian, but to unite him in fraternal charity to Christ. And thus, in loving Christ he loves his brethren – and in offending them, offends Christ equally.[2]

Prayer, the memory of baptism and frequent reception of the eucharist are all, then, powerful remedies against diffidence and fear. But the last and best is the recollection of predestination and election to eternal life, grounded in the promises of God. The Christian derives the greatest consolation from the recollection that, however often he may fall, God remains his Father, and has predestined him to eternal life. Thus he rejoices in his heart and spurns all obstacles.[3]

[1] Ibid. pp. 45v–49r.   [2] Ibid. pp. 49r–54v.   [3] Ibid. pp. 54v–56r.

The final pages of the *Beneficio di Cristo* consider possible objections. First, the reader may feel uncertain of his presence among the number of predestined souls; he may, perhaps, live continually in fear, knowing himself to be weak and liable to sin. But such considerations are declared to be temptations of the devil, who tries by every means to wean the Christian from his faith, and from the confidence which flows from it. No one is truly faithful until he believes in the Word of God, which promises the remission of sins, and peace to whoever accepts the grace of the gospel. Therefore the Christian must beware of sin and try with all his heart to behave as a son of God. If, however, he does fall, he must not on that account believe that he has become a vessel of wrath, or that the Holy Spirit has deserted him: for Christ, who had made propitiation for sin, is his perpetual advocate before the Father.[1]

The objection that, without a particular revelation, no Christian can know whether he is in the state of grace, and therefore predestined to eternal life, is disposed of as unscriptural.[2] Scripture, it is true, exhorts men to fear; and fear argues no assurance of predestination. But the fear of punishment which characterises the Old Testament must be distinguished from the filial love which is the predominant feature of the New. Fear of punishment ('timor penale') runs contrary to the 'allegrezza spirituale' which distinguishes the Christian. Scripture exhorts those who are bad Christians to fear: but only until they have tasted the sweetness of the faith, and it has begun to exercise its effects upon them. In exhorting good Christians to fear, it intends a filial, and not a penal fear – so that they may continue vigilant, and avoid whatever is displeasing to God.[3]

The work draws to a conclusion with a note of warning. Those who employ the doctrine of predestination to behave in whatever way they wish, on the grounds that their destiny is predetermined, forget that God has revealed the doctrine to make men fervent, and not cold, in His service. Thus the true Christian will hold it certain that he is predestined to eternal life, and that he is saved,

[1] Ibid. pp. 56v–6ov.   [2] Ibid. pp. 6ov–63r.   [3] Ibid. pp. 63r–68r.

not through his own merits, but by the election of God.[1] But he will also attend to the performance of good works, and the imitation of Christ, as if his salvation depended upon his own industry and diligence.[2]

These final sentences constitute a succinct epitome of all the book has argued. The final passages resume the argument once more in summary. Emphasising the tremendous benefit which the Christian derives from the crucifixion of Jesus Christ, they reiterate the doctrine that faith in the satisfaction made thereby for the sins of men, is the single mode of justification. Nevertheless, good works remain inseparable from faith: flame is accompanied by light, but flame alone burns. This is the doctrine which exalts Christ and abases human pride.[3]

The *Beneficio di Cristo* is a remarkable work, characterised by a passionate incisiveness to which a summary does little justice. Its purpose, to demonstrate how men were justified, and how they could be certain that they were, was crucial to the spiritual anxiety of the age. Its popularity was therefore inevitable, given this anxiety, and the fervour and concision of its argument; nor is it difficult to understand why it alarmed the Catholic authorities. It was not simply that, as in the case of Valdés, the visible and hierarchical structures of the Church were ignored; nor merely that a doctrine which attributed everything to faith, and nothing to good works had received explicit formulation. There was as well the militant toughness of its argument, its readiness for combat, and its consciousness of subverting the accepted norms. Above all, there was its emphasis upon predestination, already becoming an issue which was to change the whole direction of the Reformation, and to establish Geneva as a rival to Rome. And even more alarmingly perhaps, there was its anonymity.[4]

Yet even in the most impeccable quarters the work achieved an

---

[1] Ibid. pp. 68r–v.

[2] 'Onde il uero christiano da un lato tiene per fermo di esser predestinato alla uita eterna, & di douersi saluare, non gia per gli suoi meriti: ma per la elettione di Dio: il quale non per l'opere nostre: ma per monstrare la sua misericordia ci ha predestinati. & dall' altro lato cosí attende alle buone opere & alla imitation di Christo, come se la salute sua dependesse dalla industria & diligentia propria.' Ibid. p. 68v.　　　　　　　　　[3] Ibid. pp. 68v–70v.

[4] The printer's preface stated that the name of the author was withheld 'accioche

astonishing success. Beccadelli's reaction we have seen: it was a reaction shared by a number of prominent members of the hierarchy and the religious orders. Cortese had found Calvin's *Institutes* 'liable to have a corrupting effect on minds', but his enthusiasm for the *Beneficio di Cristo* was immense; Morone read the work 'con grande avidità' and circulated it in his diocese; Cardinal Madruzzo, the prince-bishop of Trent, thought it a delightful work.[1] Morone afterwards claimed that it had seemed to him to be 'molto spirituale' in its treatment of the eucharist;[2] but it seems probable that these men were attracted also by the doctrine of justification there propounded; and if they were prepared to close their eyes to the explicitly polemical tone of the book, it may be because they suspected Flaminio had had a hand in it, and because they knew that Flaminio was now under benevolent custody in the unpolemical company of Viterbo.[3]

Beccadelli's reaction, therefore, accurately mirrors the prevailing state of mind among a characteristic sector of Italian Catholics in the period following the establishment of the Roman Inquisition. He had responded enthusiastically to the book and its doctrines upon first reading it – only to learn with alarm that the book was held in disfavour by the ecclesiastical authorities. Immediately he was thrown into a quandary. On the one hand, there was the fervour and conviction which he had found so appealing in the *Beneficio di Cristo*: on the other, his allegiance to ecclesiastical authority. Not that in his mind the censor's judgement was necessarily in accordance with the real doctrine of the Church; but until a Council should deliberate upon the matter his certainty was undermined. It was a predicament he shared with others. Morone, hearing persistent 'murmurs' about the book, eventually laid it aside and never looked at it again.[4]

Certainly the Inquisition had been quick to move against the

piu la cosa ui muoua che l'autorita dell' autore': a sentiment which remained unshared by the Inquisition.

[1] Morone, *Difesa* (Cantù, *Gli Eretici*, II, 180–1).   [2] Ibid. p. 180.

[3] Morone acknowledged that Flaminio was reputed to be the author, but that he denied it: 'si diceva esser stato il Flaminio, ed esso lo negava: dopo intesi esser stato un monaco di San Benedetto, credo o siciliano, o del Regno, che non ho saputo il nome.' (Ibid. p. 181.)

[4] Ibid.

work. Cervini, as we have seen, had sent an agent to so obscure a place as Reggio to prevent its circulation, within a few months of its second appearance. Not long afterwards, a vigorous and assured reply was issued by the Dominican theologian Ambrogio Catharino.[1]

Catharino prefaced his reply with a broadside against presumptuous speculation in matters of faith, deploring the general concern of everyone, however unqualified, with the most complex questions of theology and Scripture: justification, free will, grace, providence, predestination, faith and works – together with a range of other problems which, as he declared, were so complex as to defy even the resolution and intelligence of great minds. Such universal presumption ran contrary to the injunction of St Paul: 'non plus sapere quam oportet sapere'.[2]

There followed a point by point examination and refutation of the propositions made in the *Beneficio di Cristo*. The work displays both erudition and intelligence, and it embodies a considerable measure of compressed reflection. But because its terms of reference are preordained by the object of its attack, it never achieves the directness or psychological appeal of the earlier work – and least of all its freshness. Catharino's reply remained a catalogue, and an exercise in intellectual analysis; not a manifesto written for the people.

Its publication, however, marked an important moment in the history of the Italian Church. It was the first considerable attempt in Italy to cope at the level of argument with the ideas and aspirations generated within Italy itself by the Reformation. In doing so, it employed a frame of reference on the question of justification which was close to the hearts of many of the *spirituali*, although with an emphasis which was different from theirs.[3] Catharino's

---

[1] *Compendio d'errori et inganni luterani autore, intitolato Trattato utilissimo del beneficio di Cristo crocifisso* (Rome, 1544).

[2] Ibid. p. 2r.

[3] 'la giustificatione prima de l'huomo ingiusto che si fa giusto, senza dubio non vien da l'opere, ma da la fede, ma quella che di giusto fa anchor piu giusto, vien da l'opere buone fatte in fede per dilettione...' (*Compendio*, pp. 11v–12r). This is highly reminiscent of Contarini's defence of the Regensburg agreement. Pole, as we shall see, employed the same concept of faith working through charity, or love; but he understood it in a sense quite different from Catharino's.

Compendio illustrates the growing awareness of the need to define
and clarify the guide lines of belief among Italian Catholics and,
through a General Council, among Catholics at large. The
Beneficio di Cristo, therefore, helped in its own way to precipitate
the response which found its full expression at the Council of
Trent. We have seen how this response began to take effect in
Beccadelli and Morone; we must now consider how Pole
responded to the presence in his circle of the author of the
Beneficio di Cristo.

CHAPTER SIX

Flaminio at Viterbo

Beccadelli, in his *Life* of Pole, relates that the latter invited Flaminio to Viterbo because he was worried about the opinions which Flaminio had acquired in conversation with Valdés at Naples. At Viterbo he had gently weaned Flaminio from these views, and returned him to the path of orthodoxy.[1]

The inference of Beccadelli's remarks is that Pole had dissuaded Flaminio from adhering to the views of Valdés. But Pole himself, in explaining to Carafa the reason for his invitation to Flaminio, made no mention of Valdés. Flaminio, he said, had come to Viterbo with certain opinions of doubtful orthodoxy. Pole had realised the dangers which would ensue if Flaminio, because of his ability in the world of letters, were to set himself up as a judge of complex theological affairs. He had therefore persuaded Flaminio to read the doctors of the Church; and Flaminio, responding to his guidance, remained within the Church as a devout Catholic.[2]

It has been argued by the biographer of Valdés that Pole was alarmed, not by Flaminio's association with Valdés, but by his views on purgatory and the sacrament of penance.[3] This interpretation is almost certainly correct. There is no reason to believe that Pole regarded Valdés with particular suspicion. Valdés had denied no dogmas (at least overtly), his views on justification were not dissimilar to Pole's and, like Pole, he had emphasised the importance of a personally assimilated faith. Explicitly to question

---

[1] Morandi, *Monumenti*, I, ii, pp. 326–7.
[2] Cf. Filippo Gherio to Beccadelli, 29 April 1553. (Morandi, *Monumenti*, I, ii, pp. 347–53.) Pole's conversation with Carafa is further discussed below, pp. 241–4.
[3] Fray de Sta Teresa, *Valdés*, pp. 402–4.

the official doctrine of the Church, was, however, a very different thing; and what Valdés had not overtly done, Flaminio, as we have seen, had no hesitation in doing. His views on purgatory and the sacrament of penance were exactly those which were proving so embarrassing in cities like Modena, and which Contarini and Pole had sought to circumvent in their correspondence after Regensburg. Pole's views on such questions were the same as Contarini's. They are further clarified by the testimony of Morone. The latter, hearing that Pole did not believe in purgatory, decided to test the rumour for himself. He remarked to Pole that 'many people in Italy denied purgatory': Pole, however, replied swiftly that such people were reckless and presumptuous to deny what was held by the Church.[1] On another occasion Pole informed Morone that, seeing Flaminio with his 'fine wit and fine letters' in danger of succumbing to heresy, Pole had gradually 'brought him back to the good way' ('son andato pian piano ritirandolo alla buona via').[2]

It is clear enough that by 'heresy', Pole understood an attitude which rejected doctrines such as that of purgatory, which were taught explicitly by the Church. But the doctrine of justification remained to be defined, and if Pole exercised an influence on Flaminio, there is no reason to believe that he was not himself influenced in other directions by Flaminio. In a letter to Contarini of 9 December 1541 he related the edifying and congenial nature of Flaminio's conversation:

The rest of the day I pass in this holy and useful company ('santa & utile compagnia') of Signor Carnesecchi & our Mr Marco Antonio Flaminio. Useful I call it, because in the evening Mr Marco Antonio provides me and the greater part of the company ('famiglia') with nourishment from that food which does not perish. I do not know when I have experienced greater consolation or edification.[3]

It is clear that Flaminio's arrival at Viterbo was not simply the occasion for complete submission to the guidance which Pole had to offer: he seems, indeed, to have been very much at the centre of the proceedings. It seems likely that he induced in Pole

---

[1] Morone, *Difesa*, p. 179.   [2] Ibid.   [3] *Epistolae*, III, 42.

an appreciation of Valdés. (Vittoria Colonna received at Viterbo a copy of Valdés' commentary on Romans.)[1] It was at Viterbo, too, that Carnesecchi first read Flaminio's copies of Bucer's commentaries on St Matthew and on Romans; he also read Luther on the Psalms; and he discussed the question of salvation with Flaminio and Priuli, both of whom read 'libri heretici'.[2] Carnesecchi regarded Flaminio and Priuli as his mentors ('maestri miei').[3] Both of them believed in justification by faith, while continuing to assert that good works were nonetheless necessary.[4] But neither was in total sympathy with Luther. They believed that he had spoken well on a number of issues, and that he had a good understanding of Scripture. But he had withdrawn his obedience from the Church, and had shown himself to be contumacious, thereby placing himself 'extra ecclesiam' and 'extra charitatem'. Consequently, they treated his doctrines in eclectic fashion, 'tanquam aurum ex stercore colligentes, et cetera (ut aiunt) reddebant coquo'.[5]

But there is reason to believe that if this was Flaminio's view as recollected by Carnesecchi, it was a view which he only developed at Viterbo. Carnesecchi's testimony refers to the period of time, just less than a year, which he spent at Viterbo, between November 1541 and August 1542.[6] His testimony may be examined in the light of Flaminio's correspondence at this time. On 28 February 1542, Flaminio wrote to his friend Carlo Gualteruzzi, during the course of a short visit to Naples.[7] He recommended

---

[1] *Carteggio*, pp. 238–40.   [2] 'Processo', pp. 195, 203, 213–14.
[3] Ibid. p. 205.
[4] 'il quale intendevano ancora in tal modo che non se veniva secondo loro excludere la charità, ne per consequente le buone opere che necessariamente dependono da quella'. (Ibid. p. 214.)
[5] Ibid. pp. 326–7.
[6] Carnesecchi said he spent about a year at Viterbo. (Ibid. pp. 213, 495.) In fact the period seems to have been about ten months. His father died on 29 June, 1542, and Carnesecchi was required at Florence. (Ortolani, *Pietro Carnesecchi*, pp. 40–1.) But he does not seem to have left Viterbo permanently until August 1542, as we learn from a letter of 14 August, from Priuli, in which the latter mentions Carnesecchi's departure. (Priuli to Beccadelli, Viterbo, 14 August 1542: Bodleian MS Italiano C 25, fols. 217r–220v. The account of Carnesecchi's departure occurs on fols. 217r–v.) This chronology coincides with Ortolani's account, which states (p. 41) that Carnesecchi reached Florence at the end of the summer.
[7] Paladino, *Opuscoli*, pp. 72–3.

Gualteruzzi to read the *Imitation of Christ*, which he valued above all other books apart from the Scripture. But from Flaminio's account of it, one might think that he was recommending the *Beneficio di Cristo*: for the *Imitation of Christ*, he maintained, assisted one to live a Christian life, summarised in man's 'acceptance of the grace of the gospel, that is, justification by faith'. The book, moreover, rejected 'fear' as a central motive of the Christian life. This was another of its merits: for fear of punishment was a sign of infidelity, or of an extremely weak faith. Faith in Christ relieved one of fear.[1] Therefore filial love, and not fear of punishment, should animate the Christian. Interestingly enough, Flaminio concluded his letter with the remark that he could recommend many other books which were greatly regarded 'nel mondo'; but his conscience forbade him, for he considered that they would do Gualteruzzi more harm than good.[2] Was he thinking of such heretical books as he had so recently recommended to Carnesecchi? It seems at least possible, in the light of Carnesecchi's statement that Flaminio believed Luther (and clearly Calvin) to have spoken well in many things, but to have sinned in disregarding the authority of the Church. A conviction of this kind does seem to have grown upon Flaminio at Viterbo. In a letter of 14 February 1543 written from Viterbo, and addressed to Galeazzo Caracciolo, we find further echoes of the *Beneficio di Cristo* – but without the combative overtones.[3] The sons of God, remarks Flaminio, predestined to reign with Christ, must inevitably suffer ridicule. But it was necessary to have compassion for the blindness of those who ridiculed; faith would produce a flowering of good works, and a guarantee of eternal happiness to come.[4] The significant phrase here, is that which recommends 'compassion': the *Beneficio di Cristo* had relied upon anathema.[5]

[1] Ibid. p. 72. [2] Ibid. p. 73. [3] Ibid. pp. 80–5. [4] Ibid. p. 81.
[5] Flaminio's letter opens by rejoicing at the 'felice nuova' that the gospel 'è stato seminato' in Caracciolo's heart. The news has been the cause of 'grandissima allegrezza' not only to Flaminio, but also 'al reverendissimo legato [i.e. Pole] e a questri altri signori' (*Opuscoli*, p. 80). Vinay interprets this to mean that the Viterbo group was congratulating Caracciolo 'zu seiner gelungengen Flucht nach der Stadt Calvins' ('Die Schrift "Il Beneficio di Giesu Christo"', p. 51). This would have entailed an astonishing prophetic ability on their part; Caracciolo fled to Geneva in 1551, not in 1543.

But the most remarkable indication of a change in Flaminio's outlook occurs in a letter which he wrote to Carnesecchi on 1 January 1543.[1] Flaminio referred to the discussions which he and Carnesecchi had held in recent months concerning the eucharist and the Mass: discussions which had been necessary, 'because the abominable Zwinglian sect grows more noisy in everything, and many, following the opinion of Luther', had condemned the idolatry of the Mass, and the impiety of those who heard it.[2] The rest of the letter was taken up with a lengthy defence of the Mass and the Real Presence, doctrines which, as Flaminio stressed, had always been taught by the Church, and were supported by the writings of the early fathers, as well as the Councils and the writings of contemporaries like Fisher, Pighius and Contarini. Bucer was one of the principal opponents of the eucharist, 'and in the judgement of many he has done more damage than Zwingli'; nevertheless, he had retracted his error at the colloquy of Regensburg.[3] But many, failing to follow the example of Bucer and his adherents, were misled by pride into becoming lovers of novelty and enemies of the common belief. Hiding behind a false zeal for religion, they censured their neighbours bitterly, and condemned as impious the universal sense and practice of the Church, together with those who failed to share their opinions.[4] Thus Flaminio prayed that they might be delivered from their bitter zeal, and be granted the charity and humility to refrain from reckless judgement of the practices and dogmas of the Church, and from condemnation of those, who, in true humility, reverenced and obeyed the Church.[5]

His letter concluded with a personal appeal to Carnesecchi which, in its force and urgency indicates that his strictures were addressed as much to his own conscience, and to that of Carnesecchi, as to the followers of Luther and Zwingli. If, he urged Carnesecchi, we wish to avoid shipwreck on these perilous rocks we must humble ourselves before God, and refuse to separate our-

---

[1] *Opuscoli*, pp. 74–9. The letter is written from Trent, whither Flaminio had gone with Pole, after the latter's appointment as Papal Legate to the Council. Pole stayed at Trent from November 1542 until May 1543; but the Council was postponed for a further period of time. (Cf. Jedin, *Council*, I, 468, 478.)
[2] *Opuscoli*, p. 74.   [3] Ibid. pp. 77–8.   [4] Ibid. p. 78.   [5] Ibid.

selves for any reason, however compelling it may seem, from union with the Catholic Church. To pass judgement on the things of God with the instruments of human reason is to court abandonment.[1]

By trusting thus in our own reason, he admonished Carnesecchi, we shall, in this contentious century, approach one party and hate the other, thereby losing hold of all judgement and charity. The light will seem dark, and the dark light. We shall think ourselves rich and contented when we are really poor and miserable; and we shall lack the knowledge to separate what is precious from what is vile – a knowledge which, without the spirit of Christ, can never be acquired.[2]

Flaminio's letter suggests that he had undergone a conversion to the Church, without feeling it necessary to retract the other doctrinal assumptions of the *Beneficio di Cristo*. The doctrine of the eucharist and of the Mass, as expounded in that work, are entirely in keeping with Catholic doctrine; nor is there reason to believe that Flaminio had retreated on the questions of justification and predestination. What is novel in his letter to Carnesecchi is the insistence on submission to the Church's teaching, and the emphasis upon the need for charity, rather than envenomed zeal, in sustaining one's beliefs. There is in the letter a current of passionate concern which indicates a spiritual crisis, and a decision taken perhaps with difficulty. It is clear that Flaminio had called a halt to speculations which ran counter to the Church's teaching, and that he wanted Carnesecchi to do the same. It is probably significant that the terms of his appeal, though more emotional, recall the principle which Contarini had expressed some five months earlier in writing to Pole: to trust more in the doctrine of the Church than in human understanding.

There can be little doubt that Flaminio had undergone a conversion of outlook at Viterbo. This supposition helps to resolve an apparent contradiction in Carnesecchi's testimony. At

[1] Ibid. pp. 78–9.
[2] Carnesecchi's reply, denying the validity of the Mass and the doctrine of transubstantiation may be read in *Epistolae aliquot M. Antonii Flaminii* (ed. A. Camerario, Nuremburg, 1571), pp. G5r–I1r.

one point in his evidence, Carnesecchi stated that Flaminio had questioned the divine institution of the sacrament of penance, while at another point he said that he accepted it.[1] It may simply be that the attempt to remember the events of a quarter of a century ago led naturally to such inconsistencies. On the other hand it is possible that Carnesecchi was referring to two different stages of Flaminio's development, one of which terminated, while the other took its place, with Flaminio's sojourn at Viterbo.

One final point in Carnesecchi's testimony tends to confirm this view of Flaminio's conversion. He admitted to possessing 'a fragment of a little work by Flaminio, composed in defence of the book of the *Beneficio di Cristo* against brother Ambrogio Catharino'. But the work, he explained, was never published, 'I believe because the aforesaid book was condemned and prohibited before he had finished his defence'.[2] This would suggest that Flaminio was restrained from publishing his defence of the *Beneficio di Cristo* because the book was under ecclesiastical censure. Vergerio, writing about the *Beneficio di Cristo* in 1549, was more specific: he revealed that a reply to Catharino's attack had been composed, and that its author had submitted it to a certain Cardinal. The Cardinal in question was reputed to be 'enlightened, conscious of the errors of the Church, and familiar with the sweetness of the gospel'. He was accustomed to remark that it was necessary to be prudent, and 'to await the opportune time and occasion'.[3] It can scarcely be doubted that the Cardinal in question was Pole; and that he had recommended Flaminio to suppress his reply to Catharino.

Prudence and caution were the keynotes of Pole's policy at Viterbo. His closest friends could only guess at his opinions. Carnesecchi knew nothing of Pole's convictions on the disputed issues of doctrine; he assumed that Pole believed in justification by faith alone.[4] Morone only knew that Pole 'tended to take a low view of man';[5] while Flaminio could only learn that Pole did not consider it proper strictly to speak of 'merit' in relation to anyone

[1] 'Processo', p. 194.   [2] Ibid. pp. 193, 205–6.
[3] Vergerio, *Catalogo*, pp. g5v–g6).   [4] 'Processo', pp. 290, 300.   [5] *Difesa*, p. 179.

but Christ.[1] He deliberately discouraged speculation, not merely about his own views, but about the very issues which most preoccupied him and his friends. Thus Carnesecchi and his associates hesitated to discuss Luther or Calvin with Vittoria Colonna, 'if for no other reason than out of respect for the Cardinal...who detested such curiosity ['curiosità'], in her and in everyone in general'.[2]

It was exactly this aversion to 'curiosità' which Pole urged upon Vittoria Colonna, warning her against reading Luther, Bucer, Calvin or Melanchthon, and generally recommending 'that she ought to guard herself from curiosity'.[3] But Pole also relieved her of the anxiety which had been the dominant feature of her religious life before coming to Viterbo. He advised her to abstain from excessive mortification and, as Carnesecchi interpreted it, recommended her to rely less upon external practices and to repose more confidence in Christ.[4] Carnesecchi remembered that she attributed much to faith and grace, while in her own life displaying a concern for good works. In this, she followed the advice which, she was accustomed to say, she had received from Pole: 'to believe as if her salvation depended upon faith alone, and to act, on the other hand, as if it depended upon good works'.[5]

This, she said, was Pole's reply to the question she had once asked him about the nature of his own beliefs concerning justification. He had volunteered no further information, either about this, or any other doctrine relating to faith; and she had not pressed the matter, lest she offend him with 'too much curiosity'.[6]

It is highly significant that Pole's advice closely parallels the passage which summarises and concludes the *Beneficio di Cristo*; and no less significant that it differs from that passage in omitting any reference to predestination or election. The episode suggests something of the nature and limits of the influence which Flaminio brought to bear on Pole's outlook.

[1] 'Processo', p. 550.   [2] Ibid. pp. 504–5.   [3] Ibid. p. 503.
[4] Vittoria Colonna to Giulia Gonzaga, 8 December 1541 (*Carteggio*, pp. 238–40); and 'Processo', p. 499.
[5] 'Processo', p. 269.   [6] Ibid.

It is certain that Pole believed in salvation by faith alone, and disputed the meritorious quality of works performed in grace. But he would not commit himself beyond this point for the moment. His reticence must be attributed partly to historical circumstance, and partly to a temperamental reluctance (above all after the flight of Ochino and Vermigli) to express himself upon controversial questions; especially when he feared he might be wrong.

The flight of Ochino and Vermigli, coinciding with the death of Contarini and the emergence of the Roman Inquisition, already signalised, as we have seen, the internal disintegration of the *spirituali*. Henceforward they began to suffer a notable decline of the influence which had reached its climax in the summer of 1542. As we have seen in the case of Beccadelli, the uncertainty of their situation began from this time onwards to weigh more heavily upon them.

Pole himself embodied the enigmatic stance to a supreme degree – convinced of the necessity to yield to the positive essence of what Luther had to say, while being no less convinced of its compatibility with the Church which Lutherans condemned. Prudence and restraint of utterance, coupled with insistence on submission to the Church's authority, remained his guiding principles: these, and the belief that only in a General Council could reunion be effected. For a prominent churchman publicly to support the validity of Luther's fundamental tenet would at least be injudicious, in a climate of great spiritual uncertainty, to say nothing of gathering hostility.[1] The problem was accentuated by the intellectual difficulty of reconciling opposites. The balance, hard to maintain once the problem had expressed itself, became increasingly precarious as the climate of optimism among Catholics began to wane, and was replaced by alarm at the extent of their confusion and uncertainty. Paralysis of utterance now began to affect those Catholics who, in principle convinced of the possibility of reunion with the Lutherans, were nevertheless unsure

[1] Sernini's remark that 'good people' discounted the rumour about Viterbo was balanced by the news that a close watch was being kept upon the circle by the Inquisition. (See above, n. 1, p. 73.)

how best to prepare for it outside the deliberations of a General Council. Hence the uncertainty and gradual fragmentation which beset the *spirituali* between 1542 and 1545 is reflected in the hesitations of Pole's circle at Viterbo.

These hesitations are best exemplified in Flaminio's abandonment of his proposed reply to Catharino; it is apparent, judging by his letter to Carnesecchi, that by the time the second edition of the *Beneficio di Cristo* appeared, Flaminio had revised his notions about polemical necessity; the second edition was almost certainly re-published without his consent. As for Pole, his advice to Vittoria Colonna was not so different from Catharino's 'Non plus sapere quam oportet sapere'. He was not unsympathetic to the central principles of the *Beneficio di Cristo*; his conversations with Flaminio had clearly had their influence on his own opinions; and his expression of these opinions at the Council of Trent reveals how sympathetically inclined he was to Luther (though not, it would seem, to Calvin). Nevertheless he was convinced that the place and moment for doctrinal utterance was not between the pages of polemical tracts, nor in the contentious atmosphere of the pulpit, but in the reasoned proceedings of a General Council.

Pole abhorred religious controversy, and remained distressed at the contentions which divided Christendom. He believed that those who resisted ecclesiastical authority should be reproved; but only while their revolt was still in progress. It should never be forgotten, he maintained, that although they were rebels, they were sons as well. In the event of their return to obedience, a milder countenance should be displayed. He gave as his example St Paul who, he said, was wont to flourish the rod, but to resort to it only rarely, and with reluctance.[1] On another occasion he observed that years of experience had taught him the difficulty of reconciling men who were divided on religious grounds. Whoever sought to do so must first pray for the removal of all hardness from his own heart; otherwise he would argue and contend in vain. All other remedies were, in Pole's experience, quite useless.[2]

It seems clear that these were the considerations underlying his

[1] *Epistolae*, II, 108.
[2] Ibid. p. 149, Pole to Contarini, Carpentras, 25 March 1539.

behaviour at Viterbo. He had extended the spirit of Valdés, to incorporate an explicit acknowledgement of the visible and authoritative nature of the Church. He had been deeply impressed by Flaminio's insights into the problems which had preoccupied him since his return to Italy; but he had stressed to Flaminio the importance of the usages and precepts of the Church in her teaching and sacramental offices. He liked to say that he had saved for the Church a writer whose powers would greatly have damaged her – clearly he was thinking of the author of the *Beneficio di Cristo*.[1] His endeavour had been to exercise restraint in everything: to restrain Flaminio from undue reliance upon his own opinions amid the complexities of dogma; to restrain Vittoria Colonna from excessive speculation, and from depending too much upon external practices at the expense of an interior dependence upon God. Meanwhile, he explored the dimensions of a doctrine which, in its profound appeal for him, placed every reliance upon God, in such a way as to deny the significance of human contribution in the process of salvation. It was a doctrine to which the members of his household at Viterbo – Carnesecchi, Priuli[2] and Flaminio – attached an importance quite as radical as Pole's; and perhaps more so, in that they were prepared to affirm it positively, at least among themselves; whereas Pole's temperamental reservations, and his scruples, withheld him from publicly or explicitly assenting to it. His dominant concern in fact, was silence: a concern which he had urged upon his friends until the moment should arrive when their views could be expressed without arousing scandal. It was not until the Council of Trent, when the debates began upon the crucial issue of justification, that Pole fully revealed his mind, and only then, under pressure; for by that time it was becoming clearer that the opportune moment he had waited for was not, after all, favourable to the views he had maintained.

[1] Below, p. 238.
[2] Priuli's views were well-known to his friends. Gualteruzzi wrote from Rome to Beccadelli on 12 May 1545: 'Questi nostri patroni di qua [Bembo and Cervini] vi amano al solito ambi ogni dì più quanto voi più ogni dì date loro occasione d'amarvi maggiormente con le vostre buone opere, ma non mi accusate al Signor Prioli di questa parola...' (Bodleian MS Italiano C 24, fol. 56r).

CHAPTER SEVEN

The Council of Trent:
Prolegomenon

The Council which assembled at Trent in 1545, in order to settle
the affairs of the Catholic Church, owed its existence to recent
developments in European politics, as much as to the decision of
the Pope and his advisers. Ever since the papacy had first determined on a General Council of the Church as the necessary
means to the repair of Christendom, the largest obstacle to this
gathering had been the continuance of war in Europe. From the
first summoning of a Council to meet at Mantua, in 1537; its
postponement; its resuscitation, and the decision to meet at
Vicenza in the following year; the abandoment of that decision
and finally, the abortive convocation at Trent in 1542-3, the
decisive element determining each failure had been the Habsburg–
Valois conflict. Consequently, it was only with the establishment
of peace between the Emperor and the King of France in 1544,
that the Council was finally enabled to get under way. The Peace
of Crépy marks the real beginning of the Council of Trent.[1]
From that moment it became possible for both Pope and Emperor
to act with a free hand. For Charles V, this meant a war against
the German Protestants, followed by peace terms which would
oblige them to send representatives to Trent and accept the
decisions of the Council. For Paul III it meant, above all, the long
awaited opportunity to define and clarify those elements of
Catholic belief which had been called in question by the Reformation. Thus the Bull *Laetare Jerusalem*, issued in November 1544,
two months after the Peace of Crépy, announced the purpose of

[1] For the dependence of the Council upon political developments see Jedin,
Council, I, *passim*.

52693

the Council to be the removal of religious discord (that is by settlement of controverted dogma), the reform of the Church, and finally, the liberation of the Christian people from the Turks.[1] At the same time, the committee of Cardinals charged with the responsibility for Conciliar affairs was reconstructed. It included among its members Carafa, Pole, Morone and Parisio.[2]

It had been determined that the Council should assemble at Trent in March 1545. On 22 February, less than a month before the scheduled opening, three Cardinals, Pole, Del Monte and Cervini, were appointed to preside over its affairs.[3] Their task was rendered difficult from the outset by a series of unanswered problems, both religious and political, each one of which converged upon a single question: what, within its terms of reference, should be the structure and limits of the Council? There was, for example, between Charles V and Paul III a crucial division of opinion about the priorities to be observed in the proceedings of the Council. The clarification of doctrine was, in the view of Paul III, the immediate task before the Council; the explosive issues of ecclesiastical reform he would have preferred to see handled by his own officials in the Curia. It was in the interest of the Emperor, however, that doctrinal issues be deferred, at least until the arrival of the Protestants at Trent; and until that time, their path should be made easy by a thorough programme of reform.

There was too, the related question of what efforts should be made to conciliate the Lutherans. Pole, as the leading representative of the *spirituali* at the Council, confidently expected that its decree would facilitate reunion.[4] Others, however, like Cervini, were convinced that Germany was lost beyond recovery, and that the purpose of the Council, therefore, should be to preserve Catholicism in those countries where Protestantism had not yet

[1] *C.T.*, IV, 35–8.
[2] Ibid. p. 385, 19 November 1544. The last three had been nominated as Legates to the Council in 1542.
[3] Ibid. pp. 393–6.
[4] Cf. the description by Averardus Serristorius, Cosimo de Medici's agent at Rome: 'Inghilterra, che sempre che si potesse haver sicurtà che i Luterani venissero a Trento et si sottomettessero a la determination di concilio'. (*C.T.*, XI, 944.)

firmly established itself.[1] Thus among the Legates themselves there was a fundamental difference of approach, which must be borne in mind in considering the part which Pole played in the Council.

The intention of opening the Council in March was frustrated by a succession of events, which obliged the Legates to remain at Trent for a further nine months, in the perpetual hope of opening the Council, while unsettled relations between the Emperor and the Pope prevented this.[2] Pole himself arrived in Trent only on 4 May, some seven weeks after Del Monte and Cervini had made their solemn entry to the city. His reluctance to undertake the journey was caused in part by a not altogether groundless fear of assassination at the hands of Italian mercenaries in the pay of Henry VIII.[3] But it is important not to exaggerate this cause of his delay, for there was another and more fundamental one. Pole had remained at Rome for a full month after the departure of his colleagues at the end of February, at the explicit request of the Pope. It was the latter's idea that Pole should take a holiday from public duties, and devote himself to thought about the ensuing Council. Pole seems to have accepted with alacrity, and the result of this interlude was that he compiled a treatise on the scope and nature of the Council. This treatise deserves a measure of attention, for it is of considerable interest in revealing Pole's ideas at the moment when, as he hoped, the Council was on the point of finally endorsing them.[4]

In addressing the work to Del Monte and Cervini, Pole explained how his thoughts had formed in response to a sequence

[1] For these and other questions still unsettled at the opening of the Council, see Jedin, *Council*, II, 7–12.

[2] Jedin, *Council*, I, 505–43, for an account of the reasons for delay.

[3] *C.T.*,I, pp. 183–4; cf. also, Parks, G. B., 'The Parma Letters and the Dangers to Cardinal Pole,' in *Catholic Historical Review*, XVI (1960–1), 299–317, and Jedin, *Council*, I, 509–11. The repeated exhortations of Del Monte and Cervini to begin his journey, in *Epistolae*, IV, 184–8.

[4] *De Concilio liber*, Rome, 1562; facsimile reprint London, 1962. – Pole's account of the book's origins indicates that it was begun shortly after 23–4 March 1545, when Cervini and Del Monte left for Trent (*C.T.*, I, 152), and had already been sent on to them before his own arrival on 4 May (ibid. pp. 183–4). It was probably completed, therefore, well before the end of April (*De Concilio*, pp. 1r–v, 58v).

of problems which had impressed themselves on him. He had therefore arranged and organised them in the form of a treatise, deciding to send it on to the two Legates for their perusal. He did not regard the work as a thing complete in itself; neither time nor his meagre talents would allow of that. But it would serve as an indication of his frame of mind. His purpose was merely to establish an approach to the solution of their problems, not to put forward any detailed remedies.[1]

Not surprisingly, the work is a characteristic product of the Scripturally inspired humanism which we have recognised as a dominant element in our enquiry. Couched in the form of *Quaestio-Responsio*, it explores the themes uppermost in Pole's mind, referring them to the norms provided by Scripture and the Councils of the early Church. These themes were the same as those already delineated in the Bull *Laetare Jerusalem*, and it was in similar terms that Pole declared the purpose of the Council to be the clarification of dogma, the reform of Christendom, and the establishment of peace.[2]

Thus Pole devotes some attention to the Council's structure and procedure, defining the roles played by the various representatives – the Pope, the Legates, the bishops, and finally the Christian powers. The specific interest of this part of the work lies in the exegetical method it brings to bear on questions relating to the constitution of the Church, and the relation of its members to each other within the context of the primacy of Rome. Pole defines the position of the Church in relation to the prophecies of the Old Testament. He emphasises that her authority is derived neither from General Councils, nor the consent of peoples, nor the will of princes, but from the promises of Christ to Peter; and it is within this context that he defines the duties and initiatives belonging to the various participants.

No doubt these observations were designed in part to counteract the menace of Conciliar theory. But it may also be that Pole, by the deployment of arguments drawn exclusively from Scripture and the practice of the early Church, was endeavouring

[1] Ibid. p. 24r.   [2] Ibid. p. 49v.

to provide grounds on which future Protestant delegates might be persuaded to accept the primacy of Rome. Certainly an ambition of this kind was far from alien to his temper; he was indeed convinced – in contradistinction, as we have seen to Cervini – that the whole business of the Council could virtually be defined as the recovery of union with the Lutherans, and the reform of the Church.[1]

Thus it was in the discussion of these two vital issues that his feelings were most actively engaged. The recovery of unity and the reform of Christendom had been his twin preoccupations since his days at Padua, with the Oratory of Divine Love. For years the best efforts of his mind had been devoted to these problems, while for much of this time he had felt obliged to refrain from public utterance about them. His definition of these problems therefore, at the moment when he believed them to be on the verge of resolution, possesses a high degree of spiritual insight, the fruit of long years of prayer, meditation, and reflection. There is the distinct impression that a burden has been lifted from his shoulders as he writes about these issues which he had withheld from discussing for so long, in obedience to his rule of conscientious silence. The caution which he had enjoined upon Priuli and Flaminio, and the rest of his circle at Viterbo, he now explains as the result of a determination to prevent a public scandal: never, he acknowledges, could he bring himself in former times to write about these matters – greatly though his friends had urged him – for his views could easily provide a weapon in the hands of others.[2]

Pole had been convinced, as we have seen, of the need to await the opportune moment for the expression of views which, he was aware, were highly controversial. It was not simply, as in the

1 'in praecipuis capitibus illis, quae totam fere materiam Concilii, quod nunc indictum est, continent, quorum unum est, de modo reconciliandi Germaniae populos, qui Lutherani vocantur . . . alterum, quo pacto ipsius Ecclesiae praecipua, vel potius omnia fere membra ad veteram disciplinam, & instituta, a quibus non parum declinarunt, revocentur.' Ibid. p. 57v.
2 'Quod vero nunquam mihi ipse adhuc imperare potui, ut de eiusmodi rebus scriberem, praesertim quae in alienas manus venirent: (nec enim id, cum multi amici me admodum rogarent, ulli unquam concessi) hoc nunc ultro vobis offero.' *De Concilio*, p. 58r.

Consilium of 1537, that certain proposals to reform the Church should be kept secret until the means of their fulfilment was at hand. There was also the doctrinal question which lay at the centre of Luther's reformation, and which had come to be increasingly a subject of concern in Italy. For clearly an agreement with the Lutherans would entail, above all, agreement about justification; and for Pole this meant in effect something very close to an acceptance of Luther's doctrine of salvation.

Publicly to have admitted, in the years before the Council, that Luther had been virtually right upon this issue, would have been inevitably to invite the question: had he not then been equally correct about the other issues – papal primacy, the priesthood, the sacraments, purgatory, penance, the intercession of the saints – the whole fabric of Catholicism, to which Pole remained deeply and irrevocably attached. For it was not easy in strict logic, to avow that salvation was achieved by the exclusive means of faith, while at the same time maintaining that these elements of Catholic belief were indispensable. This was a difficulty to which Pole and Contarini had adverted in their correspondence following the days of Regensburg. But for Pole, as for Contarini and Morone, and those of the Italian *spirituali* who had no thought of abandoning Catholicism, the logical dichotomy was not apparent – it appeared rather as a difficulty, and no more. If their experience of Christianity demanded an assent to the doctrine of salvation by faith alone, it demanded equally an assent to the whole complex of Catholic devotion and tradition. Their insistence that man could contribute nothing to his own salvation was matched by an insistence on man's duty to remain in communion with the Church of Rome. Thus two profoundly felt experiences were at work, and the resultant confusion which arose from the inconsistencies of these ideals (and which was reinforced by the growing climate of uncertainty), was held at bay and rendered tolerable only by the promise of a General Council. The Council, it was confidently held, would resolve these confusions and dilemmas.

Hence the jubilation which Pole felt as he finally gave utterance to views which had for years been ripening in silence, and his excitement imparted to his sentences something of the quality which had won him the affection of Contarini and of his companions at Viterbo. The rhythm of his mind and personality are so established in these pages that, of all his works, it was this one which Seripando and Morone were happiest to publish in his memory.[1]

Yet Pole's natural restraint had not been jettisoned, and if he had finally unburdened himself of his opinions, he had done so, as he acknowledged in his preface, by establishing their general principles, not by recounting them in detail. Thus throughout his discussion of ecclesiastical reform it is not the concrete programme of renewal that concerns him, so much as the frame of mind in which the problems should be met. For our purposes, nothing could be more helpful; for it is precisely this approach which reveals most clearly his psychology, and enables us to gain some understanding of the inner workings of his personality. In defining the frame of mind in which the Council's problems should be met, Pole of course is defining his own state of mind. He does so, moreover, in a way that enables us to discover in his observations the central preoccupation that coloured all his thought, illuminating its separate elements, and uniting them within a single principle. This preoccupation is perhaps best studied first in relation to the question of ecclesiastical reform. Following this procedure we shall then more easily recognise it as the irreducible element determining his doctrine of salvation.

Pole's first concern, in dealing with the question of reform, is to establish the means whereby those who hold authority in Christendom can take an effective initiative in that direction. He recommends that they should begin with themselves, stressing that the first condition of renewal in the Church is for all who exercise authority to recognise themselves as guilty men. This, he admits, is not easily achieved, for men are so constituted as vehemently to resist any such acknowledgement. They prefer instead to transfer their guilt to others. Herein, he declares, is the root of their dilemma, and the source of all their dissension and

[1] Seripando to Morone, 11 September 1561, in Jedin, *Girolamo Seripando*, II, 636–7; the English edition of this valuable work lacks the substantial appendix of the original, and many of the notes.

unhappiness. Trapped by his own self-regard, man perpetuates his misery.[1]

But, continues Pole, Christ has shown men the means of their release and, as the supreme authority, provides the example whereby others who hold power may rescue their people from disaster. In taking upon Himself the sins of all those who were subject to Him, he reconciled mankind to God. He was guiltless, yet He did not hesitate to suffer for the sins of other men. How much more readily, then, should those who by their example have often corrupted their own people, admit their guilt, making themselves answerable ('se reos facere') for the people's sins. Thus by acknowledging in equity what Christ had done in mercy, the way to mercy will be open. No remedy will be found for the present evils of the Church until her leaders publicly confess their guilt in the forthcoming Council, and become their own accusers. For the just man is the first to accuse himself of guilt: 'Justus enim, ut inquit Sapies, in principio sermonis est sui accusator.'[2]

Pole proceeds now to explain the purpose of these recommendations. He stresses that they are not designed to submit the Pope to the judgement of a Conciliar enquiry. His hope is rather that the Pope should submit to his own self-judgement, and even, in the light of that, condemn himself. For it is only in this way that he will be liberated from the claims of judgement, whether divine or human, and enabled more convincingly to judge the errors of others.[3]

Thus if, at the opening of the Council, both Pope and Emperor would acknowledge their responsibility, they would manifest the presence of the Holy Spirit, who convicts mankind of sin before He offers mercy. Just as penance was the means adopted by the founder of the Church to restore men to their true condition, so should it be adopted by all who would reform the Church, and especially those who hold His place. From their example, the rest

[1] 'imitantes prima illa humanae & terranae generationis capita, qui primi in mundum peccatum introduxere, & auxere, cum salutarem sui erroris confessionem reliquentes, alter in alterum suum peccatum transtulit, vir in mulierum, mulier in serpentum, per hunc autem modum peccatum crevit, & cum peccato omne genus miseriae.' *De Concilio*, pp. 51r–v.

[2] Ibid. p. 51v.   [3] Ibid. p. 52r.

of Christendom would follow suit: first the fathers of the Council, and then the people, and finally all nations would come to follow this initiative.

With this vision of the Church in penance, Pole reveals the dominant conviction of his life – the need for man to recognise his sinfulness, as the first step towards his liberation.[1] The consciousness of sin, and the demand for spiritual liberty, was the impetus which drove his personality, so that he understood instinctively the quandaries, however differently resolved, of Luther, Calvin, Valdés or Contarini. For it was the common spiritual experience of these men to realise the helplessness of human nature with its weight of sin, and to find release in the vision of Christ crucified, suffering atonement for the sins of men. It was faith, then, in Christ's atonement, which brought liberty. It was Pole's originality to extend this experience beyond the individual in his solitary confrontation with God, and to see it instead as the process in which humanity, through the Church, collectively attained salvation. For if the consciousness of guilt was the stimulus which led the individual to faith, it was precisely the absence of this consciousness, that, in his view, distinguished the relations of men among each other, and perpetuated their dissensions. Therefore the first step towards renewal must be a public acknowledgement of guilt.

Thus the essence of Pole's doctrine of salvation is implicit in his doctrine of reform; its hinge lies in the phrase 'Justus enim,...in principio sermonis est sui accusator.' These words express the pivotal concept around which his spiritual life was organised, and which united his views on justification with those on the reform of the Church.

This much becomes evident as we examine Pole's account of the manner in which faith establishes itself. To preach the word of God, he asserts, is to arouse alarm in the hearts of those who hear it, for it threatens to remove them from everything which they hold dear. Consequently, it is only in the exercise of charity, or love, that those who preach the word can persuade men to

[1] This theme had been adumbrated earlier in the concluding part of Pole's *De Unitate*, pp. CXXXIII v–CXXXVI r.

accept the sentence of guilt initially entailed. Their watchword, therefore must be charity, united with the word of faith: 'Predicatio caritatis, verbo fidei coniuncta'.[1]

Charity, however, as we have seen, was synonymous with the performance of good works, and Pole is therefore drawn to a discussion of the relations between faith and works. Those who disparage the value of good works offer to the idle an excuse for sloth, and to the active an occasion for ill-doing. To preach the doctrine of salvation by faith alone in this manner is to bring laws and ancient institutions into disrepute. The faith preached by the Apostles, whereby the unrighteous are justified, is, on the contrary, a faith which operates through love (that is good works).[2]

Every word in this passage must be closely scrutinised, for it throws considerable light on Pole's beliefs. There can be no doubt that he is referring to the Lutherans, and taking them to task for the disrepute in which they hold the laws and institutions of the Catholic Church. This rebellious attitude he attributes to the way in which they preach the doctrine of salvation by faith alone, so as to detract from the value of good works.[3] What is interesting, however, is his tone, amounting almost to indulgence: for although he describes their mode of preaching as perverse ('suo perverso loquendo modo'), he immediately qualifies this, adding that they preach the gospel of faith less perversely than impiously, or disloyally ('non tam perverse quidem, quam impie'), since they bring the Church's laws into contempt. Thus he does nothing to dissociate himself from the doctrine of salvation by faith alone; his objection is to those who *so* preach it as to discredit the institutions of the Church.[4] His quarrel with them, therefore, if by

[1] *De Concilio*, p. 24v.

[2] 'nec enim illos audiendos esse ullo modo censemus, qui sic solam fidem praedicant, ut piis caritatis actionibus detrahant: qui ignavis nihil agendi, impigris ad actiones male agendi occasionem, & licentiam suo perverso loquendi modo praebant: quos non tam perverse quidem, quam impie praedicare fidem existimamus; dum vel parum curare, vel prorsus contemnere leges, & maiorem instituta docent. Nec enim, quam praedicabant Apostoli, per quam iustificantur impii, fides eiusmodi fuit, sed quae caritatem operatur.' *De Concilio*, pp. 24r–v.

[3] It does not follow however, that Pole was accusing them of Antinomianism. The general tenor of the passage indicates rather, that he considered their *manner* of preaching to lend itself to a wilful interpretation.

[4] 'qui *sic* solam fidem praedicant *ut* piis caritatis actionibus detrahant' (italics mine).

inference we may so express it, is that they preach the truth, but
in such a manner as to disrupt the Church's unity. It was precisely
this point which Contarini had made to Pole in 1542. But they
had not been able to agree upon an intellectually coherent formulation which would reconcile the doctrine of salvation *ex
sola fide* with complete allegiance to the structure of Catholicism –
however confident they were that such a formulation could be
found. It is in order to accomplish this that Pole, in the above
passage, referring to the faith preached by the Apostles, and
anxious to contrast it with faith as preached in the manner he has
just attacked, describes it as 'fides...quae per caritatem operatur'.
In this way he hoped to provide a version of the doctrine of
salvation by faith alone which would respect the integrity of
Catholic belief.

It was a phrase which, in one form or another, enjoyed a large
circulation in disputes concerning justification. It had been put
forward by Erasmus in one form,[1] and had found its way into
the Regensburg agreement in another. It had been the subject of
disagreement between Contarini and his opponents in the Roman
Curia, who criticised his version of it on the grounds of ambiguity.[2]
Seripando had adopted it in 1540, but had abandoned it in 1543,
in favour of a view which eventually led him to espouse the
doctrine of twofold justice.[3] Rabelais, in recounting the advice
tendered by Gargantua to his son, made him speak of the duty to
serve God 'par foy formée de Charité, estre a lui adjoint en sorte
que jamais n'en sois désamparé par péché'.[4] The formula in fact,
was in wide usage and had for long been familiar to the scholastics; it was, moreover, a phrase alien to Luther's thought.[5]
'Charity', if it concealed a multitude of sins, was no less capable
of sheltering a variety of incompatible beliefs.

It was Pole's intention, therefore, to employ a phrase sufficiently
elastic to meet all shades of view, while privately interpreting it in

[1] *Ratio verae Theologiae* (*Opera*, v, 102–11 especially).   [2] Above, p. 59.
[3] Jedin, *Girolamo Seripando*, I, 117–34; English edition, pp. 88–103.
[4] L. Fèbvre, *Le problème de l'incroyance au XVI siècle; la religion de Rabelais*
(Paris, 1947), p. 303.
[5] Ibid. pp. 303–6. Screech (*L'Evangélisme de Rabelais*, pp. 23–41) further investi-
gates the formula.

accordance with the doctrine of salvation by faith alone, which, of course, he believed to be compatible with allegiance to the Church of Rome; and this he accepted, not in the spirit of latitudinarian inclusiveness, but quite simply, as a fact which the Council would confirm. For the moment however, in writing *De Concilio*, he was only concerned to use the phrase so as to safeguard the performance of good works, while placing the dominant emphasis on faith. Such a procedure inevitably provoked the question: why should good works be performed, if they contribute nothing to salvation?

Pole anticipates this question with a reference to Galatians, 5: 'Nunquid autem, inquit Apostolus, legem per fidem destruimus? absit: sed statuimus. Quae ergo legem roborat...hanc fidem illam esse dicimus, quae Jesum Christum redemptorem recipit.'[1] He now embarks on a more particular examination of the relation between faith and works, employing throughout the Pauline categories of discussion – faith, charity (synonymous with good works, or love), and the law.

The law, he argues, is indispensable to human welfare, both as the guarantor of human relations, and as the means whereby God directs men to His grace. But to attribute to the law the power of justifying, is to impose an intolerable burden upon men. Christ delivers man without the law.[2]

Thus man is saved by faith, not by observances. Pole is content here to assume as axiomatic that the precepts of the law, before the intervention of grace, present themselves as an insupportable burden to mankind – for this assumption was the common element in all discussions of the kind concerning justification. The law convicted man of guilt. It made him conscious of his fallen state. It forced him, therefore, to seek out the means of liberation from the accusations which it brought against him.

Whereas other writers, however, such as the authors of the *Beneficio di Cristo*, or Luther himself, proceed at this point immediately to speak of grace, and the freedom man discovers in the faith that Christ has made atonement for his sins, Pole proceeds

[1] *De Concilio*, p. 24v. [2] Ibid. p. 25r.

more carefully. Anxious to avoid the Antinomianism he had just condemned, he adopts an approach which enables him to emphasise the continued presence of the law, while yet introducing faith as the exclusive agent of salvation. Thus, he explains, the burden of the law is relieved when it becomes possible for man to enact its precepts through love: 'cum caritate vero coniuncta lex, iam non iugum grave, sed suave est'.[1] Hence Pole's attention is directed now to the actual process of justification, wherein it becomes possible for man to love the obligations which the law imposes.

He begins with an appeal to personal experience: the transition from the law considered as a burden, to the law as an expression of love, may easily be understood if each man considers his own initiation to salvation. The essence of the matter lies in an approach to God the Father, through Jesus Christ, which is achieved by faith; and a departure to other men for their salvation, which is achieved by love. Thus faith is the initial factor, giving flower in love, 'quae a vera fide proficiscitur, & cum ea...coniuncta est'.[2] But, he continues, the approach to Christ in faith entails, in the first instance, a death, in which everything that seems honourable, useful or enjoyable in life must be abandoned. This is accomplished with the aid of hope, which promises that the new life in Christ will restore man to a wealth of better goods. Nevertheless, the difficulty for human nature is considerable, and must remain so, until Christ comprises everything.

The first movements towards faith are accomplished by the Holy Spirit, who directs man, without his knowing it, to Christ: 'tanquam infantulus nescit a quo portetur'.[3] Furthermore, the Spirit moves him to a state of mind which seems quite remote from the spirit of Christ: the state of fear. The effect of this is to turn man from terrestrial concerns towards the life of heaven. He now becomes aware of the immense love which Christ has for him – but still he cannot lay aside his fears; he becomes aware indeed of further and more compelling grounds for it. He sees the seriousness of his fallen state, and that of all mankind.

---

[1] Ibid. p. 25v. [2] Ibid. [3] Ibid. p. 26v.

He begins to apprehend as well, how the forces ranged against him are stronger than he has hitherto perceived, and he understands that his battle is not merely against flesh and blood, but against principalities and powers, and the spirits of the upper darkness. At the same time, however, he becomes vividly aware of the crucified Christ, triumphantly putting all these things to rout; and feeling himself surrounded by so great a love, he begins to take arms against fear, comforting himself in the power and strength of the Lord.

Man, then, through faith in Christ, is transported to the Father; and now, Pole observes, as he concludes his treatment of the subject, there follows a mandate to depart to other men, restoring them to life and liberty. This departure is effected in the spirit of love, and man rejoices, finding peace in God. Justified in Christ, he willingly accepts the burden of the law, receiving it as the command, not now of faith, but of love.

In expressing these sentiments Pole, as we have seen, committed to paper for the first time, a sustained account of his beliefs concerning justification. The most notable feature of this account, however, is its narrowness of reference, and its almost total disregard of controversial issues. Admittedly, it had not been Pole's intention, in writing *De Concilio*, to undertake anything more ambitious than a general approach to the questions which the Council would examine. He reiterates this point at the conclusion of the work, indicating that he was conscious of the extent to which his views on the Lutherans, and on justification, as well as on the reform of the Church, needed to be amplified. He stresses that he had not offered any detailed account of his personal opinion about the means whereby the Lutherans are to be reconciled, and the Church restored to her former condition. His purpose has simply been to establish the point of approach from which the Council may proceed.[1] If the principles he has put forward prove acceptable, it will not be difficult to investigate their implications.[2]

Thus Pole's primary concern had been to formulate a *terminus a*

---

[1] Ibid. pp. 57v–58r.   [2] Ibid.

quo for the Council, conceived in very general terms. The particular point of departure he had chosen is, however, instructive, for it was designed to promote the doctrine of justification by faith only, while securing the value of good works. His solution had been very simply, to say: 'Faith justifies, and henceforth love directs men to good works' – a formula which left the vital question open. In particular, the crucial question whether works accomplished in the state of grace were meritorious, remained unanswered. It had not indeed been asked. It was not necessary for Pole's purpose to achieve so much; all that was needful was for the Council to assume a starting point which would unite the two conceptions: faith alone, and complete allegiance to the Church of Rome.

His personal interpretation of the formula, then, was still to some degree his secret, guessed at by Priuli and Flaminio, Carnesecchi and Vittoria Colonna – and by others too, less sympathetic, 'personas graves y letradas' who suspected him of heresy.[1] It was, therefore, with some intention of keeping his opinion to himself, that Pole had ventured to outline the general framework of his views, and to leave the rest unspoken. He afterwards related how, in the years before the Council, he had urged others to refrain from any self-appointed proclamation of the gospel, and had limited himself to recommending the doctrine of salvation by that faith which works through charity ('quae per dilectionem in cordibus nostris a Spiritu sancto diffusam, operatur, qua quidem qui caret, manet in morte').[2]

Thus what he had written on the eve of Trent served only to restate, or slightly amplify, the advice he had given to Vittoria Colonna: to believe as if salvation depended upon faith alone, while acting as if it were dependent on works. Beyond this he had hestitated to express his views in the years before the Council,

[1] 'Que en el card. de Inglaterra ay aquellas buenas partes que S.M.d.sabe y se veen, aliende de hazer una vida religiosa y muy onesta, mas que no embargante esto es oppinion de personas graves y letradas que esta herrado en algunas cosas dela fee, porque Roma cria de todos mostruos y que siendo uno delos legados nombrados para el concilio, me parescio avisar a S.M.d. por medio de V.M.d. desta particularidad.' Extract from instructions of Juan de Vega to Franciso de Toledo, 29 April 1545, on latter's visit to the Emperor. (*C.T.*, XI, 125.)

[2] Pole to the Cardinal of Augsburg, Brussels, 19 June 1554. (*Epistolae*, IV, 153.)

lest, as he explained to Del Monte and Cervini, 'in alienas manus venirent'; but also, as we shall see, because beyond this point his mind moved waveringly, faltering between precipitous extremes. He was conscious of living on a razor's edge. The Council would put an end to his uncertainties. Enough then, to urge that it should adopt these general principles for its discussions, gradually filling out their implications by systematic thought and argument. There can be little doubt that such in fact was the nature of his expectations in the days before the Council, when his optimism ran high, and he looked forward to a reconciliation with the Lutherans. The ensuing months however, would reveal that his conception of the Council was in harmony neither with Cervini's, who was to be the dominant force in the management of its affairs, nor with the form in which events themselves impelled it. We must now examine the tensions which arose between his personal opinions and his official role as papal representative.

CHAPTER EIGHT

Pole at Trent

In the six months which Pole spent at Trent, following the opening of the Council on 13 December 1545,[1] he displayed no very striking gift for action. This is perhaps not altogether surprising, in view of his personal and temperamental inhibitions. Seripando described him as a man 'cui nihil tam erat proprium, quam tacere'; who refrained from uttering his mind unless commanded, or impelled by necessity to speak, and whose practice it was to weigh within himself matters of moment and importance.[2] Beside his colleagues he was an amateur in matters of diplomacy. He had neither Del Monte's grasp of what could be accomplished in the limits of a given situation, nor Cervini's knowledge of the Roman Curia. He moved uneasily within the world of tactics and manoeuvre.

The real problem, therefore, is to decide why, given his political limitations, he should have been appointed to the office. Charles V, writing to his envoy Juan de Vega on 3 April 1545 – in the period, that is, before Pole's arrival at Trent – explained that in Germany it was believed that Pole was alone among the Catholics in his genuine desire for a Council, and that he had been appointed in order to impress the German Protestants. But, he continued, it was no longer believed that the Council would assemble, since so few Cardinals had been dispatched to Trent, and Pole himself had been detained in Rome so as to leave only the other two Legates, who were clients of the papacy.[3]

[1] C.T., II, 409.
[2] C.T., II, 415.
[3] Charles V to Juan de Vega, 3 April 1545 (not 9 April, as Jedin *Council*, I, 510,

This was an interpretation that was less than accurate in its essentials; but the suggested grounds of Pole's appointment may be close enough to reality. One of the most notable features of Paul III's administration had been his capacity to balance his various reform commissions with representatives of all shades of opinion, so as to attempt a harmony between the interests of the Curia and the demands of radical reformers such as Contarini. It seems likely that in appointing his Legates to the Council he had adopted the same tactics. Del Monte and Cervini could be relied upon to maintain the interests of the Curia in the face of Conciliar attack; Pole's presence was a guarantee of the papacy's commitment to a radical reform. A guarantee of this kind would be addressed in the first place to the spokesmen of reform within the Council. Beyond this, and as a corollary, it might serve to placate the Emperor, who, above all, wanted a Council which would concentrate upon reform, and appeal thereby to Protestant opinion.

In selecting Pole, moreover, the Pope would have been aware that he was choosing a man whose loyalty to Rome was firmly grounded; a man too, who was cautious, prudent, susceptible to persuasion, and unlikely to press his views too heatedly. And characteristically, in contrast to these considerations, it was an appointment which could serve another aim: to remind the Council of its essential purposes and nature. For if Pole was politically ungifted, he was a man of unquestionable spirituality, and had shown himself capable of moving others.

Thus Pole's function, in this view, would be to deflect the Council from too close an absorption in its politics and rivalries, and to recall it to the larger ends it was designed to serve.[1] Hence it may be for this reason that Pole had been detained at Rome, and allowed to rest from public duties, so as to reflect in depth upon the nature of the ensuing Council. Thus his political limitations could be relied upon to serve the interests of the papacy, while at the same time his distinctive gifts could be employed to good

n. 1 states). Extract printed in A. Von Druffel, *Karl V und die römische curie 1544–6* (Munich 1887–93, 3 vols), II, 51.

[1] Cf. P. Hughes, *Rome and the Counter Reformation in England* (London, 1942), pp. 40–1, for an estimate of Pole's activity in the Council, which emphasises his 'sense of the essentially spiritual character of the work'.

advantage. Astute political management combined with genuine spiritual purpose, seem to have been the features characterising the Pope's choice of Pole to the legation – an appointment which typifies in miniature the approach of Paul III to papal government.

It was an approach aimed at enlightened compromise. It carried within itself the possibilites for failure which threaten any policy aimed too closely at appeasement, and which lacks the internal coherence provided by a large conviction. It was the weakness of Paul III's administration that his convictions, though genuine, faltered too suddenly before the complexities of politics; he lacked the tenacity of statesmanship. Pole's weakness, on the other hand, was precisely the reverse. He was an idealist, and remained convinced that he had done his work once he had stated his ideals; politics to him, was synonymous almost, with betrayal. He was by temperament a contemplative, not a politican. Unlike Contarini or Cervini, he was unable to meet the simultaneous demands of altruism and expediency.

Pole's position, therefore, was to some extent anomalous. Remote in spirit from his senior colleague, Del Monte, and lacking that tactical finesse and vigour of Cervini, his role was from the start auxiliary. With the onset of bad health, and a growing feeling of estrangement from the directions which the Council was assuming, he left Trent at a relatively early date. The reasons for his departure must shortly occupy our attention: meanwhile, it is necessary to examine the nature and extent of his involvement in the Council.

The first weeks of the Council, following its opening on 13 December 1545, were devoted to establishing an order of business and a programme for discussions.[1] Pole exercised himself in cooperation with his colleagues' efforts to determine the voting structure, and to argue the inexpediency of the formula *universalem ecclesiam repraesentans* as a description of the Council.[2] But

[1] It is impossible to write about the Council of Trent without acknowledging the massive and definitive reconstruction of events provided by Jedin (*Council*, II). The following pages are particularly indebted to his great work.

[2] *C.T.*, II, 371–4, and 421–2; cf. also *C.T.*, IV, 578. The Legates' opposition to this phrase was related to its historical associations with Conciliarism. As Jedin has pointed out, they did not weigh the objective merits of the proposal. (*Girolamo*

by far the most important contribution which he made to the Council at this stage of its proceedings was the address which he drew up on behalf of the Legates, and which was read before the Council on 7 January by its secretary, Angelo Massarelli.[1] In this address he emphasised two themes: the need for penance or self-accusation, and the necessity to be impartial.

Each member of the Council, Pole asserted, must examine himself about his share in the responsibility for the evils which the Council was to remedy: namely, heresy, war, and the decline of ecclesiastical discipline and morals. Their purpose should be to imitate the example of Christ, in suffering the penalities of sin. There could be no doubt that the pastors of the Church had contributed ('causam dedisse') to the evils which beset her; if anyone should consider this to be an exaggeration, experience itself, which could not lie, attested it. The spread of heresy, the collapse of ecclesiastical discipline, the disobedience of Christians towards their pastors, the wars of European princes among themselves and with the Turks – all these things were attributable to the avarice, the greed and the ambition of Christian leaders.[2]

Pole went on to explain that his purpose in recalling these things was not to shame the fathers, but to draw the attention of the Council to God's judgement manifesting itself in these afflictions. The first condition of renewal was that they recognise this judgement for what it was. Unless the Council did so, it would meet in vain, and vainly call upon the Holy Spirit.

Moreover it was essential to eliminate all prejudice, and to remember, with Sallust, the necessity in matters of controversy for men to rid their minds of anger, hatred and friendship alike.[3] All men were liable to these emotions, but especially those who were in the service of princes.[4] It should never be forgotten that the Council was a place for praising no one but almighty God.

Seripando, I, 299; Eng. edn, pp. 254–5.) The quality of Pole's activity at the Council may be assessed by this description of him by a friendly witness, who speaks of him as a man 'qui cum parcius et rarius loqueretus, et ab omnibus avidissime exspectabatur et attentissime audiebatur'. (*C.T.*, II, 422, Seripando's diary.)

[1] *C.T.*, IV, 548–53; cf. also *C.T.*, II, 415.

[2] *C.T.*, IV, 550.   [3] Ibid. p. 552.

[4] It is clear from the context that Pole was referring here to such bishops as were liable to act as civil servants for their governments.

Thus the duty of the Council fathers was to intercede, acknowledging their own sins together with those of the people and their leaders. It was unfortunate that these leaders should be absent from the Council.[1] For the sins of the priesthood, of governments, and of peoples, were interwoven, in the image of Isaiah, like the strands of a rope, so that it was difficult to examine the sins of one order of society without revealing all the others. Hence the corruption of the Church was the responsibility not only of her leaders, but of the governments and peoples who encouraged it.

In conclusion, Pole admonished those bishops who came armed with mandates from their princes, to serve their princes in all fidelity and zeal, but in a manner fitting to bishops – as the servants therefore of God, and not of man. He called upon all who would address the assembly to speak freely and without fear of human opinion. Still more should they speak without hatred, even of opponents or enemies who vilified their persons. Finally, the Council should be free from all contention, keeping alive within itself the spirit of charity and peace.

The immediate effect of this homily, according to contemporary witness, was to transfix its audience, so that for a few moments everyone was silent; then they rose to their feet and joined the president, Del Monte, as he intoned the hymn *Veni Creator Spiritus*.[2] It was indeed, as Jedin remarks, the principal event of the second session, surpassing in importance the decree passed on the same day, which prescribed a rule of life for the participants.[3]

The Legates now set themselves the task of determining the order in which the Council was to examine the questions of dogma and reform. As we have seen, it was in the interest of the Emperor that the Council should concentrate upon reform, while to the Pope, the first necessity was to clarify the doctrines of the Church. The debates of 18 and 22 January dealt with this question of priorities, the Legates urging a simultaneous or parallel discussion of doctrine and reform. Against some opposition they carried

---

[1] The allusion, as we know from *De Concilio*, is to the Pope and the Emperor in particular.

[2] *C.T.*, IV, 553.   [3] Ibid. pp. 554–5. Jedin, *Council*, II, 25ff.

their point on 22 January, with Pole arguing persuasively in favour of the dependence of reform upon a true spirit of religion (that is, upon a proper understanding of doctrine).[1] With the success of this policy the Council was enabled to proceed along definite lines in dealing with the problems which confronted it.

The first question of disputed doctrine to which it now addressed itself was the relation of Scripture to the traditions of the Church. The purpose of the enquiry was to decide whether the Bible could be regarded as the exclusive source of revelation, or whether the traditions which the Church had received from the Apostles were to be accepted with equal reverence. In addition to this question it was decided simultaneously to broach the matter of reform. Hence the problem of Scriptural translation was examined, and the adequacy of the Vulgate brought in question.

For the next two months these questions were debated by the Council. Disagreements arose on the first issue about the manner of establishing the Biblical canon. Pole, together with Cervini and a number of others, was anxious that each book of the Bible be examined singly, and its authenticity pronounced upon. In this way, the objections of the Protestants to the book of Maccabees, together with the disputed parts of the New Testament, could be individually countered. The majority however, including Del Monte, was in favour of accepting without discussion the declaration of the Council of Florence concerning the Scriptural canon. The latter view prevailed, and in a vote taken on 15 February, it was decided to accept the Florentine canon without further consideration.[2]

If Pole's view had suffered a defeat upon this issue, he was more successful in urging the inclusion of Scripture and Tradition in the same decree, thus asserting their complementary roles, and the continual guidance of the Church by the Holy Spirit. Hence the

---

[1] 'videtur mihi omnino impossibile tractare nunc de moribus, omisso tractatu de religione. Qui enim mores esse possunt sublata religione aut collapsa?' *C.T.*, IV, 570–1; cf. also *C.T.*, I, 21–4, II, 424–5, and IV, 569–72, for the discussions of 22 January. There can be little doubt that the view quoted above was genuinely held by Pole, and not just officially espoused; hence it would be wrong to consider his approach to the Council to be identical with that of Charles V, in spite of similarities which later became apparent.

[2] *C.T.*, I, 30–3 and 478–81.

decree of 8 April, on Scripture and Tradition, emphasised the parity of each as a vehicle of revelation, and opposed thereby one of the main pillars of the Reformation, the belief that the Bible only was the source of revelation.[1]

On the question of the Scriptural text, however, Pole's attempt to secure the publication of Greek and Hebrew editions of the Bible met with no success. On 3 April he made a final effort to promote this aim, and it is clear from his speech that his concern arose as much from a desire to promulgate the Gospel among Eastern Christians, as from dissatisfaction with the Vulgate text.[2] It was the opinion of the Council, however, that the Latin Bible was sufficient for the moment. Accordingly, the reform decree of 8 April, while declaring the authenticity of the Vulgate, shelved all other issues, such as its translation into the vernacular, or the desirability of lay interpretations of the text.[3] The decree was therefore a victory over the proponents of a new exegesis, such as Pole and Seripando; and by limiting itself to an acceptance of the current Vulgate text, it incurred also the disfavour of the Curia, which felt that 'nothing new had been determined'.[4]

The reform discussions which followed the decrees of 8 April turned upon the role of the clergy in proclaiming the faith. It was a question which in turn raised the complex problem of episcopal residence (which was inextricably linked with Curial reform), as well as that of the relations between the regular orders and the episcopacy. Pole was in favour of maintaining the activity of the regular orders, while stressing that their function was to assist the bishop in his own diocese.[5] These issues, however, were merely touched upon in the debate, as a prelude to the major upheavals

---

[1] *C.T.*, v, 21, for Pole's successful intervention on 21 February. The decree is published by G. Alberigo *et al.* (ed.), *Conciliorum Oecumenicorum Decreta* (Freiburg im Breisgau, 1962), pp. 639–40.

[2] Jedin, who was the first to seize upon this point, explains that Pole, having lived for years in the Venetian Republic, had become familiar there with Eastern Christianity. (Jedin, *Girolamo Seripando*, p. 332, Eng. edn., p. 290.) Pole's speech in *C.T.* v, 65: 'Neque latina tantum est approbanda, sed graeca et hebraica, quia debemus pro omnibus ecclesiis providere.'

[3] Alberigo, *Decreta*, pp. 640–1; cf. also *C.T.*, I, 44, and v, 66–7, for Pole's espousal of lay interpretations of Scripture.

[4] *C.T.*, x, 939.   [5] *C.T.*, v, 135–6, 10 May 1546.

they were to cause later in the year. In the meantime, the reform decree of 17 June was little more than a first effort to facilitate an improved Scriptural and theological presentation of the faith; its most permanent feature was the duty to preach which it imposed on priests and bishops.[1]

While these matters were proceeding, however, another and more momentous issue had been raised. In their report to Rome of 15 April, the Legates suggested that the Council might initiate discussion on two of the most important controverted doctrines: original sin, and justification.[2] What this suggestion amounted to was that the Council should endeavour to define the Catholic doctrine of salvation. Such a course was precisely what the Emperor was keenest to avoid.

As yet, he had made no move against the Lutherans. It was imperative, therefore, from his point of view, that the Council should desist from formulating dogma until the Lutherans had been subdued. His supporters within the Council, in particular Cardinals Madruzzo and Pachecho, wished to see the Council deal with the question of episcopal residence; accordingly the issue was raised on 7 May, and was vigorously pressed by Madruzzo and Pachecho on the 10th.[3] Their proposal was one that touched upon the vital nerve of Curial reform; and in fact, as Jedin demonstrates, it was a carefully adjusted political move, designed to steer the Council in the direction of reform rather than dogma.[4] This attempt was linked with a visit which the Imperial ambassador, Francisco de Toledo, paid in turn upon the Legates, in which he expressed the Emperor's desire that reform should precede doctrine.[5]

Thus the interests of the Emperor and Pope had finally come into conflict. If the Council was to survive there would have to be a compromise. This was now achieved by an alteration in the hitherto rigid attitude which Rome had adopted on the question of Curial reform. As early as 22 March, the Pope had finally

---

[1] Alberigo, *Decreta*, pp. 643–6. For an account of the course of its procedure in the Council, cf. Jedin, *Council*, II, pp. 99–124.

[2] *C.T.*, X, 458–60.   [3] *C.T.*, I, 54, 125, and V, 131–6.

[4] Jedin, *Council*, II, 110–11.   [5] *C.T.*, X, 478–9. 2–3 May, 1546.

rescinded his restriction on the Council's freedom to deal with Curial reform, although he attached important qualifications to this concession.[1] But the principle had been established, and hence it became possible for the Legates to propose that the subject of episcopal residence be discussed, provided that it did not interfere with the discussion of dogma.[2] This Del Monte did on 21 May, stating that the Council would examine the problem of residence, while at the same time embarking on a discussion of doctrinal issues. The issue he proposed was that of original sin.[3]

This was a compromise which left the adherents of the Emperor without a choice. On 22 May the bishop of Cava, Tommaso Sanfelice, acting under instructions from Toledo, requested the Legates to delay the debate on original sin for a few days, until further guidance from the Emperor should come. Meanwhile, Toledo dispatched a courier to Regensburg with a request for fresh instructions.[4] But it was too late to avert the crisis. Sanfelice's intervention met with a firm refusal. On 24 May the Legates submitted to the theologians a group of questions related to the doctrine of original sin. Four days later the Council embarked on a discussion of this issue, which involved it immediately in an attempt to define the Catholic doctrine of salvation.[5]

If the direction which events had now assumed represented a dilemma for the Emperor, there can be little doubt that Pole was equally alarmed. For the Council to discuss these issues without consulting the Lutherans can have been little short of a catastrophe for him, as it could only jeopardise the possibility of a reunion. It is true that he had supported the Council's declarations on Scripture and Tradition, which had contradicted one of the essential principles of Reformation doctrine. But if the Lutherans were to appear at Trent, it would be the *sine qua non* of any agreement that they accept the parity of Scripture and

[1] Ibid. XI, 42–3; also Jedin, *Council*, II, 129–30.
[2] This was a contingency they had foreseen in their report of 15 April.
[3] *C.T.*, V, 155.
[4] Sanfelice's interview, *C.T.*, X, 496; ibid. p. 496 for Toledo's request for new instructions.
[5] *C.T.*, V, 163–4, for the questions submitted to the theologians; ibid. pp. 166–72, for the General Congregation of 28 May.

Tradition, and acknowledge the divine guidance of the Church of Rome. The very existence of the Council testified to the belief that the Bible was not the exclusive source of revelation. Hence neither Charles V nor his supporters in the Council opposed the definition of this doctrine. Pole, as we have seen, had been enthusiastically in favour of it. It is a measure of the illusion under which he laboured that he could expect, as late as 1546, the followers of Luther to accept the principle of ecclesiastical tradition, and the integrity of the Church of Rome, once it had been purged of its abuses; nevertheless, it had been his implicit assumption in writing *De Concilio*. The assumption was almost unavoidable, given his simultaneous belief in the doctrine of salvation by faith alone, together with the primacy of Rome; it exemplifies indeed, the unreal hopes which distracted the *spirituali* from too close an inspection of realities. Such an expectation could only survive by being grounded in the belief that the Council could be brought to accept everything that Luther said about salvation – and surely, it was felt, when that became apparent, there could be no problem for the Lutherans in accepting the primacy of Rome. But for the Council to proceed with its discussion of salvation, before the Lutherans had been consulted, and without giving them an opportunity to explain what they believed, was, in this view, dangerous in the extreme. And this was what occurred towards the end of May.

Thus it is reasonable to conjecture that from this point onwards, a severe tension was created in Pole's mind between his personal opinions and the demands imposed upon him by his office. To a temperament as scrupulous as his, the difficulty would be aggravated by the intensity with which he held his views on the one hand, and his high conception of duty on the other. As Papal Legate, he would clearly be obliged to suppress his innermost convictions.

It was precisely at this moment that he began to be afflicted by an illness which prevented him, on 21 May, from attending a meeting of the Council.[1] The meeting was concerned with the

[1] 'vocati sunt patres in hodiernam generalem congregationem hora 18, cui card. Polus ob adversam valetudinem non interfuit.' (*C.T.*, v, 152.)

decree on the propagation of the faith; but it is noteworthy that this was the same day on which Del Monte had proposed to the Council that it should undertake to discuss the doctrine of original sin. It seems highly probable that Pole's ailment was a direct result of this development. Nor was it simply a temporary setback. A week later Cervini, in a letter to Farnese, mentioned that Pole was suffering from a deep and continuous pain in his left arm, which was interfering with his sleep, and impeding his activity in general.[1] There is no reason to doubt that Pole was genuinely ill, although his sleeplessness may have been caused by greater difficulties than catarrh, which was the diagnosis offered by Cervini. The Conciliar discussions were now irrevocably involved in what he could only have considered to be a disastrously premature investigation of doctrines which were crucial to the main dynamic of the Reformation. The resultant anxiety seems to have induced in Pole an illness which bears all the signs of being psychosomatic, and which appears to have affected his heart.

Already it was clear that the question of original sin was inseparable from that of justification. This much had been stressed by the Legates' report of 15 April;[2] and the questions submitted to the theologians on 24 May contained a number which were directly related to the matters in dispute between Lutheranism and Catholicism. The two key questions were those which inquired whether, after baptism, certain remnants of original sin remained in man, and if so, what was their effect?[3]

The importance of these questions was that they raised the problem of concupiscence, or the inclination to sin which remained in man after he was justified. Thus they touched upon the nature of justification itself, and demanded an answer that would distinguish the Catholic position from that of Luther. The latter had maintained that concupiscence was to be identified with sin itself, although it was not imputed as such, to the man

---

[1] 'essendo venuto al Rmo. cardinale Pole una profunda et continua doglia nel braccio sinistro, causata da catarre freddo che l'impedisce il sonno et le altre attioni' (*C.T.*, x, Cervini to Farnese, 28 May 1546.)

[2] Above, n. 2, p. 123.

[3] *C.T.*, v, 164.

justified by faith.¹ It was to this question that the Council now addressed itself.

The reply given to the Legates' questions by the Spanish theologian Juan Morillo who, as Pole's theologian at the Council was later to act as an intermediary between Pole and his fellow Legates in the period when Pole had left the Council, is of some interest, in suggesting the views to which Pole himself may have adhered.² They are on the whole unremarkable, except in so far as they indicate that Pole's alarm about the discussions is likely to have been strategic for the moment rather than explicitly doctrinal. Certainly there is nothing in Morillo's views which can associate him with Luther. In his treatise on original sin, he maintained that baptism, while removing the guilt incurred by man's fallen nature, left concupiscence intact. The latter, while distinguishable from sin, acted nevertheless as a continuous force in human nature, constantly impelling it towards sin. Perfect justice, therefore, was not attainable by man in his present life.³

In exploring the issue of 'imperfect righteousness' the Council was about to move into a direct encounter with the Protestant doctrine of salvation.

Such a prospect provoked a number of the Council fathers to urge that an invitation be extended to certain Protestant divines, so that, if their views were to be condemned, they might be allowed a hearing. The matter was first touched upon by the bishop of Sinigaglia on 4 June, and on the next day his proposal was supported by four others.⁴ But no further support for the idea was forthcoming, and the Legates believed, perhaps mistakenly, that the proposal was merely a delaying tactic.⁵ On 9 June they submitted to the Council a list of erroneous views on original sin, including a number held by Luther and the Anabaptists.⁶

But if the proposal to invite the Protestants had fallen through,

---

¹ *Assertio omnium articulorum M. Lutheri per bullam Leonis X. novissimam damnatorum* (December 1520), articles 2–3, in *Luther's Works* (Eng. edn), ed. Pelikan and Lehmann (Philadelphia, 1958 ff.), vol. 32. pp. 19–31.
² *C.T.*, xii, 553–65.　　³ Ibid. p. 562.　　⁴ *C.T.*, i, 68–9, and v, 182–96.
⁵ *C.T.*, x, 512, Legates' report of 4 June; cf. Jedin, *Council*, ii, 148–9.
⁶ *C.T.*, v, 212–13.

an attempt was made to observe some measure of protocol, by arranging for a defence of their opinions to be heard. This appears to have been done in secret, and there is no record of the event in the proceedings of the Council.[1]

Yet we know that at some point in the Council's business Pole undertook, in a meeting with Del Monte and Cervini, to answer for the Protestants – lest it be said that they had been condemned without a hearing. The account is provided in a dispatch of Diego de Mendoza to the Emperor, dated 5 December 1549 – some three years, therefore, after the event.[2] Mendoza indicates that the incident occurred when it became clear that the Council was to proceed against the Lutherans without hearing them, or waiting for them to attend ('hauiendo el Concilio resoluto de proceder contra lutheranos sin sperarlos ni oyrlos').[3] We may reasonably assume therefore, that it took place at some moment between 21 May, when Del Monte presented the topic of original sin, and 9 June, when the list of condemned errors was presented. Mendoza's account of the matter is a summary of what Pole himself had said (presumably on 5 December 1549 or the day preceding) in defending himself at the Papal Conclave against the accusations brought against him by Carafa, that he had been guilty of certain errors of religion. According to Mendoza, Pole explained that he had, in agreement with his colleagues, undertaken to answer for the Lutherans, lest it be said that their views had been condemned without a hearing. Mendoza added that Pole's account was substantiated by Del Monte and Cervini.[4]

The choice of Pole for this assignment is of course significant, and it is possible indeed, that the proposal may have been his own. Certainly he can have been left in no doubt of the course on which the Council was embarked when, on 14 June, a revised draft of the proposed decree was presented to the fathers.[5] The first

---

[1] Nor does Jedin mention it.

[2] *O.S.V.*, Rom. Korresp., fasc. 9b, fols. 31r–32v; cf. also *C.S.P.S.*, IX, 483–6. The transcript of this document, which should be available in the Public Record Office, London, appears to have been mislaid. The document is, however, printed by A. von Druffel, *Beiträge zur Reichsgeschichte 1546–51* (Munich, 1873), no. 352, pp. 306–9.

[3] Rom. Korresp., fasc. 9b, fol. 32r; von Druffel, *Beiträge*, p. 308.   [4] Ibid.

[5] First draft of the decree, *C.T.*, v, 186–8; the revisions, ibid. pp. 218–19.

canon of this decree condemned the belief that in baptism, the guilt of sin was not removed, but simply concealed, or no longer imputed.[1]

These words contained an unequivocal condemnation of Luther's doctrine of salvation. The decree itself maintained that baptism removed not only the guilt of original sin, but everything essentially sinful, so that nothing was left in the baptised that was hateful in God's sight. It repudiated too, the Augustinian view put forward by Seripando on 5 June, that while concupiscence after baptism could not strictly be identified with sin, it could in another sense (*aliqua ratione*) be regarded as sin, in so far as it was a consequence of original sin, and by its presence impeded the perfect fulfilment of God's law.[2] According to Seripando, moreover, it was faith which, in conjunction with baptism, was the main element in liberating mankind from original sin.[3] Against this view, the decree emphasised that the concupiscence remaining after baptism could not be regarded as sin in the proper sense of the word, but only as an infirmity of nature, which inclined man towards sin. Baptism removed not only the guilt of original sin, but anything that could properly be regarded as sin.[4]

The distinction between these points of view was significant, and Pole felt himself obliged to intervene in criticism of the draft decree. In the debate of 14 June he made a long speech, in which he objected to the statement of canon five, that God found nothing worthy of hatred in those reborn in baptism.[5] These words, he admitted, if rightly understood, were quite acceptable, since they agreed with what St Paul himself had said. For the rest however, he would prefer to avoid using them, on account of the infirmities of human nature. It would be desirable for the decree to include a further statement on the matter, lest it be interpreted as meaning that the baptised were exempt from further sin.[6]

[1] Ibid. p. 219.
[2] Seripando's vote in *C.T.*, v, 194–5; his treatise on original sin, *Pro dictis a Polo, C.T.*, xii, 549–53; cf. also Jedin, *Girolamo Seripando*, i, 354–8 (Eng. edn pp. 314–19), and *Council*, ii, pp. 146–9.
[3] *C.T.*, v, 194–5.   [4] Ibid., p. 219.   [5] *C.T.*, i, 75–6, and v, 220.
[6] *C.T.*, i, 75–6.

It was precisely the expression 'in the reborn there is nothing hateful to God' ('in illis [renatis] enim nihil odit Deus'), to which Seripando had taken exception, on the grounds that concupiscence was displeasing to God. But it is not quite accurate to state, as Jedin does, that Pole was endeavouring to support the view proposed by Seripando.[1] It seems more likely that, as Fray de Sta Teresa argues, Pole was not directly concerned with the problem of concupiscence as such.[2] In fact his habits of thought were very different from those of Seripando. Seripando was a trained theologian, concerned with subtle and precise distinctions; Pole on the other hand, was concerned to see his spiritual experience ratified in the light of theology.[3] Thus the question of concupiscence was a highly involved theological issue, which Seripando was equipped to deal with: Pole's purpose was simply to ensure that the decree should avoid any appearance of minimising human sinfulness. It was only in this, linguistic, sense that he was concerned to make precise corrections to a vaguely worded document. Thus while no one at the Council supposed that the baptised were immune from sin, it seemed to Pole that the phrasing of the decree allowed for just such a misinterpretation.

In a broader sense, there was of course a mutual concern on the part of Pole and Seripando to avoid undue reliance upon man's efforts in the process of salvation. Indeed Seripando's treatise, *Pro dictis a Polo*, was written in defence of Pole's objection to the proposed decree; but its preoccupation, characteristically, was with the precise theology of concupiscence, and it reflects a way of thinking alien to Pole's.[4] The point is of some importance, since Pole's views are often taken to be the same as Seripando's. The danger of this approach is that Pole is liable to be classified within a definite school of theological opinion, whereas in fact he was at all times remote from the procedures and disciplines of systematic theology.[5] In this of course, he was typical of the *spirituali* who were interested in the psychology of the spiritual

[1] Jedin, *Council*, II, 156.   [2] Fray de Sta Teresa, *Valdés*, pp. 289–90.
[3] Ibid. p. 290.   [4] *C.T.*, XII, 549–53.
[5] Thus Schenk, for example (*Reginald Pole*, p. 114) associates Pole with the doctrine of twofold justice, which is an over-simplification.

life, and not in the exact distinctions made by professional theologians. The difficulty arose, however, when, as in the case of Pole,
it became necessary to find a theologically exact mode of expression. This, as we shall see, was to be a cause of real anguish to
Pole, when the debate on justification had got under way. In
discussions of this kind his only contribution could be negatively
to criticise, and to plead for greater clarity, so that the Conciliar
decrees would pay due deference to the testimony of spiritual
experience. Yet the very urge towards precise definition, which
was the main purpose of the Council, could only undermine the
broad assumptions upon which the *spirituali* depended in their
spiritual life. Thus, as the Council's work advanced, not only did
it threaten the pragmatic basis of their *credo*, but it gradually
dispelled their dream of a reunion with the Lutherans, which was
the natural consequence of their spiritual affirmations.

As yet, however, this was only beginning to become apparent.
The real significance of Pole's intervention on 14 June, was that at
last he had ventured into open criticism. His remarks intimated the
final, tentative, alarmed response of the ecclesiastical *spirituali* to the
new spirit of the Counter Reformation. The very phrasing of his
protest is revealing: 'Quod mihi dubium facit est,' 'nam in aliis non
auderem id ego affimare'. It is perhaps not too fanciful to detect
here the halting, worried accent of the eirenic *spirituali*, confronted
with the unqualified assurance which was to be the hallmark of the
Counter Reformation.[1] Certainly, this was to be the tone of
Pole's response during the ensuing months as, torn between his
loyalty to the decisions of the Church and the simultaneous disintegration of his hopes, he struggled to adapt himself to what was
happening and to resign himself to an accomplished fact.

Already, on 17 June, he had experienced his first defeat. The
decree on original sin which received the assent of the Council on
that day, remained unaltered, and his objections went unrecognis-
ed.[2] In itself, this was far from being a catastrophe; his objections
had been in a sense peripheral, prompted merely by the urge for

---

[1] This, admittedly, is to stretch the meaning of the text, which is firm enough
in its objection; but it may serve to point a general truth.
[2] Alberigo, *Decreta*, pp. 641–3.

greater clarity. But it was a measure of his anxiety that he had broken his reserve; and it seems certain that his real complaint, unuttered out of consideration for his office, was that the Council had proceeded too precipitately.

It was a complaint shared by the Emperor. On 16 June, a messenger arrived at Trent, bearing instructions for the Imperial ambassadors.¹ The latter were informed that the Emperor was opposed to the publication of decrees concerning doctrine. They were to propose instead that the Council devote itself to the reform of the Church, so as to silence the Protestants.²

The Emperor's fear was that a Conciliar decision on original sin would undermine his propaganda in the war he was to wage against the Protestants. He needed to represent it as a war against rebellious subjects, and not a war of religion. He feared too, that it would jeopardise his hopes of an alliance with Maurice of Saxony and the Margrave Albrecht of Brandenburg-Kulmbach who, though Protestants, were not members of the League of Schmalkalden. Only, therefore, when the victory had been gained, should the Council undertake to discuss disputed doctrines.³

Toledo, now that his instructions had arrived, conveyed their tenor to the Legates. But it was too late. The decree was to be submitted to the Council on the following day, and it could not be retracted at this stage. The Legates informed Toledo of this fact, and he could do nothing but accept defeat.⁴ Accordingly, on 17 June, the decree was passed at the fifth General Session of the Council.⁵ The Catholic doctrine was proclaimed, and Luther's doctrine of concupiscence stood condemned; it was the prelude to the Council's definitions on the major doctrinal issues of the day.⁶

Thus the expectations which Pole had entertained some few months earlier were now definitely threatened. Catholic doctrine

¹ *C.T.*, XI, 56–7.
² Ibid. p. 57: 'por atabar la boca alos protestantes y escusar lo que podran dezir'.
³ Cf. report from the German Nuncio, Verallo, 13 June, 1546. (*C.T.*, X, 525.)
⁴ The Legates described how Toledo, acquiescing in defeat, 'chinò le spalle et si licentiò da noi'. (*C.T.*, X, 527.)
⁵ General session of 17 June, *C.T.*, V, 238–56.
⁶ The decree is published by Alberigo, *Decreta*, pp. 641–3. Luther himself was not mentioned in the decree.

had been defined in a manner opposed to Protestant belief and the Protestants themselves had not been consulted. At this moment, two further events took place which finally betrayed whatever hopes he may have salvaged. Charles V declared war against the German Protestants; and on 21 July at ten o'clock in the morning, Cardinal Cervini introduced the subject of justification to the agenda of the Council.[1] These occurrences, with the developments which they precipitated, rendered it impossible that the Council should effect a union with the Lutherans. The Emperor's troops were now engaged against the German Protestants, while at the same time the Council was about to declare its teaching on the question which formed the cornerstone of Luther's edifice. What hope was there that it would do so in a manner favourable to the Lutherans?[2]

Pole made one final, desperate attempt to persuade the Council of the approach to be adopted on this issue. His speech of 21 June was the last he was to make before the assembly.[3] It provides a perfect mirror of the way in which he had striven to reconcile the duties of his office with the urgency of his personal convictions. His first remarks were framed in keeping with the spirit of his role as Papal Legate. He praised Cervini's speech, and pronounced it to be appropriate that the Council, having dealt with original sin and the loss suffered by mankind, should consider now the gain entailed in justification.[4]

These, it seems fair to suggest, were the words of a dutiful official; and Pole, having thus paid due respect to the demands of office, addressed the Council now from the depths of his convictions. The issue which confronted it, he stated, was both tortuously difficult, and at the same time vital to salvation. Therefore the members of the Council must pray all the more repeatedly for the guidance of the Holy Spirit. For his own part, he wished

[1] Jedin, *Council*, II, 213; the speeches of Cervini and Pole, 21 June, in *C.T.*, v, 257; Pole's speech recorded also in *C.T.*, I, 82–3.

[2] 'How could it be expected, at a moment when pope and emperor were attacking the Protestants with force of arms, that their primal doctrine – that on which the whole existence of their creed was founded – should be received as valid by a council assembled under the auspices of the two powers?' L. von Ranke, *History of the Popes* (3 vols, London, 1908) I, 158.

[3] *C.T.*, I, 82–3, and v, 257.   [4] *C.T.*, I, 82.

especially to urge the fathers to read extensively around the question, and not to shun the writings of their adversaries. On the contary, they should read them, not as the work of adversaries, but as the expression of 'another view' ('cuiuslibet alterius'). Neither should they hasten to exclaim: 'Luther said that, therefore it is false'.[1]

Pole went on to justify this admonition by explaining that it was the practice among heretics to utter truth as well as falsehood, so as more easily to lead the credulous astray. Hence, with characteristic sleight of hand he conveyed his policy directives without revealing his personal opinions. He had employed the same technique in *De Concilio*, with the purpose of defining the perspective from which the Council should examine the issues which divided Luther from the Church of Rome. Beyond this, Pole was intent on avoiding any definition of his sentiments, partly because it was difficult to find a satisfactory expression of them, and partly because of a disinclination to give scandal. It is deeply ironical that his account of the tactics used by heretics should be identical with that which Carafa had employed, in expressing to Priuli his opposition to the Regensburg agreement.[2] But this kind of irony is a recurrent feature of the evasions to which the *spirituali* were driven, in their anxiety to reconcile opposing doctrines, and it is inextricably linked with the ambiguity which marked their cause.

Pole proposed, therefore, that the members of the Council should read all works with an open mind, retaining whatever was worthy of approval, and rejecting what was not. Impartiality, he stressed, must be their guiding spirit, and he concluded his address with words which were emblematic of his whole approach, exhorting them to hold the middle way: 'Tenenda est igitur media via, nec huc neque illuc flectendum.'[3]

They were his last words to the Council. A day earlier on 20 June, a licence had arrived from Rome, permitting him to leave Trent in order to regain his health.[4] On Monday 28 June, at two o'clock in the morning, he set out from Trent, never to

---

[1] Ibid.   [2] See above, p. 56.   [3] *C.T.*, I, 83.   [4] *C.T.*, X, 531.

return. The Council's secretary, Massarelli, noted in his diary that Pole had departed for Priuli's villa at Treville, to recover from 'the illness of body and mind' which had afflicted him for forty days.[1]

Massarelli's wording is significant: it is important to notice that he speaks of Pole's mental, as well as physical health. It was not simply the pain in his left arm that motivated Pole's departure: it was also the need to recover peace of mind. The period of forty days which Massarelli specifies, indicates that his illness reached back to the middle of May, when the Council was about to embark on its discussion of original sin. There is no need to doubt the reality of Pole's affliction, physical as well as mental. His subsequent correspondence with the Legates demonstrates that his physical suffering was genuine enough, and that his doctors were seriously concerned about his health.[2] But it is difficult to avoid the conclusion that his illness was aggravated above all by anxiety, and that he had experienced something like a nervous breakdown.[3]

Pole's explanation of the motives for his departure is likely to have been privately conveyed to Del Monte and Cervini; and it may be that Massarelli had some idea of their nature, and was instructed to record them in a manner suitably oblique. Anyway, the official explanation of Pole's action remained that he had been forced by ill-health to depart. Pole's first biographer, Beccadelli, related that Pole had been obliged to leave on account of the thinness of the air, and the trouble in his arm.[4] Beccadelli's editor, Morandi, at the beginning of the nineteenth century, repeated this assertion, against the charge made by Cardinal Guise in the conclave of 1549–50, that Pole had left Trent for doctrinal reasons. Pole, however, according to the (unfortunately corrupt) source used by Morandi, 'candidly replied that God was his witness, if he had left Trent for any reason other than ill-health'.[5]

It seems possible, however, that 'candour' (Morandi's word)

[1] *C.T.*, I, 557. [2] See below, p. 165.
[3] A point first made by Fr Bernard Franck, in an unpublished essay which I am grateful to have had an opportunity to read.
[4] Morandi, *Monumenti*, I, ii, p. 302.
[5] Ibid. n. 36. Morandi's source was the text entitled *Conclave di Giulio III*, discussed in *C.T.*, II, xxvii–xxix.

may not be the *mot juste*. Pole's reply, as recorded in this version, seems more like a magnificent evasion: an appeal to God to witness the grounds which had motivated his departure (and which no doubt could truthfully be described as ill-health) – but not, we may feel, a reply to Guise's accusation. This is not to suggest that Pole maintained a secret resistance to the decrees of Trent for the remainder of his life. Such an attitude would have been inconsistent with a temperament as scrupulous as his.[1] But he was far from being ready to admit the extent to which the Council had upset him – and his reluctance is understandable, given the nature of his antagonists. But this is a question which must be reserved for treatment in a later chapter. For the moment it is sufficient to suggest that Pole left Trent for more reasons than Beccadelli indicates, or perhaps indeed imagined – though this qualification must be added with considerable reserve.

It was not intended that Pole's departure should be permanent. The Pope had given him permission to rest for a few days in a place not far from Trent, so that he could recover his repose. This much is apparent from Farnese's letter of 30 June to Pole's remaining colleagues at Trent: Pole was to return after his recovery.[2]

But Pole did not return. Instead, he acquired permission permanently to remain away, eventually securing his release from the office which had been so burdensome to him. As the Council embarked on its lengthy examination of the doctrine of justification, Pole remained secluded in Priuli's villa at Treville, afterwards transferring to Bembo's residence at Padua, and finally to Rome. Thus his departure on 28 June was final. In many ways, however, his involvement with the Council's business had just begun. We have seen how his nerve broke at the prospect of what was about to happen. We must now examine the *spirituali* who stayed for the debate.

[1] Cf. his remarks of 3 June 1546: 'Quod conscientia alicui dictat, proferendum quidem est; verum postquam semel atque iterum et tertio quis sibi satisfecerit proferendo opinionem suam, et aperte cognitum eius dictum a maiori parte non solum non probari, sed omni conatu reprobari, potest et debet ille tuta conscientia opinionem suam dimittere. Et quod amplius est a malo est.' *C.T.*, IV, 578. He was to be obliged shortly to act upon these sentiments.
[2] *C.T.*, X, 545.

CHAPTER NINE

The 'spirituali' at Trent

On 21 June 1546, with the opening of the debate on justification, the Council of Trent moved into the final and most decisive phase of its preliminary sessions. When, in the spring of the year following, the Council was suspended, the Catholic doctrine of salvation had been defined, and the ground prepared for the fundamental reforms which were to occupy the final sessions of 1562–3. Furthermore, the political alliance between Pope and Emperor, which had been the condition of the Council's operations, had been severed by the precipitate action of one man: the Papal Legate, Marcello Cervini, whose decision to translate the assembly to Bologna destroyed the Emperor's conception of the Council, and brought an eventual halt to its proceedings.[1] Three problems therefore, occupied the attention of the Council fathers in the latter part of this year: justification, episcopal residence (with the attendant problem of Curial reform), and the matter of translation; and these three problems form the tips of a triangle at which the Council touched upon the leading questions of the day – doctrine, reform, and international politics. Since it was the first of these questions which most intimately affected Pole and the *spirituali* during these months, it will be necessary to concentrate on the proceedings concerning justification. These admittedly formed the principal business of the Council in this period, but the questions of residence and of translation must nevertheless be kept in mind, if an accurate perspective is to be maintained.

It was not without reason that Cervini, introducing the topic

[1] Jedin, *Council*, II, 396–443.

of justification, described it as a matter fraught with difficulties.[1] Almost thirty years had passed since Luther had thrust it to the front as the essential theme of Christianity. Innumerable men and women throughout Europe – a whole generation – had attended to his words and experienced within themselves the powerful effects of his teaching. Luther's was the inescapable and overwhelming religious presence of the age; and even where, as in Italy, his influence was initially felt at a remove of distance and environment, it was impossible to ignore the issues he had raised. Men might never have read Luther, they might regard him as a heretic or a schismatic, and yet, in many cases, they discovered that his highly personal involvement with the problem of salvation had become theirs also. Thus, while many followed him in his denunciation of the Church of Rome, others, desirous of a reformation from within, had waited with growing impatience and uncertainty for her recovery. Throughout these years the Church remained not only unreformed, but subject to the climate of theological confusion which, in the view of the papacy, it was the first business of the Council to eliminate. Hence, when the Council finally assembled, it inevitably turned to an examination of this problem, and the conclusion of its long deliberations, the decree on justification, constituted the primary achievement of these months.

The evolution of the Tridentine decree on justification has received abundant attention and analysis in recent years.[2] It is generally agreed that three principal theological approaches were brought to bear on the solution of the problem: namely, those espoused by the Thomists, the Scotists and the Augustinians. Of these, the first (and ultimately triumphant) group, consisting largely of Dominicans, referred to the authority of Aquinas, and assumed a dominantly theocentric and logically coherent attitude towards the problem. The Scotists, on the other hand, who drew their strength from the Franciscans, placed greater emphasis upon the ethical and psychological implications of the question; while the Augustinians adopted an approach which, in its tendency, was

---

[1] *C.T.*, v, 257.   [2] Jedin, *Council*, ii, 166–96, and 239–317.

reminiscent of the formula of twofold justice which had been agreed upon at Regensburg in 1541.

Apart from the prelates who attached themselves to these schools of opinion there was, however, a fourth group, consisting almost exclusively of a small number of bishops drawn from the ranks of the Italian clergy.[1] These men, while sharing the aversion felt by the Augustinians to the medieval traditions of scholastic theology, were nevertheless unwilling to accept the formulations which the General of the Augustinians, Seripando, put forward as alternatives. Thus, weak in numbers, and intellectually insignificant if compared with the major figures of the Council, their representative significance has not always been recognised. The publication, in 1959, of an important work by Giuseppe Alberigo, on the Italian representatives at Trent, opened a new and more satisfactory perspective on their significance.[2] Alberigo, discussing the considerable literature which has grown up around the Tridentine decree on justification, points out that its primary concern has been to elucidate the opinions of those theologians who contributed to the definitive expression of the Council's judgement, as embodied in the final decree. The implication of such an approach, more theological than historical, is that the problem was of interest only to professional theologians. But as Alberigo rightly stresses, the need to clarify the doctrine of justification was at once a theological requirement and, for many people, a spiritual necessity which could brook no further delay. The Council was obliged to address itself therefore, not merely in a controversial role to the theologians of a dissident communion, but to the audience of Christendom at large. Hence, a number of fathers during the course of the debate demanded the use of very simple expressions in the formulation of the decree, so that it might be comprehensible to the unlearned.[3] It is with this aspect of the question uppermost in mind that Alberigo undertakes to redress the imbalance created by previous studies, and to examine

[1] It also included the Benedictine abbots. H. O. Evennett, 'Three Benedictine Abbots at the Council of Trent 1545–7', *Studia Monastica*, 1 (1959), 343–77.

[2] G. Alberigo, *I vescovi italiani al Concilio di Trento (1545–7)* (Florence, 1959).

[3] Alberigo, *I vescovi italiani*, pp. 337–94. A preoccupation which suggests the need for further research on the social impact of the Reformation in Italian dioceses.

instead, the problem of justification as it appeared to persons who were neither by training nor by inclination theologians.

These prelates were men who, from pastoral experience or diplomatic travels, had come into contact with circles where the claims of individual experience were valued beyond the formulations and precision of scholastic thought.[1] To certain suspiciously disposed observers they gave the appearance of being 'crypto-Lutheran'. Thus the bishop of Melopotamos, Dionisio de Zanettini – or as he was more commonly styled, Grechetto – wrote to Cardinal Farnese on 25 June, at the outset of the discussions, referring to the 'heretical and Lutheran' opinions of certain highly placed prelates in the Church. Among these he included Morone and Pole, together with Cardinal Ridolfi; while he also mentioned the bishops of Sinigaglia, Cava and Fiesole, who were at this time present at the Council.[2] Zanettini's view was that all these men were heretical in the matter of justification.

There is no evidence however, that his opinion was taken seriously by the Pope. Zanettini indeed, is most frequently remembered (or dismissed) as the victim of an incident which caused him to lose an insignificant, though doubtless painful part of his beard.[3] Nevertheless, his report is of considerable interest, since it directs attention to the *spirituali* at the Council and in the Roman Curia; and his remarks almost certainly aroused an echo of response in the minds of men like Carafa and Juan Alvarez de Toledo, the Cardinal de Burgos.[4] Zanettini was undoubtedly correct in recognising these prelates as desirous of a closer alignment between the doctrines of the Church of Rome and those of Wittenberg. The fact that in expressing this perception he referred

[1] Ibid. p. 347.
[2] As was Pole, who left, as it will be recalled, on 28 June. Zanettini counted too among his suspects the Patriarch of Aquilea, nor did he forget the influence of the late Cardinal Contarini. His letter is in *C.T.*, x, 538–40.
[3] Forcibly removed by the bishop of Cava, Sanfelice, who had been stung to fury by an insolent remark. This surrender to impulse cost the latter his departure from the Council. (Jedin, *Council*, II, 191–2.)
[4] This qualification should be added to Jedin's otherwise accurate observation that Farnese's request of 2 February 1546, bidding him send occasional reports to Rome, 'is not decisive for an appreciation of the weight attached to his accusations' (*Council*, II, 181, no. 1). On the other hand, Carafa and Toledo were far from representing official opinion.

to their beliefs as Lutheran, concentrates attention upon the varying degrees of sympathy with which they responded to the doctrine of salvation by faith alone, and prophetically adumbrates the difficulties to which a number of them were to be subjected in the years that followed the Council.

It is to this group of men, who represented the interests of the *spirituali* at the Council, that attention must now be directed. Their attitudes and opinions afford an interesting comparison with the position adopted by Pole in his retreat near Padua, and serve to illustrate the reaction of the *spirituali* to the developments which now occurred at Trent.

Perhaps the best theoretical scheme of reference for this purpose (borrowing from Alberigo), is to be found in the relationship existing between faith and works: for this was a problem about which every prelate had to assume an attitude, even if he could not effectively enter into theological discussion.[1] The advantage of this approach is that it facilitates a consideration of positions which as Alberigo states, were determined not only – or even often – by choice, or intellectual coherence, but which were rather the direct result of human and religious experience.[2]

It is furthermore remarkable that those who put forward opinions of this kind in the Council should have been, in almost every case, Italian.[3] This is not to be explained by the fact that in Italy, as Alberigo supposes, the weakness of scholastic theology (whatever the vigorous independence of thought revealed in a classical Thomist such as Cajetan) discouraged any tendency towards rigidity in theological reflection, so that an environment arose which enabled men to break loose from the intellectual monopoly possessed by the great schools of the middle ages.[4]

---

[1] Alberigo, *I vescovi italiani*, pp. 347–8.   [2] Ibid. p. 350.

[3] Almost: but not actually in every case, as Alberigo maintains (pp. 388–9). Pole's fellow countryman, Richard Pate, held views which seem to have been closer to those of Luther than any put forward by the Italians. Alberigo, however, is concerned only with the latter, and Pate falls outside his terms of reference. See below, pp. 149–59.

[4] This point is made by Alberigo (p. 389) with respect to Italy alone, but it seems applicable to Europe as a whole. Alberigo is perhaps too anxious to consider Italy as a unit separate from other European countries, although his emphasis on the indigenous quality of the ideas expressed at Trent among the Italian *spirituali* is legitimate.

After all, this was true in virtually every European country, as the influence of Erasmus indicates, and the majority of the Council fathers were Italians and Scholastics. Nor was it only in Italy that the attitudes characteristic of the *spirituali* found expression. The circle of Lefèvre d'Etaples, of Briçonnet and Margaret of Navarre, bears amply testimony to the existence of the same phenomenon in France. The experiences of the *alumbrados* point to its development equally in Spain. But it does seem that in Italy the process was carried to its furthest extension, and that there, the alternative to scholasticism almost invariably took the form of the kind of piety peculiar to the *spirituali*. It is not an accident that Valdés felt most at home in Italy.

This process was encouraged by the fact that controversial theology had been exceptionally slow in establishing itself south of the Alps.[1] Catharino's reply to the *Beneficio di Cristo* was the first really formidable intellectual response to the development of the Italian Reformation; and it did not make its appearance until 1544 – little over a year, that is, before the Council gathered. According to Alberigo, the late awakening of controversial theology is attributable to the limited infiltration of Protestant opinion; in fact, it is probably an index to the growth of Protestantism. It had to cope, too, with certain attitudes bred by the Italian Renaissance.[2]

Wherever the concern for religion became paramount among the *spirituali* it took the form initially of an interior withdrawal. The absence during the 1520s and 1530s of any notable polemical tensions encouraged a free-ranging spirituality centred upon personal experience, the expression of which bore little resemblance to the doctrine of the schools. Hence the circle of Valdés at Naples, of the Duchess Renée at Ferrara, or of Pole and his associates at Viterbo, had remained relatively free from the influences of scholastic thought and open to the influence of the Reformation. The categories of their thought were drawn from Scripture, and the limits which they recognised as proper to their speculations were determined exclusively by their attitude towards the Church

[1] Alberigo, *I vescovi italiani*, p. 389.
[2] Cf. the letter of Flavio Crisolino to Beccadelli, cited above, n. 6, p. 60.

of Rome. If, as in the Viterbo circle, the predominant attitude was one of allegiance, then Catholic doctrines such as purgatory, or the admission of penance as a sacrament, were held to be immutable; whereas in the circles of Modena or Ferrara, the influence of Luther or of Calvin was more generally received.

But there is one other factor which helps to explain the almost complete restriction, at Trent, of the outlook characteristic of the *spirituali* to prelates of Italian origin; and that is the uneven balance of representation at the Council. In the years 1545-7, Italians constituted approximately seventy per cent of those voting at the Council.[1] It would be quite wrong to believe that they voted in a bloc; the contrary was true. But the fact of their preponderance must go some way to explaining what might otherwise remain a striking and perhaps misleading, singularity: namely, the virtual exclusion of non-Italians from the ranks of those who declined to associate themselves with the dominant categories of scholastic opinion at the Council.

Among the various, and often contradictory attitudes assumed among the *spirituali*, there remained one constant element: the overwhelming demand for a personally assimilated faith, which would enable every Christian to experience within himself the effects of the divine mercy, recalling him to a life of inner peace. They remained acutely conscious, however, that the expression of this view in the form which most appealed to them (whereby faith was adjudged to be the exclusive agent of salvation) must bring them close to the position held by Luther; and they did not wish to follow Luther in his rejection of the Roman Church. Hence it is possible to observe a distinct spiritual anxiety at work amongst them, which was the result of an unresolved conflict between the testimony of their own experience, and their allegiance to the authority of the Church. The same phenomenon has already been observed in Pole and Contarini; but it is important to recognise, with Alberigo, that the expression of these attitudes at

[1] Cf. *C.T.*, v, 1037-40, for a list of those entitled to vote during this period; the list numbers a hundred such, though nothing like this number attended at any given session. Jedin (*Council*, II, 18-21, and 482-3) gives a full account of the category of persons entitled to a vote.

Trent was a significant, but nevertheless subdued echo of the dilemma which had long preoccupied an influential sector of opinion within Italy. Not one of the principal figures among the *spirituali* was present during the debate on justification. The deaths of Contarini and of Giberti, the absence of Pole, Morone and Beccadelli, left to 'exponents of the second rank' the task of representing the Italian *spirituali* at the Council.[1]

Among these exponents a distinction[2] must be made between those who, belonging to the secular clergy, had received little formal training in theology, and those who were in possession of the arduous intellectual discipline conferred by membership of a religious order. This distinction refers, clearly, not to the level of intelligence operating in these groups, but to the nature of its expression, and the directions in which it tended to develop.

The first group, drawn from the secular clergy of humanist education, comprised the bishop of Cava, Tommaso Sanfelice, whose involvement in the incident with Zanettini has already been noticed; the coadjutor of Bergamo, Vittore Soranzo; the bishop of Aquino, Galeazzo Florimonte; and the bishop of Belluno, Giulio Contarini, who was a nephew of the deceased Cardinal. With this group must be associated Pole's fellow countryman Richard Pate, who had been appointed bishop of Worcester by the Pope; the archbishop of Sienna, Francisco Piccolomini-Bandini; and finally, the bishop of Terracina, Ottaviano Raverta. The opinions of these prelates (with the exception of Pate) reveal a consistent note of diffidence, and a distinctly tentative note invests their utterance at every level. However much this may be explained by a lack of theological

---

[1] Alberigo, *I vescovi italiani*, pp. 363–4. This description, obviously, does not apply to Seripando: but there is question here, not of those *spirituali* who subscribed to the doctrine of twofold justice, but of those who eschewed any elaborate theological expression of their views. It is perhaps worth noting that had Contarini survived and participated in the Council, he would have been likely to align himself with Seripando's party, rather than with the latter group, whose views approximated closely to those held by Pole. – The latter's absence has already been explained; Morone and Beccadelli were permanently stationed at Rome, the former being engaged with his work on the Conciliar Commission, the latter in the service of Cervini.

[2] Supplied by Alberigo, *I vescovi italiani*, p. 374, n. 2.

formation, it is difficult not to suspect that there was also a circum-spect discretion which withheld them from acknowledging – above all perhaps, to themselves – their proximity to the boundaries of heresy. Certainly, it is noticeable that in the early stages of the debate, many Italian prelates were reluctant to commit themselves to an opinion.[1]

The second group comprised those who, while belonging to religious orders, did not subscribe to a traditional theology. Of these, by far the most considerable figure was the General of the Augustinians, Girolamo Seripando. Seripando's advocacy of the doctrine of twofold justice at the Council has been made the subject of ample scholarly investigation, and it is only necessary to mention here that his opinion is too often considered to have been identical with that of Pole.[2] In fact, however, support for Seripando's view was limited to certain members of religious orders, whose intellectual formation led them to prefer the theory of twofold justice to a more simple expression of their personal needs and aspirations, such as satisfied those bishops who came from the ranks of the secular clergy.[3] Nevertheless the preoccupa-tions of both groups were the same, and each represented an aspect of the climate which produced the *spirituali*. For our pur-pose, however, it is sufficient to note that Pole must be classified as occupying a position distinct from that of Seripando, and as sharing the hesitations of those who, more tentative and uncertain, found little comfort in the esoteric distinctions of a highly organised theology. It is this latter group therefore, which must now form the principal object of our attention.

On 30 June, the Legates submitted to the fathers of the Council a series of questions on the theme *de iustificatione adultorum*. The

[1] Ibid. pp. 350–2.

[2] For Seripando's campaign to establish the doctrine of twofold justice at the Council cf. Jedin, *Girolamo Seripando*, I, 354–426 (pp. 326–82, English edn), and *Council*, II, 239–98.

[3] Alberigo, *I vescovi italiani*, p. 374, n. 2. Among the members of religious or-ders, the opinions of the Dominican, Pietro Bertano, bishop of Fano, and the Benedictine abbot, Luciano degli Ottoni, were perhaps closest to those of Seri-pando. But Luciano, and Isodorus Clarius (who had taught Pole at Padua) are really *spirituali* of a recognisable cast. (Evennett, 'Three Benedictine Abbots', examines the role of the two latter.) Luciano later extended his protection to Siculo (C. Ginzburg, *Il nicodemismo* (Turin, 1970), p. 172, n. 1)

preamble to this document declared that the process of justification should be considered as referring to three distinct phases of experience. The first of these comprised the initial transition of man from infidelity to faith. A series of problems was appended as relating to this phase. The assembly was asked to consider the manner in which the merits of Christ were applied to man, the nature of God's activity in this regard, and the requirements imposed on man himself. Further problems included the role of works and faith respectively, in securing justification. All of these questions were designed to clarify the nature of the first phase, which was that of conversion. The second phase, following from the first, was concerned with the means of retaining and augmenting justification; while the third was related to the recovery of justification after loss of grace.

Among the votes of those Italians who had been most influenced by the religious sensibility associated with *sola fides*, that of Tommaso Sanfelice, the bishop of Cava, is of considerable interest. His frequent contacts with the circles of Valdés and Pole, his acquaintance with Soranzo, Carnesecchi and Morone, and his subsequent imprisonment on suspicion of heresy, under Paul IV, indicate his significance as a representative of the *spirituali* at the Council.[1] The positions which he adopted, and above all, the phraseology which he employed, are commonly considered to have been closer to Protestantism than any of the views put forward by other members of the Council.[2] On 6 July he voted on the first phase of the problem, stressing the total gratuitousness of grace in man's first movement towards faith, and suggesting thereby, the incapacity of man to dispose himself for this event. He seemed to infer as well, that faith was the exclusive agent of salvation, whereas good works were a signal of divine favour.[3] On 17 July, he voted on the second and third phases of the problem,

[1] For an account of Sanfelice, Alberigo, *I vescovi italiani*, pp. 213, 224–5, and 367; also Jedin, *Council*, II, 189–92.

[2] Alberigo, *I vescovi italiani*, p. 367. Jedin too, considers Sanfelice to have been 'more reckless than the rest [of this group] in making Luther's vocabulary his own' (*Council*, II, 190). But this view seems not to recognise the full significance of Pate.

[3] *C.T.*, v, 294–6.

touching on the value of good works when he declared that no man, although justified, might rely upon his own justice to secure salvation: he must rely instead, upon the justice of Christ, offered to God on his behalf.[1] He displayed, moreover, a tendency to oppose the role of faith and works. Having delivered himself of his opinion, the incident with Zanettini followed – the latter having declared Sanfelice to be 'either a knave or a fool' – and Sanfelice's participation in the Council ended.[2]

The opinions too, of the bishop of Aquino, Galeazzo Florimonte, enable him to be bracketed among the *spirituali* at the Council.[3] His unwillingness to espouse any rigid categories of expression is noticeable, not only in his aversion to the theory of twofold justice, but in his reluctance to attach himself to any of the formulae put forward by the theological schools. Belonging to the generation of Contarini and Giberti, he had also been acquainted with Lefèvre d'Etaples, and had moved among the circles of the Italian Catholic Reform. His terminology in the Conciliar discussions betrays a distinct note of ambiguity, markedly in contrast with the precise methods of expression which informed the dominantly scholastic treatment of these issues at the Council. Florimonte had no taste for the categories of scholasticism; nor could he see any force in the proposals offered by the advocates of twofold justice. On the contrary, he declared himself impatient of the distinction between one kind of justice and another; for him there was only one justice, that of God Himself, and it was this same justice which he believed to be inherent in the Christian.[4] His use of language, moreover, was sufficiently elastic to evade commitment upon any of the essential issues in dispute. It is impossible to know, for example (though possible to guess), what he thought about the meritoriousness of

[1] Ibid. pp. 352–4. It is true that the idea of a twofold justice is suggested here (as it is occasionally in the votes of other members of this group), but in a manner altogether less systematic and thoroughgoing than its advocates, such as Seripando, thought essential.

[2] Ibid. pp. 354–63; cf. also Jedin, *Council*, II, 191–3, and Alberigo, *I vescovi italiani*, p. 367.

[3] Cf. Alberigo, *I vescovi italiani*, pp. 209–13, 225–9, and 369–72, for a comprehensive account of Florimonte.

[4] *C.T.*, X, 685–6.

good works. But it is perhaps worth noting that he devoted some of his energy to an attack upon the *Beneficio di Cristo*;[1] and this would suggest that the *Beneficio*, despite its initial impact on men like Cortese, Beccadelli and Morone, was by now disavowed by the ecclesiastical *spirituali*.[2]

Together with Sanfelice and Florimonte, three other Italian prelates may, in a general way, be classified as supporting a view of justification which owed little to scholastic theology, while at the same time declining to embrace the alternative theory of twofold justice. The attitude of Giulio Contarini, the bishop of Belluno, indicates his concern that the Conciliar decree should avoid an undue emphasis upon human activity in the process of salvation. In his vote of 10 July, he spoke of faith as taking its effect through charity, or good works,[3] thereby employing the same enigmatic formula to which Pole had had recourse in *De Concilio*. His insistence upon the interior renewal of mankind by grace – an opinion which he shared with Florimonte – was unambiguously orthodox; but he did not hesitate to assert that man was saved by faith alone.[4] Ten days later however, he stressed his willingness to submit to the judgement of the Council, particularly in those matters which, in his earlier speech, had been thought by some to be heretical.[5] Thus a general diffidence invests his remarks which is analogous to the vagueness shown by Florimonte, and testifies to the same spiritual anxiety which inhibited the *spirituali* at the Council from any intransigent declaration of their views. It seems reasonable to assume that with Giulio Contarini, as with the other Italian members of this group, a reluctance to speak plainly indicates, not so much a deliberate concealment of dangerous opinions as a conflict of unresolved ideas, such as had appeared in the correspondence of his uncle, four years earlier, with Pole.

[1] *C.T.*, v, 365, vote of 21 July.

[2] Fray de Sta Teresa (*Valdés*, pp. 294–303) argues that some of the *spirituali* at the Council represented the spirit of the *Beneficio di Cristo*; but this is true only in so tenuous a sense as to be essentially misleading. The *Beneficio* was a vigorous and militant document, designed to combat that very diffidence which is so noticeable in the opinions of these prelates.

Finally, the bishop of Terracina, Ottaviano Raverta, seems to have shown a reluctance to depend on human works in justification, while at the same time acknowledging, with the orthodox, the reality of an inherent justice; and Bandini, the archbishop of Sienna, in his vote of 5 July, is reported to have made use of the *sola fides* formula and to have attributed every stage in justification to the activity of Christ.[1]

Apart from these Italian prelates however, the opinions of Pole's compatriot and associate, Richard Pate (who held the see of Worcester *in absentia* for Rome), indicate his importance as a representative of the *spirituali* at the Council. In his vote of 9 July 1546, Pate is reported to have said that free will consented in a merely passive way to justification – a view which clearly nullified the role of free will in preparing for conversion. He is furthermore reputed to have stated his belief that 'faith alone' was the instrument of justification, while seeming to imply as well, that good works performed after justification were not meritorious, although they remained necessary, as being in accordance with the will of God.[2]

These are opinions which taken by themselves, suggest a strong degree of affinity with Luther's doctrine of salvation; and the views which Pate is recorded as having put forward in subsequent weeks not only confirm this impression, but indicate a notable absence of the timorousness which characterised the votes of the Italians. On 20 July he stated that justice increased to the extent that faith increased; good works were the fruit of justification,

[1] *C.T.*, v, 653–4 and I, 586, l. 27, for Raverta; also *C.T.*, I, 86, for Bandini's vote. Alberigo, *I vescovi italiani*, pp. 262, 373–4, provides an interesting account of Raverta.

[2] 'Vigorniensis dissentiit ab aliis; visus est enim dicere, liberum arbitrium concurrere mere passive ad iustificationem, et solam fidem esse instrumentum iustitiae. Et visus est excludere meritum operum post iustitiam, quamvis opera dixerit esse necessaria, quia Deus vult.' *C.T.*, v, 383. – The author of this account was the Dominican theologian Marco Laureo. The fact that Pate's speeches have survived only through the reports of Laureo and (on all other occasions) Massarelli, has perhaps led to their significance being underestimated. Jedin's statement that while Pate defended the doctrine of justification by faith alone, 'it is less certain that he denied the meritoriousness of good works' is a questionable view of the above passage, and one that can hardly be accepted in the light of Pate's subsequent votes. (*Council*, II, 189.)

and a sign to man that his salvation was assured.[1] In his vote of
13 November he was even more specific: the just man not only
might, but was indeed obliged to, believe in the certainty of his
own salvation. Moreover, in defining the concept of 'inherent
justice' the Council should stipulate that it was something
imputed to the Christian soul. Otherwise the justice of Christ
would be repudiated.[2]

Here was a statement of opinion more consistently Lutheran in
orientation than any which had been put forward in the Council.
Pate had expressed his belief in the doctrine of salvation by faith
alone; he had criticised (and evidently deplored) the Council's
manner of defining the doctrine of intrinsic justice; and finally, he
had declared that the man justified by faith was bound to believe
in the certainty of his own salvation. These views, argued and
sustained over a period of months, serve to establish his position as
significantly more opposed to the doctrine which the Council
was about to define, than that of any other prelate present at
Trent.[3] Other members of the group that we have studied had
expressed a belief in salvation by faith alone; only one member of
the assembly had even distantly approached the view that the just
man must believe with certainty in his own salvation – and he had
not held fast to this position;[4] and Pate was clearly more unhappy

[1] *C.T.*, v, 364–5.

[2] 'Homo iustificatus secundum praesentem iustitiam potest esse certus certitudine fidei, se esse in gratia Dei, et qui hoc non credit, videtur de gratia Dei diffidere.' – Again: 'Quoad decretum...regavitque, ut de iustitia imputativa sic diffiniatur, ut iustitia Christi non repudiatur, cum nostra inhaerens statuitur.' *C.T.*, v, 648.

[3] Contrary to the accepted opinion that this position was occupied by Sanfelice (see above, p. 146). It may be that had Sanfelice remained at the Council as long as Pate, his expression of opinion would have been quite as definite, but this is hardly a useful line of speculation.

[4] The Benedictine abbot, Luciano degli Ottoni, is reported to have stated on 7 October: 'baptizatus tenetur credere, se esse in gratia, et quanto magis hoc credit, tanto magis iustificatur'. (*C.T.*, v, 473–4). In his vote of 23 November he merely stated that the just man might, in certain cases, be entitled to believe that his salvation was assured; but this was quite different from the Lutheran view that the justified were *obliged* to believe in the assurance of their personal salvation (ibid. p. 659). – It is difficult to see anything in his reported remarks at the Council to justify Jedin's view (*Council*, II, 289) that he subscribed to the latter opinion. For a further examination of Luciano and Isodorus Clarius, cf. Evennett, 'Three Benedictine Abbots'.

than any of them with the doctrine of intrinsic justice as it was about to be officially defined – indeed, he seems to have been alone in his objection to it.

The quality of his judgement, moreover, differs so noticeably from that of the Italians, not only in its proximity to Lutheran beliefs, but in its trenchancy of expression, that the matter seems to call for particular attention. It is so resolute a note to hear from a quarter whose attempts at harmony were as a rule uncertain that it impels a consideration of those factors which differentiated Pate's background from those of his collaborators. Such an undertaking necessitates a close attention to his earlier career: for it is here that the clue may be found, not only to his attitudes, but to his manner of expressing them. A study of Pate's career reveals two things: first, that he had become a churchman rather late in life – and secondly, that as a member of Pole's circle, he was the only representative of the Viterbo group fully to participate in the Council's business. Hence, his opinions derive an added interest, and it becomes important to examine the course of events which led him, by a devious and uncertain path, to associate with Pole. An examination of this kind, moreover, reveals how much his circumstances differed from those of the Italian prelates whose votes we have considered; so that the disparity between their respective methods of approach becomes intelligible.

In the first place he was English. Unlike Pole,[1] he had been permanently resident in Italy for less than five years at the time of his participation in the Council. As a young man, he had been a member of the group which, acknowledging for a time with equal mind the patronage of Pole and Cromwell, had been forced eventually into separate and hostile camps, over the issues of the royal supremacy and the divorce.[2] When however, the break had come in 1536, Pate had chosen to remain in the King's service: and this fact in itself makes his presence at the Council ten years later sufficiently striking to warrant further investigation.

Pate had graduated from Oxford in 1523, and had made his way to Bruges, where he studied under Vives.[3] From Bruges he

[1] Pole had spent approximately half his life in Italy at this time.
[2] Zeeveld, *Foundations*.   [3] Ibid. p. 63.

eventually moved to Paris, where he is known to have been a friend of Pole.[1] There he established himself among the circle which had gathered around Thomas Wynter, and he seems to have remained at Paris until November 1533, when he was nominated ambassador to Charles V.[2] During this period he had taken holy orders, and had become archdeacon of Lincoln, where his uncle held the diocese. As was customary among young men of promise, he went on to enjoy the patronage of Cromwell, and on 11 May 1534, his uncle wrote to the latter, thanking him for being so good a master to his nephew.[3]

But Pate does not appear to have been an altogether satisfactory servant of the King. At the end of his first year in office, he wrote to Cromwell from Madrid, excusing himself for a certain failure which had evidently been held against him. He assured Cromwell that 'I do hold up the helmet...as well as my tendre and puerile nature will (sich an oversight for lack of experience inespeciall committid) suffer me'; adding that the obscurity of his style (for which he was constantly to be upbraided) was involuntary and not studied: 'the whiche surely I do partly ascribe to thinopie off my materne tongue...and partly to the ponisshment of god, that wolde me not facile'. Nevertheless he trusted that Cromwell's indulgence, and the uprightness of his own conscience, would secure his favour with the King.[4]

Pate's optimism however, was unfounded. On 29 January 1536, Chapuys recorded a conversation which he had held with Henry VIII, during course of which the King set to dispraising his ambassador in strong terms, so as to leave the impression with Chapuys that the said ambassador was 'too good a Christian and Imperialist' for him.[5] The implication of this, quite clearly, is that

---

[1] *P.R.O.*, SP 1/55, fols. 193–4. This manuscript, a ledger kept for Pole by Thomas Starkey, is attributed by Zeeveld, (p. 66, n. 124) to the year 1528. Zeeveld further indicates that the calendared version in *L.P.*, IV (3), no. 6004 (ii), which ascribes the document to 1529, is also mistaken in the description of the document which it provides. – The list of expenses, which reveals a number of Pole's associates at this time, includes an item for 'Mr Patys' (f. 194v).

[2] *L.P.*, IV (2), no. 4514, VI, no. 1481 (12).   [3] *L.P.*, VII, no. 639.

[4] *P.R.O.*, SP 1/188, fol. 186, 11 December (1534?); calendared *L.P.*, VII, App. 2, no. 42.

[5] Chapuys to Antoine Perrenot, 29 January 1536, *P.R.O.*, 31/18/2/2 (Vienna Transcripts); calendared *L.P.*, X, no. 201. Cf. also, *L.P.*, X, no. 297.

Pate's opinions on the divorce, if not the royal supremacy, were little to the King's admiring. It is significant therefore, that in a dispatch which Pate addressed to the King on 14 April 1536, Pate took it upon himself to plead for the legitimation of Princess Mary; and he reported Granvelle's view that if Henry would acknowledge the authority of the Pope, his marriage with Anne Boleyn might be recognised.[1]

This dispatch was written from Rome, on the eve of Pole's breach with the King. Pate, of course, could not have known that the breach was coming (the contrary, in fact was expected by most Englishmen, including as we have seen, Starkey); but it would seem, nevertheless, that he was well disposed to the position which Pole had in fact adopted. That the latter thought no less kindly of him in return, may be inferred from an affectionate reference which appears in a letter written to Priuli at this time, from Venice, in which Pole speaks of 'our' ambassador to Charles V.[2]

When however, a month later, the final separation was decided, by the dispatch to England of Pole's manuscript, Pate chose to remain in the service of the King. But the services of one so implicated in the company, and perhaps the sympathies, of papal loyalists, were inevitably suspect; and on 12 March 1537, Thomas Wyatt was appointed to replace him as ambassador to the Emperor.[3] Pate was issued with a summons to return, and on 15 October, he was present at the christening of Edward VI.[4]

His behaviour in the subsequent three years seems to have removed whatever doubts of his allegiance may hitherto have troubled Cromwell and the King. He was restored to his position as ambassador in April 1540.[5] This time, his despatches were appropriately weighted with attacks upon the Church of Rome.[6]

---

[1] *L.P.*, X, no. 670.

[2] *Epistolae*, I, p. 447; abstract in *L.P.*, X, no. 619. The letter was written on 30 March 1536, but a postscript was added on 3 April, which is the date given (inaccurately therefore) in the calendar.

[3] *L.P.*, XII (1), no. 537.   [4] *L.P*, XII (2), no. 911.

[5] *L.P.*, XV, nos. 468–9, and 530.

[6] Which he considered to rest upon 'an only presumed authoritie'. *P.R.O.*, SP 1/160, fol. 28, Pate to Henry VIII, Ghent, 11 May 1540 (calendared *L.P.*, XV, no. 665).

But the fall of Cromwell drew from him a strain of opinion which, however politic, was probably in accordance with his inner sentiments. Cromwell, he wrote, had been 'a plaine gentile a traytor and an heresiarche'; while he had been in power, foreigners believed that piety and religion had disappeared from England: they thought the Mass had been abolished and the sacrament of the altar rooted out. Now, however, Pate has made sure that the contrary is known.[1]

But if the King's caution in religious matters, following the fall of Cromwell, was directed in some measure to appease the Emperor, it did not extend to a desire of reconciliation with the Pope. Hence the discovery of letters directed to Pate by a member of Pole's entourage, John Heliar, finally set seal to this phase of his career.[2] His first, and no doubt desperate reaction was to temporise. He wrote to Henry on 3 October, expressing his hope that he would not be judged to consist 'other in therrour that many alate yeres hath brought wilfullie to a confusion or in the numbre of those that while they were fownd nother cold nor yet hoote but tepide hath byn thought worthie an utter vomete'. The author of the incriminating letters was a 'traitour not yet sufficiently instructed by scripture to kno what is obedientiam volo et non sacrificium'. But Pate and his chaplain (Seth Holland, who was also inculpated) were loyal men, and not 'such as his letters directed to us myght giue a suspition to a iudge not fauorablie inclined and affected'.[3]

Pate followed up his protestations with a letter to the Privy Council, in which he sought to demonstrate his loyalty by

[1] *P.R.O.*, SP 1/161, fol. 103, Pate to Norfolk, Bruges, 12 June 1540 (calendared *L.P.*, xv, no. 876).

[2] *L.P.*, XVI, no. 129. Heliar, who graduated from Oxford in 1532, had held a living in East Meon, Hampshire, where Pole's mother lived. Having spent several years at Louvain, he joined Pole at Rome in 1537, and a year later became penitentiary of the English Hospice there. (G. B. Parks, 'The Reformation and the Hospice, 1514–59', in *The English Hospice in Rome*, p. 205.)

[3] *P.R.O.*, SP 1/163, fol. 66, Pate to Henry VIII, Brussels, 3 October 1540 (calendared *L.P.*, XVI, no. 119). The fact that Pate did not argue that he had severed his connections with Heliar subsequent to the period in which the incriminating letters were addressed to him, would suggest that they were of recent origin.

vigorous denunciations of the 'Bishop of Rome' and his adherents.[1] This in turn was followed by another letter to the King, and elaborate expressions of devotion.[2] But his time was up. By the end of November, he was in receipt of 'letters of comfort' issued by the King, requesting his return to England.[3]

Instead of yielding to the summons, he waited until early January, travelling with the Emperor to Germany, and from there he took his leave, 'feigning a curiosity to see Cologne'.[4] By 13 January, he had passed through Spires, and was on his way to Rome.[5] The Constable of France, Montmorency, wrote: 'L'on dict de luy que secrettement il avait tousjours este bon chretien, soutennant nostre religion.'[6]

At Rome he was received effusively, and on 8 July, 1541, he was appointed to the see of Worcester.[7] His friendship with Pole was quick to reassert itself, and the latter, writing to Contarini on 1 September, recommended Pate as one to whom he was bound by ties of race, cause and love.[8] The connection was maintained, for Pate was a member of Pole's suite in November 1542, when the Legates made their first (and premature) visit to Trent; and he accompanied Pole again in 1545, when on 4 May they made their entry to the city, this time successfully to await the inauguration of the Council.[9]

Thus Pate's background, prior to his participation in the Council, was strikingly different from that of any other member of the assembly. It is clear enough that he had indeed been 'neither cold nor yet hot' in the King's support, and that all the while he had maintained an underground connection with the members of Pole's entourage. Whether he was specifically committed to

[1] P.R.O., SP 1/163, fol. 70, Pate to the Council, 4 October 1540 (calendared L.P., XVI, no. 122).

[2] L.P., XVI, no. 258.　　　　　　　　　　[3] Ibid. nos. 269, 295 and 308.

[4] P.R.O., 3/13/11, fasic. 6, fol. 2v, 'feignant d'allez vers la ville de Coullonge, come pas curiosité de le veoir'. Marillac to Francis I, 12 January 1541 (calendared L.P., XVI, no. 449; cf. also, ibid. no. 448).

[5] L.P., XVI, no. 452.

[6] P.R.O., 31/3/11, fasic. 4 (abstract), 11 January 1541 (calendared L.P., XVI, no. 446).

[7] L.P., XVI, no. 981.　　　　　　　　　　[8] Epistolae, III, 30.

[9] C.T., IV 303, n. 3, and I, p. 183.

Pole's service is another question, and one to which Heliar's letters, had they survived, would doubtless provide an answer; but it seems unlikely. It would seem more probable that during the years before 1541, he was intent on advancing his career, and keeping his opinions to himself. Such evidence of his opinions as we have considered, suggests a predominantly Catholic orientation; and there is one other source which tends to support this impression. In 1539, he was one of a substantial majority of divines to approve a series of proposals which were dominantly orthodox.[1] Thus he declared himself in favour of transubstantiation, private Masses, auricular confession, and the distribution of communion in both kinds; together with the view that it was permissible for priests to marry. Of these, the first three formed an essential part of Catholic belief and practice; and the latter two, while committing him to the Anglican establishment (such as it then existed) were not in theory incompatible with allegiance to the Church of Rome. Moreover his strictures against the papacy in his later dispatches convey the impression of a rather nervous anxiety to prove his worth, and in the circumstances, can hardly be considered a definitive expression of his views.

The fact that his religious disposition was Catholic did not, as we have seen, prevent him from adopting an attitude towards salvation which approximated closely to the views of Luther. This, after all, was a commonplace among the *spirituali*. What is unusual in Pate is the thoroughness and resolution with which he gave voice to his sentiments. Perhaps he had had enough of circumspection by the time he came to Italy. But it is a sufficiently remarkable occurrence to prompt the question whether he had held these views before his arrival at Rome.

It is of course quite possible that his opinions had been formed outside the *milieux* of the Italian *spirituali*; and this would help to explain their singularity. In the years before 1541 he presumably had ample opportunity of reading Luther, or of coming into contact on his travels, with Protestant communities. On the other hand, his arrival in Italy coincided with the preparations for the

---

[1] *L.P.*, XIV (I), no. 1065.

colloquy of Regensburg; he himself had given notice of the forthcoming event when, shortly before his flight, he reported that fifty doctors and learned men had assembled at Worms, 'whither Bishop Vergerius is sent, as the ambassadour of Venice told me, of the Queen of Nauar'.[1] Thus he was in Italy at the time when excitement ran highest about the possibility of reaching an agreement with Lutherans. When, in the early summer, a settlement was reached on the article of justification, it can hardly have been possible for anyone living at Rome, and particularly an official of the Church, to avoid consideration of the issues involved. Throughout this time, moreover, he was in close touch with Pole, and this friendship was sustained in the years following. It can scarcely be doubted, considering his intervention in the Council, that he was deeply interested in the deliberations of Pole and his associates, or that, by the time he came to Trent, he was thoroughly familiar with the attitudes of the Viterbo circle. It seems reasonable to conclude, therefore, that his expression of opinion at the Council reflects not only the preoccupations, but the tendencies, of the Viterbo group. In this case, his opinions derive an added interest, since in his advocacy of them he displayed no sign of that 'tendre and puerile' nature which he had confessed to Cromwell, but argued with a vigour and deliberation which are quite unusual.

His resolute manner of expression, is therefore entirely explicable, if it be remembered that he had been subject to none of the restraining influences which normally withheld the *spirituali* from too forthright an expression of their views. He had lived outside Italy for the greater part of his life; he was unfamiliar with the environment which produced the *spirituali* and the 'diffidentia' against which the *Beneficio di Cristo* had inveighed. He himself had been a stranger to scholastic theology for most of his life, and had moved in circles where diplomacy and politics had formed the principal staple of conjecture. He had become a bishop almost overnight, without the trappings of a conventional ecclesiastical career. He had been exposed suddenly, to ideas

---

[1] *P.R.O.*, SP 1/164, fol. 39, Pate to Gardiner and Knevet, Valentianes, 1 December 1540 (calendared *L.P.*, XVI, no. 308).

which seemed to offer a solution to the principal religious problem of the day, and to promise an effective means of re-establishing religious unity. What could be more natural than that he should enthusiastically assent to these ideas, and be impatient of the reservations which more timorous, or more subtle minds might have? He may have allowed himself to be persuaded into circumspection in the years immediately before the Council; but once the Council had been summoned he seems to have seen no further grounds for hesitation. And if the Council seemed unsympathetic to his views, this may have occurred to him as a still greater incentive to argue them with constancy and force. Such at least, we may imagine to have been Pate's motives, who in his own career had discovered the limited utility of circumspection, and whose natural disposition was apparently impatient of half-measures.[1] He was, we may suppose, at heart a resolute man, given to direct expression. It seems probable therefore, that Pate's activity at the Council provides the solitary instance in which the attitudes of the Viterbo circle publicly received an integral expression, and were carried to their logical conclusion. This would suggest that Pate's views, while not necessarily identical with those of Pole, represented the implications of the latter's thought, and in areas perhaps, which Pole himself did not wish to explore. Certainly Pole's opinions, when he finally revealed them, were not dissimilar to those of Pate; but they were confined to a narrower range of inquiry. They were expressed, moreover, with a caution and reserve, and an anxiety to qualify everything, which were characteristics, not only of the man, but of the larger movement which he represented; and they were expressed in private.

Thus it is remarkable that the two most vigorous of the *spirituali* at the Council, Pate and Sanfelice, should be the two who had come into greatest contact with Pole and his associates at Viterbo. A third associate of the Viterbo group, Soranzo,

---

[1] Despite his uneasy years of service with the King; this after all, was a compromise arising from his reluctance to break completely with his country, and to live in exile. No such considerations operated to restrain him at the Council; and besides, he may have been weary of experiments in subterfuge.

arrived at the Council on 12 February, displayed some unhappiness over the decree on Scripture and Tradition,[1] and departed to his diocese before the debate on justification got under way.[2] But the interventions of Pate and Sanfelice sufficiently represent the outlook of the Viterbo group. Their votes, contrasted with those of Giulio Contarini, or of Florimonte, reveal a thorough-going commitment to a doctrine of salvation which, in the case of Sanfelice, displays a tendency that was definitely Lutheran, and in the case of Pate, is virtually indistinguishable from the views of Luther.

Nevertheless, they were at one with the other *spirituali* in their reluctance to adopt scholastic theological constructions to contain their views. The result was that members of this group as a whole found it exceptionally difficult to express, in a considered manner, the attitudes which they wished to see embodied in the Conciliar decree. For in the theological climate of the sixteenth century, as Alberigo states, the refusal of the approaches provided by scholastic theology, presented, for those who wished to remain orthodox, difficulties of extreme complexity.[3] Hence the views expressed by the *spirituali* in the Council (leaving aside the advocates of twofold justice) remained essentially a series of individual requests, varying in emphasis from man to man, that the efficacy of Christ's merits should in no way be obscured by an emphasis upon the human contribution to salvation.

It is partly by inference therefore, that one can observe in the votes of these men, the state of their proximity to Luther's thought. In the case of Pate, there is almost an exact degree of correspondence, and there can be little doubt that he was convinced of Luther's orthodoxy on the fundamental question of salvation. In this respect (though not in its details) his opinion was identical to that expressed by Contarini four years earlier, when he was on the point of death; and Pate would surely have agreed as well, that the schism could be easily resolved, once agreement had been reached on a matter which was not basically in dispute. This, in the view of Contarini, as of Pate, and Pole, and the other *spirituali*

[1] Jedin, *Council*, II, 92–3.   [2] Alberigo, *I vescovi italiani*, pp. 255–6.
[3] Ibid. p. 384.

was to be in large measure the function of the Council: to reform and reunite the Church.

In the case of Sanfelice, it is less easy to determine the precise degree of correspondence between his views and those of Luther. He did not stay at the Council long enough to allow retrospectively, an accurate assessment to be made. In so far as it is possible to form an estimate however, and to contrast his declared attitude with that of Pate, it would seem that the correspondence between his views and those of Luther was less absolute; and it was even less so in the case of Florimonte, or of Giulio Contarini. It remains to be considered how Pole and the rest of his circle reacted to the developments which occurred after his departure.

CHAPTER TEN

Pole's protest

The reversal of Pole's hopes at the Council of Trent was the occasion of a personal crisis more serious in its implications than that which he had experienced a decade previously, in severing his connection with his country. For this time the very attachments and beliefs which had forced him ten years earlier to that decision, were gradually revealing themselves to be incompatible with the most cherished convictions of his spiritual life. Now, as the summer wore on, and the Council continued its deliberations, it became impossible for him to escape from the head-on conflict which he had sought to evade in departing from the Council. It was becoming increasingly evident that departure was in any real sense impossible. He still held the office of Conciliar Legate, and his leave, in any case, had been granted as no more than a temporary respite, to enable him to recover his health. Thus he found himself obliged to remain in permanent contact with the Council, to receive and answer letters from his fellow Legates, and ultimately, to deliver his opinion on the matter which he least wished to examine, now that his expectations had been shattered. It is necessary to consider, therefore, the events which led to his final protest, followed by a reluctant submission, at the beginning of October 1546, of a memorandum on the proposed decree concerning justification, together with an account of his own views on the problem.

On 1 July 1546, three days after his departure from the Council, Pole arrived at Priuli's villa in Treville. He looked forward to a short period of rest, following which, if his health was still uncertain, he would move on to Venice, or the baths at Padua.[1] During the daytime he took a little exercise in his carriage or on horseback, and he felt himself beginning gradually to improve in this cool mountain retreat where, years before, he had been accustomed to escape from the oppressive heat of summer. But the pain in his left arm continued; his nights were generally restless; and his doctors warned him that he must take great care if he were to avoid the risk of becoming paralysed.[2] His hopes of complete isolation from the Council's business were short lived; for it was the intention of Cervini and Del Monte to enlist Pole's services on the questions which preoccupied the Council. Thus on 2 July he received a communication from the Legates, dated 30 June, which included a copy of the proposals concerning justification.[3] A pattern was thereby established – and it was maintained throughout the next four months, which formed the period of Pole's convalescence. On this occasion, Pole replied immediately, assuring the Legates that the proposals seemed to him to be 'of the first importance, and worthy of great consideration'; and he dutifully begged them to keep him further informed through the agency of Richard Pate.[4] There can be little doubt, however, that he privately considered this development to set an ominous precedent.

On the other issue, entirely political in content, as to whether the Council should remove from Trent, Pole displayed little hesitation in complying with the Legates' requests. His own inclination was to preserve the Council at Trent, rather than allow it to be suspended indefinitely, or transferred to another location.[5] Consequently he did what was in his power to restrain those prelates who, because they feared the proximity of Trent to the theatre of war or who, suffering from financial shortage, and anticipating what they believed to be the inevitable suspension of the Council, had departed for the more congenial regions of Padua and Venice. When, in extension to these difficulties the town became threatened with an outbreak of typhoid, Pole,

[1] *Epistolae*, IV, 188.
[2] Ibid. pp. 189–90.
[3] *Epistolae*, IV, 189.
[4] Ibid.
[5] *C.T.*, XI, 944.

acting in accordance with the Legates' instructions, endeavoured to persuade such prelates as were not genuinely ill to return to Trent.[1] He kept the Legates informed too, of the intentions of the Imperial ambassador, Diego de Mendoza, who, passing through Treville, had explained to Pole his attitude to the proposed translation of the Council.[2]

He remained steadfast nevertheless, in his own reluctance to return to Trent, or to commit himself in writing on the problem of justification. But the issue was not to be avoided. On 11 August, Seripando presented to the Legates a preliminary draft of a decree on justification.[3] This was a document which, despite the fact that it was inspired almost exclusively by Scripture and the commentaries of St Augustine, embodied a view of justification which was quite inimical to Pole's. It condemned, for example, the opinion that all virtuous actions performed before justification were assessed by God as sinful, and judged worthy of eternal punishment; it asserted, on the contrary, that virtuous works were a necessary preliminary to justification.[4] It contained an unequivocal condemnation of the Lutheran doctrine of salvation by faith alone, and the allied doctrine that the only justice available to the Christian was that of Christ himself, imputed to the Christian soul.[5] It denied the right of any man to consider himself certain of predestination to eternal life.[6] It condemned the view that the divine precepts were incapable of fulfilment with the aid of grace.[7] It stressed the necessity for auricular confession and the performance of expiatory satisfactions such as alms-giving, prayer, and other spiritual exercises.[8] Finally, it expressly and vigorously denounced all those who argued that good works could contribute nothing to salvation; and it declared instead, that salvation should be conceived of as a divine reward.[9]

This document admittedly, was far from representing the final

[1] *Epistolae*, IV, 197–8.
[2] *C.T.*, x, 591–2. Cf. also Jedin, *Council*, II, 229.   [3] *C.T.*, v, 821–8.
[4] Ibid. pp. 823–4. Canons 1 and 2. It seems probable that Pole subscribed to the opinion here condemned (see below, pp. 185–6). Not all the other Lutheran doctrines condemned in subsequent canons were held by Pole; but their categorical rejection struck him as decidedly impolitic.
[5] *C.T.*, v, 824, Canon 3.   [6] Ibid. p. 826, Canon 4.   [7] Ibid. p. 826, Canon 5.
[8] Ibid. p. 827, Canon 6.   [9] Ibid. pp. 827–8, Canon 7.

outcome of the Council's deliberations on justification. In fact it was superseded only a fortnight later by a revised version, compiled once more by Seripando, and embodying a view of salvation which rested upon the theory of twofold justice.[1] It was, therefore, no more than a preliminary sketch of the programme which Seripando was to defend in the ensuing months. But it serves to indicate how far removed were the proponents of this theory from any belief in the possibility of doctrinal reconciliation with the Lutherans. For the whole of Luther's doctrine had been thoroughly rejected in this document. Thus the idea of twofold justice, which had been the basis of the Regensburg agreement, had been radically transformed into a more militant version which owed little either to the form or spirit of the earlier expression of this theory. It may be that this was one more reason why the later version held so little appeal for the *spirituali* at the Council, whose views were more pragmatic, and in certain cases more eirenic.[2] It was certainly one of the principal reasons which led Pole, with a mixture of dismay and indignation, to repudiate the document.

His first reaction was to say merely that the decree dealt with many things deserving of 'more mature consideration'. He dispatched his friend Vincenzo Parpaglia, the abbot of San Saluto, with this message, adding that he himself would need considerably more time to inform himself upon the issue, which in his view was as complex as it was important. Certainly he did not consider that he could do so in a few short days.[3]

Parpaglia departed for Trent on 22 August with this message.[4] His mission was the result not merely of a desire on Pole's part to reveal his impressions of the proposed decree; it had a wider and more acute significance. For now, in the middle of his seventh week of absence, Pole was under considerable pressure from both Rome and Trent, not only to declare himself upon the matter of justification but to return to Trent, and resume his duties as

---

[1] *C.T.*, x, 828–33, which, as Jedin demonstrates, wrongly ascribes the document to 19 August, instead of 29 August (*Council*, II, 239, n. 1). This document was in turn superseded by the September draft discussed below, pp. 174ff.

[2] See above, pp. 137–60.   [3] *C.T.*, x, 623, n. 5.

[4] *Epistolae*, IV, 193.

papal Legate.[1] Either prospect filled him with intense dismay. It was Parpaglia's function, therefore, to dissuade the Legates from their purpose. Consequently, his instructions included a request from Pole, which amounted almost to a plea for mercy: he begged the Legates to place themselves in his position, and have the same consideration for him that they would wish him to feel on their behalf.[2]

He followed this up with a letter on 25 August stressing the danger to his health which would occur were he to act immediately on the Pope's instructions and return to Trent.[3] His left arm, shoulder and eye, he complained, still caused him grievous trouble, and his doctors assured him that he was in real danger of being crippled for life.[4] It seemed to him therefore, that he could better accomplish the Pope's wishes in attending to his health, and he was determined on sending Parpaglia to Rome the moment he returned from Trent, so that the Pope might better appreciate how matters stood. Meanwhile, he added, he intended to remain in the hands of his doctors, and to refrain from going on to Padua, until he better understood the Pope's intentions. Parpaglia returned that evening, on 25 August, and the next day he set out for Rome.[5] There, he succeeded in persuading the Pope and his advisers that Pole was in no condition to return to Trent. Accordingly, on 28 August a letter was addressed to Pole in which he was empowered by the Pope to act as he thought best, and to remove to Padua or Venice if he so desired.[6]

Thus Pole was finally released from the necessity of returning to Trent. But there had been no concessions issued to relieve him of the duty of opening his mind on the question of justification. His reluctance to comply with this demand may be gauged by the almost desperate tenor of his instructions to Parpaglia on the latter's setting out for Trent. Pole, after all, had had ample

---

[1] *C.T.*, x, 613, letters of 16 and 22 August to the Cardinal Camerario. Cf. also op. cit., n. 3, as well as p. 623, n. 5.

[2] That is in respect to the fatigues of office, which were the constant themes of their complaint.

[3] *Epistolae*, iv, 193–5.

[4] 'Mi metteria in pericolo manifesto di rimaner stroppiato in tutta la mia vita', *Epistolae*, iv, 194.

[5] Ibid. p. 195.   [6] *C.T.*, x, 613, n. 3.

time in the years before the Council, to consider the problems associated with justification. That he should so earnestly request permission to refrain from uttering his opinion indicates, therefore, the gulf which he felt to exist between his own views and those which were predominant at the Council. His reluctance to speak now is explicable only as the result of a scrupulosity so severe as to be bordering on the neurotic; and it tends to confirm the impression that Pole was suffering from a nervous breakdown.

In the end, these accumulating pressures, and his anxiety about developments at Trent, drove him to take preventive action. While he was still awaiting the outcome of Parpaglia's mission to Rome, he wrote to Cardinal Morone, on 28 August, explaining his opposition to the Conciliar deliberations. His letter was nothing less than an attempt at direct intervention, on the highest level, to halt the Conciliar proceedings.[1] Morone passed his letter on to Cardinal Ardinghello, who in turn was requested to show it to the Pope.[2] In this letter Pole argued with force and cogency the inexpediency of dealing with so crucial an issue at the present time; and he revealed, as a result, the intensity of his fears about the likely outcome of a Conciliar decree on justification.

Pole opens with a reference to the dissatisfaction which he hears is prevalent at Rome concerning the brevity of his instructions to Parpaglia. He declares his resolve to explain more fully to Morone what he feels about the issues which the Council is discussing – although he is sure that he can say nothing that is not already known to Morone and his colleagues on the Conciliar commission. Nevertheless, he continues, the two issues which lie before the Council, concerning justification and episcopal residence, are crucial to the whole programme of renewal and reform. No article of dogma, he declares, does not in some manner touch upon the problem of justification, and depend upon a correct decision in that matter; while in the sphere of conduct, the same is true concerning the residence of bishops. It seems to Pole, therefore, that in things which require so much mature considera-

---

[1] *C.T.*, x, 631–3, Pole to Morone, Treville, 28 August 1546.
[2] *Epistolae*, iv, 180–2, Pole to Morone, Padua, 17 September 1546. That Morone was the recipient of this letter is demonstrated below, n. 2, p. 71.

tion, the Council must not allow itself to be driven by the pressures of time into making a precipitate decision. This is particularly true with regard to justification – for no pronouncement has survived from any previous Council to guide the fathers in their deliberations. The essence of this doctrine, of course, has never been abandoned, for it contains in itself the foundation of the Church, and the completion of every other dogma.[1] Nevertheless, it has never been treated by any other Council in the form in which it now presents itself; and since it makes a great difference in which words, and in what sense, it is to be understood, it is hardly desirable that the explication of this question, which for fifteen hundred years has lain untouched, and in a kind of silence, should be compressed into the space of a single month or two.[2]

Moreover, Pole continues, a precipitate decision would admirably suit the Church's enemies. For they seek and desire nothing so much as that the Council, in its resolution of this problem, should provide them with an opportunity of attacking the teaching of the See of Rome and of the Councils. Their first efforts had been to withdraw popular allegiance from the Holy See by pointing to abuses in the sphere of conduct. When they realised that these were insufficient grounds for defection, they had tried to undermine the Church in doctrine – and in nothing so much as this very issue of justification.[3]

This particular view of the Reformation throws considerable light on Pole's attitude towards the Protestants. It confirms once again that his objections were based less on their charges of corruption (or their doctrine), than their disruption of the Church's unity. The principal object of his life, since 1537, when he had sat on the reform commission, had been to deprive the schismatics of all just grounds for grievance, by acknowledging, within the Church of Rome, the very things which they believed

---

[1] 'De iustificatione vero, licet, quod ad rem ipsam attinet, numquam verus eius sensus defuerit, ecclesiae ut pote quae fundamentum sit et caput omnium, ut diximus dogmatum.' *C.T.*, x, 631.

[2] 'quare cum multum intersit, quibus verbis et quo sensu intelligatur, quod mille quingentis annis intactum est et quasi in silentio iacuit, huius explicatio non videtur unius aut alterius mensis spatio debere coarctari'. *C.T.*, x, 632.

[3] *C.T.*, x, 632.

to have been betrayed. The public ratification of this acknowledgement was to have been the purpose of the Council. Now it
was clear that the Council was heading in the opposite direction.
Pole therefore continued to plead for the necessity of listening
to the Lutherans, if the Church were not further to be weakened
by a refusal to explore their doctrines. For having maintained that
they have chosen to assail the Church with doctrine, he goes on to
explain that they know more about this particular doctrine than
the Catholics.

For twenty years, he states, they have energetically studied it,
almost as one man. They have written about it, argued in dispu-
tation, and perpetually conferred on it between themselves. The
result is, that though in other matters of importance they may
disagree,[1] in this affair their judgement is unanimous.

All these considerations, he continues, persuade him that it is
necessary to proceed with care, and to allow such time for the
discussions as is fitting for questions of such magnitude. This
approach will have the effect of reinforcing the Council's authority in other matters: and nothing, he reminds Morone, is more
needed at this time than authority, when everyone is departing
from the obedience of the Holy See.[2] Thus it is vital to proceed
at a more timely pace.

But, he adds, it is equally important that a greater openness of
mind should be displayed, with less rancour towards the opposing
party. It is necessary to consider their objection to too many
'works' among the adherents of the Holy See: an objection which
they consider to be vindicated by the manner in which this issue
is being treated as something already settled, without so much as
a consideration of the terminology which they employ – so that
there is apparently a reluctance to agree with them even in matters
of vocabulary.[3]

It is interesting to observe that Pole here shifts the ground of
argument from a consideration of the objective difficulties which
should restrain the Council from coming to a precipitate decision,
to a sustained criticism of the manner in which it is conducting its

[1] Pole is doubtless referring here to the doctrine of the Eucharist.
[2] *C.T.*, x, 632.   [3] Ibid.

enquiries. His principal grievance now emerges as the Council's refusal to consider the wealth of Protestant experience, which in his view, it would be disastrous to ignore. Hence he reveals the basic disposition animating him: to deplore the Protestant schism on the grounds of its denial of the Roman Primacy and consequent disruption of the Church, while at the same time sympathising with its positive doctrinal content. Yet, characteristically, he conceals the extent of his sympathies by reverting only to the considerable expertise and the impressive unanimity which Protestants have acquired upon the central issue. It is easy to recognise as implicit in his remarks the belief that, whereas Protestants were in the right upon this issue – which they had thoroughly examined and about which they were all agreed – the Council was about to declare itself in a manner at once both precipitate and rash, and to provide its enemies thereby with a powerful weapon.

Pole considers that these Protestant objections are altogether valid if the Council is to persist in avoiding their terminology (which often means avoiding Scriptural terminology) simply because it is in use with Protestants.[1] He himself realises that the fathers of the Council are prompted, not as the Protestants believe, by mere partisan hostility, but by a genuine zeal for piety. The authors of the present decree are the best and most learned of men. They have convinced themselves that the more they retreat from the vocabulary of their adversaries, and the more keenly they oppose them, by so much more are they deserving of the Church's regard. But, he adds, they ought to be restrained by their superiors.[2]

With these remarks, Pole introduces his appeal for a suspension of the Council's business. Referring to the current version of the decree, he mentions that, from all he has heard, the Legates have been very far from giving their approval to it, and that there is in fact a plan to replace it with a revised draft.[3] Surely, he urges, this is the moment for a complete reassessment: an opportunity to defer the issue, and to wait for a more representative assembly.

[1] Ibid.   [2] Ibid.
[3] Which had been virtually completed by the time Pole wrote. It was submitted to the Legates next day, 29 August. See above, n. 1, p. 164.

That there are difficulties, he acknowledges; but he can see no other remedy. Let there be more time given to a study of the question, so that the best informed opinions may be brought to bear on the decree. In this way it could be so constructed as to be received without hesitation by the universal Christian world. A larger Council, with bishops attending from all parts of the Christian world, would carry more authority, and would so establish the consensus of the universal Church, as to attract the obedience of every Christian.[1]

Thus there can be no longer any question about Pole's opinion of affairs at Trent. His choice of expression indicates the death of a conviction, and the nourishment of an ailing hope, that the Council might yet be the instrument of reconciliation in the schism. He had made it abundantly clear that he thought the present condition of the Council thoroughly insupportable: narrow, precipitate, and unrepresentative. He brings his letter to a close with a repeated stress upon the dangers of the current situation: in no other Council, he complains, have so few prelates been assembled, or such important issues been proposed. Yet now this crucial issue, which embraces everything, and around which there is greater controversy than the Church has ever known, is about to be determined by no more than fifty bishops, at the very most,[2] and proposed for the consent of the whole Christian world. This procedure, he repeats in conclusion, will diminish the authority of the decree – particularly if it should be published singly, and without the decree on ecclesiastical reform, which everybody is awaiting.[3]

Pole's arguments, however, went unheard. His one success had been to acquire a personal dispensation to remain away from Trent, and he had to be content with that. Early in September he removed to Padua, where he took up residence in Bembo's villa.

---

[1] *C.T.*, x, 632.

[2] Sixty-six persons entitled to a vote were present at the General Session of 17 June 1546 (*C.T.*, v, 253–5); at the next General Session, 13 January 1547, which passed the decree on justification, sixty-eight such people were in attendance (ibid. pp. 817–19); during the debate of 28 August, the day on which Pole wrote, twenty-eight people spoke, though doubtless more were present (ibid. pp. 418–419).

[3] *C.T.*, x, 632.

Here he was able to enjoy something of the tranquillity which he so much desired. He had the advantage of a study and a garden, two things which, as he wrote to Vittoria Colonna, had always been especially delightful to him.[1]

He fully believed that in writing to Morone he had acquitted himself of the obligation to deliver his opinion.[2] In this however, he soon found himself to be mistaken. For Rome had requested his opinion not on policy, but on doctrine; and now the question was repeated more emphatically, and in such a way as to leave no room for doubt about precisely what was asked of him. Throughout September he was under constant pressure from both Rome and Trent, to declare his belief concerning the doctrine of justification.[3] Finally the request became an order, from the Pope himself, to set in writing his opinion on the matter.[4] This development left Pole no choice but to comply.

At the beginning of October he received from Pate (who was presumably acting at the instigation of Del Monte and Cervini) a copy of the revised draft on justification, currently under discussion at the Council.[5] His dismay was absolute, and he did nothing to conceal it from the Legates. He could not see, he told them, how he was to express himself upon the matter: his absence from the Council precluded him from any appreciation of so many things in the decree about which he felt the need for further information. Besides, his illness was grievously afflicting him, so that he was in little condition to think, let alone write, about matters of such great importance. Even when he passed a quiet night he would find in the morning that his arm was causing him worse pain than usual. However, he concluded

---

[1] *Carteggio*, p. 311.

[2] *Epistolae*, IV, 180–2, Pole to Morone, Padua, 17 September 1546. Quirini was unable to specify the recipient of this letter, but a brief comparison with a letter which Pole sent to Cardinal [Sforza?] on 25 September establishes the point beyond doubt (ibid. pp. 182–3).

[3] Ibid. pp. 180–2.

[4] *C.T.*, x, 633, n. 1. Minute addressed to Pole requiring him to put his opinion on the proposed decree in writing. It is dated September 1546. (An evident misprint attributes the document to 1545. Internal evidence renders this date extremely unlikely.)

[5] This was the version known as the September draft, which replaced the draft of 29 August. (Jedin, *Council*, II, 241–4, and below, pp. 174–89).

wearily, 'in order to obey His Holiness, and to fulfil my obliga-tion, I shall not neglect to look at [the decree] and to examine it as best I can'. He promised to convey his opinion with the assistance of an intermediary, *viva voce*.[1]

In the event however, and fortunately for our purposes, he wrote it down. Four days after acknowledging receipt of the proposed decree he forwarded to Trent an account of his views, probably enclosing a memorandum on the issue, together with a commentary on the draft decree. His emissary in this task was Dr Juan Morillo, whom he described as 'mio familiare'; and the circumstance is not without some interest.[2] Morillo was a Spanish theologian who had come to Trent in the service of the bishop of Chiaramente. Little is known of his career, apart from what Carnesecchi revealed in 1567.[3] According to the latter, Morillo, with his bishop's permission, entered Pole's service after the first recess of the Council – early, therefore, in 1547. Afterwards he had moved to Paris, where Carnesecchi met him in 1553 or 1554. They saw a little of each other at this time, and Morillo seemed in all things to be orthodox – 'except', according to Carnesecchi, 'in the article of justification'. The last that Carnesecchi heard of Morillo was that he had become involved in heresy – whether Lutheran or Calvinist he could not say – and he had been obliged to leave Paris for this reason. He died on his way to Germany or Switzerland. As to whether Morillo had been in agreement with Pole on the article of justification, Carnesecchi was unable to say: he had never attempted to discover what Pole thought about the matter. All he knew was that at the time of the Council Morillo had conferred with Pole, and then reported his opinion to the Legates.

[1] *Epistolae*, IV, 199–200, Pole to the Legates, Padua, 5 October 1546.
[2] Ibid. pp. 200–1. Pole to the Legates, 9 and 18 October 1546. Morillo left Padua on the first of these dates, travelled to Trent, where he explained Pole's views, and departed, apparently, on 14 October. Two days later, Massarelli wrote in his diary, 'This morning I recorded Cardinal Pole's vote concerning twofold justice'. (*C.T.*, V, 496, n. 2.) It seems reasonable to conclude therefore, that Morillo had carried a written version of Pole's opinion to the Legates, and that the latter having examined it, passed it on to Massarelli a few days later. An alternative view would be that Pole wrote his commentaries after Morillo had gone. Either way, they were composed at some point between 5 and 16 October; and as I prefer to believe, before 9 October.
[3] 'Processo', pp. 514–16.

But to have established the connection is enough; and since we know that it was Pate who had sent Pole the copy of the draft decree (through acting, clearly, on the instructions of the Legates) it would seem possible that Pate himself had been responsible for the choice of Morillo. Hence it is possible to observe the line running from Pole at Treville to Pate, Morillo, and the *spirituali* at the Council. The coincidence of their outlook is clearly established in the communiqué which Pole entrusted to Morillo; but before this can be studied, it is necessary to consider the revised version of the decree on justification which formed the subject of Pole's commentary, and the occasion of his memorandum on the issue – both of which he probably composed, as we have seen, between 5 and 9 October 1546. In these four days he finally revealed, in as candid a manner as he could, his exact state of mind about the issue which had caused him so much anguish in the past few months, and about which his opinion had for years been the object of the keenest speculation among both his admirers, and those who, less well disposed, had observed his enigmatic silences with growing distrust.

CHAPTER ELEVEN

The reluctant theologian

The September draft of the decree on justification was constructed with a view to distinguishing the Catholic doctrine of salvation from that of Luther.[1] This, in Pole's opinion, was a fundamental error of approach; hence it was hardly to be expected that the document itself would please him. It consisted of eleven articles, expounding in a forthright manner what the Church believed and taught. Twenty-one canons were appended, in which heretical – and particularly Lutheran – beliefs were solemnly declared anathema. Thus there was no more concession in this document to the weight of Lutheran theology than there had been in the July draft, which Pole had so vehemently criticised.

The opening paragraph proclaimed the necessity of clarifying the Catholic doctrine of salvation, because of new and erroneous ideas which had disturbed the Church. There followed an account of the conditions which gave rise to the need for justification. Man was born the child of wrath, and was enslaved by sin. The law of Moses had shown him, not how he could be saved, but how much he stood in need of divine mercy. When at last, through the merits of Christ's sacrifice, mankind had been redeemed, salvation became possible to those who, accepting divine grace, were reborn as sons of God. Henceforward it became possible for man to grow more justified from day to day, increasing in divine favour.[2]

---

[1] *C.T.*, v, 420–7. Jedin gives a full account of its origin, and of the developments it underwent before being presented to the Council on 23 September 1546 (*Council*, II, 239–44).

[2] *C.T.*, v, 420–2 (Preamble, and articles I-V).

So far there was little in the proposed decree that ran contrary to Luther's teaching. In the middle of article V, however, there suddenly appeared a quotation from the epistle of St James which turned the whole course of the argument in a profoundly anti-Lutheran direction. This epistle, which Luther had rejected as 'an epistle of straw', emphasised the importance of good works in the process of salvation. In particular, chapter two, verse twenty-four proclaimed that man was justified not only by faith, but also by good works: 'Videtis quoniam ex operibus iustificatur homo et non ex fide tantum.'[1] This verse, it became clear, was to serve as a keystone to the Catholic doctrine of salvation.

Not that good works were considered to contribute significantly to conversion. Justification, it was stated, occurred gratuitously, through the operation of the Holy Spirit. But man, according to articles VI and VII, was capable of preparing and disposing himself for this event. In these articles, therefore, the Lutheran scheme of salvation stood implicitly condemned. Nevertheless, it was emphatically stated that justification was initially achieved by faith alone, without any preceding merit on man's part.[2] No one, it was asserted, could be counted justified until the merits of Christ had been communicated and imputed to him.

This particular choice of expression is interesting, and to a degree, surprising. For despite its clear intention of resisting Lutheran theology, article VII came very close to suggesting that the justice whereby man was made acceptable to God was not to be distinguished from the personal justice of Christ.[3] The implications of such a view, that no specifically individual justice could be attributed to man, ran contrary to much that the document asserted elsewhere. Jedin observes that this passage is ambiguous, in that it fails to indicate whether Christ's justice is to be regarded as identical with the grace of justification.[4] But the overall tenor of the passage seems to indicate that the two concepts were indeed

[1] Article V (*C.T.*, v, 422).
[2] Articles VI and VII (*C.T.*, v, 422–3).   [3] *C.T.*, v, 423.
[4] Thus the article refers to the reception of Christ's justice 'as if it were our own' ('ac si nostra esset et nos ea praestitissemus'); Jedin, *Council*, II, 243.

thought of as identical. Hence the doctrine of intrinsic justice, which the document upholds elsewhere,[1] is here passed over in silence and replaced, virtually, by the doctrine of imputation. How is this anomaly to be explained?

Perhaps the explanation is to be found in the words of article VII: 'Ita non sunt duae iustitiae'. The purpose of the argument at this juncture was to repudiate the theory of twofold justice. In order to accomplish this the contrary viewpoint was asserted. Thus in refuting what was considered to be an artificial distinction between Christ's justice and that of man, the article emphasised their identity. It thereby came close to supporting the Lutheran doctrine of imputation, and effectively contradicted the principal emphasis of the whole document: that man was intrinsically renewed by grace.[2]

This was the effect, but not the intention of the argument: for article VII continued with an assertion that man was not merely reputed to be justified, but was actually and intrinsically so ('iustificati non modo reputamur, sed vere iusti nominamur et sumus'). The ambiguity therefore remained unresolved, though the intentions of the argument were plain. It was on the ambiguities however, which Pole seized, in an effort to interpret the text in a manner corresponding to his own ideas.[3]

The concluding articles of the September draft dealt with the nature of justifying faith, and stressed the auxiliary activities of hope and charity in the work of sanctification. Care was taken to distinguish 'faith' from mere confidence in the divine forgiveness.[4]

There followed an account of man's growth in justification through obedience to the law of God and cooperation with His grace. Article VIII condemned the view that without a special revelation the justified man could be certain of his own salvation.

---

[1] Cf. p. 177 below; but indeed the doctrine is upheld in the subsequent part of article VII itself.

[2] Whether or not this explanation is correct, it is clear that the Council had a long way to go before arriving at a satisfactory account of the doctrine of intrinsic justice; and in fact this clarification was achieved only in the arduous debates which followed the appearance of the September draft. (Jedin, *Council*, II, 249–261.)

[3] Below, pp. 178–9.   [4] Article VII (*C.T.*, v, 424).

Finally, the doctrine of salvation by faith alone was explicitly rejected, and the meritoriousness of good works again proclaimed.[1]

The twenty-one canons which were appended to these articles reasserted the essential elements of the Catholic doctrine of salvation, and condemned all doctrines to the contrary. The first heresy to be condemned was Pelagianism. Canon I denounced the view that man could be justified without the aid of grace. The remaining canons were directed to a condemnation of the Lutheran system of salvation (although neither Luther nor his supporters were mentioned by name), and to a definition of Catholic teaching on the issues in dispute. Thus it was clearly stated that man could dispose himself for the initial grace of justification;[2] that he could contribute by good works to his own salvation;[3] that he was intrinsically justified by grace, and not merely reputed to be so;[4] and that the precepts of God's law were capable of being fulfilled with the assistance of grace.[5] The view that all human works accomplished before justification were gravely sinful, was explicitly condemned;[6] and the final canon resumed the whole argument, anathematising the belief that good works were devoid of merit in the sight of God.[7]

The proposed decree reached Pole, as we have seen, early in October. It told him all he needed to know about the imminent decision of the Council, and confirmed his fears about the course which events had now assumed. Hence his commentary on the September draft[8] is of considerable interest, not only because it was his first attempt to write in detail on such matters, but because his confidence in his own opinions had perhaps now reached its lowest point. It is noticeable that such criticisms as he ventured, invariably arose from a standpoint significantly different from that of the proposed decree; yet their manner of expression was restrained, and on the whole, diffident. It is as though he feared to place himself at too great a distance from the decision of the Coun-

[1] Article IX, *C.T.*, v, 425.
[2] Canon III (ibid. p. 426).
[3] Canon VI and Canon XIV (ibid. pp. 426–7).
[4] Canon VII (*C.T.*, v, 427).
[5] Canon X (ibid.).
[6] Canon XIX (ibid.).
[7] Canon XXI (ibid.).
[8] *C.T.*, xii, 674–6.

cil. Yet he did not hesitate to make his criticisms clear. It is perhaps reasonable to assume, that such dissenting views as he expressed were likely to have been the result of long-standing and intense conviction. Even in these instances he can occasionally be seen to retract an earlier criticism, in favour of the view embodied in draft decree. An impression of inconsistency and vacillation is thereby created. It is difficult to escape the conclusion that Pole's commentary on the September draft was the product of an uneasy mind, wavering between uncomfortable alternatives.

The form of the September draft, he acknowledged, appealed to him. He admired the principle of a preliminary explication of the problem, followed by separate canons in which the matter could be dealt with more particularly. But the content of the document, with its heavy obscurity about matters which should be 'common and familiar' was in many ways distressing to him.[1]

In particular, he objected to the obscurity of article VII which, as we have seen, did not clearly distinguish between the personal justice of Christ and the grace residing in the justified soul. Pole claimed that this article, in tending to identify the justice of Christ with the phenomenon of grace, placed too much emphasis upon the role played by the theological virtues in salvation.[2] His own opinion, which he considered to be in accordance with the view of Scripture, was that justification arose from a wider (and as it turned out, rather different) sequence of events.[3]

Thus Pole objected to article VII on a number of grounds, the most important of which was the stress it laid upon the theological virtues – in particular, we may suspect, upon the virtues of hope and charity, which resulted in good works. It is highly significant that he contrasted this emphasis with what the article had earlier

---

[1] *C.T.*, XII, 674.

[2] That is the virtues of faith, hope and charity. Pole's remark was equivalent to a complaint about the excessive emphasis which, in his view, the draft decree placed upon human effort in salvation.

[3] 'Optaret, ut hic cautius provideretur, ne hic locus contradiceret iis, quae superius dicta sunt de communicatione et imputatione iustitiae Christi in nos et inferius canone VII dicuntur; atque etiam sacrae scripturae nec satis cum ipso sensu veritatis convenire videntur, qui non in sola charitate aut etiam cum aliis virtutibus theologicis constituunt rationem iustificationis nostre, sed constituunt eam in variis quasi partibus.' (*C.T.*, XII, 674.)

stated about the justice of Christ, 'communicated and imputed' to the Christian soul.[1] He considered too, that an emphasis of this kind ill accorded with the contents of canon VII. Whether he was correct in this is hardly important; what is interesting is that canon VII attributed justification to the grace residing in the Christian soul, and not merely to the remission of sin, or the imputed justice of Christ.[2] In adverting to canon VII, Pole drew attention to the variety of forces at work in justification. From there he proceeded to single out for particular attention the remission of sins, which, he claimed, was the principal agent of justification. The effect of his argument, therefore, was to minimise the contribution made by man himself to his original conversion.[3]

In the first place, Pole maintained, justification was achieved through the remission of sins, which occurred as a result of the satisfaction merited by Christ. Only when this had taken place, was it possible for man to progress in sanctification: and sanctification, he explained, was imparted to mankind together with the gift of charity, and the other theological virtues.[4]

The significance of this viewpoint was that it drastically reduced the power of man to dispose himself for conversion. This in turn implied an idea of the 'servile will', helpless to extricate itself from sin, and embedded in a nature that was utterly and in every element corrupt. Such was the view that Pole went on to develop and it is clear from what follows that his conception of human nature in its natural condition was in every respect similar to that of Luther.[5] It was a view altogether more pessimistic than that embodied in the draft decree. Luther held that justification occurred as a totally gratuitous intervention on the part of God. In

[1] Above, p. 175. [2] *C.T.*, v, 427.

[3] Thus Pole seized upon the ambiguities of article VII to turn the argument in his own direction. It is doubtful however, whether he paid due attention to the claim of article VII that man's original conversion occurred gratuitously, through the operation of the Holy Spirit. What he remained apparently unable to accept was that man could *cooperate* with grace in his conversion.

[4] 'Primum in remissione peccatorum data satisfactione ex meritis Christi, deinde in sanctificatione, que fit per Spiritum sanctum, qui datur nobis cum caritate et aliis virtutibus theologicis.' (*C.T.*, xii, 674.)

[5] Or to that reflected, for example, in the opening pages of the *Beneficio di Cristo*.

this respect, the Catholic position was identical with his. But Catholic theology insisted equally upon the preliminary role of natural virtue in disposing man to accept the grace of justification. For Luther – and, as it is evident, for Pole – there was no such thing as 'natural virtue' in the fallen state of man.

Pole indeed, maintained that St Paul (Rom. 4.7) attributed the greater part of justification to the remission of sins. Man remained entirely passive in the process of justification, since, as Pole continued, he enjoyed no spiritual resources which would enable him to correspond at this stage to the will of God. The virtue of charity, he pointed out, did not reside in the unjustified.[1] Consequently the first, and most important stage of justification consisted in the remission of man's sins. The instrument of this remission was the justice of Christ, imputed to the Christian soul, and effecting satisfaction on its behalf.

Thus through the justice of Christ, imputed to the Christian soul, the wrath of God was turned aside and the virtue of charity implanted (so that the justified man was henceforth enabled to perform good works).[2]

It must be remembered that the word 'charity' is closely related here to the word 'grace', which in turn raises the question of the nature and significance of the justice imparted to the Christian soul. Pole had spoken of the 'imputed justice of Christ'; yet he had also spoken of the 'gift of charity' which accompanied it. This would suggest that he did indeed acknowledge the existence of a justice intrinsic to the Christian soul. In this detail therefore, his position was quite different from that of Luther. It was not yet clear, however, what significance he attached to the notion of intrinsic justice. Seripando's question, written in the margin of the manuscript, went to the heart of the problem: 'Quid ergo est, quod iustos intrinsece et reipsa efficiat?'[3]

---

[1] 'Num charitas non potest esse cum impietate peccati' (*C.T.*, XII, 674).

[2] 'necesse est ergo, ut prius saltem nostra remittantur nobis peccata quam habeamus charitatem, et ut prima ac potissima pars iustificationis sit ipsa remissio peccatorum et solutio debitorum eaque necessaria atque essentialis, et hec non fit propter charitatem, quam nondum habemus tunc, sed potius contra, quia remittuntur nobis peccata propter aliam iustitiam, nempe Christi nobis imputatem, pro nobis satisfacientem, et per illan placata ira Dei datur nobis charitas'. (Ibid.)

[3] *C.T.*, XII, 675.

Pole's attempt to cope with this question rested on the assertion that the justice of Christ was imputed to the Christian soul.
It imparted not only the gift of charity, but a simultaneous remission of sin. Hence the justice of Christ constituted an important part of man's intrinsic justice, and was the point of origin to
which all else should be referred.[1]

It will be seen that this interpretation, which bears a resemblance to the theory of twofold justice formulated at Regensburg,
was in essentials orthodox, although Lutheran in emphasis. But
it is significant that Pole made no attempt to recommend the
doctrine of twofold justice in itself. It seems likely indeed, that the
theory held as little importance for him as it did for the other
spirituali at the Council. What is reflected in the above account is
no more than a remnant of the idea which gained currency at
Regensburg: that part of it which related man's intrinsic justice to
the personal justice of Christ. It amounted to little more than an
acknowledgement that intrinsic justice did in fact exist: but
whether it could in any sense contribute to man's personal salvation was a question which remained unanswered. It was not a
question which Pole wanted to investigate. In effect, he preferred
to attribute everything to the imputed justice of Christ.

Thus the elements of orthodoxy can be seen to exist within his
system; what is not apparent is how they were reconciled in his
mind with other, often contradictory attitudes, which he felt
equally obliged to incorporate. It must be remembered that he
had at no time been able to establish his opinions on these questions in an intellectually coherent way. Alberigo's remark, that
'in the theological climate of the sixteenth century the refusal of
the approaches provided by scholastic theology presented, for
those who wished to remain orthodox, difficulties of extreme
complexity', is amply vindicated in the case of Pole.[2] Again, he
was writing under conditions of great strain, after a lengthy and

[1] 'Item quod iustitia Christi imputata nobis non solum efficit, ut charitas
donetur nobis, sed etiam ut absolvamur a peccatis, soluta iusta satisfactione, que
pars est iustitie essentialis et necessaria, ad quam tanquam ad suum genus debet
referri.' (Ibid.) Pole added that the imputed justice of Christ enabled man to fulfil
the precepts of the law, assisted by grace.
[2] Alberigo, *I vescovi italiani*, p. 384.

exhausting illness. He was, moreover, obliged to express himself with reference to a document which, purporting to be the testament of orthodox opinion, must necessarily have carried weight with him; and at a time when his own opinions were even more hesitant and uncertain than before. Hence it would be unrealistic to expect any sustained consistency in what he wrote. He was in two minds, and therefore likely to contradict himself.

He did so in discussing the issue of free will. In the early part of his commentary he had suggested that before justification the human will was incapable of cooperating with divine grace, or of disposing itself for conversion.[1] Later, in commenting on the third canon of the draft decree, he adverted once more to this question.

Canon III maintained that the human will was capable of disposing itself for conversion, and of freely accepting or rejecting the grace of justification. It condemned the view that man remained an entirely passive recipient throughout the process.[2]

This was a patently unequivocal assertion: free will was an active agent in man's justification. Yet Pole discovered, or thought that he discovered, a contradiction in it; and that he did so, indicates the unsettled state of his opinions. He had already suggested, though not explicitly, that free will played a very minor part, if any, in man's first justification. His objection to canon III began by developing this train of thought. There was in this canon, he maintained, a suggestion that justification could be attributed at least in part to human virtue, and not in its entirety to divine grace. Hence it opened the way to human self-glorification.[3]

So far, Pole's line of objection was consistent with what he had

[1] Above, p. 180.
[2] 'Si quis, Deo tangente cor hominis per motionem et illuminationem Spiritus Sancti, dixerit hominem ipsum tamquam exanime quoddam organum ita divinam illam motionem recipere, ut [eam] praeventus non possit libera sua voluntate moveri nec vocanti Deo atque excitanti consentire, ut esse ad obtinendam iustificationis gratiam disponat ac praeparet, sicut etiam posset dissentire: anathema sit.' (*C.T.*, v, 426.)
[3] 'In III canone libere arbitrio tribuitur facultas et virtus, qua seipsum possit preparare ad gratiam et consentire ipsi cum ipsa gratia vocante et excitante, quasi saltem ex parte iustificatio sit tribuenda virtute nostre, et non tota gratia Dei et virtuti ipsius, et sic saltem de ea parte possimus gloriari.' (*C.T.*, xii, 675.)

before maintained or suggested. His next statement however, in which he claimed to detect a contradiction in the canon, is so remarkable a misinterpretation of what was actually expressed, that at first reading it appears to be quite unintelligible. In giving leeway to human self-approval, Pole observed, canon III actually sanctioned what it had earlier, and properly condemned: namely, the view that free will remained inert during the course of justification.[1]

On the face of it, this looks as if Pole were simultaneously affirming and denying the freedom of the human will to accept or reject the grace of justification. As such, it is a senseless statement. It is, however, profoundly revealing as to his state of mind: for what seems to have happened is that midway through his objection he abandoned it, and accepted the view actually embodied in canon III. He can hardly have been fully conscious that this was what had occurred; but the proposal which he went on to make was in every way a reiteration of what canon III explicitly stated. He argued in fact, that the power of free will to dispose itself for justification should be attributed to the action of divine grace.[2]

The phrase 'per gratiam Dei' was of course indistinguishable from the provisos already included in the canon: 'Deo tangente cor hominis per motionem et illuminationem Spiritus Sancti'; and again: 'vocanti Deo atque excitanti'. Yet the fact was not apparent to Pole's mind as he wrote. A possible explanation is that he had originally misread the sense of canon III, taking the phrase about human passivity ('hominem ipsum tanquam exanime quoddam organum') as descriptive of man's actual condition, because that was how he himself conceived of it; and in that case, the canon would certainly have appeared to him to contradict itself. Yet he concluded his objection with the remark that such a conception of the human will had been 'properly condemned'. What can have occurred then, to bring about this glaring inconsistency in his own observations?

[1] 'Idcirco probat quidem, quod superius recte damnatum est, liberum arbitrium habere se in iustificatione tanquam exanime.' (Ibid.)

[2] 'optaret tamen, ut poneretur hic potius quam praeparare se et consentire et alia omnia potest facere liberum argitrium per gratiam Dei'. (Ibid.)

It can only be that, working under pressure, and in a state of considerable mental turbulence, he attributed to the document a contradiction which in fact existed in his own mind. Two strong and mutually opposing forces, it would seem, were at work in him. The first urged him to consider unredeemed human nature as the entirely passive recipient of divine favour; the second, to acknowledge the possible authority of the document in front of him. During the course of his remarks on canon III, it may be assumed, the second of these forces asserted itself, displacing his original objection. It is a measure of his uncertain frame of mind that such a transformation should occur without his becoming fully conscious of it.

How completely he had reversed his original opinion may be appreciated when the phrase 'per gratiam Dei', which he thought desirable of insertion, is contrasted with his earlier suggestion that natural virtue had no place in the unjustified.[1] What possible leverage could there be for grace, unless man's natural virtue was capable of reacting to it? Or did grace, without need of leverage or cooperation, automatically release the captive will? The first of these alternatives was the one that ultimately became established in the Tridentine decree on justification. The second was that proposed by Luther. Pole, at the time of his commentary on the September draft, was clearly wavering between these two alternatives, unable wholeheartedly to accept one or to reject the other.

His intellectual anguish was doubtless all the greater in that he had been from the outset a reluctant theologian. The issues which he had been asked to write about were not, in his view, proper objects for intellectual dissection. Like all the *spirituali*, he was concerned only with the practical attitudes which should inform and motivate Christian living: and of these, the chief and most apparent, was that the Christian had no one but Almighty God to thank for his salvation. To proceed beyond this, and to conjure with the intricacies of an abstruse theology, was alien to his whole approach and temper.

[1] Above, pp. 179, and 182.

Consequently he could respond only to the particulars of the proposed decree, and with a consistency which fluctuated in proportion to the complexity of the issues which he dealt with. His opposition to canon IV for example, was strikingly in contrast to the hesitant and unsure objections which he had raised to the preceding canon. The fourth canon of the draft decree had condemned the proposition that remorse for sin, arising from the fear of hell, must be considered gravely sinful in the unregenerate.[1] Pole rejected this assertion out of hand. Servile fear, he implied, could in no circumstance be considered anything but sinful in the unregenerate.[2] The arguments of the scholastics, he maintained, could be brought to bear upon the issue; and he demonstrated his point by means of a syllogism which, it may be suspected, was designed to refute scholasticism with its own weapons.

In scholastic theology, he asserted, there was no such thing as a morally indifferent act, and therefore nothing which was not either meritorious or sinful; merit however, occurred as a result of grace; therefore servile fear, arising neither from grace nor from the love of God, could be of no assistance to the unregenerate ('paene esse valde utilem ad conversionem et peccatores suo modo ad resipiscentiam plurimum iuvare').[3]

There is no need to examine the merits of this argument, or to inquire whether the scholastic categories which it employed were characteristic of Pole's mode of thought. But it is worth noting that he did not explicitly admit the validity of the concept 'merit' in relation to good works; and we know from other sources that he was in reality unwilling to do so. What is furthermore remarkable, is that his argument reverted to the tendency which had earlier revealed itself, to regard the state of fallen man as utterly devoid of anything that could be considered 'virtue'. There can be little doubt that such was in reality his true conviction,[4] in contrast to the concessions which he had made in dealing with canon III. Even here, however, there remained some measure

---

[1] *C.T.*, v, 426.

[2] Similar sentiments had been expressed in Flaminio's letters, and in the *Beneficio di Cristo*.

[3] *C.T.*, XII, 675.

[4] For further evidence of which cf. below, pp. 189–90.

of compromise, and it is noticeable that he stopped short of actually contradicting the claims of canon IV. He did not assert that servile fear was positively sinful (although this was the implication of his remarks); he merely stated that it was 'hardly useful' as an instrument of regeneration. Hence it is possible to observe, once again, the deference which withheld him from fully challenging the claims of the proposed decree; and it would seem probable that this was the direct result of the uneasiness which he felt about his own position, as the Council moved closer to an official declaration of its teaching.

Nevertheless, he continued the same line of assault in his criticism of canon XIX,[1] which stigmatised the view that all human works were sinful, before justification.[2] Pole attacked this canon with the same argument which he had used before: no action could be pleasing to God unless it was inspired by charity. The scholastics, he pointed out, taught that there was no such thing as an indifferent act. Thus the inference of Pole's remarks was clear: all works performed before justification were sinful. Significantly, however, Pole again stopped short of making the inference explicit. He would not directly contradict the claims embodied in the text before him. But his comment upon it reveals it as certain beyond doubt that Pole's conception of human nature in its fallen state was identical with that of Luther.[3] Natural virtue was a delusion; man was trapped in sin, his will frozen and immobile. He remained powerless to choose anything but what was contrary to the divine commandments; and there was no question that he could in any way dispose himself more favourably in the eyes of God, or prepare himself freely to accept the grace of conversion.

[1] Pole attributed the argument to canon IX by mistake – unless the reference to canon IX is simply a misprint; the argument he attacked was undoubtedly that of canon XIX (*C.T.*, v, 427).

[2] 'Si quis dixerit, opera omnia, quae ante recuperatam iustificationem fiunt, quacumque ratione facta sint, esse peccata: anathema sit.' (Ibid.)

[3] 'Item dicendum arbitratur ad id quod, canone IX [*sic*] asseritur, quod non omnia opera impiorum sunt peccata, cum certum sit, ea omnia esse defectus in lege Dei et non assequi finem precepti, qui est charitas de corde puro, etc. Et sic anathemizatur ii omnes scholastici, qui non agnoscunt actus indifferentes seu medios.' (*C.T.*, xii, 675.)

Or rather, there had been no such question. Pole's conviction, here so firmly expressed, was in reality undergoing a process of erosion induced by self-doubt, coupled with an anxiety to submit to the authoritative teaching of the Church. For the September draft was regarded by the Council as the basis for a future declaration of dogma. Faced with such a challenge, Pole's confidence in his own opinions suffered pause; and his uncertainty is manifest in every line. He did not hesitate to express his dissatisfaction with the Council's line of thought; but his objections were never stated with a force proportionate to their intensity.

His concluding criticisms reflected the spirit of the commentary as a whole: hesitant disagreement, tentatively argued, and suggesting an altogether more radical difference of opinion than he would allow himself to express. The decree, he noted, condemned the view that the precepts of God were incapable of fulfilment by those living in the state of grace.[1] Would it not be preferable, he inquired, further to elaborate this statement, lest it be construed as meaning that man was capable of *perfectly* fulfilling the divine commandments (thus enabling him to glory in his own achievement)? The decree should refrain from suggesting that man was saved through the perfect observance of God's law – as though to imply that the merits of Christ were not more than sufficient for salvation. Rather should it stress the need to embrace the merits of Christ and depend perpetually on them.[2] It was the familiar complaint: if man were to be allowed any responsibility in his own salvation, the sufficiency of Christ's merits would be brought in question. The logic of such a position was inescapably Lutheran.

Pole's final objection revealed the same spirit of uncertain criticism which he had brought to bear throughout his commentary on the draft decree. Canon XXI of the September draft had stated unequivocally that man, with the assistance of divine grace was capable of meriting salvation.[3]

Here was the crux of the whole question, the point which,

[1] Cf. canon X of the September draft: 'Si quis dixerit, Dei praecepta homini etiam iustificato et sub gratia constituto esse ad observandum impossibilia: anathema sit.' (*C.T.*, v, 427.)

[2] *C.T.*, xii, 675. [3] *C.T.*, v, 427.

more than any other, separated the Lutheran and Catholic conceptions of salvation. To Luther, a statement of this kind was nothing other than Pelagian: in attributing power to man, it detracted from the power of God. It was of no use to protest that such power derived entirely from Christ's merits, and must perpetually be referred to Him: the very attribution of 'merit' to man's works was a limitation placed upon the power of God. As such, it was a blasphemy.

Against this view, the Council had produced a document which supposed the interior regeneration of the soul by grace; in his restored condition, man, possessing now the grace conferred upon him by the sufferings of Christ, could merit a heavenly reward through the performance of good works.

Obviously these views could not be reconciled. Pole, therefore, was faced with a clear choice: there was no room for evasion. He had, as we have seen, acknowledged to his friends in private, that he did not think the word 'merit' could ever justly be applied to human action. It might reasonably be supposed, then, that he would resolutely oppose the doctrine proclaimed in canon XXI. In fact nothing of the kind occurred. The article undoubtedly disquieted him; he made his objection; but the objection was oblique in the extreme, and almost half-hearted. He went no further than to suggest that the merits of Christ be more fully acknowledged in the canon. Otherwise, he felt, it might appear to be Pelagian in inspiration.[1]

This remark came close to implying a formal acquiescence in the view embodied in the draft decree. By thus implicitly acknowledging the doctrine of human merit, however uneasily, Pole had aligned himself with the Tridentine doctrine of justification. The alignment, however, such as it was, had been attained with difficulty, and it was not in accordance with the dominant orientation of the commentary. Hence it is impossible not to feel that he had allowed himself to be edged reluctantly into an acceptance of Tridentine orthodoxy. As the gulf between the Lutheran and Catholic doctrines became ever more apparent, Pole found him-

[1] *C.T.*, xii, 676.

self forced to abandon the middle ground which he had occupied, and to choose between positions which he had hitherto regarded as compatible.

In his commentary on the September draft Pole had concentrated most of his attention on the problem of justification in its initial phase. He had been largely concerned with the question of conversion, and had shown himself to be intent on disputing the element of human self-preparation which the document allowed for. Only peripherally had he touched upon the crucial doctrines which distinguished Luther's teaching from Catholicism: the doctrines of imputed righteousness and of salvation by faith alone. He had been content merely to correct an emphasis which he had felt to be erroneous. In doing so, he had revealed his basic disposition; but in a manner both sporadic and oblique. The reasons for this indirectness of approach have already been examined, but it is important to recognise in addition, that his own views were to a degree obscured by the very nature of the task in hand. He had been engaged in commentary, not in exposition. His arguments were formed with reference to an existing text. Consequently his own views emerged only by implication, and were not arranged into a coherent whole.

Turning, therefore, to the declaration which he drew up simultaneously with his commentary on the September draft, it is possible to observe more easily the exact state of his opinions on the issues in dispute. In this document, entitled *De iustificatione annotatio*,[1] Pole finally revealed the extent of his commitment to the doctrine of salvation by faith alone. Abandoning equivocation, he showed himself to favour a view of justification which was in essentials Lutheran.

As usual, he employed an exegetical approach, appealing to Scripture and to personal experience in support of his opinions. His opening sentence was an uncompromising declaration of belief – an affirmation that 'good works' could contribute nothing to salvation.[2]

---

[1] *C.T.*, XII, 671–4.
[2] 'Nunquam vere dici potest, hominem coram Deo iustificari ex operibus tam

The implications of this statement are quite clear: Pole is avowedly committing himself to a view of justification which is distinctively Lutheran, and opposed to the doctrine which was becoming manifest at Trent. It must be noticed that he considers the interior condition of man to be in all circumstances sinful, whether before or after justification ('qui ex nobis ipsis semper mali sumus'). Thus not only are all works performed before conversion actually sinful: but even works accomplished in the state of grace are good only in so far as they proceed from God. They cannot be considered to contribute to man's justification.[1]

Pole elaborates this statement further, remarking that man, once converted, stands continuously in need of justification. He is perpetually driven to seek pardon for his sins: and this pardon he apprehends through faith in Christ ('per misericordiam in Christo, quem fide apprehendimus').[2] It is not, therefore, through observation of the law that man is justified, but through the divine pardon promised in the Gospel and revealed to all believers.[3] The word of God, he continues, resides in man, forever accusing him of sin, and constantly impelling him to look for refuge in the mercy of Christ. Such is the testimony of Scripture and experience ('et testimonio scriptuarum et experientia constet').

Hence the dichotomy which Luther had experienced between the aspirations of the spirit, and the actual accomplishments of human nature, was felt with equal intensity by Pole. Confronted with this dilemma, he recognised the inner paradox presented by the Christian faith: 'How is it', he inquired, 'that having died to sin [in baptism or conversion] we continue all the while to sin?'[4]

It was this question which Luther had detected at the heart of

extra gratiam factis, que nonnisi peccata sunt, quam in gratia, que etsi, quatenus quidem ab illa proveniunt, et bona dicuntur et sunt, quia tamen in nobis et a nobis fiunt, qui ex nobis ipsis semper mali sumus, nunquam sic bona esse possunt, ut per ea coram Deo iustificemur.' (*C.T.*, XII, 671.)

[1] This was a view which had been specifically condemned in the September draft (cf. above, n. 2, p. 177 and n. 1, p. 187).

[2] *C.T.*, XII, 672.

[3] 'Nempe per eam, quam in evangelio per remissionem peccatorum promisit et exhibet credentibus, non autem, per eam, quam in lege per impletionem mandatorum promisit et retribuit operantibus.' (*C.T.*, XII, 672.)

[4] 'Qui enim peccato mortui sumus, quo pacto vivemus in illo?' (Ibid.)

Christianity. The answer that had forced itself upon him with a startling clarity was that man was not made righteous by striving: righteousness was imputed to him. He remained a sinner but was accounted just: *semper peccator, semper iustus*. Faith in Christ ensured his acceptance before God, and Christ's justice was put to work on his behalf. Thus, with all the exaltation of discovery, Luther had offered a release to countless souls, who, fearing the prospect of damnation, could yet find no escape route from the tyranny of sin. The doctrine of imputed righteousness provided the principal dynamic of the Reformation.

It is to this doctrine that Pole implicitly adverts in reply to the question he had raised. Turning to St Paul's epistle to the Romans he cites the text: 'Quicunque enim spiritu Dei aguntur, ii sunt filii Dei' (Rom. 8.12); and significantly adds 'Et in eo non peccant quidem, qui Dei spiritu aguntur; eo, quod sunt filii Dei non peccant.'[1] In effect, his comment was equivalent to a statement that sin was not imputed to the sons of God: man, once justified remained a sinner, and was at the same time perpetually just. To illustrate the paradox, Pole resorts once more to Scripture, referring this time to the first epistle of St John: 'Qui enim natus est ex Deo, non peccat' (1, Jo. 5.18). This statement, remarks Pole, comes from a writer who was fully aware of the permanence of sin in man; and he refers back to a text which he had cited earlier: 'Nam "si dixerimus", ait Joanes Apostolus, "quia non peccavimus, mendacem facimus eum et verbum eius non est in nobis." ' (1, Jo. 1.10).[2]

Thus, explains Pole, the flesh wars against the spirit, and the will chooses what it wishes to avoid (Gal. 5.17; Rom. 7.18ff). Such, he observes, was the experience of St Paul himself, who, devoted to the law of God, found himself nonetheless subject to the law of sin. But because the word of God resided in him he was raised up from despair through the mercy of Christ, and was enabled in the exercise of faith and hope to thank God for his salvation.[3]

This same remedy, moreover, is available to every Christian.

[1] Ibid.   [2] Ibid.   [3] Ibid.

However often he may fall, he has only to disavow his sins, and turn for pardon to Almighty God. Hence there is no need to despair, so long as he retains his confidence in God.[1]

It is interesting to observe that Pole here selects the passage of St Paul which most closely approximates to Luther's doctrine of salvation. The justice of Christ is offered to the sinner as a garment ('per velamen'). Thus, in the certitude of faith, the sinner trusts in the promise of salvation. Luther interpreted this to mean that the 'garment' of Christ's righteousness shielded the sinner from divine wrath; sin was not thereby dissolved, so much as ignored. Pole, while not explicitly acknowledging the doctrine of imputed justice, seems nevertheless to imply agreement with the Lutheran position. He insists upon the continuous necessity to observe the laws of God; but, as he has already stressed, observances do not justify the sinner. Only faith in Christ's redeeming power can bring salvation.[2]

The only sure foundation therefore, is the word of God. Pole emphasises the necessity to trust only in the mercy of Christ, through which sins are remitted. Supported by his faith, the sinner looks forward to salvation.[3]

It may be of interest to notice the phrase 'non in nostra iustitia confisi'. Pole here seems to acknowledge the existence, however ineffective, of a justice intrinsic to the Christian soul. This suggests that, in theory at any rate, he may not have been fully committed to the doctrine of imputed righteousness, so that it is possible to detect here once again, an unresolved ambiguity. The

[1] 'non desperet nec per aliam viam se veniam a Deo impetraturum confidat, ea una excepta, quam per apostolus Paulus nobis ostendit, cum ait: "Confidentiam habentes in introitu sanctorum in sanguine Iesu, quam initiavit nobis viam novam et viventem per velamen, id est per carnem suam, et sacerdotem magnum in domo Dei; accedamus cum vero corde in certitudine fidei, aspersi corda a conscientia mala, et abluto corpore aqua munda. Detineamus confessionem spei nostrae indeclinabilem; fidelis est enim, qui promisit."' Hebr. 10.19–23. (Ibid. p. 673.)

[2] 'Sed nunquid hoc de nullo alio preter ipsum unum dici poterit? Minime id quidem: "Omnes enim peccatores sumus et gloria Dei semper indigemus", ut scilicet per fidem coram eo iustificemur.' (*C.T.*, XII, 673.)

[3] 'Sustinemus autem, quicunque vere est et ex corde in illum credimus, non in nostra iustitia confisi, sed in verbo eius, in quo promisit penitentibus et in eum credentibus, se gratis nobis per misericordiam suam in Christi nomine peccata remissurum. Quare hoc fide innixa in illo semper anima nostra speravit, sperat et sperabit in finem.' (Ibid.)

phrase as it occurs is reminiscent of the doctrine of twofold justice agreed upon at Regensburg in 1541. But, as was noted at that time, the doctrine was capable of Protestant interpretation; and this is certainly the sense which Pole imparts to it. Moreover, the phrase occurs casually, and it is apparent that it carried little significance for Pole. If the gift of grace conferred a state of personal righteousness on the Christian, it was not sufficiently important to warrant attention. Penitence and faith were the supreme requirements ('penitentibus et in eum credentibus'); everything else was subordinate to these.

Thus, remarks Pole, as his argument draws to a conclusion, the saints themselves cannot escape from sin. Perpetually accused by God, they seek perpetual refuge in His mercy, so that, through penitence and faith, they are snatched up from their sins.[1] Man, therefore, remains intrinsically sinful. Once justified in faith, however, he can proceed with confidence and gratitude before the throne of grace, there to seek constant forgiveness of his sins.[2]

This concluding excerpt reveals the psychology which shaped Pole's attitudes, and establishes the similarity of his beliefs with those of Luther. Thus in this brief declaration, after years of silence, Pole had finally revealed, as clearly as he could, the nature of his ideas concerning justification. It is easy to see why he had earlier hesitated publicly to commit himself upon the issue; as he had himself admitted, his views might have provided ready propaganda for the enemies of Rome.[3] Consequently he had waited for the 'opportune moment' of the General Council – only to discover that his expectations were delusory.

Particularly striking in this treatise is the absence of the compromise formula to which Pole had hitherto resorted in discussions about justification. There is no mention of the phrase 'fides

[1] C.T., XII, 673.
[2] 'Accedamus igitur cum fiducia ad thronum gratiae' illius, quicunque in ille et per illum iustos nos et sanctos per veram fidem agnoscimus, quamvis iidem in nobis ipsis inusti et peccatores simus, de iustitia, quam ex illius ineffabili dono tam in illo quam in nobis ipsis habemus, ei gratias agentes; de peccato vero, que nostra tantum culpa nunquam in nobis absunt, veniam sine intermissione ab eodem postulantes.' (C.T., XII, 673-4.)
[3] Above, pp. 114-15.

quae per caritatem operatur' which had occupied such an important place in *De Concilio*. This phrase, as has already been noted,
was essentially ambiguous. Permitting as it did, a wide range of
interpretations, it was ideally suited to the conditions which
existed before Trent. Pole himself (at a later date) came close to
acknowledging that he had employed it during these years because of its general inclusiveness.[1] He did not add, as he might
have, that it had enabled him to shelter his opinions without
thereby denying them.

Now, however, the time for compromise was over. Pole had
been confronted with a document which contradicted everything
he felt. He had been required to deliver his own judgement on the
question, and, after futile efforts at evasion, he had eventually
complied, under duress. There was no effort at concealment in the
account which he had given. The doctrine he propounded was
straightforward and familiar: it was the doctrine of salvation by
faith alone. Pole's belief about the matter was essentially the same
as Luther's. Man was justified by faith; his sins were discounted;
his good works bore witness to the word of God residing in him;
they did not merit a heavenly reward. Such was the essential
mechanism of salvation, pithily expressed in Luther's paraphrase:
semper peccator, semper iustus.

But where Luther had been intent on following the logic of his
affirmations, Pole had been restrained by a faith different from
that proclaimed by Luther: faith in the Church, as the repository
of Christ's presence and teaching. It was this faith which had
formed a principal theme of his conversations at Viterbo, and he
had urged it upon the more impatient members of his group, as
the necessary completion to their personal belief in Christ.

Now the two doctrines had come into conflict. The Council
had pronounced (or was on the point of doing so) against belief in
salvation by faith alone. It had made it certain beyond doubt that
there was no ground for reconciliation with the Lutherans. This
much had been implicit in its proceedings from the month of
May 1546; it was confirmed by the events of the summer; and

---

[1] Below, pp. 203–4.

by October, when Pole received the draft of the proposed decree, it was apparent to him that there could be no further ground for hope.

Three months later the situation was made finally explicit. The decree on justification which was passed in January 1547 propounded a doctrine totally opposed to that of Luther.[1] It asserted that faith and works were contributory to salvation; that man was made intrinsically just by grace, and became utterly transformed in consequence; and that his good works were therefore worthy of reward.[2]

With this decree, the Council of Trent established a new conception of the Reformation: or one that was new at least, to the *spirituali*. It eliminated their belief in the possibility of a doctrinal *rapprochement*. Another way of thinking had become predominant, in which there was no longer any question of uniting Christendom by conferences or debates. The Counter Reformation had emerged as an historical force, proposing the definitive Catholic response to the revolution heralded by Luther.

Cochlaeus wrote enthusiastically from Germany to congratulate Cervini on the text of decree. He expressed his satisfaction that it had been kept intact from the 'curious innovations' desired by certain leading figures in the Church, and that the way had now been closed to their 'new fantasies'.[3] As Jedin remarks he probably had Pole in mind.[4] Certainly it was the end of Pole's belief in any likelihood of reconciliation with the Lutherans. His last words to the Council had been an exhortation to hold steadfast in the middle way; the ensuing months revealed to him that there was no middle way. It must now be determined in what manner Pole and his associates at Viterbo received the Council's doctrine of salvation.

---

[1] Alberigo, *Decreta*, pp. 647–57.
[2] For the definitive analysis, cf. Jedin, *Council*, II, 307–10.
[3] Cochlaeus to Cervini, 29 March 1547 in W. Friedensburg, 'Beiträge zum Briefwechsel der katholischen Gelehrten Deutschlands im Reformationszeitalter', *Zeitschrift für Kirchengeschichte*, XVIII (1898), 620–1.
[4] *Council*, II, 312. A later reference to Pole in the letter tends to confirm this judgement (see below, p. 197).

CHAPTER TWELVE

Pole and the
Tridentine decree

It has already been established that by the time Pole wrote his commentary on the September draft, his mind had begun to waver between two views of justification: that to which he had subscribed for years, and that embodied in the draft decree. The latter clearly exercised a powerful influence over him, purporting as it did, to summarise the official teaching of the Church, inspired and prompted by the Holy Spirit. We may assume that there would be in Pole a strong disposition to accept the teaching of the Council for this reason. He had himself publicly upheld the principle of submission to the general consensus of the Council.[1] Yet there remained one last escape route for him, if he wished to choose it: the Council's decisions could not strictly be considered binding until they had received the official approval of the Pope. Since the Council terminated only in 1563, its decree did not receive papal ratification within Pole's lifetime.[2] Consequently he could have privately disowned the Council's declaration on justification, while remaining orthodox in his allegiance. It is necessary therefore, to proceed with care, in plotting the exact course of his reaction to the conciliar decree.

There can be no doubt about his intense dissatisfaction. He told Morone that the form of the decree displeased him, and that he considered its argument to be too elliptical.[3] From the first,

[1] See above, n. 1, p. 136.
[2] As Morone reminded his interrogators in 1557. He added that, before the Council, he had adhered to the doctrine of justification as expounded at Regensburg, but had accepted the decision of the Council once it was proclaimed. (Cantù, *Eretici*, p. 178.)
[3] Ibid., p. 179: 'Non mi parlò della sostanza, ma disse che aveva desiderato l'or-

moreover, he remained implacably opposed to any plan of publishing the decree. He was, indeed, among the group of Cardinals on the Conciliar commission who argued against publication in the early days of January 1547. Their objections, however, were only partially successful. The Pope discountenanced their arguments, but remained opposed to an official promulgation, lest it should appear to anticipate his approval of the Conciliar degrees. Accordingly, the decree was printed unofficially, for private circulation.[1] Two months later Cochlaeus, writing on 29 March, noted that Pole's name was missing from the list of signatures attached to the printed version of the decree.[2]

The omission is significant. What is more remarkable, however, is that two years later, Pole was still intent upon publicly dissociating himself from the text of the decree. Towards the end of 1548 a printed edition of the Conciliar decrees was brought out at Bologna. There were 150 copies in all. Early in November two copies were dispatched to Cardinal Cervini at Rome. Attached to each copy were three *capsulae*, to receive the official seal of the three Legates who had presided at the Council. On 6 November Cervini acknowledged receipt of the two volumes. He promised to append his seal, and to find out 'whether the most reverend and illustrious Cardinal Pole will be pleased to do the same'. Cervini's choice of expression suggests that he may have expected a refusal. This, at any rate, was what he got. When, 350 years later, the German scholar Ehses examined the surviving volume at the Vatican Archives, he discovered that the third capsule, reserved for Pole's seal, remained empty.[3] Clearly Cervini had tried and failed to win Pole's cooperation. Nor was Pole's resistance simply temporary. A year later, in September

dine del decreto in altro modo, e che gli pareva che avesse compilato molte cose insieme, le quali più comodamente si sariano potute dividere in molti articoli.'

[1] *Nuntiaturberichte aus Deutschland*, Bd. I, vol. IX, p. 455, n. 1; cf. also, Jedin, *Council*, II, 312, n. 1, and pp. 315–6.

[2] He added that he was 'intensely concerned' about Pole's health. It seems possible that he was thinking of Pole's spiritual, no less than physical condition; the passage in which he speaks of Pole follows immediately upon a statement concerning his ambition to devote the last years of his life to refuting heretics. *Zeitschrift für Kirchengeschichte*, XVIII (1898), 621.

[3] *C.T.*, V, pp. xxv–vi.

1549, an ampler edition of the Conciliar decrees was published, once more at Bologna: and Pole again refrained from sanctioning it with his seal or signature.[1]

These facts plainly indicate that for some years after the suspension of the Council, Pole withheld from approving the decree, or supporting the campaign to publish it. In his resistance, however, he could no doubt point to the example of the Pope, who had refused to sanction an official publication, lest it prejudice the ultimate papal ratification which the decrees must eventually receive.

There is, however, another piece of evidence which has commonly been adduced in favour of the view that Pole supported the Council's doctrine of salvation.[2] This is a volume published at Louvain in 1569 – eleven years after the death of Pole – entitled *A Treatie of Iustification*, and described as 'Founde emong' the writings of the Cardinal.[3] It set forth the doctrine of justification as proclaimed at Trent. In addition to the main text, it contained a translation of the Conciliar decree, and a number of writings by the early fathers, 'all newly translated into English'.[4]

The first thing to be noted is that there is nothing in the title to support the view that Pole actually wrote the work. It was simply 'Founde emong the writinges of Cardinal Pole of blessed memorie'. The fact that Pole's name is invoked in such a way suggests that the connection was intended to enhance the authority of the publication; it is all the more remarkable, therefore, that the composition of the work is not explicitly ascribed to him.

The form of the treatise, moreover, is quite dissimilar to any known work of Pole. It employs a thoroughly scholastic mode of exposition, as opposed to the exegetical approach of Pole.[5]

[1] Ibid. p. xxvi. The fact was remembered, and registered against Pole, as the records of the Roman Inquisition show. ('Compendio', 286.)

[2] Schenk, *Reginald Pole*, p. 112, n. 11; Jedin, *Council*, II, 279, n. 1.

[3] *A Treatie of Iustification. Founde emong the writinges of Cardinal Pole of blessed memorie, remaining in the custodie of M. Henrie Pyning, Chamberlaine and General Receuier to the said Cardinal, late deceased in Louaine* (Louvain, 1569).

[4] Title-page.

[5] A point first made by J. Fischer, 'Essai historique sur les ideés reformatrices des Cardinaux Jean Pierre Carafa (1476–1559) et Reginald Pole (1500–58)' –

Thus we find, for example, a traditional account[1] of the 'two principall and sovereigne powers of the sowle, the one called reason and understanding, the other will' for which it would be difficult to find a parallel in any of Pole's spiritual writings. Again, there are frequent citations from the fathers of the Church, including references to St Thomas and St Bonaventure,[2] which must surprise anyone familiar with Pole's style of argument. It was not usual for him explicitly to employ patristic (let alone scholastic) evidence to make his case; he preferred as a rule, to rely exclusively upon the word of Scripture.[3]

Thus the evidence suggests that Pole possessed this work; it does not suggest that he wrote it. In 1569, however, a group of English exiles living at Louvain would have had good reason to emphasise the connection between a text so unquestionably orthodox, and the 'blessed Memorie' of their departed country-man. It was not so many years since Pole had seemed to certain of his continental co-religionists to be a kind of heretical fifth columnist;[4] and a suspicion of this kind had only recently been revived at Rome, during the trial of Carnesecchi. Hence national pride might very well have dictated the publication of this impeccable material 'Founde emong' Pole's writings. Moreover, the work was clearly intended for circulation among English Catholics, for whom the memory of Pole constituted an important element in the growing recusant tradition.[5] On balance, therefore,

doctoral dissertation for the University of Paris (Paris, 1957), p. 364, n. 53. Fischer rejects the attribution of the *Treatie* to Pole, although not all his reasons are convincing. I find it difficult to agree with Fischer's view that Pole left the Council for no other reason than ill-health, and that his ideas on justification were not basically different from those which underlay the Council's teaching (ibid. pp. 268–70).

[1] *Treatie*, p. 8a.
[2] Ibid. p. 17a.
[3] Fischer, 'Essai historique', p. 364, n. 53, was the first to notice this point, and to note, in addition, that 'le nom de l'editeur est passé sous silence' – an omission which he rightly regards as suspicious in itself. It is perhaps worth noting that a contemporary hand on the title page of the copy in the Cambridge University Library ascribes the translation to Thomas, Lord Copley.
[4] Below, pp. 220ff.
[5] This, presumably, is Fischer's meaning when he writes: 'Il nous semble plutôt qu'on sit voulou sous le couvert de Pole, faciliter l'entrée en Angleterre des Canons de Trente.' ('Essai historique', p. 364, n. 3.)

it does not seem that the *Treatie of Iustification* is of direct help in elucidating Pole's ideas.

Turning to the remaining evidence, however, it is possible to detect certain positive indications that Pole altered his ideas on justification, so as to bring them into line with the decision of the Council. It has already been suggested that, as early as 1547, he had shown a distinct tendency (in his commentary on the September draft) to modify his objections to the statement issued by the Council. But this tendency had not been strong enough to reconcile him to the publication of the text, and he deliberately withheld his signature from the printed version for at least three years after the suspension of the Council. Whether he considered the publication of the Council's judgement to be merely premature, since it would inevitably end all chance of reconciliation with the Lutherans, or whether he remained opposed in principle to the doctrine which had been defined at Trent, must remain a matter of conjecture. If, however, the truth lies in the latter circumstance, his objections were impermanent, and by 1554 he had adopted the Tridentine doctrine of salvation.

This much is apparent from a letter which he wrote in that year to the Cardinal of Augsburg, defending himself against certain charges which were being levelled at him by Italian Protestants in Switzerland.[1] Among other things, he was accused of having known the 'true Gospel', particularly with regard to justification, but of deliberately suppressing its advance in Italy.[2] In reply to this charge, Pole acknowledged that he had at one time adhered to the doctrine of salvation by faith alone ('nos fide, sine operibus justificari'); but, he maintained, he had acquired the belief directly from St Paul, and had interpreted the text in accordance with the Church's teaching ('ab apostolo Paulo accepisse, Interprete Ecclesia'); never had he presumed, in the Protestant manner, to interpret the text according to his own private judgement. Nonetheless, he had not fully understood the problem

---

[1] *Epistolae*, IV, 150–8.

[2] 'me Evangelicam nosse veritatem, praesertim quod ad justificationem attinet, sed magna cura, ac studio prohibuisse, quominus illa apud Italos divulgaretur'. (Ibid. p. 152.) This is unmistakably a reference to Pole's conduct in the years before the Council, and particularly to his policy at Viterbo.

until he had studied the epistle of St James in the same light of the Church's teaching. There he had learned, what the Church had never doubted, that man was justified by works ('nos ex operibus justificari').[1]

It is important to remember that this is the language of the Counter Reformation, employed to describe a situation which had been radically altered by the Council of Trent. As such, it is a tacit acknowledgement of the change wrought in Pole's beliefs by the decision of the Council. He could not, in these years, easily acknowledge that he had ever adhered to an heretical opinion; he knew that he had never intended to be anything but orthodox. The fact that the opinion in question had been officially declared heretical only in the years 1546–7, must not be allowed to obscure a proper appreciation of the difficulty which confronted Pole. He had to defend himself against the charge of heresy; or to be exact, against the charge of having privately adhered to an opinion which he now regarded as heretical. He spoke of his former attitudes in the light of a recently acquired conviction, which inevitably altered the perspective of his earlier experience. It would not be proper to assume that because he spoke in a manner which he could not have adopted ten years earlier, that he was necessarily acting hypocritically. He had simply submitted to the judgement of the Church, in accordance with a principle which had been continuously present in his conception of the Christian life.

Thus the phrase 'Apostolo Paulo...Interprete Ecclesia' must be understood as referring to the *intention* with which Pole had read the epistles of St Paul in the years before the Council: an intention manifestly orthodox. The fact that his interpretation of St Paul had been considered by the Council to be heretical was, on the other hand, distinctly embarrassing, and even dangerous, as he was soon to learn.

The Council of Trent, then, had turned Pole's attention to the epistle of St James; an epistle which, with its emphasis upon the role of works, had appeared to Luther as entirely worthless. It is noteworthy that Pole attributed his change of view, not to the

[1] Ibid., p. 152.

intervention of the Council, but to a simple reading of the Scriptures in the light of the Church's teaching. Evidently he remained unwilling to acknowledge the distress which he had experienced at the Council; it was, no doubt, a painful and humiliating memory. His reluctance to do so, however, involved him in a consequent evasiveness, which in turn contributed to the distrust which he aroused among the more vigilant and suspicious members of his own communion; while at the same time it confirmed him in the odium of those Protestants who vilified him as a renegade.[1]

In writing to the Cardinal of Augsburg, therefore, Pole had recourse to the epistle of St James. He did so in order to defend a point of view which he had in reality adopted as the result of a profounder and more unsettling experience than he was willing to acknowledge. His choice of text is highly significant, for it was an inevitable set-piece of the Counter Reformation.[2] In that epistle, remarked Pole, the apostle James adverted to the story of Abraham in order to illustrate that man was justified by works.[3] St Paul, however, had used the same text to demonstrate that salvation was by faith alone.[4] Hence, the Protestants, observed Pole, concentrated on the Pauline text exclusively, whereas the Church combined both texts in her teaching. Thus the Protestants separated what the Church considered jointly; they thereby separated themselves from the Church, and disturbed it with that doctrine [of justification] which was revealed in order to

[1] Below, pp. 220ff.

[2] Cf., for example, chapter X of the *Treatie of Iustification* (pp. 60a–62b), 'That there is no contrarietie betwene S. Paule and S. Iames, concerning the doctrine of Iustification, and howe they are to be understood.' The similarity of this exercise to the argument of Pole in the above letter cannot be taken as proof that the *Treatie* was written by Pole; the argument, after all, was essential to any informed discussion of what the Reformation was about.

[3] James 2.21–5: 'But wylte thou understande (thou vayne man) that fayth wythout dedes is deade? Was not Abraham oure father iustifyed thorowe worckes, when he had offered Isahac his sonne upon the aulter? Thou seeste, how that fayth wroughte wyth his dedes, as through the dedes was the fayth made perfecte: and the scripture was fulfylled, which sayeth: Abraham beleved God, and it was reputed unto hym for righteousness, and he was called the frend of God. Ye se then howe that of deades a man is iustifyed, and not of fayth onelye.' (Rouen Bible, 1566.)

[4] Romans 4.1–25.

establish concord between God and man. For his own part, Pole had learned to understand the two texts equally, following the guidance of the Church.[1]

Having thus defined the nature of his belief, and the process of development which it had undergone, Pole turned to the other charge which had been laid against him: that he had deliberately suppressed the doctrine of justification *ex sola fide*, in the years before the Council. Certainly, he observed, there had been many people in the principal Italian cities of that time who had intemperately misinterpreted the Pauline texts. He could not say, however ('tamen illud dicere non possum') that he had been responsible, as his accuser argued, for sending messengers or letters to these cities, urging greater moderation, or a temporary concealment of these views ('aut eam ad tempus occultarent').

The most he would acknowledge was that he had occasionally cut short the speculations of those who, meeting in little groups and circles, had sought to penetrate the mysteries and doctrines of religion and especially the doctrine of justification. He had urged them to refrain from despicable and intemperate discussions, reminding them that it was not their calling to pronounce upon or preach the Gospel.[2]

It is true, as we have seen, that Pole had exercised restraint upon his own circle of immediate friends: Priuli, Flaminio and Vittoria Colonna. He was convinced that the time for public utterance had not yet arrived. Meanwhile, in the privacy of the Viterbo circle, he had espoused an approach to the doctrine of justification which, supporting as it did a broad range of interpretation, had served as a temporary formula, until the Council should decide the issue finally. The formula 'fides quae per caritatem operatur' had enabled him to offer a satisfactory middle view. It had served to indicate the practical necessity of works, while not obscuring the essential role of faith. It was neither Pelagian nor Lutheran in inspiration. The interpretation which Pole had given to it in his heart of hearts was virtually indistinguishable from the belief of Luther; as a pastoral device, however, it had as he now observed,

---

[1] *Epistolae*, IV, 152.   [2] Ibid.

proved acceptable and had helped to eliminate contentious bickering, for the interim.[1]

The doctrine which Pole had recommended at Viterbo had indeed been that of 'fides...quae per dilectionem operatur'.[2] But he had understood it in a sense quite different from that which he now gave to it. For now, in 1554, Pole interpreted the formula in a manner which was in all respects compatible with the decision of the Council. Man was justified in the performance of good works; his faith was thereby made complete ('Nos ex operibus justificari, fidemque ex eis consummari'). Salvation, therefore, was achieved by faith and good works. Yet earlier in the same letter, Pole had admitted to having once believed in the doctrine of salvation by faith alone; and it was not so many years since he had begun his 'Note on justification' with the remark: 'Nunquam vere dici potest, hominem coram Deo iustificari ex operibus.'[3]

The Catholic doctrine of salvation had been established and defined at Trent. Seven years afterwards, Pole, accepting the doctrine there enunciated, looked back on his earlier life in the light of that decision. He remembered his former attitudes as incomplete, but not erroneous; and he thereby confused intent with actuality.

The selectivity with which his memory worked is, perhaps, further illustrated by his remarks, in the same letter, on the attitude assumed by the Council towards the Protestants. He recalled his own efforts to persuade the Council that it should adopt a kindly tone towards the Protestants, and that it should regard them not as 'rebels' but as 'rebellious sons' ('non eos nobis tales videre oportere, rebelles quidem, sed filios rebelles').[4] This approach he noted, had been shared by others who were then his colleagues; and the judgement of the Council had been framed in accordance with that view.[5]

It is perfectly true that the Conciliar decrees refrained from personal recriminations. The originators of the views condemned at Trent were not specifically singled out by name. But Pole had

[1] *Epistolae*, IV, 152.   [2] Or alternatively, 'quae per caritatem operatur'.
[3] Above, n. 1, p. 189.   [4] *Epistolae*, IV, 157.   [5] Ibid.

sought for much more at the time; he had been driven into near-despair by the Council's whole approach to the doctrine of salvation, and had especially deplored its neglect of Protestant theology. All this seems now to have been forgotten; there is, apparently, no recollection of the defeat experienced at the Council by the *spirituali*. Admittedly, it was not strictly incumbent on him to recall all this in the present circumstances; his purpose was merely to rebut the charge that he had been guilty of intemperate abuse about the Protestants.[1] Nevertheless, it is evident how much his basic attitudes had altered.

By 1554 the doctrinal lines had been drawn for seven years; and it is plain that Pole, despite his initial aversion to the Council's doctrine of salvation, had accepted it as binding, and had reconciled himself to its official promulgation. At first, as we have seen, he had refused to associate himself with the publication of the Conciliar decrees. He may still have hoped, as late as 1549, that a papal decision would revoke the Council's judgement. On the other hand, he may simply have felt that an official publication was still premature, and that it was advisable to delay the impact of the Council's final, uncompromising stand. It is even possible that he hoped for a future revision, by the Council itself, of the decree on justification. The Council, after all, had only been suspended; future sessions might provide the opportunity he hoped for. By 1554, however, the Council had once more assembled and had once more been suspended: but not before it had become apparent to all observers that the last hopes of reconciliation between Protestants and Catholics had disappeared.[2]

Further evidence confirms the supposition that a fundamental change was wrought in Pole's ideas during the years which followed the first sessions of the Council. Certain dialogues which he wrote for his own use, and for circulation among his friends reveal the transformation of his views on justification. Of these, a treatise entitled *De Reformatione Ecclesiae* is the most informative.

[1] *Epistolae*, IV, pp. 156–7; cf. also, below, pp. 258ff.
[2] For the sessions of 1551–2, and the abortive attempt to maintain Protestant observers at the Council, cf. Jedin, *Geschichte des Konzils von Trient*, III (Freiburg im B., 1970), 219–399.

The text of this document was frequently rewritten and revised, so that it exists in a number of alternative versions.[1]

The first draft was almost certainly composed before 1545. There is no suggestion in the text that the General Council has been summoned; there is, on the other hand, a reference to those 'who consider that a general council is necessary at the present time'.[2] The second version contains a number of passages which are scored through, and occasionally, rewritten in the margin. One such passage deals with the desirability and purpose of good works. It stresses the 'peace and consolation' which may be acquired in the performance of good works. All human action of this kind is directed to the attainment of interior peace ('quo omnis labor dirigi debeat, id est quies nostra').[3] It is noticeable that no other effective value is attributed to the execution of good works: they are not spoken of as meritorious, or deserving of heavenly reward.

Yet this passage is marked out, apparently for revision, and the rewritten version (at the base of the folio) has a significantly different emphasis.[4]

Good works are not considered to be void or useless in the sight of God. The statement is repeated a few sentences later, in the same marginal revision: good works yield a return of inner peace, not only in the future, but during man's own lifetime ('nobis mercedem quietis et consolationem, nondum futuram...'). The phrase 'fides quae per dilectionem operatur' recurs too, in this passage: but Pole now interprets it in a sense which admits the meritorious value of good works performed in grace. Thus it is not unreasonable to assume that the alterations here recorded

[1] Vat. Lat. 5964, vols. I and II, also Vat. Lat. 5969, fols. 174r–290v; a further copy exists in the Biblioteca Nationale, Naples, Cod. IX A 14. Fischer, ('Essai historique', App. 2, pp. 10–12) classifies the variant texts in the Vatican collection. The latter, with the exception of Vat. Lat. 5969, are on microfilm at the Bodleian (Bodleian MS Film 30).

[2] Vat. Lat. 5964, I (Bodleian MS Film 30) fol. 2r; cf. also ibid. fols. 52r and 135r. Fischer ('Essai historique', p. 291) also considers that the document was first composed at some date before the Council met.

[3] Ibid. fols. 68v–69r.

[4] 'Intelligamus et sciamus laborem nostrum non inaniturum Domino, sed pro eo requiem et mercedem copiosam in celis nobis habet [?] repositam.' (Ibid. fol. 68v.)

were inserted after the Council's doctrine of salvation had been finally determined. There can be no doubt, from what we know already, that the unrevised version reflects the views which Pole adhered to in the days before the Council; while his letter to the Cardinal of Augsburg propounds a view which is in every respect identical with that set forth in the marginal revisions.[1]

Finally, Pole's English papers, which date from the period of his return to England, contain a number of sermons which are peripherally interesting in relation to the question at issue.[2] In the last of these sermons, he preached of the necessity for works.[3] It would be unreasonable to expect too much from a source of this kind; his purpose was entirely pastoral, and he was not engaged in any theological exercise of high refinement. He sought merely to persuade the people that they must diligently work on God's behalf, and eschew the doctrine of salvation by faith alone: 'And this cann nott be settled wyth knowledge alone, where to settle them [i.e. faith, hope and love], butt they must be ioyned wyth works, which be requyred orneuer the constience can be settled by faith. Butt of faith begyneth the furst settling'.[4]

Works, therefore, completed faith, and the two combined to gain man his salvation. Pole's case was amply buttressed with quotations from the epistle of St James, so that people might

see how necessarie the doctrine of workes must be ioyned wyth the doctrine of faith, and wythall see, to hym that shall receiue frute by the celestiall vocation and doctrine, how necessarie it is thatt he worke, which can nott be frutefullie done afore he be well instructed, nott onlie of the kynde off works that must be ioyned wyth the faith or rather to procede of the zeale off faith, to receiue the frute off bothe, butt also of the meanes how to worke.[5]

The 'meanes' were those recommended by the Church. Those

---

[1] The same development may be noticed in another treatise of Pole's, entitled *De Prudentia et Sapientia Humana*, where the following occurs, in a passage marked, apparently, for deletion: 'Ipsa nunc Dei imago per opera eam quaerentibus, est quasi lapis in uia, ad quem offendentes cadunt, pii uero non querentes operibus, sed fide eam inveniunt.' (Vat. Lat. 5964, fol. 430r.) The words are strikingly reminiscent of the advice given by Pole to Vittoria Colonna. (Above, p. 96.)

[2] Vat. Lat. 5968, fols. 379r–482v (Bodleian MS Film 33).
[3] Ibid. fols. 447r–482v.   [4] Ibid. fol. 447v.
[5] Ibid. fol. 448r.

who would 'bryng furte by their workes ony blessed fructe acceptable to god' must perform them in the framework of the visible Church, 'under the spirituall obedience off his curate, in hys own vocation.'[1]

The tenor of these remarks is obvious enough. Taken in conjunction with the foregoing evidence, it can scarcely be doubted that Pole, by the time of his return to England (and perhaps even earlier), had overcome his objections to the doctrine of justification which had been defined at Trent. This does not mean that he was capable of expressing the doctrine with the same precision which the Council had displayed. On the eve of his return to England he was requested by Pope Julius III to compose something for publication on the theme of justification. He did so; but the outcome was considered to be unduly 'brief in certain matters, and even confused'. It was not deemed suitable for publication.[2] This is hardly surprising: it was one thing to accept the decree out of obedience; but to eliminate the 'confusion' which awaited those of the *spirituali* who survived into the 1550s was beyond human contrivance. Events, as we shall see, only conspired to deepen their confusion.

[1] Vat. Lat. 5968, fol. 457v.
[2] J. I. Tellechea Idigoras, 'Una denuncia de los Cardenales Contarini, Pole y Morone por el Cardenal Francisco Mendoza (1560)', *Revista Española de Teologia*, XXVII (1967), 33–51.

CHAPTER THIRTEEN

The Tridentine decree
and the
end of the Viterbo circle

To the members of Pole's circle, the Conciliar debate on justification and its final outcome appeared as little other than disastrous. Two members of the group, Priuli and Flaminio, had declined from the outset to have any official connection with the Council. Unlike Pole, they had, perhaps, a realistic appreciation of its likely outcome.

Early in 1546 the post of secretary to the Council was offered to Flaminio. He replied with a graceful but uncooperative elegy. The post was then offered to Priuli, who refused it with less accomplishment but equal firmness.[1] Both men were in good standing with the papal secretary, Farnese, so that they could turn down the offer without incurring his disfavour. But they were vehemently distrusted in other quarters, as advocates of the modern heresy which had caused the Church so much disquiet. On 11 March 1546, the troublesome Zanettini wrote from Venice to Cardinal Farnese. He complained rabidly of Pole, of his 'moderna et insana dottrina', and of his two 'favourites', only one of whom, however – Flaminio – he cared to mention by name. The other he preferred to leave anonymous, 'per bon rispetto', and for the time being.[2] It has been conjectured with some probability, that the second of these 'favourites' was Priuli,

---

[1] C.T., x, 290, 322, 374; cf. also E. Costa, 'Marc Antonio Flaminio e il cardinale Alessandro Farnese', in Giornale Storico della Letteratura Italiana, x (Turin, 1887), 384–7. The post was finally given to Massarelli (Jedin, Council, II, 79–80).

[2] 'Circa il cardinal Polo già io scrissi che la oration predita è sua farina et tanto più che tien apresso di sé doi favoriti di quella mala semenza del episcopo morto di Verona [Giberti] già notati di questa moderna et insana dottrina, l'un chiamato Flaminio, l'altro non scrivo per bon rispetto; havisarò poi al tempo et loco.' Cited by A. Stella, 'Guido da Fano, eretico del XVI secolo, al servizio dei re

who, belonging as he did to the Venetian patriciate, could not be denounced without losing the goodwill of the Venetian government.[1]

Thus both Priuli and Flaminio were known for their support of quasi-heretical opinions. It is hardly to be expected, then, that they would react enthusiastically to the Council's treatment of the 'moderna et insana dottrina' which they upheld.

Flaminio in particular, as part-author of the *Beneficio di Cristo*, must have been profoundly disturbed by the Council's declaration; nor is there any evidence that he was immediately inclined to exchange his own views for those embodied in the decree.[2] A year after the decree had been accepted, Flaminio still held to a view of human nature which was utterly at odds with Tridentine doctrine. Considered in itself, he believed, human nature was unrelievedly corrupt ('una uilissima massa di peccato'); anything that was worthy in mankind came from the Spirit of Christ who purified His elect by means of a lively faith ('il quale purga, et rigenera mediante la uiua fede in suoi eletti').[3]

This is very much the language of the *Beneficio di Cristo*. But Flaminio remained firm in his attachment to the Church of Rome. In the same letter he warned against the self-deceptions which could so easily occur under the guise of zeal. The principal of these, he considered, was that which lay in wait for those who took it upon themselves to proclaim the gospel, without having been appointed to the task. He himself had no time for the sort of people who, however ignorant, set themselves up as theologians, and bitterly inveighed against the theologians and preachers of the Church.[4]

d'Inghilterra', in *Rivista di Storia della Chiesa in Italia*, XIII (Rome, 1959), 196–238, p. 210.
    [1] Ibid.
    [2] Prosperi, *Tra Evangelismo*, p. xvii, n. 12, suggests that Flaminio may have published an anonymous attack on the Tridentine decree.
    [3] Letter from Flaminio to ?, Rome, 31 December 1547, in D. Atanagi (ed.), *De le lettere di tredici uomini illustri* (Rome, 1554), pp. 318–23. The context indicates that Flaminio's correspondent was a lady. Maddison mistakenly ascribes the letter to 10 February 1547 (*Marcantonio Flaminio*, pp. 174–5). The letter may have been written to Giulia Gonzaga.
    [4] Atanagi, *De le lettere*, p. 321.

It is interesting to notice that Flaminio employed almost the exact terms which Pole adopted in writing about the same problem to the Cardinal of Augsburg; and his remarks recall too, the warning which he had addressed to Carnesecchi five years earlier. There can be no doubt that Flaminio, from the time of his sojourn at Viterbo, had taken Pole's advice to heart: those who preached the Gospel must be first commissioned by the Church. It is quite clear too, that by the Church, he understood the Church of Rome: for, as he continued, the Church was hierarchically ordered, like a court, and was best served when everyone performed his duty, not usurping the functions of another.[1]

Thus Flaminio, while remaining orthodox in his attachments may yet have decided to neglect the Council's teaching on justification and to avail himself of the fact that the decree had not yet been ratified by the Pope. On the other hand, the passing of time, and the influence of established belief, may have exercised a gradual effect on him: for in another, and perhaps later letter, he expressed the opinion that diligence in striving for the image and likeness of God could reproduce, in a man's life, something of the goodness and purity of God.[2] Certainly this was a view which seemed to invest human action with a positive supernatural value. As such, it is significantly different from the approach adopted in the *Beneficio di Cristo*, and from the concept of the 'elect' to which Flaminio remained attached as late as 1547.

Finally, one of Flaminio's later poems reveals, according to his most recent biographer, certain signs of a spiritual realignment. Professor Maddison observes that the seventeenth lyric of the *Carmina Sacra* 'tells of his conversion or possibly reconversion from something bordering on Lutheran heresy to orthodox Catholicism'.[3] The trouble is, that it is impossible to be certain about the period to which the poem refers, since it specifies nothing more precise than 'olim aberrans a grege...' There is

[1] Ibid.
[2] Ibid. p. 353, letter to Ulisse Bassiano, s.a.
[3] Maddison, *Marcantonio Flaminio*, p. 190. The poem in question is entitled 'Gratias agit Christo cuius beneficio e maximis periculis sit ereptus, e ad un viam salutis reuocatus.' In the edition which I have used, it is number 19 among the *Carmina* (*De Rebus Divinis Carmina*, Paris, 1550, p. 24).

every reason to suppose that Flaminio was referring to the occasion of his visit to Pole's household at Viterbo. Hence the poem is of little value in helping to elucidate Flaminio's attitude to the Conciliar decree.

On 17 February 1550, Flaminio died at Pole's household in Rome.[1] Cardinal Carafa, hearing of Flaminio's condition, and anxious to be present at his last moments, hurried to Pole's residence; on his arrival he concealed himself, and heard Flaminio recite the creed, and profess his faith in the Church of Rome ('se cum Orthodoxa Romana Ecclesia omnino sentire'). Not content with this, he whispered in the ear of the presiding priest, urging him to require of Flaminio that he make a declaration of his belief concerning the eucharist; to which proposal Flaminio replied with a profession of faith in the doctrine of transubstantiation. Overcome with joy, Carafa emerged into Flaminio's line of sight, and sitting down beside him, conversed with him easily in his last moments. Flaminio, having confessed his sins, and then received the eucharist while Carafa stood by and assisted, died peacefully, in communion with the Church.

Maddison remarks that this account of Flaminio's death 'is taken by those who are anxious to prove that Flaminio was an orthodox Catholic as an indication that he had recanted'; 'but', she adds, 'the creed is accepted by all the major Protestant Churches and Flaminio was always orthodox about transubstantiation'. Thus, she maintains, it was on the doctrine of justification that Flaminio should have been examined.[2]

Nevertheless, it is perhaps worth noticing that Flaminio is supposed to have expressed himself as *altogether* ('omnino') in accordance with the Church of Rome: and it seems at least possible that he considered the Tridentine doctrine of justification to form part of that allegiance. Moreover, there is surely matter for reflection in the fact that Carafa did not, apparently, examine Flaminio's belief about this doctrine. Flaminio had been (at one time anyway) notoriously suspect on the issue in question, and

[1] The following account of Flaminio's death is taken from A. Caracciolo, *Vita Pauli IV* (Cologne, 1612), pp. 54–5.
[2] *Marcantonio Flaminio*, p. 202, n. 44.

his opinions had been well known to those who held authority: nor was it, indeed, a doctrine about which Carafa was insensitive. Could it be that Carafa had already found Flaminio's opinions on the question to be orthodox? Certainly the evidence suggests that his relations with Flaminio were much improved during these years: Flaminio, after a severe illness during which Carafa had prayed for him, even composed a poem in Carafa's praise.[1] Despite such conjectures, however, Maddison is undoubtedly correct to leave the matter open. The state of evidence does not permit a firm conclusion about Flaminio's reaction to the Conciliar decree. It remains, therefore, a matter of opinion. Some will perhaps agree that the balance remains slightly tilted in favour of the view that Flaminio ultimately accepted the Council's declaration; others, doubtless, will prefer uncertainty.

As for the other members of Pole's circle, it seems likely that, with varying degrees of unhappiness, they followed him in accepting the decision of the Council. In the case of Priuli, as of Vittoria Colonna, the role played by Morone was considerable. At the outset, they both reacted to the developments at Trent with an anxiety similar to that which Pole had felt. Vittoria Colonna, indeed, on learning of Pole's departure from the Council, expressed the deepest satisfaction: God, she felt, had ordained things in a manner just short of miraculous, in detaching Pole from so disturbing a condition of affairs.[2]

Five months later, however, she had altered her opinion. In a letter to Morone, written during the period of her final illness, she expressed both hope and confidence that Priuli would be induced to accept the Council's judgement on the matter.[3] Her letter makes it plain that Morone had played a large part in her own change of attitude, and that he had undertaken to assist Priuli, who appears to have been suffering from a breakdown. This letter, indeed, sheds considerable light on the reaction of Pole's circle to events at the Council; but it is couched in such deliberately guarded terms that it calls for a measure of close interpretation.

---

[1] Caracciolo, *Vita Pauli IV*, pp. 52–4.
[2] 'Processo', p. 549. [3] *Carteggio*, pp. 312–14.

Vittoria Colonna began by thanking Morone for the letter which he had written to Priuli. The latter, she wrote, had returned to Rome in poorer health than she might have hoped. As Morone remarked, he was suffering from 'too much satisfaction.' It would be well if Morone were to invite him for a year to Bologna: the change would enable him to recover some badly needed weight, and would restore his spirits.[1]

It is not entirely frivolous to enquire whether the word 'health' may not here be used to indicate a state of spiritual, rather than physical breakdown. There is talk, certainly, of 'gaining weight'; but, more significant perhaps, is the reference to the recovery in spirits which Priuli might experience at Bologna. He is to become 'più vivo che non pare'.[2] As recently as October (little over a month, that is, before Vittoria Colonna's letter), Priuli's health had been sufficiently in trim to permit of a journey between Padua and Trent on Pole's behalf.[3] On the other hand, events at the Council must unquestionably have thrown him into a condition of despondency. It is not unreasonable to assume that for Priuli, as for Pole, the Council was the occasion of a spiritual crisis. Hence it seems possible that these references to his health are in reality a subterfuge for remarks about his spiritual condition.

It may be thought unreasonable to hunt for obscure meanings in what seems to be a simple enough statement: Priuli was not feeling well. But the necessity to read between the lines arises from one remarkable and arresting statement: 'too much satisfaction is consuming him' ('la troppo satisfactione lo vada consummando'). It can hardly be supposed that Priuli was in any sense 'satisfied' with what was happening at Trent. What meaning, then, has this particular construction?

The text makes it apparent that the expression had originated with Morone. The fact that it was taken up by Vittoria Colonna, and referred to as in some way apposite, indicates that she considered the phrase exactly adequate for what it was intended to convey. It is significant, therefore, that the word 'satisfaction' will support a secondary meaning; and one that in the theological

---

[1] *Carteggio*, pp. 312–14.
[2] Ibid.
[3] Below, p. 218.

climate of the moment, was distinctly apposite. The concept of 'satisfaction', indeed, lay at the heart of the doctrinal quarrel about salvation.

The doctrine of satisfaction was inseparable from the doctrine of good works. If the latter were considered to be meritorious, then mankind could indeed offer an effective satisfaction for sin and contribute thereby to salvation. This, of course, had been the view upheld at Trent. The Council, indeed, had affirmed that man could not only participate in, but appropriate Christ's merits, so that human endeavour was endowed, in its teaching, with redemptive value.

Viewed in this light, Morone's phrase is charged with an inner meaning which illuminates the nature of Priuli's malady. The words 'too much satisfaction is consuming him' can be understood to mean nothing less than that Priuli was suffering from acute distress at the proceedings of the Council. There can be no doubt that he had experienced a nervous breakdown. But there was more to it than that.

Exactly how serious the problem was, may perhaps be inferred from Vittoria Colonna's remark, categorical in its assurance, that he was 'not well': and that his 'illness' ran contrary to the hopes which she had entertained ('non è tornato lì sano come io vorrei'). This conveys the impression that Priuli's crisis may have taken a form which represented a threat to his continued orthodoxy: an interpretation supported by the tone of the passage immediately following, which once again suggests a measured and deliberate attempt to speak in paradox and riddle. It would be unwise, she considered, to 'experiment' too much: Priuli should be allowed to advance little by little to the position which Morone occupied, so that he would be obliged to reason 'in the pelagian way'; then, perhaps, he would enjoy a 'a healthier countenance and a more pious disposition'.[1]

The 'position which Morone occupied' was one of simple acquiescence in the doctrine of justification put forward at the Council. Only recently, however, had he come to hold these

[1] *Carteggio*, p. 313.

views. Formerly, his opinions had been close to those of Pole and Contarini. At the time of the Regensburg agreement, he had accepted the compromise arrangement with an easy mind. Afterwards, he had been profoundly impressed with the *Beneficio di Cristo*. It was only at the time of the Council, as he later explained, that he had come to recognise the doctrine which it promulgated as the true and definitive teaching of the Church.[1]

It was this same process of submission to the Council's judgement which Vittoria Colonna wished to foster in Priuli. He was to be assisted gradually to accept the doctrine that good works contributed in an essential (and meritorious) manner to salvation. Hence her use of the revealing word 'pellagianamente'. To the *spirituali* the doctrine of good works had seemed equivalent, almost, to Pelagianism. Yet now it was apparent that the doctrine was about to be defined as orthodox: both faith and works, grace and human effort, were to be regarded as essential to salvation.

Priuli, apparently, was a long way from accepting this. He seems indeed, to have been more adversely affected by the proceedings of the Council than even Pole had been. Of all the *spirituali* in Pole's circle he was clearly most in danger of abandoning the Church. Such, at least, would seem to be the implication of Vittoria Colonna's observation that he stood in need of a more pious disposition ('più piatosa anima'). Thus his state of mind bore a certain resemblance to that of Flaminio on his arrival, six years earlier, at Viterbo; and it is instructive that Vittoria Colonna recommended exactly the procedure which Pole had adopted at that time. There were to be no 'experiments', no violent harangues; Priuli must be led gently, just as Pole had spoken with Flaminio, 'pian piano'.

In the event, Priuli stayed within the Church. Beyond this, there is no evidence that he accepted the decision of the Council. But the fact that he retained his close friendship with Pole for the remainder of the latter's life, and that he never chose to live for any length of time outside Pole's circle, suggests perhaps, that he eventually reconciled himself to the situation which had been

[1] Cantù, *Eretici*, p. 178.

created by the Council. But again, as in the case of Flaminio, this remains a matter of conjecture, and can be offered as no more than probability.

There can be no doubt, however, that Vittoria Colonna had submitted to the Council's judgement, and that Morone had been the decisive influence in eliciting her consent to its proceedings. Never in her life, she wrote, had she been more in debt to anyone. She was full of appreciation for his persuasiveness 'in deigning to consider another name than that of Jesus'.[1]

The phrase 'si degna nominare altro che Iesu' clearly indicates the nature of Morone's influence. He had persuaded her that not 'Christ alone', in the sense understood by Luther, but Christ working through the efforts of the sinner himself, represented the process whereby salvation was attained. Thus he had convinced her of the possibility, and indeed the necessity, of a personal contribution to salvation.

This is the last letter of Vittoria Colonna to which a date can be assigned.[2] For two months now, she had been seriously ill.[3] In the middle of January 1547 she transferred from the convent of Sant' Anna to the Palazzo Cesarini, which stood nearby. There she made her will on 18 February, and died a week later, at the age of 57.[4]

With her death, the Viterbo circle came to an end.[5] There was nothing left for it to do. Most of its members passed into relative obscurity, for a time. But their memory had not been erased, and the events of the ensuing years combined to throw them once more into the foreground of attention. It is dramatically appropriate that the first hint of what was to emerge occurred at exactly the moment when the programme of the *spirituali* was suffering its last reversal. In the same year that the Council was engaged in clarifying the Catholic doctrine of salvation, Pietro

---

[1] *Carteggio*, pp. 313–14.   [2] Ibid. p. 314, n. 3.

[3] Cf. Pole's letter to her, 4 October 1546, in a postscript to which he expresses his concern at the news, which he has just received, that she is ill. (Ibid. pp. 309–312.)

[4] Ibid. p. 314, n. 1.

[5] Shortly afterwards, Pole retired from the Legation of the Patrimony. (Below, p. 219.)

Carnesecchi received his first summons to appear before the Roman Inquisition.[1] At Rome he was examined by Juan Alvarez de Toledo, the Cardinal de Burgos, who was Carafa's principal collaborator. Carnesecchi, however, enjoyed powerful friends. Pole intervened on his behalf with a letter to the Pope; the charge was dropped, and no more was heard about the matter for a time.[2] But this brief alarm signalled the gathering of forces which would in time endanger the security of all, however devout, who had been associated with the 'moderna et insana dottrina' proscribed at Trent. As Zanettini had inferred, the time and place were yet to be determined.

For the moment, however, it only seemed necessary that the *spirituali* should adjust gradually to the new situation which the Council had created. On 18 October 1546, Pole wrote to the Legates, thanking them for their courteous reception of his commentaries on the September draft. The pain in his arm, he informed them, had not quite left him, although he was no longer obliged to purge and dose himself ('Finito ch'io hebbi di purgarmi, & dozzarmi').[3] Five days later he received permission to return to Rome. He dispatched Priuli to Trent, to explain the nature of the papal dispensation which had finally relieved him of his troublesome office.[4] On 27 October he set out from Padua for Rome. Priuli arrived at Trent on the same day, and the official termination of Pole's office was formally noted by the Council's secretary, Massarelli.[5]

Travelling slowly along good roads, and in excellent weather, Pole arrived at Rome on 16 November, feeling considerably better for the journey.[6] Once there, he settled into a new life at the Curia.[7] Early in 1547, he was replaced as governor of

[1] R. Gibbings, *Report of the Trial and Martyrdom of Pietro Carnesecchi* (Dublin, 1856), pp. 12–19; 'Processo', pp. 554–6.

[2] Amabile, *Il santo officio della inquisizione*, p. 148, n. 1. The records of the Inquisition note that Pole supported Carnesecchi 'cum vocatus esset Romam responsurus de fide sub Paulo III' (Corviersi, 'Compendio', p. 284); Carnesecchi also enjoyed the support of Cosimo I who intervened on his behalf. (Ortolani, *Pietro Carnesecchi*, pp. 64–8.)

[3] *Epistolae*, IV, 201.   [4] Ibid. pp. 201–2, and *C.T.*, X, 701, n. 1.
[5] *C.T.*, I, p. 449.   [6] *Epistolae*, IV, pp. 202–3.
[7] Jedin, *Geschichte*, III, pp. 173, 186, 207.

Viterbo.[1] Thus he was free to spend his time in relative seclusion, slowly recovering his peace of mind.

But his seclusion was not allowed to remain absolute. The city was alive with rumour: speculation about his possible future ran hand in hand with murmurs about his mysterious past and his ambiguous connections. The Pope, now in his eighty-first year, was evidently close to death. Among the candidates for his succession Pole was obviously an important figure. A distinguished aristocrat, of high intelligence, and occupying a position of considerable prominence in the movement of reform, he seemed in the eyes of so many to possess the qualities which would be most needed to guide the Church into a condition of renewed authority. To others, however, he was irrevocably compromised by his associations, and his evident dissatisfaction with the Council. He had been friendly with Vermigli and Tremelli, who had since apostasised to Switzerland. He had surrounded himself with men who had been closely associated with the renegade Ochino; only lately, he had sheltered one of them against a charge of heresy. Worst of all, he was known to have held opinions which the Council had declared to be heretical. Were these the qualities which were to support the Church in its campaign against the spread of heresy?

On 19 July 1547 the Imperial ambassador, Diego de Mendoza, reported to the Emperor. He discussed Pole's suitability as a candidate for imperial favour in the event of the Pope's death. He considered that Pole was a person 'for whom it would be well to do something, for he has an upright conscience'; but was careful enough to add: 'unless this talk of "Justification" does him harm (and it is not of as small account as they say)'.[2]

Mendoza proved himself to be an astute and well-informed observer; when the Pope died, two years later, his reservations were verified. The ensuing decade witnessed multiple recriminations and reprisals against the *spirituali* and their figurehead, the Cardinal of England.

---

[1] His successor was Pietro Angelini, bishop of Sutri and Nepi. He was appointed on 31 March 1547. (Bib. Com. Viterbo, MS 331 II C VII 10 *Riforme* 43; fols. 39v–40r.) [2] *C.S.P.S.*, IX, 508–9, App.

CHAPTER FOURTEEN

Recriminations

In the years immediately following the first sessions of the Council of Trent the sufferings of the *spirituali* began. The innate opposition between Reformation and Counter Reformation could no longer fail to be observed. All the religious parties, henceforward, recognised themselves to be in simple confrontation; and the ambiguity which had marked the cause of the *spirituali*, even as it began to dissolve in the face of altered circumstance, became almost overnight the target of a concentrated and confident attack from opposed quarters.

Nowhere more than in Italy had confessional differentiations been more slowly recognised as final. Once the boundaries had been clearly indicated, it therefore became imperative for all the main contestants to persuade the fainthearted that there was neither neutral ground nor prospect of cessation in the conflict which had broken out. From Geneva, Calvin, since 1544, had inveighed against the 'delicate protonotaries' who concealed their Protestant sympathies beneath the guise of external Catholic conformity, and who appealed in self-defence to the example of Nicodemus, who came to Christ by night.[1] Calvin's concern was to invite them, if necessary through exile, into open profession of their allegiance. From Rome, Carafa and his supporters had long observed the circles of Italian *spirituali* with distrust bordering upon alarm: their covert attachment to erroneous

[1] Calvin's point was that Nicodemus thereafter emerged to bear uncompromising witness. *Excuse de Jehan Calvin a Messieurs les Nicodemites, sur la complaincte qu'ilz font de sa trop grand' rigueur* (Geneva, 1544), in *Three French Treatises*, ed. F. M. Higman (London, 1970), pp. 131–53. C. Ginzburg, *Il nicodemismo* (Turin, 1970), studies Nicodemism as a European phenomenon.

beliefs; their extension of patronage to crypto-Protestants; their evident discomfiture at the Council of Trent – all these things, he was determined, must now be singled out for diligent attention: the future of the Italian Church was too important to be left to wavering pastors. In 1549 he was installed as Archbishop of Naples,[1] the very centre in which the teaching of Valdés had taken shape. Although he deputed his activities to a vicar, the change was in a real sense symbolical. It marked the ascendancy in Italy of the drive which had begun in 1542, to ensure that the Catholic faith remained the religion of the Italian people.

Thus, among all religious parties, the call to doctrinal purity and candour was now paramount: those whom Calvin had addressed as Nicodemists were now called upon by Protestants to emerge and demonstrate their faith with clarity. From the Catholic side, they were required to demonstrate their resolute adherence to the teaching of the Church and of the General Council. Inevitably, in the course of all this, there were bound to be reproaches and recriminations, charges of treachery, hypocrisy, or clandestine subversion; and in 1548, the death of Francesco Spiera so dramatised the crisis that it became impossible to ignore it.

Spiera was a successful lawyer with a large family. He lived at Cittadella, near Padua. Converted to Protestantism, he persuaded his family to share his new beliefs, and finally began to preach in public. He attracted a certain following among the poor. He was brought to trial, and convicted as a heretic. Fearing that his children would be disinherited, he recanted in 1546; and thereafter fell into despair, convinced that he was damned for his betrayal of the truth. For two years he languished in a terrible depression; visitors came from Padua to comfort him in his affliction: among them was the bishop of Capo d'Istria, Pier Paolo Vergerio, a former disciple of Valdés, himself now under investigation by the Roman Inquisition. In 1548 Spiera died, still despairing of salvation. His example was publicised and exploited by Vergerio to discredit Nicodemism and to arm the conscience

---

[1] Amabile, *Il Santo Officio della Inquisizione in Napoli*, pp. 142–3.

of Italian Protestantism: Spiera, according to Vergerio, had finally discredited the policy of clandestine faith. Henceforward, Nicodemism became, in the propaganda war conducted by Vergerio, the supreme object of opprobrium. It did not disappear, but it was subjected to a newly intensified assault. Those who, rejecting the path of Lutheranism and exile chosen by Vergerio, clung silently to their equivocal beliefs, had now to suffer the ridicule of exiled Protestants, no less than the denunciations of the Catholic authorities.[1]

The spirit of militancy and suspicion was bound to affect the ecclesiastical *spirituali* who survived into the 1550s. The acrimony of disillusioned Protestants, whose hopes in these moderate prelates had been high, was directed against them throughout this decade with no less force than that of the *zelanti* in the Roman Inquisition, who still feared a secret adherence on their part to the doctrine of justification (and its implications) which had been condemned at Trent.

Increasingly, these animosities came to be turned upon the man who, more than anyone, represented the interests of the *spirituali* in the Curia. It was in these years that Pole's name became anathema to people who were otherwise at odds in the religious struggle. To the Italian Lutherans who gathered around Vergerio, Pole was the symbol of ultimate betrayal: the man who 'understood' the doctrine of salvation; who had promised (or seemed to have implied) its imminent recognition by the General Council; but who, when the time had come, had abandoned the truth in order to align himself with the cause of Rome. To Cardinal Carafa and his followers, Pole was no less an object of distrust: had he not adhered to the very doctrine which Vergerio upheld – did he not perhaps still do so?

Thus for Pole, and those who had been associated with him, these years took on the aspect of a rearguard action conducted against the simultaneous assaults of militant Lutheranism, and of

[1] Cantimori, *Eretici Italiani*, pp. 57–70; 'Nicodemismo e speranze conciliari nel Cinquecento italiano' translated in E. Cochrane (ed.), *The Late Italian Renaissance 1525–1630*, (London, 1970), pp. 244–65; and 'Italy and the Papacy'. Church, *The Italian Reformers*, contains an interesting study of Vergerio.

the *zelanti*. Yet in the case of Pole there is a further paradox which heightens the complexity of his situation, and lends a certain irony to the merely personal dilemma which he encountered. In the last years of his life, he became the agent of a persecution more notorious and extensive than that which he was himself obliged to endure. From 1554, until his death in 1558, he was entrusted with the supervision of the Counter Reformation in his native country. As Papal Legate, he held with Queen Mary the ultimate responsibility for the policy which brought some 285 people to their death, charged with the crime of heresy.[1] If, occasionally, he intervened to stay the hand of a too-zealous executioner, these incidents must not be taken as a sign that he had abandoned the general conviction of his age: that no state could permit within its territories more than one religion. They may suggest, perhaps, that he was uncertain about the operation of the principle;[2] but his acceptance of the principle itself indicates the limits which Christian humanists attached to the legitimate and public expression of religious opinion. These limits were not, perhaps, so narrow as the rules which guided the proceedings of the Roman Inquisition once Carafa had become Pope Paul IV.[3] They did not rest on the assumption that the private expression of heretical opinion was sufficient ground for imprisonment:[4] and for this reason they provoked the scandalised opposition of Pope Paul IV. But they were not so broad as to permit the spread of open heresy. With the publicly unregenerate, with men who strove to subvert the Commonweath through the propagation of heretical doctrines, Pole was ruthless in his dealings. They were the declared enemies of Christ, servants of Satan who, once all attempts to reconcile them had proved futile, must be prevented from corrupting others: they must pay the penalty with their lives.

The vehement aspect of Pole's temperament, indeed, is rarely more apparent than in his hostility to organised religious dissent;

[1] These figures are based on the estimate given in A. G. Dickens, *The English Reformation* (London, 1964), p. 266.

[2] Cf. Schenk, *Reginald Pole*, pp. 152–4.

[3] In 1555.

[4] Or, under Pius V, for death, as Carnesecchi's execution indicates.

and it is in striking contrast to the leniency which he displayed towards those who showed a willingness to reserve their opinions, or submit themselves, as Flaminio had done, to charitable and persuasive discourse. During his time in Italy, where heresy was more circumspect, he had revealed this element of his personality most clearly. In England his personal kindness faltered before the responsibilities of power. Clemency was not, it never had been, extended to the publicly unregenerate; and now the Commonwealth was threatened by sedition: were not the cobblers, weavers and tradesmen who met their deaths at Smithfield the declared enemies of Christ, intent on the disruption of the realm? He issued his injunctions: they must gently be exhorted to the truth; if they persisted in their errors, they must be handed over to the secular arm for punishment.[1]

Thus in the last years of his life Pole was subjected to the penalties which followed the extinction of the cause espoused by the *spirituali*, while at the same time he remained committed to the very machinery of coercion implanted in the structure of society and of the age, which their diffuse and generous aspirations had never seriously, or at a fundamental level, questioned. It is this paradox which forms the theme of his declining years and calls for a minute investigation: not only as illustrating the tensions, spiritual and circumstantial, which afflicted his complex personality, but as affording too, a partial glimpse of the uncertain twists and clashes through which the Catholic Church advanced towards a resolution of the challenge posed to its identity by the Reformation.

The following pages will be concerned with the difficulties experienced by Pole and his associates in the period of the newly militant Counter Reformation. They will examine these developments in relation to the apparent anomaly of his role in Marian England: a role which derived not from any attempt to compensate for his earlier opinions, but from the logic of an ecclesiastico-political position which he had never abandoned. The anomaly, therefore, is an historical illusion, induced by change of circum-

[1] D. Wilkins, *Concilia Magnae Britanniae et Hiberniae ab anno MDXLVI ad annum MDCCXVII*, 4 vols (London, 1737), IV, 173–4.

stance; but it serves to illustrate the historical limitations of the cause and policies adopted by the *spirituali*.

The first sign of trouble for Pole and his associates came in 1549, two years after the suspension of the Council. In the spring of that year, the Papal Nuncio at Venice, Giovanni della Casa, published an index of prohibited books. Among the works which he condemned was the *Beneficio di Cristo*. A few months later Vergerio, safely entrenched in the Grisons, launched a broadside against Casa's index.[1] During the course of his attack he made a veiled reference to Pole and his 'enlightened' policy of caution. A certain Cardinal, he claimed, was in possession of 'un dolce libro', a defence of the *Beneficio di Cristo*. This Cardinal had a reputation for enlightenment; he was said to realise the errors of the Church, and to savour the sweetness of the gospel; certainly, he was possessed of many excellent virtues: let him, therefore, now permit the publication of this 'good book', and defend it. Otherwise, his reputation would prove to have been false, and he would be seen to lack that spirit which so many had attributed to him.[2]

The Cardinal in question, continued Vergerio, was accustomed to remark on the necessity to be prudent, to await the right occasion and the opportune moment. These were wise counsels; but surely the occasion and the opportune moment had arrived? Thus it would be possible to observe how now the Cardinal was about to act: it was to be hoped that he would have the courage to declare himself, 'together with his whole school'. Certainly it would be time enough.[3]

Vergerio's impatience indicates the new refusal of Italian Lutherans to support the counsels once afforded by the *spirituali*. It demonstrates too, his recognition that there was no longer any place for mediation: the *spirituali* must declare themselves. Perhaps he was uncertain about the likely alignment of the Viterbo group; perhaps he merely sought revenge. In any case, he chose his tactics with deliberation, quietly alerting them to the dangers of their situation. He would not as yet denounce them openly; he would content himself with subtle allusions which, by their

[1] *Il catalogo de libri, li quali nuovamente...sono stati condannati* (s.l., 1549).
[2] *Il Catalogo*, p. g5v.   [3] Ibid. p. g6r.

very anonymity, would alarm the guardians of orthodoxy and underline the presence of an enemy within. Thus, if the Viterbo group should maintain the cause of Rome, they could be certain that their past would be employed judiciously against them. As it turned out, Vergerio had an exact measure of the situation.

In the same year in which Vergerio's pamphlet appeared, the Holy See fell vacant through the death of Paul III.[1] The ensuing conclave, in which the Cardinals met to elect his successor, lasted from November 1549 until February 1550; it was one of the longest in the history of the Church.[2] For the Italian Nicodemists, this occasion was fraught with a particular significance. If Pole were to be elected Pope, there was some hope that men like Carnesecchi could breathe freely; perhaps even, that the decree on justification might be reversed.[3] But if the hopes of *spirituali* and Nicodemists were fixed on Pole, others were equally determined that no one who had been tainted with the suspicion of heresy should ever be elected to the chair of Peter. Consequently, it was during the papal conclave of 1549–50 that Pole first became aware that he had made a public enemy in Carafa.

A papal election was also an important event in the rivalry between the French and Spanish. The Cardinals were divided first along national and political lines; and while some of them – notably Pole himself, Cervini and Carafa – were prompted by purely ecclesiastical motives, the majority voted in accordance with the interests of the Emperor or the King of France.[4] It was the extreme difficulty of reaching an agreement between the Imperial faction, headed by Farnese, and the French party headed by de Cupis (until the arrival, on 12 December, of an urgently-awaited contingent of four French Cardinals led by Guise), that prolonged the conclave in a deadlock for nearly three months.

1 On 10 November 1549. (*C.T.*, II, 4.)

2 Pastor provides a full account (*Popes*, XIII, pp. 1–44). Massarelli's contemporary account is published in *C.T.*, II, pp. 1–145.

3 There is no evidence that Pole had any such intention; the possibility may have presented itself to observers like Carnesecchi. ('Processo', p. 207.)

4 Pastor, *Popes*, XIII, 5–6 describes the formation of the parties, and makes the point that Cervini was well able to take account of political considerations, without, however, being dominated by them. Jedin, *Geschichte*, III, 219ff. provides a recent and authoritative survey of the conclave.

It is not the purpose of the following account to describe the manoeuvres which delayed a settlement. Nevertheless, it is essential to bear in mind the actual circumstances in which the charge of heresy was first publicly directed against Pole. Carafa spoke as an independent Churchman, intent on preserving the papacy from error; prelates like de Cupis, and later Guise, seized upon the charge as an effective means of excluding the Imperial candidate.

For most of the time Pole was the candidate favoured by the Imperial party. In the first days of the conclave, before the four French Cardinals arrived to redress the balance of the parties, he seemed almost certain to be elected.[1] His own attitude towards this prospect was astonishingly detached. Flaminio wrote that Pole would more willingly emerge from the conclave as a Cardinal, than as Pope: adding that no one would believe this, unless they knew him intimately.[2] Certainly, Pole betrayed no sign during these months that he was remotely interested in the prospect. He declined to engage in lobbying, convinced that he must do nothing to advance his cause, and that he must remain the passive servant of the Lord.[3] He told his supporters, when they sought to elect him by acclamation (before the French Cardinals arrived), that he would rather enter through the door than through the window;[4] and the incident reveals that he was content to let the matter rest in the hands of providence. It is possible, indeed, though by no means certain, that he entertained doubts about his capacity for the position.

On 29 November, nineteen days after the death of Paul III, the Cardinals entered into conclave.[5] Pole was accompanied by Priuli and two attendants.[6] Already the Imperial Cardinals had settled upon Pole as the candidate whom they would support. Thus, when the first ballot was held on 3 December, Pole secured twenty-one votes, and the Spanish Cardinal de Burgos, Juan Alvarez de Toledo – who was also an Imperial candidate – came

[1] Pastor, *Popes*, XIII, 12, n. 2.
[2] Atanagi, *De le lettere di tredici uomini illustri* (Rome, 1554), p. 357.
[3] *Epistolae*, IV, 53–65; also *C.T.*, II, 64, n. 1 and 70.
[4] *Epistolae*, IV, 63, and Pastor, *Popes*, XIII, 14, n. 4.
[5] *C.T.*, II, 4, 26–7.   [6] Ibid. pp. 125, 128.

next, with thirteen votes.[1] On the following day Pole's votes rose to twenty-four, only four short of the necessary two-thirds majority. The pro-French party took alarm. It seemed as if Pole must certainly be elected in the next ballot. The French ambassador, d'Urfé, informed the Cardinals that the four awaited Frenchmen were already at Corsica: if the electors would not delay for them, the French king would refuse to acknowledge the election. Prompted by this announcement, the Imperial Cardinals resolved upon a different tack: they would proclaim Pole as Pope, elevating him by homage. Accordingly, on the night of 4 December an advance deputation of two Cardinals was sent to Pole, only to be told that he rejected such a method of election.[2]

Nevertheless, the Imperial Cardinals entered the conclave next morning with firm hopes that Pole would be elected. A number of their colleagues had assured them during the night that, if Pole were to secure twenty-six votes, they would add their own votes in his favour, by way of accession. Thus, on the morning of 5 December, when the ballot had been counted and Pole's vote stood at twenty-three, excitement in the conclave was near breaking-point. Cardinal Carpi rose to add his vote for Pole; he was followed by Cardinal Farnese. Only one further vote was needed to ensure Pole's election. A heavy silence followed, interrupted by the dean's inquiry whether any more votes were to be cast. The silence continued. No further vote was forthcoming. Thus the meeting was adjourned, and the Cardinals departed with a considerable sense of anti-climax.[3] Pole had been within one vote of the papacy; henceforth his chances receded every day.

This much, however, was not immediately apparent, and Pole

[1] The Emperor's personal preference was for Toledo; should his fortunes not succeed, he would support Carpi, Pole, Morone or Sfondrato. The Imperial Cardinals, however, were not aware of the Emperor's wishes when the conclave opened; and as it turned out, Pole proved to be a more successful candidate than Toledo. (Pastor, *Popes*, XIII, 10.)

[2] *C.T.*, II, 42–3; Druffel, *Beiträge*, p. 311, n. 10; Pastor, *Popes*, XIII, 10–15. Pole at first admitted that the method of acclamation, or 'adoration', was in accordance with the law; but as the two Cardinals departed, he sent a messenger after them withdrawing his consent. It was on this occasion that he announced his preference for the door rather than the window (above, p. 227). Cf. his letter concerning these events, *Epistolae*, IV, 53–65.

[3] *C.T.*, II, 43–7.

continued to head the ballot for some time, even after the arrival on 12 December of the four French Cardinals under the leadership of Guise. But he was never to be as near the papacy again. Hence his failure invites consideration. It is impossible, of course, to ascertain the hidden cause or causes which withheld from him the single necessary vote. The diarist Massarelli records[1] that Pole's exclusion was attributed to 'various and diverse causes', among which he enumerates the fact that Pole was not Italian ('quia externus esset'); that he was too young; that he had little experience of business ('quia in rebus, quas ad rem publicam gerendam pertineant, parum versatus est'); and that as some people feared, he would be liable to wage a war against England. Of greater weight than any of these, however, according to Massarelli, was the suspicion that in matters of faith he was inclined towards novel and heretical opinions; particularly in the matter of justification. There was a feeling that he had not in every detail accepted the decree on justification which had been proclaimed in the Council of Trent.[2]

Massarelli concluded his account with the observation that no one suspected of heresy had ever occupied the chair of Peter. The remark suggests that he was rather shocked by what he had heard about Pole; and it may be that he was led too easily to suppose that herein lay the principal cause of Pole's exclusion.

Nevertheless, it was exactly this consideration which prompted Carafa to alert his colleagues to the danger which confronted them. As early as 2 December, when the order of business was still to be established, Carafa was overheard to say that 'he could name a day' when Pole would be obliged publicly to acknowledge his involvement with dubious or heretical opinions. The effect of this remark was to create a stir of excitement among the pro-French party, who began to confer busily among themselves. Toledo, as one of the leading Imperial candidates (also Carafa's chief collaborator on the Inquisition) took the opportunity of sending a messenger to Pole, urging him to exculpate himself from the charge of heresy. Pole, however, replied that he had no

[1] Ibid. p. 47. [2] Ibid.

intention of refuting such a calumny in public until he should know who his accuser was. If anyone should wish to present himself in that capacity Pole would so confute him, with the help of God, that he would regret his temerity in spreading rash accusations.[1] Privately, though, he gave such a good account of himself that he successfully countered the poor opinion which Toledo had of his beliefs, and seemed to have emerged happily from the affair.[2]

The morning's activity, however, continued to be delayed by excited discussions between Toledo and the pro-French Cardinals. Accordingly, Cervini and Morone urged the commencement of normal business, so that they might settle without further delay the form of election to be adopted.[3] Scarcely was the business concluded, however, when Carafa leapt to his feet and delivered an attack on Pole, accusing him of 'certain errors' in religion.[4] The whole college was thrown into confusion.[5] Pole alone, apparently, remained unperturbed. He replied easily, treating Carafa as a madman ('como a loco'), turning aside his arguments with a mixture of casual banter and dialectical skill ('now laughing, and now quoting holy scripture in his support'), defending his role at the Council of Trent, and generally acquitting himself so well that he thoroughly discredited Carafa.[6]

Thus the morning of 2 December concluded with a tactical triumph for Pole. But the matter was not permitted to rest there. Carafa's charges were too serious to be passed over and forgotten; and they were too useful to be neglected by the pro-French party. It was not simply that Pole had cherished certain heretical opinions: Carafa also maintained that he had harboured in his household at Viterbo a veritable 'platoon of heretics'.[7] Such accusations

---

[1] *C.T.*, II, p. 47, n. 2. [2] Ibid. [3] Ibid.
[4] Report of Mendoza to the Emperor, 5 December 1549 (Druffel, *Beiträge*, pp. 306–9; also in *C.S.P.S.*, IX, 483–6).
[5] *Beiträge*, p. 483. [6] Ibid. p. 309, n. 2.
[7] This information is derived from Caracciolo's MS *Life* of Carafa, written in the seventeenth century, but drawn from original letters and papers. The MS version is far more extensive than the printed *Life* (published in 1612; see above, n. 1, p. 212). Copies of the MS are to be found in most of the major European libraries. The relevant section, concerning Carafa's charges against Pole at the conclave reads as follows: 'Appresso il Card:l Theatino ricordò a i Padri la

must have been distinctly welcome to Pole's enemies within the conclave.

Beccadelli relates that three charges in all were brought against Pole at this time (he does not say by whom): the first was that of heresy; the second, of over-indulgence to heretics in his legation at Viterbo; and finally, it was rumoured that he had a natural daughter in a convent at Rome. In reply, Pole pointed to his history of dedication to the Holy See, and the pacific character of the Viterbese; as for the third charge, his accusers would find 'to their great confusion' that the girl was a poor orphan, 'the child of an Englishwoman who had died at Rome', and that Pole had undertaken to provide for her education.[1]

The last of these charges was probably spread about *sub rosa*; there is no mention of it in the surviving records of the conclave. The other two, however, are connected; and the first of them must have been particularly embarrassing to Pole's supporters. After the arrival of Guise and his supporters on 12 December the argument was willingly pressed into use. Guise, at this time a young man of twenty-three, skilful and assured in political manoeuvre, immediately assumed the leadership of the French party. The parties were now equally balanced, and for over a month they remained locked in *impasse*, as Pole and Carafa (occasionally replaced by other candidates) approached, but never attained the necessary two-thirds majority. Carafa had been put forward by the French on 15 December, not because they wished to see him Pope, but because as an austere and zealous reformer he was an acceptable counter-candidate to Pole. Henceforth the conclave degenerated into an exhausting and repetitive battle of nerves as each side sought to wear down the endurance of the other.[2]

On 17 December Guise came out with an attack on Pole. The latter, he claimed, had departed suddenly from the Council of Trent because he wanted to evade the discussions on justification.

lentezza, e conuenienza in Materia d'heresie, quando egli fu a Viterbo Legato della Romagna, il tenue in Casa un Drapello d'heretici, e di persone sospettissime' (BM Harl. 1763, fol. 149v).

[1] *Monumenti*, I, ii, pp. 303-4.   [2] Pastor, *Popes*, XIII, 20ff.

His avidity for the papacy was prolonging the conclave: would he not now withdraw his candidature? Pole, in reply, denied that he cherished any personal ambitions for the papacy: he was content to leave things in the hands of providence. God knew all movements of the human mind, and he was not unaware that Pole had left the Council for no other reason than ill-health.[1]

It is not easy to know what the cumulative effect of these accusations may have been. Massarelli's opinion, that Pole was excluded from the papacy principally because his orthodoxy had been called in question, probably reflects little more than Massarelli's scruples. Pole's public standing was at no time in jeopardy before the reign of Paul IV. He continued to occupy an important position in the counsels of the Church, and no objection was raised to his appointment as Papal Legate to England following the death of Edward. More probably he failed because of other reasons: because he was a foreigner and, like Adrian VI, uncompromising in his zeal to eliminate ecclesiastical abuses.

When at length the parties finally resolved their differences, they settled on a man who was unlikely to offend too grossly the susceptibilities of the Roman Curia, but whose dedication to the cause of reform was sufficiently genuine to appease the zealous. Cardinal Del Monte had been Pole's senior colleague at the Council of Trent; he was a man whose hasty temperament was offset by a genial enjoyment of good company; he had a sound knowledge of jurisprudence, and was widely experienced in the politics of the Curia. When on 8 February 1550 he was elected Pope,[2] the Church seemed to have survived the dissensions of recent months with a kind of exhausted equanimity. But new dissensions were shortly to emerge.

Julius III began his reign by establishing a number of commissions to deal with ecclesiastical reform. One of his first concerns was to revivify the Roman Inquisition. On 17 February 1550 he appointed seven commissioners to deal with the protection of the faith: de

[1] 'ita eum e Tridentina synodo ob solam adversae valetudinis caussam discessise non ignorat'. (*C.T.*, II, 64, n. 1.)
[2] *C.T.*, II, 143.

Cupis, Carafa, Cervini, Sfondrato, Morone, Crescenzio and Pole.
Their ambit was not simply the affairs of Italy, but the preservation of the faith throughout Europe; nevertheless, Italy remained
the principal theatre of operations.[1] Another commission was
appointed to deal with the reform of the datary, and on 19
April 1550 a third commission was set up, to supervise the workings of the General Council which was shortly to be reconvened
at Trent.[2] Thus from 1550 to 1553 Pole, as a member of each of
these commissions, was kept busy with the discussion and formation of papal policy. He remained steadfast in his zeal to eliminate
corruption, protesting vigorously when the Pope elevated a
seventeen-year-old relative to the rank of Cardinal. The occasion
prompted the Pope to remark that he regarded Pole as Quintilian
regarded Cicero: 'what he wrote and spoke appeared to be the
first thing that came into his head; but in reality it was the result
of the very subtlest art, as were all the words uttered by the
Cardinal of England'. The Pope added that he had been 'not a
little taken aback by this'.[3]

The decision to recall the Council involved Pole, towards the
end of 1550, in active consultations with the Pope and with his
colleagues on the Conciliar commission. In January 1551 a bull
was published summoning the Council; and on 1 May the second
period of the Council of Trent was inaugurated.[4] In the course
of time decrees on the sacraments appeared; measures against
clerical abuses were proposed; but within a year the Council was
again suspended, wrecked by the refusal of Protestant observers
to accept the Council in its present form, and the renewal, in
April 1552, of war in the Imperial territories. On 28 April, the
Council was suspended.

When Pole heard the news (28 April was Good Friday), he
felt 'as if the dead body of Christ were before my very eyes';[5]
and although his hopes of ecclesiastical renewal soon recovered,[6]

---

[1] Ibid. p. 157; Pastor, *Popes* XIII, pp. 210–24.

[2] *C.T.*, II, 168; *C.T.*, VII, 3.

[3] Dispatch of Don Juan Manrique de Lara, 18 November 1551. (*C.S.P.S.*, X, no. 662.)

[4] Pastor, *Popes*, XIII, 99ff. Jedin, *Geschichte*, III, 219–399.

[5] *Epistolae*, IV, p. 71; *C.T.*, IX, 1138.   [6] *Epistolae*, IV, 71.

they did so more by faith in the inexhaustible vitality of the Church than by any immediate sign of its activity. For Pole these years were marked by isolation and defeat: the defeat of his expectations at the Council in 1546–7; the death of his closest friends, Vittoria Colonna and Flaminio; the rejection of his candidature at the conclave in 1549–50 (however much he accepted it in the spirit of detachment); and now, the eruption of war and the enforced postponement of the Council's work. A sense of isolation had been deeply impressed upon him at the conclave, where he found himself surrounded by men with whom he had 'virtually nothing in common...neither country nor kindred'; whose habits and customs, as he wrote, were mostly alien to him, and with few of whom he enjoyed any close friendship.[1] Every event, it seemed, conspired to reinforce his sense of exile.

He soon withdrew from his work upon the Roman Inquisition: it seems that he found its procedures insupportable. It was not that the tribunal had yet advanced to the policies which marked it under Paul IV. Carafa, indeed, still thought it unreasonably moderate.[2] But in one important respect it now departed from the earlier restraint which characterised it under Paul III: it began to examine people who formerly had been almost exempt from its enquiries – who, many of them holding high positions in the Church, were suspected of sympathising with questionable or heretical doctrines. The Council of Trent had eliminated any doubt about the Church's doctrine of salvation; the flight of Vergerio had underlined the dangers which still existed in high places: henceforth, the Inquisition's range of operations was extended to incorporate every category of person, and the tribunal itself was strengthened by the new certainty about what constituted orthodoxy. The result was that equivocation, which had been the hall-mark of the *spirituali* and Nicodemists, became little less reprehensible than formal heresy. Few people died,[3] but more and more people began to come within the purview of enquiry and suspicion. After February 1551, Pole's name is missing

---

[1] *Epistolae*, IV, pp. 60–1.   [2] Pastor, *Popes*, XIII, 216.
[3] Cf. Vergerio's comment, Pastor, *Popes*, XIII, 219.

from the list of Cardinals who sat on the tribunal; and there is evidence that he was alarmed by the inflexibility which marked its dealings.[1]

There was every reason why he should have been. The principle of limited clemency to which he held had now been abandoned: private expressions of unorthodox opinion had become hardly more acceptable than open heresy. In addition to this, men who had been associated with his own group at Viterbo were now being summoned for interrogation. On 20 March 1551, Flaminio's friend Galeazzo Caracciolo fled from Naples; by 8 June he was in Geneva, where he became one of Calvin's most devoted followers.[2] Three days after Caracciolo's flight, the bishop of Bergamo, Vittore Soranzo, was arrested and taken to Castel S. Angelo.[3]

Like Caracciolo, Soranzo had been in close contact with the circle of Valdés at Naples; he was, indeed, a thoroughly representative figure among the *spirituali*. Venetian by birth, he had been educated at Padua, where he was a contemporary of Pole and a friend of Morone.[4] He had served with Sanfelice at the court of Clement VII, and had spent a year at Naples in 1540–1. After the death of Valdés, he had spent some time at Viterbo, and had remained in close contact with Pole and his friends until 1544, when he was appointed to Bergamo. There he devoted himself to pastoral activity, broken only by a brief sojourn at the Council of Trent, which he abandoned before the discussions on justification began.[5] In 1550 complaints were made about his preaching. The Venetian ambassador protested about these 'calumnies'; but the Pope replied that Soranzo had certainly compromised himself at Trent, where he had denied the existence of free-will and opposed the preaching of good works.[6] On 21 May 1551 the

---

[1] Below, pp. 243ff.

[2] P. Paschini, *Venezia e l'inquisizione*, p. 99.   [3] Ibid. p. 74.

[4] Cantù, *Eretici*, II, 189. On Soranzo, cf. P. Paschini, *Tre ricerche sulla storia della Chiesa nel Cinquecento*, pp. 91–151; also Alberigo, *I vescovi italiani*, pp. 56–8 and 76–9.

[5] Alberigo, *I vescovi italiani*, pp. 255–6.

[6] 'Lui venne al Concilio et nello sagiassemo bene; ma lui persiste, non vuol credere che habbiamo libero arbitrio, ne vuol che si predicha di esso, né delle opere'. (Cf. Paschini, *Venezia e l'inquisizione*, p. 63.)

Venetian ambassador reported that certain Cardinals were 'greatly incensed' against Soranzo: they thought of him as having many accomplices, and wanted to deprive him of his diocese: but, he added, the Pope had no intention of letting this happen.[1] On 26 June Soranzo confessed to the ownership of a book containing writings by Luther, Bucer, Melanchthon, Ochino 'and other writings concerning the diet of Ratisbon in 1541'.[2] He was released on the same day but was not reinstated in his diocese for a while.

In the same year that Soranzo was arrested, Appolonio Merenda, who had been Pole's chaplain at Viterbo, was summoned to Rome for questioning. Like Soranzo, Merenda had lived at Naples for a time, as chaplain to the bishop of Policastro. In 1541, he took up residence at Viterbo where, according to Carnesecchi, he never expressed any unusual opinion, except on the issue of justification 'in its most simple form.'[3] He left for Calabria after a year and, although Priuli invited him back in 1544, he never returned to Viterbo. Instead, he spent some time at Mantua and Verona. On being summoned once again to Rome he was accused of sacramentarianism, tried, and deprived of his benefices in 1553.[4] Ignoring the command to live in Rome, he departed for Venice and Padua in 1555; during the reign of Paul IV he fled to Switzerland.

Thus by 1551 the Inquisition had begun to move against the former associates of Valdés and Pole. The fact did not pass unnoticed in Switzerland. It was now apparent to Vergerio that his warning of 1549 had been ignored: the Viterbo group had not emerged in opposition to the Church of Rome. But the alternative which he had tacitly indicated was indeed occurring, and without his having to assist the process: Soranzo's arrest seemed to herald the destruction of all those who, as Vergerio saw it, had compromised their consciences in order to stay within the Church. Some idea of his reaction, and that of his compatriots in

[1] Ibid. p. 75.   [2] Paschini, *Tre ricerche*, p. 140.
[3] *Processo*, p. 526. Carnesecchi adds that, by the 1550s, Merenda was friendly with Ochino, Vergerio and other Italian exiles in the Valtelline.
[4] Amabile, *Il S. Officio della Inquisizione in Napoli*, p. 142.

Switzerland, may be derived from a passage which appears in the second edition of Francesco Negri's *La tragedia del libero arbitrio*.[1] This work, which was an allegorised attack upon the papacy, had first appeared in 1546. Negri took the opportunity, on its second appearance in 1551, of inserting a fresh passage rejoicing in the discomfiture of Pole and his friends. He was convinced that Pole would shortly suffer the same fate as Soranzo: for, as he observed, Pole and the Patriarch of Aquilea,[2] no less than Soranzo, were all guilty of the same inconsistency which vitiated whatever good qualities they might possess: they understood the doctrine of justification, they resisted at least some abuses in the Church – but they continued to attend Mass and to pay homage to the Pope.[3]

This was the same complaint which Vergerio had made in 1549, but in more specific terms: Negri had no hesitation in naming the people whom he was attacking. The time for compromise was past: if Pole would not declare himself, it would not be long, remarked Negri, before his crimes caught up with him. Already the Pope was preparing to hunt down all three: Soranzo was in prison; Pole and Grimani stood in danger since the arrest of Merenda and of Grimani's doctor, Giovanni Susio;[4] and the trial of the two latter would draw the attention of the Inquisition to their patrons.[5]

Negri's prediction was well-founded. It was inevitable that in such circumstances Pole's name should increasingly recur in the records of the Roman Inquisition. Yet it was not necessary to proceed formally against him. His views could be casually elicited in conversation, and he could be politely requested to explain his

[1] Published in 1551 (?) *s.a.*, *s.l.* Negri was a Benedictine monk who left Italy in the 1530s. He was a close friend of Vergerio and Ochino, and collaborated in Vergerio's propaganda campaign. (G. Zonta, 'Francesco Negri l'eretico e la sua tragedia "Il libero arbitrio"', in *Giornale storico della letteratura italiana*, LXVII–LXVIII (1916), pp. 263–324 and 108–60. Zonta argues that the second edition came out in 1550, but Paschini (*Tre ricerche*, p. 136, n. 4) points out that it cannot have been published before 1551, when Soranzo was first imprisoned.)

[2] Giovanni Grimani.

[3] Zonta, 'Francesco Negri', p. 139; reproduced in Paschini, *Tre ricerche*, p. 136.

[4] Susio was summoned to Rome by de Cupis in July 1550, but nothing was found against him and he was released after a month. (Ibid. p. 137, n. 1.)

[5] Zonta, 'Francesco Negri', p. 139; reproduced in Paschini, *Tre ricerche*, p. 136.

circumstances. This is what in fact occurred in the spring of 1553, as we learn from a letter of Filippo Gherio.[1]

According to Gherio, three members of the Inquisition approached Pole separately at this time. In the last week of April Cervini explained to Pole that the Inquisition held three things against him. The first was his close friendship with Flaminio; the second was his disagreement with the doctrine of justification defined at Trent;[2] and the third was his reputed radicalism in conversation. This last charge arose from a remark which had been made by a witness under examination, who once heard from Pole 'things which left him scandalised'; although, as he admitted, having afterwards taxed Pole upon these issues, his mind had been put at rest.

In reply, Pole observed that he could answer nothing to the third charge, since he did not know what he was supposed to have said. The witness himself had apparently testified to its essential harmlessness. As for his friendship with Flaminio, Pole could not deny that Flaminio was wavering a little when he first joined Pole's household. Pole had recognised his ability and his consummate literary judgement. He had seen the danger that Flaminio might wish to exercise it upon questions of theology. Accordingly he had set him to reading the doctors of the Church, and had persuaded him to content himself with that. Flaminio had died an exemplary death. Pole therefore felt that his own connection with him should be a matter more for gratitude than reproach, since by receiving him into his household he had recovered him for the Church. Had Flaminio been estranged, he could have done great damage, considering that his fine intelligence was united with 'an incomparable style in writing about sacred things'.[3]

Pole's account of his relations with Flaminio is, as we have seen, substantially true. But it does not sufficiently indicate the probable religious influence which Flaminio exerted upon Pole himself: and it did not meet the suspicion that Flaminio's 'incom-

[1] Filippo Gherio to Beccadelli, Rome, 29 April 1553. (*Monumenti*, I, ii, pp. 347-53.)
[2] 'che non sentiva della justificatione in conformità del l'articulo fattone nel Concilio di trento'. (Ibid. p. 347.)
[3] Ibid, p. 350.

parable style' had already done sufficient damage. Pole, therefore, does not seem to have been altogether frank. His reluctance to speak fully about such delicate issues is evident in his reply to the most damaging criticism of all: that he disagreed with the Tridentine doctrine of justification. There had been no question, he told Cervini, of any serious disagreement. The Council fathers had seen his opinion before the decree was drawn up, and that opinion had not been at variance with the decree. He may have stated a preference for 'a certain difference of words' which, had he written the decree himself, he would have employed. But the sense of the decree would not have been altered.[1]

Here, if ever, there was evasion. Pole's opposition to the decree had arisen from much more than a 'certain difference of words'. He came close to admitting as much himself, in writing to Truchsess a year later: yet even then, he failed to recollect the fundamental division which had existed between his own approach and that of the Council.[2] This, as we have seen, was probably not consciously deceptive: it was more a matter of emotion recollected in tranquility. But on the occasion of his conversation with Cervini there were certain deliberate omissions of which Pole cannot but have been aware: his root-and-branch aversion to the concept of merit, for example. If he evaded discussion of these issues now it was not, in all likelihood, because he still opposed the Council's declaration; but because he knew that the Inquisition would not be mollified by the simple truth. If he were to disclose everything to the best of his abilities he would never escape the damaging assertion that he had been a heretic: and he could not accept that this had been the case. Consequently, he chose to dismiss the matter lightly, as a trifling question of detail. Cervini, of course, cannot have been deceived. He had been Pole's senior colleague at the Council; he had almost certainly conversed with him about these issues; and he had seen the memoranda submitted by Pole under duress. But he was a good-hearted man, and knew that Pole's loyalty to the Church had never been in question. So he went

[1] Ibid. p. 347. [2] Above, p. 204.

away 'thoroughly contented, enlarging upon the goodness and quality of cardinal Pole'.[1]

Gherio further related that Cardinal Carpi (who frequently served upon the tribunal of the Inquisition)[2] called about this time on Pole's friend, Vincenzo Parpaglia, as he was passing through Viterbo. He told Parpaglia that 'many things had been heard against Cardinal Pole', and that he had seen certain 'writings or scribblings' which, in order to protect Pole, he had suppressed.[3] It may be that Carpi was merely testing Parpaglia, and that no such writings existed: on the other hand it is distinctly possible that he was referring to the memoranda which Pole had composed in 1546. Whatever the truth, Parpaglia (who had acted as a messenger between Trent and Padua on that occasion, and who, as a member of Pole's entourage, can scarcely have been ignorant of his doctrinal anxieties) made no mention of it to Pole until nearly Easter.[4] At this time, Pole was staying at St Paul's Outside the Walls, in preparation for his departure from Rome.[5] Hearing, however, that Carpi had arrived in Rome, he sent a message to him, expressing a wish to visit him.

When he saw Carpi he learned about the rumours concerning him which, according to Gherio 'were in sum, nothing but generalities...nothing concrete, but everything in the air and in the clouds, without conclusiveness'.[6] Pole then raised the matter of the 'scribblings' about which Parpaglia had spoken; but he did so very carefully, first speaking of his regard for Carpi, and his belief that Carpi held him in equal esteem. He then expressed his regret that Carpi should have suppressed the papers in question, adding that 'in attempting to please him he had given him great displeasure'. Carpi replied that he had said nothing about any

[1] *Monumenti*, I, ii, p. 347.
[2] Carpi was a member in January 1552, together with Carafa, Toledo and Cervini. In April 1553 his name is missing from the list of Cardinals-Inquisitor, but it reappears later in the same year. (Pastor, *Popes*, XIII, 217, n.1.)
[3] *Monumenti*, I, ii, p. 347–8.   [4] Ibid. p. 348.
[5] 'se ben'era andato a San Paolo con disegno di non tornar più a Roma'. (*Monumenti*, I, ii, p. 348.) Taken literally, Gherio's expression seems to imply that Pole intended to leave Rome forever: it is possible that he thought of entering the Benedictine monastery of Maguzzano (Schenk, *Reginald Pole*, p. 121).
[6] Ibid.

papers to Parpaglia, that he had the highest regard for Pole's integrity and learning in religious matters, and that he had never heard anything to Pole's discredit. He then began to speak about business matters.[1]

Carpi, it is clear, had said rather too much to Parpaglia; and the incident reveals the uneasy mixture of familiarity and suspicion with which Pole was treated in these years by certain of his colleagues in the Curia. Their suspicions are by no means unintelligible. Pole's carefully ambiguous attitude in the years before the Council; his friendship with men of dubious doctrinal sympathies; his known aversion to the proceedings of the Council – all these things, considered in the atmosphere which followed Vergerio's departure for Switzerland and his campaign against the 'equivocators' at Rome, understandably prejudiced the minds of many people: and Pole's dismissive attitude towards the whole affair carried a certain detectable note of disingenuousness. There was ample reason to investigate Pole's disposition. His very inability to explain the matter frankly (either to himself or anyone else) contributed to the atmosphere of suspicion and distrust.

On the other hand, it seems that the Inquisition was at this time genuinely desirous of reaching an understanding, so that that whole matter might be forgotten. Carafa, during these months, made a number of indirect approaches to Pole which finally resulted in a meeting and an amicable settlement, for a time at least. The bishop of Sagona, who was a supporter of Carafa, began to approach Pole's friends, explaining that Carafa had no part in the calumnies which were circulating about Pole. He spoke thus to Gherio and Parpaglia, requesting them in turn to say as much to Pole. Gherio responded by arranging frequent meetings between Pole and the bishop, and the latter returned constantly to Carafa, full of admiration of Pole.[2] The result of all this was that when a meeting finally occurred between Pole and Carafa it ended in their reconciliation.

It occurred spontaneously, towards the end of Lent, while

---

[1] *Monumenti*, I, ii, p. 348.

[2] Carafa also employed another mediator, a certain Don Bernardino. (Below, p. 242.)

Pole was still at St Paul's Outside the Walls, preparing for his journey from Rome. One night at about eight o'clock Carafa arrived at St Paul's on the first stage of his devotional journey round the Seven Churches.[1] He stayed there for a long time in prayer. Pole, who was spending the evening in his room in conversation with the Master of the Sacred Palace, Girolamo Muzzarelli, heard that Carafa was in the church, and that he had been there for almost an hour. Feeling that it would be discourteous to ignore him, he approached the church, and found Carafa on the point of leaving. The latter, seeing Pole arrive, dismounted quickly from his carriage: the two men met, and returned to Pole's room. They remained in conversation there for over two hours.[2]

At first they spoke of general matters, treading the ground softly. Carafa mentioned a friend, a certain Don Bernardino, who had done much to mediate between himself and Pole; and the latter replied with a eulogy of this man, recalling his attempts to ease the scandal which their strained relationship was causing. There followed many expressions of mutual regard, until at last, Carafa delicately raised the matter of Pole's connection with Flaminio. To this, Pole replied that his exile, the dangers he endured, the deaths he had suffered in his family on account of religion, were sufficient testimony of his allegiance: he had abandoned everything for the Holy See. He did not think that he deserved so much distrust, or that 'every little thing' should render him suspect. On the contrary, if he were to have been found in conversation with Luther himself, it should more readily be supposed that he was endeavouring to convert him than that he was himself being led astray.[3] He then recounted the story of his friendship with Flaminio, and Carafa received it with the same satisfaction which Cervini had earlier displayed.[4]

At this point, however, there occurred a sharp misunderstanding.

[1] This would suggest that the meeting took place on the night of Holy Thursday.
[2] Every so often, a servant of Carafa's would enter with a reminder that it was getting late; only to receive a genial retort from Carafa that he must not be reproached for enjoying the company of Pole, 'for it was a long time since he had enjoyed it'. (*Monumenti*, I, ii, p. 349.)
[3] Ibid.   [4] Ibid. p. 350.

Carafa suggested that Pole should publish something on his own behalf: a remark to which Pole took immediate exception, inquiring heatedly whether he was to publish an *apologia*? Should he not first be permitted to know who his accuser was, or of what he was accused?[1] Carafa replied hastily that there was no question of an *apologia*: publicly to defend himself would be disastrous, since it would imply that he had lived under suspicion.[2] Carafa's idea was rather that he should publish something which would redound to his own honour. But Pole professed himself indifferent to questions of honour. Had he been concerned with honour he would long since have appealed to public opinion to judge the calumnies which had been brought against him. As matters stood, he was an adequate judge of his own conscience; and in short, he refused to publish anything. Carafa persisted for a while, but without making any headway.[3]

The conversation then began to range upon a number of wider issues. Pole raised the subject of the Inquisition, remarking that he approved the end envisaged, but could not countenance the manner of its proceedings.[4] Instead of harshness, he urged the way of charity and mildness ('la via della carità et mansuetudine'). Carafa, after a lengthy discussion, was brought to the point of agreement, and even professed himself averse to the manner of inquisitorial proceedings at Rome. He was about to take up residence in his diocese at Naples, and would employ the policy recommended by Pole. He then returned to the question of Pole's familiarity with persons of suspected views. He spoke in

[1] 'E che! ho da scrivere una apologia? facciasi che io veda quis me accusat aut qua de re accusor.' (Ibid.)

[2] 'siquidem omnis defensio vel ad crimen, vel ad suspicionem criminis depellendum adhibetur' (*Epistolae*, IV, 98).

[3] Pole, allowing himself to be mollified, acknowledged that he was indeed accustomed to amuse himself with writing. He tried to do so with care and diligence; but he wrote for himself, and not for others. He treated his writings as an animal treated its offspring: rearing them to maturity, and then forgetting them. (*Monumenti*, I, ii, p. 351.)

[4] Pastor (*Popes*, XIII, 222) believes that Pole was protesting here against the use of torture. This may be true; but it is not certain that torture was a usual instrument of interrogation; and the particular incident recorded by Pastor occurred four months after Pole's conversation with Carafa. The context suggests that Pole was adverting to the investigation of people like Soranzo who, by any charitable estimate, were loyal to the Church.

particular of Giulia Gonzaga, mentioning that her name was on the list of suspects. Pole, however, spoke of his regard for her and explained that he wished to win her with courtesy, since there was no other good way to do so.[1]

The outcome of this conversation was that after two hours Carafa departed with a higher estimate of Pole than he had enjoyed for years. But despite the mutual expressions of good feeling, there seems to have remained – on Pole's side at least – an undercurrent of reserve. Neither man had been completely generous in restoring the foundations of goodwill. Thus, when Pole adverted to the remarks which, according to other Cardinals, Carafa had made about him, the latter replied that he should not trust their accounts; and when Carafa, at the end of their conversation, regretted that he had not earlier discussed these things with Pole and put an end to rumour, Pole somewhat inflexibly observed that it had not been for want of trying on his part. He had frequently endeavoured to approach Carafa in consistory, but the latter had always fled the opportunity of discussion, and had on at least one occasion shown signs of spite.[2]

Nevertheless, the meeting ended in amity, and Carafa departed with assurances of his esteem for Pole. He even told him that he hoped Pole would some day become Pope.[3] That same night, moreover, he spoke to his colleagues on the Inquisition. He told them that Pole was the best and most blameless of men, and he repeated his belief that when the next Pope was to be elected there could be no better candidate than Pole. To others he spoke of Pole's devotion to the faith, and explained that everything which had been said against him was mere calumny.[4]

Pole, in his turn, was overcome with joy. After Carafa's departure he called Muzzarelli back to his room and told him of his great happiness that a reconciliation had occurred – a happiness made complete by the very fact that it was unexpected.[5]

The following day, Carafa invited Muzzarelli and two other Dominicans to dine with him. He recounted the story of his

[1] *Monumenti*, I, ii, p. 351.　　　　　　　[2] Ibid. p. 352.
[3] See below, n. 3, p. 275.　　　　　　　　[4] *Monumenti*, I, ii, p. 352.
[5] *Epistolae*, IV, 92–3.

reconciliation with Pole and expressed himself anxious to assist Pole in every way, so as to remove the malicious fictions which had been devised against him. He begged Muzzarelli to write to Pole,[1] telling him of his readiness to assist Pole, and his hopes that Pole would publish his work on the Anglican schism.[2] Muzzarelli complied with his request, and begged Pole on his own behalf to publish something of his other writings.[3] Pole, however, in a lengthy reply explained his reluctance to do so. He did not number himself among the writers; he preferred to settle controversial matters by discussion; nevertheless, if the Pope urged him, he would agree to publish a new edition of his *De Unitate*.[4]

There had once been a moment, he told Muzzarelli, when he was almost persuaded by his friends to publish something in his own defence, against the rumours which were circulating about him. He was in considerable doubt about the right course to adopt, being torn between alternatives. He consulted the Pope, who advised him against publishing anything. Nothing, he had pointed out, had been publicly imputed against Pole. Neither had anything worthy of response been said about him privately. Pole's honour and that of the College of Cardinals in general would be brought into disrepute if it were known that there had been complaints about him. Thus the Pope had besought him to desist from publishing an *apologia*, and Pole accordingly had determined on remaining silent. As Carafa had observed in their recent conversation, he could publish nothing which would not reveal him to have been suspected of some crime; whereas by remaining silent he could avoid unpleasantness. Carafa had spoken prudently, and as a friend.[5]

But if he refused to write a defence of himself, it was not, he felt, for want of provocation. He complained to Muzzarelli of informers who were troubling the Inquisition with damaging

[1] Who was on the point of leaving Rome.
[2] That is Pole's *De Unitate*. Carafa had read parts of it when it was being composed, and had strongly approved of it. (*Epistolae*, IV, 91–2.)
[3] Ibid. p. 93.
[4] The Pope, it appears did not so urge him. Instead, as we have seen, he begged him to write something on the question of justification, but the result was considered to be too 'confused' for publication.
[5] *Epistolae*, IV, 94–8.

stories and suggestions. One of them, a man named Theophilus – a name which Pole considered to be inappropriate – had recently sought to bring into disrepute certain devoted servants of God and the Church. He had openly stated that in matters of religion these men were in agreement with the enemies of Rome: and he had named Contarini, Morone and Pole. He had done his best to render Pole suspect in the eyes of the Church, arguing that in matters of faith Pole was at one with the very people who were busily attacking him for his allegiance to Rome.[1]

This remark suggests that the efforts of Vergerio and Negri had not been altogether fruitless: their attacks on Pole and his associates had evidently been brought to the attention of the Inquisition. But now it seemed as if their efforts were of no avail: the real truth, wrote Pole, was now established, and the informer had discredited himself in the eyes of God and man.[2] Hence Pole stood in need of no defence. He appreciated that Muzzarelli had never thought of asking him for one: unless perhaps, in the one particular, concerning Pole's familiarity with certain persons of suspected faith. Pole had frequently been told, even by people zealous for his reputation, that he too readily allowed himself to be approached by such persons. He was warned that the more kindness he displayed, the more he left himself open to attack; and was exhorted, therefore, to desist from encouraging such attacks. Perhaps Muzzarelli was of the same opinion: if so, Pole would freely explain the reasons for his approachability ('facilitas') in these matters – but at another time, for he had already exceeded the limits of his letter. Thus he would content himself with observing that if he had been familiar with persons of this sort, there had never been very many of them, to the best of his knowledge: and anyone who appreciated the limits of his approachability, his reasons for it, or the persons involved would, if he were fair-minded, consider him to be worthy not of blame but of praise, and would exhort him to continue in this policy.[3]

This was essentially the same line of defence which Pole had employed with Cervini and Carafa. It was patently sincere. There

---

[1] *Epistolae*, IV, p. 102.   [2] Ibid. p. 101.   [3] Ibid. p. 104.

can be no question that Pole was genuinely indignant that his efforts to preserve people like Flaminio or Carnesecchi for the Church should be construed as a suspicious inclination to consort with the enemies of Rome. Nevertheless, such a construction was eminently understandable in the circumstances of post-Tridentine Italy, and Pole's inability to recognise this fact only testifies to the virtual extinction of the opportunities for reconciliation which the *spirituali* had believed to exist in the years before the Council.

What is therefore most noteworthy in the above passage is the observation that there were limits to the 'facilitas' which Pole was prepared to exercise. The private expression of religious doubt, or even of heretical sentiments, was tolerable in so far as it could be met by 'the way of charity and mildness'; but the public advocacy of heretical doctrines, or the obstinate refusal to retract them was another matter. Pole was not opposed, as he had assured Carafa, to the purpose of the Inquisition: merely to a narrowness and inflexibility in its approach, and probably to its methods of informing. It is necessary to remember this, if we are not to discover in his management of affairs in England a contradiction which did not in fact exist. It was merely that conditions in England had long since passed the limits within which he was prepared to exercise 'facilitas'.

Pole concluded his observations on this topic with what seems like a reference to the attacks from Switzerland. Perhaps it might be felt that open or notorious heretics would construe his 'facilitas' as an indication that he was among their number. He did not himself know whether such a thing may occasionally have happened, or if it had, the identity or number of such people. But the circumstance was anyway irrelevant. St Paul himself had had to suffer calumnies of this kind when his opinions were taken up by impious men. That was when he was still alive: to-day, how many others used his writings to justify their errors! Thus if an occurrence of this kind were to be taken as a criterion of faith, not even Paul himself could be regarded as a Catholic.[1]

[1] Ibid.

Pole, it is true, cannot have known the identity or number of those Protestants who claimed him as an ally, or who regarded his 'facilitas' as a sign of approbation. There is evidence, indeed, that even after the Council, numbers of Italian Nicodemists spoke of him as a kind of patron; and it was this very attitude which in part prompted the further denunciations of Vergerio.[1] There is no reason to suppose that Pole was personally familiar with these people; and there is even evidence, surprising as it may seem, that he did not believe that Vergerio was the instigator of the Protestant attack on him.[2] But he was clearly aware that he had a reputation for knowing 'the truth' concerning justification, even if he had never publicised it: and it was this circumstance which, in conjunction with his 'facilitas', had led others to suppose that he was all the while a covert heretic. Thus Pole's indignation at the use which Protestants were making of his reputation was tantamount to an assertion that there had never been any disparity between his doctrine and the doctrine of the Council. If he sincerely believed that, he was confused; if not, he was being highly evasive. The truth is probably that he was confused, and that his confusion involved him in evasion.

A year later, as we have seen, Pole was prepared to acknowledge that he had suffered a correction in his doctrine of salvation: but he made no explicit mention of the Council. It was the authority of Scripture which, interpreted by the Church, had led him to correct his views upon the matter.[3] And when at the same time he came to put his views on paper, the result was too confused to be thought worthy of an *imprimatur*.[4] Perhaps the experience at Trent was too difficult to comprehend in an age which scarcely acknowledged the concept of development in Christian doctrine,

[1] Below, pp. 264ff.

[2] This is hard to understand, in view of the fact that by the time in question Vergerio was appending his own name to the attack. (See below, p. 260.) Two years later, Pole was still reluctant to believe that Vergerio was his accuser, as appears from a question put by Priuli to Roger Ascham, whether 'Vergerio' were not a pseudonym for Sturm: 'His persiquivit a me, an non putarem *Praefationem Vergerii*, praefixam libro Poli a te fuisse scriptam.' (Ascham to Johann Sturm, Greenwich, 14 September 1555, in *Works* ed. Giles (London, 1865) I, ii, pp. 447–448.)

[3] Above, p. 200.

[4] Ibid. p. 208.

and at a time which was reluctant to distinguish easily between material and formal heresy. But however much Pole's self-perception may have been obscured by the prevailing character of thought, or however much it was impaired by spiritual pride, or caution, or self-deception, the result was that a distinct note of equivocation was introduced into his statements – over and above the note of hesitancy which characterised his usual pronouncements. Contemporaries did not miss it: Massarelli observed it at the papal conclave;[1] Carafa as well as Vergerio took account of it in their opposite ways; and it was this remaining ambiguity which, in part at least, undermined the reconciliation which had been so laboriously achieved between Pole and Carafa.

Suspicion, it would seem, was endemic to Carafa's mind. It could be forgotten for a while in a violent upsurge of emotional generosity: but under another impulse it would start smouldering again. His temperament was absolute: equivocation seemed to him the mask of treachery. Thus he could be driven emphatically to revoke a friendship formed in a moment of exaltation or religious fervour. Carafa had spoken to Flaminio as he lay dying, with a mind relieved of all suspicion: three years later he regarded it as highly questionable that anyone should have been friendly with Flaminio; later again he was heard to observe that Flaminio deserved the stake.[2] Suspicions crept back into his mind and fed upon each other; gradually they hardened into certainties; amnesties conferred in emotion would be repudiated in emotion, and the victims would be summoned for renewed interrogation. For most of his life his worst impulses were restrained to some extent by colleagues or superiors. The interrogations were restricted to his inner mind, or found their way merely into conversation. There they might be quelled for a moment by a charitable word (for he was capable of generosity); or inflamed again by what seemed like culpable indifference. It was only when he became Pope, and was charged with the responsibility of protect-

[1] 'Ex qua nota, etsi Polus ipse ab aliquibus impetitus [se] purgare conatus fuisset, non usque adeo tamen et iis verbis, quibus decebat (ut aiunt), fidem suam expressit, ut omnem prorsus suspicionem tolleret et multorum mentes ad bene de eo quoad fidem sentiendum revocaret.' (*C.T.*, II, 47.)

[2] Below, p. 278.

ing Christendom, that the barriers to action were removed, with the severest consequences for those who were unfortunate enough to suffer his distrust.

But in 1553, it seemed as if the old wounds had at last been healed. Satan had been overcome, wrote Pole, in his attempt to form an enmity between him and Carafa.[1] It seemed indeed, as if the difficulties of Pole's recent past had been forgotten; and when in the summer of that year Queen Mary succeeded to the English throne, a new and apparently more hopeful phase in Pole's career began. On 6 August he was appointed as Papal Legate to England,[2] and although political considerations prevented him from taking up his office until the end of 1554,[3] he re-entered his own country, after a lapse of more than twenty years, with a new sense of providential destiny and purpose.

[1] *Epistolae*, IV, 93; cf. also 105–6.   [2] Ibid. pp. 109–10.
[3] R. Ancel, 'La reconciliation de l'Angleterre avec le Saint Siège sous Marie Tudor: Legation du Cardinal Polus en Angleterre (1553–4)', *Revue d'histoire ecclesiastique*, X (1909), 520–36 and 744–98. Documents in *Nuntiaturberichte aus Deutschland*, Abt. I, 1534–59, Bd. 13 (Index, p. 464).

CHAPTER FIFTEEN

Reprisals

The scope of this enquiry does not permit a full investigation of Pole's Legatine career in England.[1] It is generally supposed that his conduct of affairs was devoid of inspiration. Yet if it be remembered that for the last years of office he was under papal censure, and tormented by the difficulties of the situation; that for the last nine months of the period he was seriously ill; that in the time available to him he summoned a national synod which dealt with ecclesiastical reform in a manner sufficiently original as to influence the later development of the Counter Reformation;[2] and that his period of office extended to no more than four years in all, it may seem that the verdict of 'sterility' usually

[1] The Cambridge dissertation of R. H. Pogson will supply this deficiency. I am deeply grateful to him for his erudite and helpful criticism of this chapter. The fullest published account is by P. Hughes, *The Reformation in England*, II, 184–330. Cf. also D. M. Loades, *The Oxford Martyrs* (London, 1970).

[2] Particularly in respect to seminary legislation and pastoral visitation. Cf. *Reformatio Angliae, ex decretis Reginaldi Poli Cardinalis, Sedis Apostolicae Legati, Anno MDLXI*. The decrees recommend the establishment of schools for the education of priests, 'tamquam ex seminario'. The work was published at Rome in 1562, on the eve of the Tridentine decrees on seminary training. Pole's influence on the pastoral directives of St Charles Borromeo is of particular importance. Cf. J. I. Tellechea Idigoras, 'El formulario de vista pastoral de Bartolomé de Carranza' in *Anthologia Annua*, IV (1956), 385–437. Further remarks concerning Pole's seminary legislation, and its indebtedness to Giberti, in H. Jedin, 'Domschule und Kolleg Zum Ursprung der Idee des Trienter Priesterseminars' in *Kirche des Glaubens*, II, 348–59 (formerly in *Trierer Theol. Zeitschrift*, LXI, 1958, 210–23). J. O'Donohue, 'The Seminary Legislation of the Council of Trent', *Il Concilio di Trento e la Riforma Tridentina, Atti del Convegno Storico Internazionale, Trento 2–6 Settembre 1963* (2 vols, Rome, 1965), pp. 157–72, adds to the same author's study of *Tridentine Seminary Legislation* (Louvain, 1957) – the best and fullest account of Pole's posthumous influence at Trent.

passed upon his policies owes a little to the retrospective colouring which they received in the light of subsequent events.

A little; but the primary event for which the reign of Mary is remembered was one for which Pole held, with the Queen, a responsibility undiminished by his reluctance to participate in its disquieting actualities. The Marian persecution ended with the accession of Elizabeth; England was removed from the direct influence of the Catholic revival; but what little it had received of that influence was enough to ensure that the religious energies associated elsewhere with the movement should seem, in the minds of Englishmen, irrevocably darkened by the memory of human suffering, and the fear of its recurrence under Spanish power. The possibility that such memories might recede was obviated by a work of literature which transmuted them into the national consciousness.

Nobody could accuse Foxe of impartiality. It might seem significant, therefore, that his account of Pole should be so lenient. He considered that 'Pole's lightning was for the most part kindled against the dead'. Thus, while he caused the bodies of Fagius and Bucer to be disinterred, and had their bones burned before the populace of Cambridge, nevertheless 'peradventure...he thought by this means to discharge his duty toward the Pope', rather than by causing bloodshed among the living.[1] Yet Foxe's 'peradventure' must be taken for no more than its is worth; and it only means that he was not familiar with Pole's sermons or writings.[2]

For Pole was not averse to the principle of persecution. On the contrary, he shared the general conviction of his age – a conviction shared by Cranmer and Calvin no less than Pole and Mary – that the protection of the faithful from corrupting influence (by force if necessary) was the first duty of a Christian pastor. To

---

[1] *The Acts and Monuments of John Foxe. With a life and vindication of the work* (ed. Townsend, London, 1843–9), VII, 91. Foxe also relates how Vermigli's wife was disinterred and buried on a dunghill. (Ibid. and VIII, 296–300.) Later in the century Robert Persons recorded the story, which he heard from Sir Francis Englefield (who claimed to have witnessed the event) that Pole, acting on Mary's orders, had the body of Henry VIII removed from its embalment and committed to the flames. J. J. Scarisbrick, *Henry VIII* (London, 1968), p. 497.

[2] As appears from his rather vague notice of Pole later in the work. (*Acts and Monuments*, VIII, 307–8.)

show mercy to the reprobate and unrepentant was an act of cruelty to the Christian Commonwealth.[1] In Italy his principle had been that 'sinners who were not obstinate or public should be induced with charity to return to the good way'.[2] In England, however, he encountered heresy which was both obstinate and public – or was forever threatening to become so, in the eyes of a regime which feared popular upheaval, and which was strongly disposed to identify it with religious dissent.

Occasionally he was moved to urge a warning against the excessive severity of some of his subordinates.[3] But he also rebuked the citizens of London for having 'sore offended God by gyvinge favour to heretykes'. He exhorted them to 'tempre your favour under such maner, that yf you can converte them by any wayes unto the unyte of the Chryche, then doo it...but yf ye cannot, and you suffre or favour them, there cannot be a greater work of crueltye ageynst the commonwelthe'.[4] These words exemplify his attitude, and indicate the limits which he had acknowledged in defending his 'facilitas' a few years earlier. The people must be on their guard against 'these heretykes pretendynge to dye constantly for the fayth of the Chyrche'. Constancy without truth was not enough: 'yt ys not the constancy that is prysed in the chyrche to dye for our owne opinion'.[5]

'Opinion' was a snare for the unwary. Heretics, as he wrote on another occasion, were not to be confused with the martyrs of the early Church, although they might persuade themselves that they were such: 'not understonding that the payne doth nott make

[1] Thus as early as 1550 he wrote: 'Nec tamen quae dixi de mansuetudine, & clementia huius pastoris, sic intelligi volo, ut propterea a subversis & contumacibus, quales in tanto grege multos reperire est necesse, iustas ac meritas poenas excludam. Quod si fieret, non clementia, sed insignis crudelitas esset appellanda. Quin vero id affirmare non dubitamus, nullum alium esse magistratum, qui seuerius fontes castiget, & puniat, sed non prius, quam omni adhibita benignitate atque clementia, se nihil proficere animaduertit. Quod enim supplicium grauius infligi cuiquam potest, quam ut e communi filiorum Dei commercio, in manus Sathanae, tanquam e coelo ad inferos tradatur, & abiiciatur?' (*De Summo Pontifice*, Louvain, 1569. This work was composed during the conclave of 1549-50, as appears from the preface. The excerpt cited above appears on pp. 75v-76r.)

[2] Morandi, *Monumenti*, I, ii, p. 326.

[3] Strype, *Ecclesiastical Memorials*, III, ii, pp. 29-30, and Foxe, *Acts and Monuments*, VIII, 154, 307-8.

[4] Strype, *Ecclesiastical Memorials*, III, ii, p. 487.   [5] Ibid. p. 499.

them martyrs, butt the cause and nott suche a cause that they imagine of their owne brayne, butt suche as ys approved by the churche, and nott that ys condemned by the church, as theires ys.'[1] The trouble was, as he assured the people, that every man had made himself 'a studier of Scripture to learne it of his owne wytt and labour', and from there would make himself a teacher 'as experience showeth the multitude of teachers and preachers att this a late tymes past'.[2] From this confusion had arisen the spiritual anarchy which destroyed the unity of Christendom. The people, therefore, must learn another way, 'how wythout readeng yow yourself may receiue frute and comfort of euery word of god'.[3]

The real issue, therefore, was authority. The doctrine of Christ was indeed contained in 'the Evangell, whiche euerye good man shud haue both in hart and in mouth, and showe the same in his deades'. All were agreed on this; but how it was to be interpreted was not for everyone to say:

And thatt the same is the doctrine of peace, herein is no controuersie att all, in thys both the catholyke and the heretike wyll agree, but when itt cometh to this poynct of whome this doctrine shuld be learned...here now begynneth the greater trouble and dissention in religion.[4]

Scripture, it was plain, must be interpreted in accordance with the Church's teaching. The Bible would 'do...meruellous good taken in tyme and place and wyth all dew circumstance'; but read with a contentious or rebellious mind it was both 'noysom and pernicious'.[5] The way to salvation was not through Scripture alone. It was necessary to have too, 'ceremonies and traditions, which at no tyme the Church lacked, and all this was taught wythout booke, being at thatt tyme thatt the Apostles beganne to teache in Gierusalem no booke of the new testament wrytten, but all was received of the Apostles'.[6]

Thus Scripture, properly understood, would bring a man to

[1] Vat. Lat. 5968 (Bodleian MS Film 33), fol. 256v.
[2] Ibid. fol. 396v.
[3] Ibid. fol. 397r.
[4] Ibid. fol. 256v.
[5] Ibid. fols. 433r, 435r.
[6] Ibid. fol. 438v.

know the word of God. Nevertheless, 'they are most apte to receyve light, that are more obedyent to follow ceremonyes, than to reade: for those be *parvuli*; and suche to whome the Scripture gyveth light'.¹ The ultimate key to salvation, however, was 'neyther the ceremonies which the heretykes doe rejecte, nor yet the Scrypture whereunto they doe so cleave',² but the living activity and practice of Christianity itself. The mercy of God would be revealed only to those who would themselves show mercy.³ Fasting, prayer, penitence and mercy were the basis of a Christian life.⁴ The people, therefore, must understand two things: 'both what the churchye ys, what pryvyleges and graces be graunted to them that be of that bodye, and the waye howe to enjoye them'.⁵

Pole's pastoral emphasis, therefore, was clearly laid upon obedience and works. The days were past when he presided over little groups which fervently discussed the helplessness of man. Man, within the bosom of the Church, had all the help he needed to secure salvation. This was not, of course, a new conclusion: what had changed was the direction of his pastoral emphasis. For the cities of northern Italy in 1542, he had recommended preaching as the means of pastoral regeneration: the 'simplex evangelium', without scholastic theology.⁶ His experience in Italy had taught him the dangers of unrestricted preaching – the necessity for preachers, as he now wrote, explicitly to respect the ceremonies, laws and constitutions of the Church.⁷

It was better to have no preaching than bad preaching. Obedience, the fruit of his experience in Italy, was the first requisite of holy preaching. In Italy, in the privacy of the Viterbo circle, he had taken works for granted, without regarding them as the inner constituent of Christian living. They were not the source of sanctity, but its result. His one concern was that they should not

¹ Strype, *Ecclesiastical Memorials*, III, ii, p. 503.   ² Ibid.
³ Ibid. p. 505.   ⁴ Ibid. p. 506.
⁵ Ibid. p. 509.   ⁶ Above, p. 67.
⁷ 'nec tamen nego necessariam esse verbi praedicationem, sed nisi vel ante sit vel simul constituta Ecclesiastica disciplina, dico potius obesse, verbum quam prodesse, quia hoc carnales homines ad inanem aurium delectationem non ad salutarem animi disciplinam & alimentum transferunt'. (*Epistolae*, v, 73. I am grateful to R. H. Pogson for showing me the significance of this quotation.)

be thought of as a currency to purchase salvation from a contractually obliged God. Salvation was by faith alone: ceremonies and works were necessary because commended by God and the Church. At Modena, Morone had forbidden the Jesuits to preach the doctrine of merit: Loyola's protest had been silenced because of the ascendancy of the *spirituali* at the Curia. In England, in the years which followed Trent, Pole's pastoral emphasis was on obedience and merit, and Morone was Cardinal Protector of the realm. The *spirituali* had passed through the experience of Trent; *sola fides* was an embarrassing memory from the past. Morone apologised in person to the Jesuits.[1] At Trent, Pole had urged the publication of the Bible in Hebrew, Greek and Latin. In England, he submitted to the advice of Dominican scholastics to reconstitute the syllabus at Oxford so as to replace the teaching of Hebrew ('which commands small audiences') with the study of scholastic texts.[2]

Change indeed; but the change was regulated by a constant – the principle of obedience to the Church, the guiding principle of his existence throughout his years in Italy as now in England. The eirenic aspirations of the *spirituali* had disappeared at Trent. What survived was their contribution to the pastoral renewal of the Church: their concentration on the bishop as its director, on the priest as its agent, on the seminary as its training ground, on holiness as the sacramental fruit of pastoral obedience, of collective as well as individual devotion – the Mass, the eucharist, the confessional were in Europe the mainspring of the Catholic revival.[3] Pole's reforming legislation in England was in part a transplant from the Verona of Giberti.[4] His plans were resumed in the Milan of Borromeo.[5] From Milan they were exported to the dioceses of Catholic Europe.[6] But in Europe the Jesuits played a vital role which was denied to them in England.

---

[1] Below, p. 270.   [2] *Epistolae*, v, 47.
[3] Jedin, 'Das Bischofsideal der Katholischen Reformation', *Kirche des Glaubens*, II, 75–118.
[4] Jedin, 'Domschule und Kolleg', ibid. II, 348–59. For the indigenous English influences, cf. J. O'Donohue, *Tridentine Seminary Legislation*, pp. 110–19.
[5] Tellechea Idigoras, 'El formulario de vista pastoral'.
[6] G. Alberigo, 'Carlo Borromeo come modello di vescovo nella Chiesa posttridentina', *Rivista Storica italiana*, LXXIX (1967), 1031–52.

Loyola wrote to Pole, offering his assistance.[1] Pole's failure to accept the initiative evoked the bitter comment of the Count of Feria: 'The Cardinal is a good man, but very lukewarm; and I do not believe the lukewarm go to Paradise, even if they are called moderates.'[2] Pole's neglect to invite the Jesuits to England will perhaps always remain something of a mystery. It can hardly be explained as a delayed reaction to the rift between the *spirituali* and the Jesuits in 1542–3: that rift had been healed by the time of his return to England.[3] He was not slow to rely upon the traditional preaching orders, the Dominicans and Franciscans. Perhaps it was the flair for individuality and initiative in the Jesuits that he may have shirked from as an inconvenience, preferring to postpone the risk of adventurous preaching until ecclesiastical discipline had been reestablished.[4] As the research of R. H. Pogson demonstrates,[5] he wanted to establish the norms of discipline before arranging for their detailed implementation. (After his experience of the Italian cities it is not difficult to understand why.) Perhaps the Jesuits were too original for him. Perhaps he saw them as an unwelcome instrument of greater Spanish influence. Feria's remark must be given its political implications.

To certain of Feria's compatriots, Pole's conduct of affairs in England was also unduly moderate in other things, not least in what they considered his slowness in pursuit of heresy.[6] It is perhaps as well to reflect on this, before wholeheartedly accepting the terrible description 'carnifex et flagellum Ecclesiae Anglicanae' applied to Pole by his successor in the diocese of Canterbury, Matthew Parker.[7] Schenk was possibly correct in arguing that Pole experienced some doubt about the extent to which the

[1] J. H. Crehan, 'St Ignatius and Cardinal Pole', *Archivium Historicum Societatis Iesu*, xxv (1956), 72–98.
[2] *C.S.P.S.*, XIII, no. 415.
[3] As Salmeron's deposition indicates. (Below, p. 270.)
[4] *Epistolae*, v, 73.   [5] Unpublished Cambridge dissertation.
[6] It was said that Pole's friend Carranza 'andaba descontento del Legado, por verle más blando de lo que el quisiera en el castigo de los herejes'. This was in August 1555. Cited by J. I. Tellechea Idigoras, *Bartolomé Carranza y la Restauracion Catolica Inglesa (1554–1558)*, Rome, 1964, p. 200.
[7] Cf. Dickens, *The English Reformation*, p. 266.

principle of persecution should be applied; he was certainly correct in his assertion that Pole's 'occasional, haphazard clemency can hardly be said to matter very much'.[1] Principle demanded the suppression of whatever scruples he may occasionally have experienced; and the responsibilities which he believed to be inseparable from his office quickened his apprehension of the dangers to the Church and Commonwealth, making him mindful of the necessary limits to 'facilitas'. His responsibility for the persecutions of the reign was one which he himself acknowledged. The historian is perhaps best advised simply to register the fact, and then resist if possible the urge to extenuate or vilify, according to his inclination.

Abroad, Pole's English policy attracted the attention of his Protestant enemies. Already, in the spring of 1554, Vergerio was planning fresh assaults. On 30 March he wrote to Bullinger, informing him that he had come upon a copy of *De Unitate*.[2] Never, he considered, had a work been written which attacked the Protestant position with greater heat or eloquence. He intended to publish an excerpt from it, in which Pole spoke of the Protestants as similar to Turks, and urged the Emperor to take up arms against them. He would append his own *scholia* to these remarks. Thus Pole's hypocrisy would be revealed to all, and Pole would be discredited if he were to appear at a religious conference.[3] Having accomplished this, Vergerio would see to it that the whole work was afterwards published with additional *scholia*.

Vergerio was evidently afraid that Pole would be sent as a papal delegate to the impending religious conference for the settlement of Germany. Thus he caused a copy of *De Unitate* to be sent to the representatives of his patron, Duke Christoph of Württemberg, so that they would suffer no illusions in the forthcoming conference which, as they believed, was to be held at

---

[1] Schenk, *Reginald Pole*, pp. 152–4.

[2] Letter cited by F. Hubert, *Vergerio's publizistische Thätigkeit* (Göttingen, 1893), p. 135, n. 361.

[3] At this time, Pole was still living on the continent, awaiting permission to enter England. The preliminaries to the Peace of Augsburg were at hand.

Nuremberg.[1] Shortly afterwards, his edition of the relevant excerpt from the book appeared, under the title *Oratio R. Poli*.[2] A prefatory note by one 'Athanasius' to a certain 'pastor of Augsburg'[3] adverted to a promise which Pole was declared to have given to the pastor in question to the effect that in the event of a religious conference being held he would support 'our doctrine'. It was best, therefore, that Pole's address to the Emperor should be published, so that his dissimulation might be recognised for what it was.[4] There followed a lengthy passage from *De Unitate* in which Pole, by a rhetorical device, addressed the Emperor and warned him that 'a new enemy, more terrible than the Turks' had now appeared.

This text was published by Vergerio in order to discredit the policy of religious talks in Germany;[5] it enabled him in addition to denounce Pole as a renegade. Pole, he maintained, was worse than the ancient Pharisees: for he differed from them in understanding the truth against which he contended. He had been motivated by two things in publishing his work against the Protestants: fear of denunciation by Carafa, on account of his doctrinal views, and ambition for the papacy, which he coveted.[6]

In reality, of course, Pole had never published the work, and it had not been written against the German Protestants, but against Henry VIII; and his address to the Emperor had been a device to frighten Henry with the threat of a continental alliance directed against England. It was only in passing that he had made the briefest of allusions to the German schism.[7] But these allusions

[1] Vergerio to Duke Christoph, 19 April 1554 (E. von Kausler and K. Schott (eds.), *Briefwechsel zwischen Christop Herzog von Württemberg, und Petrus Paulus Vergerius*, Tubingen, 1875, p. 68).

[2] *Oratio R. Poli, qua Caesaris animum accendere conatur & inflammare...cum scholiis Athanasii* (1554, *s.l.*, but Augsburg?).

[3] Between 1545 and 1547 Ochino was pastor to the Italian Protestant community at Augsburg.

[4] *Oratio*, preface.   [5] Below, pp. 266ff.

[6] *Oratio R. Poli*, pp. Ciiiv and Civv.

[7] Thus, in the passage published by Vergerio: 'Do you not see that this seed of the Turks [i.e. heresy] has been widely sown among us? I wish only that it were so insignificant that you could not see it. But you have seen it in your Germany. How greatly we should mourn this! However, the seed of the Turks has not been completely sown there. Public authority has not thus far forced everything else to be dominated by the command of one man. For there is no reason for complete

were enough for Vergerio to indicate Pole's attitude towards the schism; and his plan to publish a complete edition of *De Unitate* doubtless derived its inspiration from the tone of emotional hostility which pervades the book, and Pole's occasional references to the disruption of Christendom which the Reformation had effected.

About the same time that this excerpt from the work appeared, Pole received an anonymous letter accusing him of perfidy, and threatening to publish 'very soon' an edition of *De Unitate*. Among other things, he was reproved for having suppressed the book in order to prevent it from falling into Protestant hands; and there was reference as well to a certain pastor of Augsburg (presumably Ochino) with whom Pole was supposed to have conferred, promising to support the Protestant cause. There can scarcely be any doubt that the author of this letter was Vergerio, although Pole was altogether bewildered by it, and supposed that it was by a German.[1]

This anonymous letter is unfortunately lost, but its contents may be inferred from an account of it given in Pole's letter of 20 June 1554 to the Cardinal of Augsburg, Otto Truchsess.[2] Parts of this letter have been already discussed; but so much of it is taken up with a rebuttal of the accusations made against him in the recent anonymous attack that a further account of it is called for. It is certain that Pole had not yet seen a copy of *Oratio R. Poli*;[3] but Vergerio's letter seems to have repeated, and further amplified, the accusations levelled at him in that work. Thus Pole found himself obliged to deny that he had ever been to Augsburg in his life. He had, it was true, spent some months at Dillingen very recently, in the household of Truchsess himself: but he had never met or conferred with any representative of the Protestant persuasion, or promised to espouse their cause at a religious conference.[4]

---

despair about the genuine church of the Germans. It may blossom forth again and produce the beautiful fruits of Catholic truth after oppression by this deceitful seed. But this seed is now sown in England.' (Dwyer, *Pole's Defense*, p. 272.)

[1] *Epistolae*, IV, 151, 154. [2] Ibid. pp. 150–8.

[3] See below, p. 262. The work may not even have appeared yet, though this seems unlikely. [4] *Epistolae*, IV, 154.

There was, however, more to deny than that. Pole had been further accused of secretly acknowledging the gospel, especially in regard to justification, while at the same time endeavouring to prevent the doctrine from being publicised in Italy. In reply to these charges, Pole provided Truchsess with a brief history of his religious opinions. He explained his former attitude to the doctrine of justification, and related his attempts to restrain all impatient and immoderate proclamation of religious doctrine.[1]

He denied, moreover, that he had ever canvassed for the papacy, or urged a Franco-Imperial war against the Protestants.[2] He might have spoken harshly of Protestants, referring to the corrupt influence which they exerted upon others, and arguing that a putrid member should be severed from the body; but he had always advocated first the adoption of gentle measures of persuasion. He had always opposed the use of war as a way of winning back the Protestants. For this reason, indeed, he had had to suffer the reputation of excessive mildness, and had been suspected of favouring the Protestant cause.[3] At the Council of Trent he had exhorted the fathers to display paternal love in all their judgements; for even open heretics should be regarded not so much as rebels, but as rebellious sons.[4] He had not been alone in this opinion, and the Council fathers had readily adopted it.[5] Far from feeling hostile towards the people of Germany, his own sentiments, like those of all Englishmen, were deeply friendly. The very fact that Germany had received the faith from an Englishman, St Boniface, should serve as a spiritual bond between the countries. It was all the more regrettable, therefore, that the Germans should rebel against the Church and, their example having been followed by England, endeavour to draw all others after them.[6] In conclusion, Pole begged Truchsess to investigate any rumours that a pirated edition of *De Unitate* was about to

[1] Above, pp. 200–4.
[2] *Epistolae*, IV, 154–6. The latter imputation, as we shall see, was the one which Vergerio was most anxious to publicise.
[3] Ibid. pp. 156–7.　　　　　　　　　　　　　　　[4] Ibid. p. 157.
[5] Ibid. This seems like a breathtaking feat of intellectual reconstruction, in view of Pole's feelings on the Council eight years earlier.
[6] Ibid. pp. 157–8.

appear: if so, he begged him to publish an authentic version, which Pole would dispatch to him, along with a new preface which he had composed. If, however, Truchsess should hear nothing, he should postpone the matter until Pole had sent an agent of his own to make further inquiries.[1]

Pole's alarm at Vergerio's accusations is apparent. If he were to suffer a public attack, he would be obliged publicly to defend himself.[2] Hence his willingness to permit a new, authenticated edition of *De Unitate* to appear, arose from his need to undercut the charge of secret complicity with heresy. Such an accusation, at a time when he was about to take up office in England, would need convincing refutation. Not only would it damage his authority in England, but it would also jeopardise his recently consolidated standing with the Roman Inquisition. It was imperative, therefore, that Vergerio's attack be met.

But it was not. Truchsess, apparently, could find out nothing, and Pole's inquiries were no more successful. By the end of the year he was installed as Papal Legate in England, and was preoccupied with other matters. Early in 1555, however, he received a copy of *Oratio R. Poli*. He straightaway sent his manuscripts to Truchsess to be published, if the latter saw fit.[3] But Truchsess, it would seem, did not see fit; for when in 1555 an edition of *De Unitate* appeared, it was under the auspices not of Truchsess, but of Vergerio, and it was dedicated to the Protestant elector John Frederick of Saxony.[4]

The work was provided with a preface in which Vergerio openly revealed himself as Pole's antagonist. He accused Pole of having suppressed the *De Unitate* on its first appearance. By keeping it from general circulation, Pole had been able to present himself as a friend of the true faith, so as more easily to insinuate himself into the confidence of Protestants.[5] By implication, therefore, Vergerio was publishing the work in order to reveal

[1] *Epistolae*, IV, p. 158; cf. also, p. 151.
[2] Ibid.   [3] *Epistolae*, V, 60–2.
[4] *Reginaldi Poli, Cardinalis Britanni, pro Ecclesiasticae unitatis defensione libri quatuor...nunc primi in Germania editi...* (1555, s.l., but Strasburg). Cf. Vergerio to Duke Christoph, 23 October 1554: 'Deinde dedi imprimendum librum Cardinali Poli Angli cum antidotis.' (*Briefwechsel*, p. 71.)   [5] Preface, p. ii.

Pole in his true colours; and, lest anyone be impressed by Pole's eloquence in defence of Rome, he appended to the text a series of anti-Papal tracts by Calvin, Bucer, Brentius and Melanchthon.

Thus, by 1555, Vergerio's campaign against Pole was operating at full pitch. Nor was it restricted to the printed word. There exists in the Vienna state archives a copy of a manuscript propaganda sheet in which the charges against Pole and his associates are repeated.[1] The document is undated and unsigned. It is written in the form of a private letter, but its tone and contents indicate that it was intended for circulation. From the early 1550s Vergerio had been responsible for the infiltration to Italy of propaganda sheets which were then distributed to different places.[2] These sheets often took the form of 'open letters', both manuscript and printed, in which the propaganda war was carried forward.[3] It seems reasonable to assume, therefore, that the Vienna manuscript is a propaganda circular inspired by Vergerio; and since it refers to the treatise *Discorso di Pace*, which Pole published in 1554 or 1555 it almost certainly belongs to the same period.[4]

The letter opens with an attack on the *Discorso*. Two main points are singled out for criticism. The first is that Pole has implicitly equated the Turks with 'those who embrace the pure doctrine of the Gospel'. The second is that he has ventured the opinion that the combined power of France and the Empire would scarcely be sufficient to repress the Protestants.[5]

Against the first of these points the author complains that the

---

[1] *O.S.V., England, varia*, fasc. IV, 1555–98 (formerly fasc. V), fols. 7r–9r. (Calendared in *C.S.P.S.*, XIII, no. 227, but the translation is surprisingly misleading in places.)

[2] Cf. Beccadelli, in a letter of 16 May 1551: 'Tratto ho qualche cartello o in stampa o in penna che mi vengono alle mani di mille furfantaria contro il Concilio et la sede Romana et frati, le quali sono mandate sotto coperta di lettere senza nome in diverse luoghi, et a iudicio mio et d'altra ancora è farina del Vergerio già vescova di Capo d'Istria, il quale sta ne Grisoni et sparge di qua questi veleni'. Cited in Paschini, *Venezia e l'inquisizione Romana da Giulio III a Pio IV* (Padua, 1959), pp. 75–6.

[3] In September 1553 Beccadelli complained that 'questo sventurato [Vergerio] non cessa et con lettere et con messi et suoi libriciuoli che va stampando ogni dì di subornare et infamar molte persone'. (Ibid. p. 102.)

[4] *Discorso di Pace di Mons. Reginaldo Polo Cardinale Legato a Carlo V Imperatore, et Henrico II Re di Francia (s.a., s.l.).*

[5] *O.S.V., England varia*, fasc. IV, fol. 7r. Cf. *Discorso*, fols. Bi v–Bii r.

bad opinion in which the Emperor and the French king hold 'our doctrine' derives from the activity of 'papal legates and friars, especially confessors' who inflame the minds of princes. He then turns to deliver a personal attack on Pole who, 'with all the great profession which he makes of sincerity and goodness' is not ashamed to say that Protestants are similar to Turks.[1] Is it possible that Priuli is of this opinion, since some say that he dictated the discourse to Pole?[2] Perhaps one day some brave man may confront them face to face. He would ask them if they were not the same men who at Rome, at Viterbo, at Venice and at Trent had warmly prevailed upon all whom they could trust to keep it secret that in the matter of justification (among other things) the enemies of Rome were altogether in the right; that man was justified by the sole merit of Jesus Christ, apprised in faith; and that he could contribute nothing further by his works?[3]

This was the most extensive, detailed and damaging attack delivered against Pole so far. It continues with the conjecture that perhaps Pole and Priuli have now abandoned this opinion: or perhaps, on the other hand, they still believe it in the secret of their hearts, while at the same time condemning it openly, which would be worse. There then follows an attack upon the papal policy of endeavouring to secure peace between France and the Empire: the purpose of which policy, it is argued, is to unite the forces of the two powers against the Lutherans.[4]

This preoccupation is highly revealing, for it points to the root motive animating Vergerio's campaign against Pole in the years 1554–5. Pole, as well as Morone, enjoyed a reputation among Lutherans as moderate men and conciliators, who were anxious to restrain the aggressive spirit of the Inquisition. Vergerio had noted with alarm how many Italians ('meos caros compatriotas') looked to Pole as to an apostle: men who, recognising that salvation was by faith alone, nevertheless conformed with the

[1] *O.S.V.*, *England varia*, fasc. IV, fol. 7r.
[2] Ibid. (*C.S.P.S.*, XIII, no. 227 reads 'this course'; which alters the meaning rather considerably.)
[3] Ibid. fol. 7r.
[4] Ibid. fols. 7v–8r.

Reprisals

external rituals of Catholicism, pleading by way of excuse the example of Pole.[1]

Vergerio was referring to Italians like Carnesecchi whom Calvin designated 'Nicodemists', and whose most outstanding spokesman, Giorgio Siculo, had been executed at Ferrara in 1551.[2] Siculo was a Benedictine monk, a prophet and a visionary. He wielded great influence among Italian Protestants, especially in the Grisons, where Vergerio was attempting to organise the Italian Lutheran community. As a young man he had been a member of the same community as Benedetto da Mantova; at one time of his life he was recommended to Pole; and he continued to interest the Inquisition for some years after his death.[3]

Siculo represented an important current in Italian heterodoxy; the tendency, as Cantimori puts it, to remain independent of the principal doctrines of the Reformation, while nevertheless opposing the existing form of the Church.[4] Inspired prophecy and simplified piety were the characteristic features of his doctrine. For Siculo, as for Vergerio, the Spiera case raised the problem of how to comport oneself in the face of persecution. Unlike Vergerio, however, Siculo maintained that Spiera had been mistaken in allowing himself to be trapped in a situation which led him to abjure his beliefs. It was better, he felt, that men should openly continue the practice of Catholicism, while secretly keeping their opinions to themselves until such a time as the Church should alter her condition.[5]

To many Italians who shared Siculo's approach, Pole and Morone seemed like harbingers of comfort, visible evidence that the Church might yet accommodate itself to their desires. Thus, for example, the 'compatriots' of whom Vergerio complained.[6]

[1] Vergerio to Duke Christoph, 19 February 1555. (*Briefwechsel*, p. 100.)
[2] The following account of Siculo is based on Cantimori, *Eretici Italiani*, pp. 57–70. Caponetto demonstrates that Siculo was a friend and disciple of Benedetto da Mantova (*Dizionario*, VIII, 439–40). A. Rotondò promises a chapter on Siculo, based on new documents, in a forthcoming study of heresy at Bologna and Modena in the sixteenth century. Cf. 'Per la Storia dell' eresia a Bologna nel secolo XVI' in *Rinascimento*, 13 (1962), 125, n. 1.
[3] Caponetto, 'Benedetto da Mantova', *Dizionario*, VIII, 439–40; Rotondò, 'Per la Storia dell' eresia', p. 126, n. 1.
[4] *Eretici italiani*, p. 62.   [5] Ibid. p. 64.
[6] Carnesecchi, on learning of Pole's death, considered that one of the threads

265

Others, who found their way to Switzerland, cast one final despairing glance in their direction, as if asking their indulgence. Ochino and Vermigli had done as much in 1542; and ten years later, at the beginning of Lent, an Augustinian preacher, Celso Martinengo, wrote from Milan to the Vicar General of his order in Rome, lamenting that he could no longer reconcile Christian liberty and charity with the religion he had known in Italy. Could he do so, he would be 'the happiest man in the world'; but he could not. He thought of Soranzo, who might have consoled him [but Soranzo was in Rome for questioning]; and he begged his superior to recommend him to Soranzo, Pole, Morone and Grimani. Within a few weeks Martinengo was at Geneva, where he became the first pastor of the Italian Lutheran community.[1]

In the light of such circumstances as these, it is not difficult to understand Vergerio's hostility to Pole. By refusing to sever his connection with the Church of Rome, Pole was providing comfort to the timorous Niceodemists who, unlike Martinengo, renounced the challenge of the gospel, and conformed to the appearances imposed by residence in Italy. Yet we must look beyond this for an explanation of the incessant propaganda which he directed against Pole in the two years 1554-5.

Early in 1554, as we have seen, Vergerio elaborated a particular strategy for his campaign; and during the ensuing period he carried it out to its last detail. He had informed Duke Christoph at that time, of his intention to provide the latter's delegates at Nuremberg with a copy of *De Unitate*. He would inform them too, of the 'story' which lay behind Pole's strictures on the Protestants.[2] The 'story', as we have seen, was that Pole had suppressed the book in order to persuade the Protestants that he was really on their side. It was therefore imperative that Pole be discredited in the eyes of Protestants, at a time when they were about to negotiate a settlement with the Emperor. The representatives of

which kept him in Italy was now broken. He later told the Inquisition that he had not wished to discredit or offend his patrons, Pole and Morone, by departing for Switzerland. ('Processo', pp. 305-8.)

[1] Paschini, *Tre ricerche*, pp. 142-3.
[2] *Briefwechsel*, p. 68, 19 April 1554.

Rome must not be allowed to approach the conference table with bland words and promises of peace: the moderates in particular, men like Pole and Morone, must be shown up as hypocrites.

This interpretation is further confirmed by the fact that Duke Christoph was implacably opposed to a policy of concession by the Protestants.[1] Hence, during the period 1554-5, as events moved towards a religious settlement in Germany, Vergerio, working on the Duke's behalf, endeavoured to destroy the impression that Pole – and by extension the moderate Roman party – was well disposed towards the Protestant cause. He was moved no doubt in part by indignation at what he thought of as their treachery; but his indignation was not unmixed with fear that a religious peace in Germany, followed by peace between the Empire and France, would isolate the Lutherans and leave them prey to political destruction. Hence Pole's *Discorso* advocating peace between the two great powers positively invited his repudiation. Exactly this preoccupation may be observed in the final onslaught which he delivered against Pole in 1555.[2] On 9 February he wrote to Duke Christoph, informing him that he had composed a further work revealing the manner in which Pole was conducting the affairs of England. He referred in the same passage to Morone: a man who, like Pole, thoroughly understood 'the truth', and so deceived the uninformed. They belonged to the same stable: to see one was to see the other.[3] Ten days later he wrote again, complaining of his compatriots who were so easily misled by Pole. He hoped to show them how 'their apostle' was presently comporting himself in England.[4] Accordingly, there appeared in 1555 a little book entitled *Epistolae duae*, in which the power of

---

[1] Cf. L. Spitz, 'Particularism and Peace: Augsburg 1555' in *Church History*, xxv, 1956, 110-26.

[2] Yet another attack on Pole appeared in this year, entitled *Giudicio soprà le lettere di tredici huomini illustri publicate da M. Dionigi Atanagi & stampate in Venetia nel l'anno 1554*. It was published anonymously, but there can be little doubt that the author was Vergerio. (See above, n. 4, p. 40.) The burden of the complaint was that Pole had restrained Flaminio from advancing into the fullness of truth, and that by the exercise of 'sottilissima astutia' he had persuaded many others to keep their opinions to themselves, while all the time promising that the Church would eventually recognise the truth of what must be temporarily concealed. (Cf. Schelhorn, *Amoenitates Historiae Ecclesiasticae*, II, 7-15.)

[3] *Briefwechsel*, pp. 92-3.   [4] Ibid. p. 100.

Rome came virulently under fire.[1] The first letter dealt bitterly with Catholic pamphleteers like Muzio and Casa, and linked their efforts with the threat of an Imperial war against the Lutherans;[2] the second, with heavy irony, was entitled *De Studio, et Zelo pietatis Cardinalis Poli.*[3]

This letter, the last which Vergerio directed against Pole, repeated the familiar charges at greater length, and with greater vehemence than before; and it contrasted Pole's former policy of moderation with his persecution of the English Protestants. Had Pole not formerly avowed his belief in the doctrine of salvation by faith alone, and expressed his strong desire to promote it when the 'time and opportunity' should arise? Had he not frequently asserted that his adherence to the papacy was but dissimulation, to be cast off when the right moment should occur? Had he now abandoned his beliefs, and sinned against the Holy Spirit; or had he never been sincere at all in his religion?[4] He had restored England to communion with the Church of Rome; he had imprisoned Cranmer, and consigned to martyrdom men like Hooper, Rogers, and Dr Rowland Taylor. He had elevated Stephen Gardiner to the see of Winchester, while Ponet, a true pastor of the Church, went into exile.[5] In short, he was triumphant: the power of Rome, the reign of hypocrites, was now established. But Pole would pay for this triumph in the deepest pit of hell, tormented by eternal fire. Rome, moreover, was deluded in believing that the fall of England heralded the imminent return of Germany. Morone had been chosen as the Papal delegate to Augsburg – a man, like Pole, well-versed in treachery; but his hypocrisy was known in advance: who had seen one, had seen the other.[6]

It is clear that Vergerio, in attacking Pole, hoped to discredit the pretensions of the papal delegates to Augsburg, and to discourage

---

[1] *Epistolae duae, duorum amicorum, ex quibus uana, flagitiosaque Pontificum, Paulitertii, & Iulii tertii, & Cardinalis Poli, & Stephani Gardineri pseudoepiscopi Vuintoniensis Angli, eorumque adulatorum sectatorumque ratio, magna ex parte potest intelligi.* (Anon, *s.a., s.l.,* but 1555.) Copies of this rare work are to be found in St John's College, Cambridge (0.20¹⁰) and the Biblioteca Nazionale, Florence (Guicc, 2.4.5²).

[2] Ibid. fol. A4r.   [3] Ibid. fols. B1r–B4v.   [4] Ibid. fol. B1r–v.
[5] Ibid. fols. B1v, B3r.   [6] Ibid. fol. B4v.

the Protestant estates from compromise. But his policy was a failure. Later that year Duke Christoph rode home from the conference at Augsburg, sadly reflecting on the ruin of the gospel and the triumph of particularist interest.[1] Nevertheless, Vergerio must have derived much gratification in learning, two years later, of Morone's imprisonment; and in publishing, shortly afterwards, the charges preferred against Morone by the Roman Inquisition.[2]

Carafa's reconciliation with Pole did not survive the passage of time, the renewal of rumour and suspicion, the corroborative evidence, possibly, of Vergerio. On 23 March 1555 Julius III died, and Carafa forgot his fervent hopes that Pole would some day become Pope. Instead, he became Pope himself, after the brief interval of Marcellus II, who reigned for three weeks and then died.[3] At the ensuing conclave his suspicions about Pole and Morone were revived, for their opponents once again cast aspersions on their orthodoxy.[4] The charge was no more than a political counter, but Carafa was disposed to take it seriously. Certain Jesuits and others who had formerly entertained a poor opinion of Morone's doctrine testified at this time to his present orthodoxy; but their remarks were taken as an indirect accusation against his past.[5] On 22 May 1555 Carafa was elected Pope, taking the name Paul IV. He straightaway began inquiries about Morone.[6]

One of Loyola's most devoted followers, Alfonso Salmeron, was summoned to make a deposition, and he revealed the history of Morone's earlier attitude to the principal questions of the Reformation.[7] Salmeron had been sent to assist Morone in his diocese of Modena in 1543. Morone, however, had prevented

[1] Spitz, 'Particularism and Peace', p. 121.
[2] *Articuli contra Cardinalem Moronum, de Luteranismo accusatum, et in carcerum coniectum (s.a., s.l.,* but 1557 or 1558).
[3] *C.T.*, II, 248, 253, 260, 266.
[4] Pastor, *Popes*, XIV, 58; *C.S.P.S.*, XIII, no. 197.
[5] Cf. J. I. Tellechea Idigoras, 'Una denuncia'.
[6] At the same time, he confirmed Pole in his Legation; but not before referring the matter to the Inquisition. (*Epistolae*, V, 136–9, and below, p. 273.)
[7] P. Tacchi Venturi, *Storia della Compagnia di Gesù in Italia,* I, ii (3rd ed., Rome, 1950), pp. 154–8.

him from preaching the doctrine of justification 'contra il senso lutherano'. Salmeron believed that his intention had perhaps been Catholic; but neither his meaning nor his words were so. Morone had denied that good works could merit anything – unless, perhaps, eternal punishment. He had also favoured a certain preacher, a Franciscan friar named Pergola, who was subsequently examined by the Inquisition. Some years later, however, Morone had discussed these questions once again with Salmeron, and had revealed a mind utterly changed and altogether Catholic. He had begged Salmeron's forgiveness for the scandal and offence which he had earlier given him. He had expressed himself loyal to the Church's teaching, and submissive to what had been determined by the Council of Trent on the subject of justification.[1]

The effect of Salmeron's remarks was to absolve Morone of deliberate or persistent error; but to confirm in Carafa the suspicions which he entertained of him. Now that he was Pope, his policy was simple, and unshakeable. He intended to restore the political superiority of Rome, and to eliminate the contagion of heresy which, as he believed, had affected even the higher reaches of the Church. The first of these objectives took expression in overt hostility to the Spanish monarchy, threatening as it did the independence of the Holy See and of his native Italy; and it led him to embark upon a policy which, after a year and a half in office, resulted in war between the papacy and Spain.[2] During the course of this conflict, which broke out in September 1556, the second of his objectives began to manifest itself, with results that were disastrous for the remaining *spirituali*.

The Pope's hostility to Pole was openly demonstrated on 9 April 1557, when he announced in consistory the recall of all his agents in the territories of Philip II. On this occasion he made a particular reference to Pole, revoking his Legation 'nominatim'.[3] Pole was overwhelmed by the decision. He wrote to the Pope on

[1] Ibid. In 1547 Loyola instructed Salmeron to visit Morone again, and demand an explanation of what had passed between them in 1543.
[2] H. Lutz, *Christianitas afflicta. Europa, das Reich und die papstliche Politik im Niedergang der Hegemonie Kaiser Karls V (1552–1556)* (Göttingen, 1964); Pastor, *Popes*, XIV, 90–174.
[3] *C.T.*, II, 306.

25 May, urging him to appoint another Legate in his place: England could not survive without a Papal Legate.[1] His request was met in form, if not in spirit. On 14 June, an octogenarian Franciscan, William Peto, was appointed as Cardinal and Legate for England, and he was obliged to hold office despite his protests that he was incapable of doing so effectively.[2] Pole, as Archbishop of Canterbury, retained his position as 'legatus natus'; but on the same day that Peto was appointed he was recalled to Rome.[3]

The reason for his recall was directly related to the arrest and imprisonment of Morone, on 31 May 1557.[4] At the same, time, Sanfelice and Soranzo were arrested.[5] One 12 June, the Venetian ambassador reported that the Inquisition was making enquiries about Pole.[6] This was followed by a move against Priuli. During the reign of Julius III, Priuli, at the instigation of the Venetian government, had been promised the see of Brescia on the death of its incumbent, Durante di Duranti. In June 1557 Paul IV revoked all appointments to benefices by accession. His motive, according to the Venetian ambassador, was to prevent the advancement of Priuli, who was notoriously suspect in the Pope's opinion.[7]

Thus in the middle of 1557 the machinery of the Inquisition began to move in earnest against the surviving *spirituali*. The news of Pole's recall, however, came to him only indirectly; for the Queen now saw to it, despite his protests, that all letters from Rome were prevented from reaching him.[8] In October 1557 the Pope sent his nephew, Carlos Carafa, to Flanders, to demand Pole's extradition; but the Queen obstinately refused permission

---

[1] *Epistolae*, v, 27–31.

[2] *C.S.P.V.*, vi, ii, no. 937, dispatch of Bernardo Navagero, 18 June 1557.

[3] Ibid.

[4] Pastor, *Popes*, xiv, 290–1, and App. 46–7. On 1 June, the Pope hinted that Pole was involved in the case against Morone (*C.S.P.V.*, vi, ii, no. 914).

[5] Pastor, *Popes*, xiv, 284, 312. Paschini *Tre ricerche*, pp. 145ff.

[6] *C.S.P.V.*, vi, ii, no. 933.

[7] Navagero to the Council of Ten, 18 June 1557: 'il pontefice ha detto a qualche Cardinal, che nella casa del R. mo Polo, ove sono tanti appestati parlando di heresia, non vi è persona più del Priuli' (*P.R.O.* 31/14/87, fol. 110; cal. in *C.S.P.V.*, vi, no. 939).

[8] Below, n. 3, p. 273.

for Pole to leave the realm. Carlos Carafa carried with him a list of the charges against Pole; and the circumstances reveal how determined the Pope was to secure a confrontation between Pole and Morone. Although political hostilities had ceased, following the Spanish victory of St Quentin in August 1557, the Pope remained intent on completing the second of his objectives. Indeed, from this time onwards, he devoted all his energies to that end. As the months passed, it became increasingly clear to him, as it had been earlier clear to Vergerio, that between Pole and Morone there was no difference: or rather, it seemed to him that Morone was no more than a disciple. The master conspirator, he was convinced, remained at large.[1]

Pole, meanwhile, did not neglect to plead his cause. His personal envoy, Niccolò Ormaneto, travelled to Rome to intercede with the Pope;[2] he himself wrote constantly, urging reason, moderation and restraint; and in the autumn of 1557 he drew up a lengthy *apologia* defending himself against the Pope's attack.

This document, composed towards the end of August 1557, was never sent to Rome. Pole, on re-reading it, threw it into the fire.[3] A copy of the document survived, however, and it has recently been published.[4] In essence, the letter is a protest: an indictment of the Pope's misguided policy, and a review of the long history of Carafa's animosity to Pole. The tone of the document is one of grief and hurt resentment; bewilderment that a servant of the papacy should be obliged so to defend himself; and a certain passionate determination to recall the Pope to his true duties. In this respect, it is reminiscent of Pole's earlier appeal to Henry VIII, which it resembles in emotional eloquence and indignation: and it was destined to have even less effect. It is perhaps in keeping with the history of the *spirituali* that their final

[1] *C.S.P.V.*, VI, ii, no. 1067. Cf. below, p. 278.
[2] Ibid. nos. 981, 1002.
[3] *Monumenti*, I, ii, pp. 325–6 (Beccadelli's *Life*).
[4] J. I. Tellechea Idigoras, 'Pole y Paulo IV: Una celébre Apologia inedita del Cardenal Inglés (1557)', *Archivium Historiae Pontificiae*, IV (1966), 105–54. The document, printed on pp. 133–54, is convincingly ascribed to the month of August 1557 (p. 109). The original is in the Inner Temple Library, Petyt MSS, no. 538, vol. 46, fols. 391r–426v.

protest should have been hurled into the fire by its author, and a copy relegated to a private desk. Its contents were communicated piecemeal to the Pope in later letters, and through personal envoys; with more restraint, but with the same lack of effect.

Pole's letter opened in bewilderment. He considered it to be without precedent that a Pope, suspecting a Cardinal of heresy, should revoke his Legation without specifying the offence. The Pope's treatment of Morone was no less unprecedented. He had placed Morone in custody without fair trial. He had linked his case with that of Pole. For his own part, Pole had no wish to experience the same fate.[1] He could only plead that the Pope suspected them unjustly, and insist (following the example of St Paul) that the Pope was in the wrong.[2]

Pole then turned to a consideration of the Pope's recent dealings with him, complaining of the latter's underhand methods of procedure. Pole had learned that the brief recalling him to Rome (which, through no fault of his own he had been prevented from reading)[3] spoke of a general assembly of Cardinals to deal with Church reform. What could be more honourable? What better reason could there be for Pole's recall? But the Pope's actions revealed his true intentions. Pole would not allow himself to be deceived by bland words. For when the Pope referred the decision to confirm Pole's Legation, not to the Cardinals in consistory, as was customary, but to the Inquisition, he revealed the true state of his opinion about Pole. Then, when the decision to renew Pole's office was in question, he deferred the matter until after Morone's arrest, and finally deprived him of his Legation altogether, replacing him with another man. He thereby revealed his conviction that Morone's case was linked with Pole's, and that he had arrested Morone in order to find out something further about Pole. Again, in the same consistory in which he deprived Pole of his office, he debarred Priuli from his rightful advancement to the see of Brescia, thus once more making it apparent what he thought of Pole and his associates. Finally, Pole had learned from

---

[1] *Apologia*, p. 134. [2] Ibid. pp. 134–5. The reference is to Gal. 2.11.
[3] The Queen having withheld from him every communication from Rome (ibid. pp. 136–67).

correspondents that the Pope referred to him in private, adverting to his long-standing suspicions about Pole, and his knowledge that for many years Pole's household had been a refuge for heretics. In particular, the Pope had named Flaminio, openly referring to him as a most perverse heretic. Expressions of this kind released Pole from further hesitation, and provoked him to reply.[1]

Pole's reply took the form of a review of his relations with the Pope. He pointed out that this was not the first time that the Pope had put about this fable. He had first raised the matter in the conclave following the death of Paul III. Together with de Cupis, he had conspired to blacken Pole's name with a charge of heresy. The Cardinal de Burgos (Toledo) had generously mediated between Pole and de Cupis, so that the latter eventually assured Pole that he considered him to be 'the best man in Rome'. Pole had then decided to call upon Carafa, seeing that they were estranged, and to effect a reconciliation, if that were possible.[2]

Pole reminded the Pope how, during the course of that interview, he had remarked upon the ways of providence, which had permitted him twice in his lifetime to be condemned by the two men whom he most revered – Henry VIII and Carafa himself – for the crime of *laesae majestatis*.[3] He had then recounted to Carafa how, at the time of the latter's appointment to the College of Cardinals, Paul III had entertained some doubt about his suitability. Contarini and Giberti were urging the nomination of Carafa; at the last moment the Pope showed signs of vacillation, and thought of appointing Aleander in his place. On the night before the nomination, the Pope summoned Pole, thinking to gain his support for his contemplated change of course. He had heard that a disagreement had arisen between Pole and Carafa, and supposed that Pole would therefore support the cause of Aleander. The Pope did not at first disclose the reason for his change of plan, but implied that it was serious. At length, however, he revealed that Carafa had fallen under some suspicion of impiety. At this suggestion, Pole blazed up with indignation and

---

[1] *Apologia*, pp. 138–9. [2] Ibid. p. 140.
[3] Carafa, he meant, was accusing him of *laesae majestatis divinae* (ibid.).

(as he afterwards realised) passing the bounds of propriety, he extolled Carafa's piety at the expense of Aleander's. He then flung himself at the Pope's feet, and beseeched him to ignore this calumny against Carafa, whose probity was such that Pole would stake his soul upon it. To these entreaties, and those of Contarini and Giberti, the Pope replied by reverting to his earlier decision; the next day Carafa was appointed.[1]

At the end of Pole's account of this incident, Carafa had shown himself to be already conscious of, and appreciative of Pole's intervention on that occasion. He had warned Pole to be on his guard against the sort of rumours which circulated in a papal conclave; and Pole had then departed, thinking that the whole comedy, or tragedy, was at an end.[2] Rumours, however, had persisted, so that at length another interview took place, which ended in Carafa promising his support for Pole at the next papal conclave.[3]

Yet now the Pope was once again incriminating Pole, and lending his ears to complaints about him. The Pope, however, had only to observe Pole's actions, to see how ill-founded were these rumours. Even if such complaints were justified; even if Pole had once assented to heretical doctrines (which was far from being the case); even if he had sided openly with heretics and fought against the Church; surely his present campaign against heresy, fought in the name of the papacy and of the Church, must absolve him of all further suspicion? His whole life had been spent in obedience to the Church of Rome. His present labours were devoted daily to the protection of the faithful. Were his efforts, then, to be brought to nothing by the very representative of Christ who was their beneficiary?[4]

Pole had been informed that the Pope believed himself to be prompted by the highest motives: he wished, for the sake of his successor, to purify the college of electors from all imputation of heresy, by removing its two most suspect members.[5] It was an accusation which Pole considered to be no less unjust than that of David against Saul. He could appeal only to God: 'Domine vim patior, responde pro me.' [Is. 38.14]. God, he was assured, would

---

[1] Ibid. p. 141. [2] Ibid. p. 142. [3] Ibid.
[4] Ibid. pp. 142–3. [5] Ibid. p. 143.

reply on his behalf; and the whole Church would hear and understand. He would reply with deeds, not words: for Pole's deeds testified his belief. The years of bitterness which as a young man he had experienced on account of his allegiance to the faith, were ample evidence (no less than his spontaneous peace efforts in the present war, to restore the harmony of Christendom) that he was a loyal servant of the Church.[1]

Pole turned now to a vindication of his right to speak thus to the Pope. The role of Cardinals was to assist the Pope in governing the Church. Therefore it was both the right and duty of a Cardinal to admonish the Pope if his actions sprang from human error rather than divine encouragement. Let the Pope consider, then, how Satan was misleading him in his proceedings against Morone and himself. The Pope, in imprisoning Morone, had publicly declared that he was motivated by considerations of God's honour and the dangers to the Church. He had said the same thing privately in respect to Pole. But if the Pope were to deliberate upon the matter, and to inquire whether his decision came of God, he would see that its effect was to disrupt the work of Christ Himself. Pole had led the people of England back into obedience to the Church. To undermine that work by questioning Pole's faith, and removing him from his Legation, must rejoice the hearts of heretics and schismatics, and cause grave scandal to the faithful. For the sake of his flock, therefore, Pole must resist the inclination of the Pope, and urge him to examine whether his decision came of God. The Pope was risking the destruction of the Church in England. In his attempt to purify the College of Cardinals he had in reality brought it into disrepute, with charges more damaging than any brought by heretics. He was behaving like a sleepwalker, blind to the actual dangers threatening the Church. Pole, therefore, was exercising his Christian duty as a Cardinal, and his right, in endeavouring to awaken him: for the Pope was misusing his *plenitudo potestatis* in his conduct towards Morone and himself.[2]

Pole and Morone, however, had done nothing to deserve his

---

[1] *Apologia* pp. 143–5. For Pole's peace efforts, cf. Lutz, *Christianitas Afflicta*.
[2] *Apologia*, pp. 147–53.

blame. On the contrary, they had laboured in his service: their one fear was that in persecuting them he was crippling his own proper influence. Therefore they prayed that Christ might lead him constructively to exercise his powers towards them; lest, in default, the universal Church should suffer.[1]

It was a moving appeal, and a fitting postscript to the history of the *spirituali*. Together with Morone, Pole had worked to maintain the unity of the Church; and, with Morone, he had suffered repudiation by the chief pastor of that Church. The remaining months of his life were dragged out in disgrace; Morone, more fortunate in his time, survived to find himself absolved of all suspicion, and entrusted with the supervision of the final moments of the Council which, in its first sessions, had been the cause of so much suffering to Pole.

For the moment, however, Morone was the key figure in a case which continued to preoccupy the Pope throughout the latter part of 1557. In the second week of October, Salmeron was again interviewed about his connection fourteen years earlier with Morone. He related once more the details of Morone's views on justification, explaining that Morone had forbidden him to preach the doctrine of merit. Salmeron had written about this to Loyola at the time, and had been recalled to Rome as a result. Loyola had referred the matter to Pope Paul III, complaining that Salmeron's faith and the honour of his order had been called in question; the Pope, however, had bidden them proceed no further in the matter.[2] Asked about the *Beneficio di Cristo*, Salmeron replied that he had been told of a book 'qui postea damnatus est' which Morone freely circulated at Modena.[3] But he did not believe that Morone had ever been a heretic: he had been simply ill-informed about the article of faith in question; and afterwards (at the conference of Augsburg in 1555) he had apologised for his former conduct to Salmeron, and acknowledged that he had been in the wrong.[4]

[1] Ibid. p. 154.
[2] Tacchi Venturi, *Storia della Compagnia di Gesù in Italia*, I, ii, pp. 162, 168.
[3] Ibid. p. 169.
[4] Ibid. p. 163. This was the second occasion on which Morone apologised to Salmeron, the first having been in 1547, after the Council of Trent. (Above, p. 270.)

Thus, as time passed, the details of Morone's life emerged in a light which confirmed the Pope in his worst fears. Obsessed with the idea of heresy, and the danger which it constituted to the future of the Church should an heretical Cardinal succeed him, he grew every day more convinced that the real instigator of these evils was still at liberty in England, surrounded by his circle of accessories. Of these, Priuli was the principal; and when, at the end of 1557, the see of Brescia fell vacant, the Pope stood firm in his refusal to permit the accession to Priuli.[1] On 30 March 1558 Pole wrote a long letter protesting against the decision, in terms which recall his *apologia*.[2] At the same time he wrote to Cardinal Scoto assuring him of his innocence and loyalty to the Church, and requesting Scoto's mediation with the Pope.[3] These letters followed a personal appeal transmitted to the Pope at the beginning of 1558 by Pole's envoy Giovanni Francesco Stella.[4] Stella was instructed to remind the Pope of Pole's lifelong devotion to the Church; of his relations with Carafa over the years; and of the damage suffered by the Church on account of his misguided policies.

In essence, therefore, the burden of Pole's *apologia* was communicated to the Pope. But the latter was deaf to all appeal. For some months now, a 'process' had been built up against Pole,[5] and its contents confirmed the Pope in his hostility. When, in October 1557, the Venetian ambassador approached him about Priuli's right of accession, he burst out in anger, exclaiming that Priuli belonged to 'that accursed school, and that apostate household, of the Cardinal of England.' Pole was the master, Morone the disciple; Flaminio too, had been a member of the group, and would have been burned had he survived. The Pope added that were his own father a heretic, he would himself carry the faggots to burn him.[6]

---

[1] Cf. the report of Bernardo Navagero to the Council of Ten, 5 November 1557 (*P.R.O.* 31/14/87, fol. 111; calendared in *C.S.P.V.*, VI, ii, no. 1075); also Paschini, *Alvise Priuli*, pp. 143ff.

[2] *Epistolae*, v, pp. 31–6 (calendared in *C.S.P.V.*, VI, iii, no. 1209).

[3] Ibid. pp. 62–5.

[4] B.M. Add. 41,577, fols. 259r–260v, *Instruttione al R.do Monsr Stella*, 10 January 1558. (Cal. in *C.S.P.V.*, VI, iii, no. 1135.)

[5] *Epistolae*, v, 32. [6] *C.S.P.V.*, VI, ii, no. 1067.

By this time, it is clear, the Pope had worked himself into a state of fury about Pole and his associates. He could think of little else but heresy; it was even rumoured that he would abandon all business except that of the Inquisition.[1] There can be no question that his rancour had been fed by the list of charges which the Inquisition had compiled on Pole; and an examination of this list reveals that Pole was seen, indeed, as the source and origin of disaffection in the Church.[2] He was the principal agent of subversion, 'doctor et complex Moroni'; his theological ideas were Lutheran;[3] he had departed from the Council of Trent rather than be present for the decree on justification;[4] and he had sheltered and encouraged a variety of heretics, including Flaminio, Priuli, Carnesecchi and Vittoria Colonna.[5] It is a sufficiently extensive range of charges to explain the Pope's anxiety to arrest Pole and confront him with Morone. It is also a significant commentary on the predicament of the surviving members of the Viterbo circle who remained in Italy.

On 8 October 1557, Carlo Gualteruzzi noted that 'il povero Monsignor Carnesecchi' had been summoned to appear at Rome.[6] Carnesecchi, however, had recourse to his protector Cosimo I, with the result that he managed to evade the call to Rome. In March 1558 he was deprived of his ecclesiastical benefices; but he escaped the scaffold for a time, until the day when, nine years later, he went to his death 'fashionably dressed in a white shirt, with a new pair of gloves and a white handkerchief in his hand as though to his wedding'.[7] Soranzo died in

---

[1] Amabile, *Il Santo Officio della Inquisizione*, p. 230.

[2] 'Compendio'. It is worth noting that while this is a record of the charges against Valdés, Pole, Morone, Priuli, Flaminio, Vittoria Colonna, Soranzo, Sanfelice, Carnesecchi and many others, the space allocated to Pole (pp. 283–6) is approximately four times larger than that devoted to any of the others (with the curious exception of Vittoria Colonna, who receives about half as much attention as Pole).

[3] 'Idem Polus defendit et nititur probare doctrinam Lutheranam de Justificatione esse veram, et improbat Theologiam Scholasticam, et persuadet purum et simplex evangelium esse praedicandum' (ibid. p. 284; cf. also p. 286).

[4] Ibid. p. 286.   [5] Ibid.

[6] Bodleian, MS Ital., C 24, fol 81r.

[7] Ortolani, *Pietro Carnesecchi*, pp. 88–93, 164–5, and Cantimori, 'Italy and the Papacy', *N.C.M.H.*, II, 267.

prison at Rome in 1559; Sanfelice was released the following year.[1] Merenda had long since fled to Switzerland. The rest of Pole's circle were in England, safe from the demands of Paul IV.[2]

But Pole's life was drawing to an end. In the spring of 1558 he fell seriously ill; by September, he knew himself to be dying.[3] Sick with quartan fever, he lasted for two further months, until 17 November. On that day, the Queen died at St James's, at seven o'clock in the morning; twelve hours later she was followed by Pole, in his palace across the river.[4] In his will he stated that he had been always loyal to the Catholic faith and to the Holy see.[5]

Carnesecchi, remarking on Pole's death, observed that 'in the eyes of the world' he had died unhappily, 'being regarded in Rome as a Lutheran and in Germany as a Papist'.[6] Carnesecchi's judgement is an apposite comment on the fortunes of the *spirituali* and their figurehead. But a more comprehensive verdict may be found in Starkey's *Dialogue*. At one point in the conversation, Pole is represented as enlarging upon the necessity for 'wyse and polytyke men' to have regard for prudence: there are moments when the advice of a wise man may be 'laughyd at, and no thyng at al hyt shold be regardyd, no more than a tale tollyd among deffe men'. Therefore 'hyt apperyth some respecte ys to be had both of tyme and of place'.[7]

The expression of a complex policy should be deferred until the opportunity exists for its fulfilment: here we may discern the guiding principle which shaped Pole's outlook, and imparted to his bearing an enigmatic air which puzzled his contemporaries,

[1] Paschini, *Tre ricerche*, pp. 150–1; Alberigo, *I vescovi italiani*, p. 225.
[2] Pate took up residence at Worcester in 1555; he was deprived of his see in 1559, imprisoned in the Tower the next year, and released in 1562. He made his way to Louvain, and died there in 1565. (*C.S.P.V.*, VIII, nos. 82 and 186; cf. also, *D.N.B.*) Priuli left England in 1559, and died, apparently on his way to Italy (Paschini, *Alvise Priuli*); Rullo left in the same year, and returned to Italy, where he was examined by the Inquisition in 1566 (Amabile, *Il Santo Officio della Inquisizione in Napoli*, p. 142). He died in prison in 1567 (de Frede, *La Restaurazione Cattolica*, p. 128). Giulia Gonzaga died in 1566. Her papers were confiscated by the Inquisition. Pius V, having seen them, is said to have declared that had she lived he would have had her burned alive. (Amabile, p. 182n.)
[3] *C.S.P.V.*, VI, iii, no. 1265. [4] Ibid. no. 1286.
[5] *Epistolae*, V, 181–7. [6] 'Processo', p. 301. [7] *Dialogue*, pp. 21–3.

and often made his actions seem at odds with his presumed intentions. His predicament in Italy was such that circumstances left him with no other choice. Hence Lupset's answer is not without a certain irony:

Wel, Master Pole, as touchyng the respecte both of tyme and place, I thynke hyt ys some thyng to be consydered...How be hyt, I thynke agayne also that theyr hys nother so much respect of tyme nother of place to be had, as many men juge, whych thynke the hyest poynt of wysdome to stond therein; and so naroly and so curyously they pondur the tyme and the place, that in al theyr lyfys they nother fynd tyme nor place.[1]

For Pole, the time and place were to have occurred at Trent. There, however, he discovered that circumstances had eluded the course devised for them by expection. As a result of this development, he was forced into an evasion of his past: a past which had itself depended on concealment as a prelude to the opportune moment which the Council would provide. But in the circumstances which existed after Trent, evasion proved to be impossible; and his discredited and abandoned ideals were turned against him in a way which left him powerless to protect himself. Like Starkey's counsellor, he found himself among deaf men.

[1] Ibid. p. 23.

Epilogue

The cause of the *spirituali* was marked by evasion and dissimulation. These are not good for a man's character. It was against a background of dissimulation sustained and accentuated over a period of twenty years that Pole returned to assume the direction of the Church in his own country, and to become the agent of a persecution which by the standards of a later age is nothing less than horrible. Morone apologised to the Jesuits for his opposition to them in the 1540s. It is difficult to imagine Pole apologising.[1] He did not easily climb down, and when honour was at stake he was insufferable. He never forgot that he was a nobleman, and the memory was compounded by the fact that he was living among foreigners. Partly character, and partly circumstance, combined to make him secretive; intransigence was his second nature, caution came first. There was in him a mixture of pride and stubborn timorousness. He kept his secret thoughts even from his closest friends. Carnesecchi and Priuli could only guess at his opinions; Contarini was bewildered by his failure to support him in his task at Regensburg. He could disappoint people. His silent and reserved deportment earned from the outset the distrust of Carafa; his very spontaneity seemed calculating to Del Monte who, having known him for years, was 'not a little taken aback' by his capacity to mix 'the subtlest art' with what appeared like 'the first thing that came into his head' – and Del Monte had spent a lifetime at the Roman Curia.

And yet despite these things, he kept his friends. In the final analysis, his virtues are more impressive than his failings. Priuli,

---

[1] 'E che! ho da scrivere una apologia?' (Above, n. 1, p. 243.)

Contarini, Flaminio, Seripando, Morone, Vittoria Colonna, saw more in him than his defects of character. Contarini was magnanimous, and could forgive; he overlooked Pole's weakness. When he disappointed people it was more usually for the sake of principle and conscience – Starkey and Vergerio are examples in point. In the most difficult times he remained loyal to his friends. He protected Carnesecchi when it was impolitic to do so. He resigned from the Inquisition, protesting when it moved against his friends, and when he might have protected himself by remaining silent. He consistently defended the memory of Flaminio, when Flaminio, being dead, might easily have been sacrificed to the more immediate and whispering counsels of expediency. Here, pride came to the assistance of instinctive loyalty; and loyalty, in the end, was his most signal virtue. It was in loyalty to More and Fisher that he allowed his convictions to overcome his anxieties both for himself and for his family, and to make the agonising choice publicly to adopt the cause in which they died.

In 1541, on learning of his mother's execution by Henry VIII, he remarked that God had given him the grace of being the son of 'one of the best and most honoured Ladies in England...but now He has wished to honour me still more, and increase my liability, because he has made me in addition the son of a martyr'.[1] In many ways his own life was a martyrdom. In 1535 he had to choose between his country, his friends, his prospects of advancement, the safety of his family, on the one hand, and what he believed to be the unity of the Church, as guaranteed in the teaching authority of the Pope; he chose the Church. In 1546–7 the consequences of that decision obliged him to choose once more between a teaching authoritatively formulated in a General Council, and his own most intimate spiritual experience; once again, he obeyed the Church. In the last years of his life he suffered the destruction of his reputation by the head of the Church for the sake of whose office he had endured both exile and the renunciation of his spiritual autonomy. He suffered without public protest. He wrote a manifesto in his own defence,

[1] Morandi, *Monumenti*, I, ii, p. 329.

and then burned it. He would not exacerbate the scandal caused by the Pope's anger by engaging in an open quarrel.

Is it surprising if a certain vehemence, a stiffness of demeanour, a more than occasional touch of self-righteousness are also elements in his character; these, and the encompassing atmosphere of evasiveness about matters which in frankness required the candid ventilation of what was in his mind? His abrupt and disturbing declarations of principle, covertly prepared, were at least directed against people who had it in their power to hurt him: Henry VIII and Julius III (who was simply a little 'taken aback', but not so much so as to lose confidence in Pole's intrinsic worth). His strategies of concealment, his evasions, were the expressions of timidity and a desire for self-protection. Self-protection meant the protection too, of others close to him – in England his family, in Italy his friends. He did not like to be unpopular. He liked a quiet life. He chose a form of life which gave him neither popularity nor the conditions of learned ease he most enjoyed: the study and the garden which he could have chosen, at the price of conscience. It might be said that he lacked moral courage in everything but the essentials, which is what makes his courage in the essentials so outstanding. He was never anything but uncomfortable as a public figure. Uneasy in office, he was at home with individuals. His capacity for friendship, and the friends he made, his gentleness and courtesy to those in difficulties – it is above all, his courtesy (which was in him a spiritual quality as much as a natural virtue) which enabled him to put others at their ease, and to assist them towards the discovery of peace of soul. Interior peace, reflected in his most intimate writings, the *De Concilio* and *De Reformatione*, was what attracted others to him, and drew them into the presence of something savouring, quite unmistakeably, of personal holiness. He was most at peace in the Benedictine settings where he had made so many of his friends; it is perhaps instructive that having resigned from the Curia he took up residence in a monastery. Perhaps he would have been happiest there. He was, quintessentially and in all things, a man of prayer.

His life was a sequence of disappointments and reversals: hated by his countrymen, living among foreigners, attacked by his co-religionists after the Council of Trent, denounced as a renegade by others who could not forgive his submission in obedience to the teaching of the Church. There was little in the external appearance of the Church to sustain, in his own lifetime, the faith he placed in her recovery. He did not live to see the final stages of the Council of Trent, which Morone's diplomacy brought to so skilful a completion, and which saw the adoption of the proposals initiated by Giberti at Verona (proposals repeated in the legislation of his own London Synod) for the better formation of a zealous priesthood. He did not live to see these proposals take root in the Milan of Borromeo and the parishes of Europe. In his own country his opportunities and aspirations were cut short by his death and by the accession of Elizabeth. The example of the persecutions, followed by the return of the Protestant exiles, succeeded only in persuading most of his fellow countrymen that John Foxe made better reading then a papal dispatch. He was remembered more kindly and to better effect at Milan and Trent, and by Beccadelli, who helped to keep his memory alive in an age when he would have been made happy by the signs of vitality and sanctity beginning to stir again throughout the Church.

Bibliography of Material Cited

PRIMARY SOURCES

MS Sources

CAMBRIDGE
University Library   Add. MS. 4876 (transcript).

LONDON
B.M.   Add. MS. 41,577.
    Harleian MS. 1763.

P.R.O.
S.P.   S.P. I/55, 105, 160, 161, 163, 164.
Transcripts   31/3/11; 31/14/87; 31/18/2/2.

NAPLES
Biblioteca Nazionale   Cod. IX A 14.

OXFORD
Bodleian Library   MSS. Italiano C 24, C 25.
Microfilm   MSS. FILM 30 of Vat. Lat. 5964 (Vatican Library).
    MSS. FILM 33 of Vat. Lat. 5968 (Vatican Library).

PARMA
Biblioteca Palatina   Cod. Pal. 1009, 1010, 1022, fasc. XI.[1]

VATICAN
Archivio Vaticano   Arch. Consist. Acta Miscell., 18.
Biblioteca Vaticana   MSS. Vat. Lat. 5964, 5968, 5969.

VIENNA
Österreichisches   MS. England, varia, fasc. IV (1555–98).
Staatsarchiv   Rom. Korresp., fasc. 9b.

VITERBO
Biblioteca Comunale   MSS. 331 II C VII, 7, 8, 10 (*Riforme* 40, 41, 43).

Printed Sources

Alberigo *et al.*, G. *Conciliorum Oecumenicorum Decreta* (Freiburg im B., 1962).

[1] In 1965 these MSS. were in the close keeping of Professor Tommaso Bozza at the Biblioteca Nazionale, Rome.

Allen, P. S. *et al. Opus Epistolarum Desiderii Erasmi Roterodami* (Oxford, 1906–58), 12 vols.

Anon. *Trattato Utilissimo del Beneficio di Iesu Cristo Crocifisso* (Venice,1543). *The Beneficio di Cristo*, translated, with an introduction by Ruth Prelowski, in *Italian Reformation Studies*, ed. John A. Tedeschi (Florence, 1965), pp. 21–102.

Ascham, R. *Whole Works*, I, ii (ed. Dr Giles, London, 1865).

Atanagi, D. *De le lettere de tredici uomini illustri* (Rome, 1554).

Babington, C. *The Benefit of Christ's Death* (Cambridge and London, 1855).

The Beneficio di Cristo see under Anon.

The Bible in Englyshe (Rouen, 1566).

Brieger, T. 'Aus italienischen Archiven und Bibliateken', *Zeitschrift für Kirchengeschichte*, V (1882), 574–622.

Calendar of Letters, Despatches and State Papers relating to the Negotiations between England and Spain, ed. G. A. Bergenroth *et al.* (London, 1862–1954), 13 vols and 2 supplements.

Calendar of State Papers and Manuscripts, Relating to English Affairs, existing in the Archives and Collections of Venice, vols. IV–VII, ed. Rawdon Brown (London, 1871–90).

Calvin, J. *Excuse de Jehan Calvin, a Messieurs les Nicodemites sur la complaincte qu'ilz font de sa trop grand' rigueur* (*Three French Treatises*, ed. F. M. Higman, London, 1970).

Camerario, A. *Epistolae aliquot M. Antonii Flaminii* (Nuremberg, 1571).

Casadei, A. 'Lettere del cardinale Gasparo Contarini durante la sua legazione di Bologna (1532)', *Archivio storico italiano*, CXVIII (1960), 77–130, 220–85.

Catharino, A. *Compendio d'errori et inganni luterani autore, intitolato Trattato utilissimo del beneficio di Cristo crocifisso* (Rome, 1544).

Concilium Tridentinum: Diariorum, Actorum, Epistolarum, Tractatuum Nova Collectio, ed. S. Merkle *et al.* (Freiburg im B., 1901ff).

Corpus Catholicorum, VII, ed. F. Hünermann (Münster in Westphallen, 1923).

Corpus Reformatorum, IV, ed. C. Gottlieb Bretschneider (Halle, 1837).

Cortese, G. *Gregorius Cortesius Card. Omnia quae huc usque colligi potuerunt, sive ab eo scripta, sive ad illum spectantia*, ed. A. Cominus (Padua, 1774).

Corviersi, C. 'Compendio di processi del Santo Uffizio di Roma', *Archivio della Società Romana di Storia Patria*, III (1880), 261–91, and 449–73.

Costa, E. 'Marc Antonio Flaminio e il cardinale Alessandro Farnese', *Giornale storico della Letteratura Italiana*, x (Turin, 1887), 384–7.

Crehan, J. 'St Ignatius and Cardinal Pole', documents and commentary, *Archivium Historicum Societatis Iesu*, xxv (1956), 72–98.

Dittrich, F. *Regesten und Briefe des Kardinals Gasparo Contarini* (Braunsberg, 1881).

Druffel, A. von *Beiträge zur Reichsgeschichte 1546–51* (Munich, 1873). *Karl V und die römische Curie 1544–6*, 3 vols (Munich, 1887–93).

Erasmus, D. *Opera Omnia*, 10 vols. (Leyden, 1703–6).

Ferrero E. and Muller, G. *Carteggio di Vittoria Colonna* (Turin, 1889).

Flaminio, M. *De Rebus Divinis Carmina* (Paris, 1550).

Foxe, John. *The Acts and Monuments of John Foxe. With a life...and vindication of the work*, ed. G. Townsend (London, 1843–9, 8 vols.).

Friedensburg, W. 'Beiträge zum Briefwechsel der katholischen Gelehrten Deutschlands im Reformationszeitalter', *Zeitschrift für Kirchengeschichte*, xviii (1898), 233–97, 420–63, 596–636.

'Das Consilium de emendenda ecclesia, Kardinal Sadolet und Johann Sturm von Strassburg', *Archiv für Reformationgeschichte*, xxxiii (1936), 1–69.

Gasquet, F. A. *Cardinal Pole and his Early Friends* (London, 1927).

Gee, J. A. *Life and Works of Thomas Lupset* (New Haven, 1928).

Gibbings, R. *Report of the Trial and Martyrdom of Pietro Carnesecchi* (Dublin, 1856).

Jedin, H. 'Contarini und Camaldoli', *Archivio italiano per la storia della pietà*, ii (1959), 51–117.

Kausler, E. von and Schott, K. (ed.). *Briefwechsel zwischen Christoph Herzog von Württemberg und P. P. Vergerius* (Tübingen, 1875).

Le Plat, J. *Monumentorum ad historiam Concilii Tridentini potissimum illustrandam spectantium amplissima collectio*, iii (Louvain, 1783).

Letters and Papers, Foreign and Domestic, of the Reign of Henry VIII, ed. J. S. Brewer and J. Gairdner (London, 1862–1910), 21 vols. in 33 parts.

Longolius, C. *Orationes duae...Longolii vita* (Florence, 1524; facsimile reprint, Gregg Press, Farnborough, Hants., 1967).

Manzoni, G. (ed.). 'Estratto del processo di Mons. Pietro Carnesecchi', *Miscellanea di Storia Italiana*, x (1870), 187–573.

Melanchthon, P. *Confessio Fidei exhibita invictiss. imp. Carolo Caesari Aug. in Comiciis Augustae Anno M.D.XXX. Addita est Apologia confessionis* (Augsburg, 1535).

Monti, G. M. *Ricerche su Papa Paolo IV Carafa* (Benevento, 1923).

Morandi, L. *Monumenti di varia letteratura tratti dai manoscritti di Mons. Beccadelli* (Bologna, 1797–1804, 2 vols. in 3 parts).

Morone. *Difesa*, see Cantiù, C. *Gli eretici* (secondary sources).

Nuntiaturberichte aus Deutschland, Abt. 1 (1533–59) (ed. German Historical Institute in Rome, Gotha, 1892 ff: in progress).

Paladino, G. *Opuscoli e Lettere di Riformatori Italiani del Cinquecento* (Bari, 1913).

Parks, G. B. 'The Parma Letters and the Dangers to Cardinal Pole', *Catholic Historical Review*, XVI (1960–1), 299–317.

Pelikan, J. and Lehmann, H. *Luther's Works* (Philadelphia, 1958–9), 55 vols.

Piccolomini, P. 'Documenti Vaticani sull' eresia in Sienna durante il secolo XVI', *Bulletino Senese di storia patria*, XV, 1908, 295–305.

Pole, R. *Pro ecclesiasticae unitatis defensione, libri quatuor* (Rome, *c.* 1537; facsimile reprint, Farnborough, Hants., 1965).

    Défénse de l' Unité de l'Eglise, ed. and trans. N.M. Egretier (Paris, 1967).

    Pole's Defense of the Unity of the Church (Westminster, Maryland, 1965), ed. and trans. J. G. Dwyer.

    Discorso di Pace (*s.l.*, *c.* 1554–5).

    De Concilio liber. Ejusdem De baptismo Constanti...Imperatoris. Reformatio Angliae ex decretis eiusdem (Rome and Venice, 1562)

    De Summo Pontifice (Louvain, 1569).

    Epistolae Reginaldi Poli S.R.E. Cardinalis et Aliorum ad Ipsum, ed. A. M. Quirini (Brescia, 1744–57, 5 vols.).

    See also under Vergerio.

Schelhorn, J. G. *Amoenitates Historiae Ecclesiasticae* (Frankfurt and Leipzig, 1737–8, 2 vols.).

Starkey, T. *A Dialogue between Reginald Pole and Thomas Lupset*, ed. J. Cowper, in E. Herrtage, ed., *England in the Reign of Henry VIII* (London, E.E.T.S., 1878). Another edition edited by K. Burton (London, 1948).

Strype, J. *Ecclesiastical Memorials relating Chiefly to Religion...under King Henry VIII, King Edward VI, and Queen Mary I* (Oxford, 1822, 3 vols. each in 2 parts).

Tacchi Venturi, P. *Storia della Compagnia di Gesù in Italia*, I, ii (*Documenti*) (3rd edn, Rome, 1950).

Tellechea Idigoras, J. I. 'Pole y Paulo IV: Una célebre Apologia inédita del Cardenal Inglés (1557)', *Archivium Historiae Pontificiae*, IV (1966) 105–54.

'Una denuncia de los Cardenales Contarini, Pole y Morone por el Cardenal Francisco Mendoza (1560)', *Revista Española de Teología*, XXVII (1967), 33–51.

A Treatie of Iustification. Founde emong the writinges of Cardinal Pole of blessed memorie, remaining in the custodie of M. Henrie Pyning, Chamberlaine and General Receuier to the said Cardinal, late deceased in Louaine (Louvain, 1569).

Valdés, Juan de. *XVII Opuscules by Juan de Valdés*, translated and edited from the Spanish and Italian by John T. Betts (London, 1882).

The Hundred and Ten Considerations of Juan de Valdés, translated and edited from the Italian by John T. Betts, in Benjamin B. Wiffen, *Life and Writings of Juan de Valdés* (London, 1885).

Vergerio, P. P. *Il catalogo de libri, li quali nuovamente nele mese di Maggio nel anno presente 1549 sono stati condonnati...e aggiunto...un indicio e discorso del Vergerio* (s.l., 1549).

Giudicio soprà le lettere di tredici huomini illustri publicate da M. Dionigi Atanagi & stampate in Venetia nel l'anno 1554.

Oratio R. Poli, qua Caesaris animum accendere conatur & inflammare... cum scholiis Athanasii (published anonymously, 1554, s.l., but Augsburg?).

Epistolae duae, duorum amicorum, ex quibus uana, flagitiosaque Pontificum, Paulitertii, & Iulii tertii, & Cardinalis Poli, & Stephani Gardineri... eorumque adulatorum sectatorumque ratio, magna ex parte potest intelligi (published anonymously, s.a., s.l., but 1555).

(ed.). *Reginaldi Poli...pro Ecclesiasticae unitatis defensione libri quatuor* (Strasburg, 1555).

Articuli contra Cardinalem Moronum, de Luteranismo accusatum, et in carcerum coniectum (s.l., c. 1557–8).

Wilkins, D. (ed.).*Concilia Magnae Britanniae et Hiberniae ab anno MDXLVI ad annum MDCCXVII*, 4 vols. (London, 1737).

SECONDARY SOURCES

Unprinted

Fischer, J. 'Essai Historique sur les Idées Reformatrices des Cardinaux Jean Pierre Carafa (1476–1559) et Reginald Pole (1500–58)' (Doctoral dissertation submitted to the University of Paris, 1957).

Franck, B. 'Reginald Pole' (unpublished essay).

Printed

Alberigo, G. *I vescovi italiani al concilio di Trento* (Florence, 1959).
'Carlo Borromeo come modello di vescovo nella Chiesa post tridentina', *Rivista Storica italiana*, LXXIX (1967), 1031–52.

Amabile, L. *Il Santo Officio della Inquisizione in Napoli* (Citta di Castello, 1892).

Ancel, R. 'La reconciliation de l'Angleterre avec le Saint Siège sous Marie Tudor: Legation du Cardinal Polus en Angleterre (1553–4)', *Revue d'historie ecclesiastique*, X (1909), 520–36, and 744–98.

Bainton, R. 'Four Reviews', *Italian Reformation Studies in Honor of Laelius Socinus*, ed. John A. Tedeschi (Florence, 1965).

Bakhuizen van den Brink, J. N. *Juan de Valdés réformateur en Espagne et en Italie* (Geneva, 1969).

Bataillon, M. *Erasme et l'Espagne* (Paris, 1937).

Becker, W. *Immanuel Tremellius* (2nd edn, Leipzig, 1890).

Bowker, M. *The Secular Clergy in the Diocese of Lincoln* (Cambridge, 1968).

Bozza, T. *Introduzione al Beneficio di Cristo* (privately printed, Rome, 1963).

Buschbell, G. *Reformation und Inquisition in Italien um die Mitte des XVI. Jahrhunderts* (Paderborn, 1910).

Bussi, *Istoria della città di Viterbo* (2nd edn, Rome, 1743).

Cantimori, D. *Eretici italiani del Cinquecento* (Florence, 1939).
'La Riforma in Italia', *Problemi storici e orientamenti storiografici* (Como, 1942).
'Italy and the Papacy' (*N.C.M.H.*, II, 251–74).
'L'Influence du manifeste de Charles Quint contre Clement VII (1526) et de quelques documents similaires de la litterature philo-protestante et anticuriale d'Italie', *Charles Quint et son Temps* (Paris, 1959), 133–41.
'Nicodemismo e speranze conciliari nel cinquecento italiano', *Studi di Storia* (Turin, 1959), 518–36. Translated in E. Cochrane (ed.), *The Late Italian Renaissance* (London, 1970).

Cantù, C. *Gli eretici d'Italia* (Turin, 1865–6, 3 vols.).

Caponetto, S. 'Benedetto da Mantova' (*Dizionario Biografico Degli Italiani*, VIII, Rome, 1966, 437–41).

Caracciolo, A. *Vita Pauli IV* (Cologne, 1612).

Cessi, R. 'Paolinismo preluterano', *Rendiconti dell' Accademia nazionale dei Lincei*, Cl. di sc. mor. sto. e filol., ser. VIII, vol. XII (1957), 3–30.

Church, F. C. *The Italian Reformers* (New York, 1932).

Cistellini, A. *Figure della Riforma Pretridentina* (Brescia, 1948).

Crehan, J. 'St Ignatius and Cardinal Pole', *Archivium Historicum Societatis Iesu*, XXV (1956), 72–98.

de Frede, C. *La Restaurazione Cattolica in Inghilterra sotto Maria Tudor* (Naples, 1971).

De Maio, R. *Savonarola e la Curia Romana* (Rome, 1969).

Dickens, A. G. *The English Reformation* (London, 1964).

Dionisotti, C. 'Monumenti Beccadelli', *Miscellanea Pio Paschini*, II (Rome, 1949), 251–68.

Dittrich, F. *Gasparo Contarini* (Braunsberg, 1885).

Douglas, R. M. *Jacopo Sadoleto* (Cambridge, Mass., 1959).

Ebeling, G. *Luther* (Tübingen, 1964, Eng. trans., London and Philadelphia, 1970).

Elton, G. R. 'Reform by Statute: Thomas Starkey's Dialogue and Thomas Cromwell's Policy', *Proceedings of the British Academy*, 54 (1968), 165–88.

Evennett, H. O. 'Three Benedictine Abbots at the Council of Trent 1545–7', *Studia Monastica*, I (1959), 343–77.

Fèbvre, L. *Le problème de l'incroyance au XVIe siècle; la religion de Rabelais* (Paris, 1947).

Fenlon, D. 'The Counter Reformation and the Realisation of *Utopia*', *Historical Studies: Papers Read to the Ninth Conference of Irish Historians* ed. J. Barry, 9 (Dublin, 1973).

Ferrara, O. *Gasparo Contarini et Ses Missions* (translated from Spanish by Francis de Miomandre, Paris, 1956).

Gilbert, F. 'Cristianesimo, Umanesimo e la Bolla "Apostolici Regiminis"', *Rivista Storica Italiana*, 79 (1967), 976–90.

'Religion and Politics in the Thought of Gasparo Contarini', *Action and Conviction in Early Modern Europe: Essays in Memory of E. H. Harbison*, ed. T. K. Raab and J. E. Seigel (Princeton, 1969) pp. 90–116.

Ginzburg, C. 'Due note sul profetismo Cinquecentesco' *Rivista storica italiana*, LXXVIII (1966), 184–227.

Il nicodemismo (Turin, 1970).

Gleason, E. G. 'Sixteenth Century Italian Interpretations of Luther', *Archiv für Reformationgeschichte*, 60 (1969), 160–73.

Haile, M. *The Life of Reginald Pole* (2nd edn, London, 1911).

Hall, B. 'The Colloquies between Catholics and Protestants, 1539–41',

Studies in Church History, VII, ed. G. J. Cuming and D. Baker (Cambridge, 1971), 235–66.

Headley, J. 'Thomas More and Luther's Revolt', *Archiv für Reformationgeschichte*, 60 (1969), 145–59.

Heath, P. *The English Parish Clergy on the Eve of the Reformation* (London and Toronto, 1969).

Hubert, F. *Vergerio's publizistische Thätigkeit nebst einer bibliographischen Ubersicht* (Göttingen, 1893).

Hughes, P. *The Reformation in England* (3 vols., London, 1950–4).
Rome and the Counter Reformation in England (London, 1942).

Imbart de la Tour, P. *Les Origines de la Réforme*, III *L'Evangélisme* (Paris, 1914).

Jayne, S. *John Colet and Marsilio Ficino* (Oxford, 1963).

Jedin, H. *Girolamo Seripando* (Würzburg, 1937, 2 vols.; Eng. edn, London, 1947).
A History of the Council of Trent, vols. I, II (London, 1957, 1961).
Geschichte des Konzils von Trient, vol. III (Freiburg im B., 1970).
'Gasparo Contarini e il Contributo Veneziano alla Riforma Cattolica', *La Civilta Veneziana del Rinascimento* (Florence, 1958), 103–24. (Vol. IV of *Storia della Civiltà veneziana* (*Conferenze*), published by Fondazione Giorgio Cini, 1955ff).
Kirche des Glaubens Kirche der Geschichte: ausgewahlte Aufsatze und Vortage (Freiburgim B., 1966, 2 vols.).

Jung, E. M. 'On the Nature of Evangelism in Sixteenth-Century Italy', *Journal of the History of Ideas*, XIV (1953), 511–27.

Küng, H. *Justification* (4th edn, Einsiedeln, 1957, Eng. trans. London, 1964).

Knowles, D. *The Religious Orders in England*, III, *The Tudor Age* (Cambridge, 1959).

Loades, D. *The Oxford Martyrs* (London, 1970).

Leclercq, J. *Un humaniste érémite, le bienheureux P. Giustiniani, 1476–1528* (Rome, 1951).
Alone with God (London, 1962).

Logan, O. M. T. 'Grace and Justification: Some Italian Views of the Sixteenth and Early Seventeenth Centuries', *The Journal of Ecclesiastical History*, 20 (1969), 67–78.

Longhurst, J. *Erasmus and the Spanish Inquisition: the case of Juan de Valdés* (Albuquerque, 1950).

Lortz, H. *The Reformation in Germany* (2 vols., London, 1968).

Lovatt, R. 'The *Imitation of Christ* in late Medieval England', *Transactions of the Royal Historical Society*, 5th ser., 18 (1968), 97–121.

Lutz, H. *Ragione di Stato und Christliche Staatsethik im 16. Jahrhundert* (Munster, 1961).

Christianitas afflicta. Europa, das Reich und die papstliche Politik im Niedergang der Hegemonie Kaiser Karls V (1552–1556) (Göttingen, 1964).

Luzio, A. 'Vittoria Colonna', *Rivista storica mantovana*, I (1885), 1–52.

Mackensen, H. 'The Diplomatic Role of Gasparo Cardinal Contarini at the Colloquy of Ratisbon of 1541', *Church History*, XXVII (1958), 312–37.

'Contarini's Theological Role at Ratisbon in 1541', *Archiv für Reformationgeschichte*, LI (1960), 36–49.

Maddison, C. *Marcantonio Flaminio: Poet, Humanist and Reformer* (London, 1965).

Mann, M. *Erasme et les debuts de la réforme francaise, 1517–1536* (Paris, 1933).

Matheson, P. *Cardinal Contarini at Regensburg* (Oxford, 1972).

McConica, J. K. *English Humanists and Reformation Politics* (Oxford, 1965).

McNair, P. *Peter Martyr in Italy. An Anatomy of Apostasy* (Oxford, 1967).

Meyer, H. 'Die deutschen Protestanten an der zweiten Tagunsperiode des Konzils von Trient 1551–2', *Archiv für Reformationsgeschichte*, LVI (1965), 166–209.

New Cambridge Modern History, II (ed. G. R. Elton, Cambridge, 1958).

Nicolini, B. *Ideali e passioni nell' Italia religiosa del Cinquecento* (Bologna, 1962).

Nieto, J. C. *Juan de Valdés and the Origins of the Spanish and Italian Reformation* (Geneva, 1970).

O'Donohue, J. *Tridentine Seminary Legislation, its Sources and its Formation* (Louvain, 1957).

'The Seminary Legislation of the Council of Trent', *Il Concilio di Trento e la Riforma Tridentina. Atti del Convegno Storico Internazionale, Trento 2–6 Settembre 1963*, 2 vols. (Rome, 1965), I, 157–72.

Ortolani, O. *Pietro Carnesecchi* (Florence, 1963).

'The hopes of the Italian reformers in Roman Action', *Italian Reformation Studies in Honor of Laelius Socinus*, ed. John A. Tedeschi (Florence, 1965), 11–20.

Parks, G. B. 'The Reformation and the Hospice', in *The English Hospice in Rome: The Venerabile Sexcentenary Issue*, vol. XXI (May 1962, printed at the Catholic Records Press, Exeter), pp. 193–217.

Pas, P. 'La doctrine de la double justice au Concile de Trente', *Ephemerides Theologiae Lovanienses*, XXX (1954), 5–53.

Paschini, P. *Un Amico del Cardinale Polo: Alvise Priuli* (Rome, 1921).
Pier Paolo Vergerio il giovane e la sua apostasia (Rome, 1925).
Tre ricerche sulla storia della chiesa nel cinquecento (Rome, 1945).
Venezia e l'inquisizione Romana da Giulio III a Pio IV (Padua, 1959).

Pastor, L. von *History of the Popes*, vols. X–XIV (London, 1910–24).

Phillips, T. *A History of the Life of Reginald Pole* (2nd edn, London, 1767).

Pommier, E. 'La societé vénitienne et la réforme protestante au XVIᵉ siecle', *Bollentino dell' Istituto di Storia della Società e dello Stato Veneziano*, I (1959), 3–26.

Post, R. R. *The Modern Devotion: confrontation with Reformation and Humanism* (Leiden, 1968).

Prosperi, A. *Tra Evangelismo e Controriforma: G. M. Giberti* (Rome, 1969).

Raab, T. K. and Seigel, J. E. (ed.). *Action and Conviction in Early Modern Europe: Essays in Memory of E. H. Harbison* (Princeton, 1969).

Ranke, L. von *History of the Popes* (London, 1908, 3 vols.).

Renaudet, A. *Préréforme et humanisme à Paris pendant les premieres guerres d'Italie (1494–1517)* (Paris, 1916).

Ricart, D. *Juan de Valdés y el pensamiento religioso europeo de los siglos XVI-XVII* (Mexico, 1958).

Rotondò, A. 'Atteggiamenti Della Vita Morale Italiana Del Cinquecento: La Pratica Nicodemitica', *Rivista Storica Italiana*, 79 (1967), 991–1030.
'Per la Storia dell' eresia a Bologna nel secolo XVI', *Rinascimento*, 13 (1962), 107–56.

Rupp, G. *The Righteousness of God. Luther studies* (London, 2nd impression, 1963).

Scarisbrick, J. J. *Henry VIII* (London, 1968).

Schenk, W. *Reginald Pole, Cardinal of England* (London, 1950).

Screech, M. *The Rabelaisian Marriage* (London, 1958).
L'Evangélisme de Rabelais (Geneva, 1959).
Marot Evangélique (Geneva, 1967).

Seebohm, F. *The Oxford Reformers* (3rd ed., London, 1887).

Signorelli, G. *Viterbo nella storia della Chiesa*, III, ii (Viterbo, 1940).

Spitz, L. 'Particularism and Peace: Ausgburg 1555', *Church History*, XXV (1956), 110–26.

Sta Teresa, D. de *Juan de Valdés 1498(?)–1541, Su pensamiento religioso y las corrientes espirituales de su tiempo* (Rome, 1957).

Stella, A. 'Guida da Fano, eretico del XVI secolo, al servizio dei re d'Inghilterra', *Rivista di Storia della Chiesa in Italia*, XIII (Rome, 1959), 196–238.

'La Lettera del Cardinale Contarini sulla Predestinazione', *Rivista di Storia della Chiesa in Italia*, XV (1961), 411–41.

Tacchi Venturi, P. *Storia del Compagnia di Gesù in Italia*, 2 vols. in 2 parts (3rd edn, Rome, 1950–1).

Tedeschi, J. A. (ed.). *Italian Reformation Studies in Honor of Laelius Socinus* (Florence, 1965).

Tellechea Idigoras, J. I. 'El formulario de vista pastoral de Bartolomé de Carranza', *Anthologioa Annua*, IV (1956), 385–437.

Bartolomé Carranza y la Restauraciõn Católica Inglesa (1554–1558) (Rome, 1964).

Toussaert, J. *Le sentiment religieux en Flandre à la fin du Moyen Age* (Paris, 1963).

Tucker, M. A. 'Gian Matteo Giberti, Papal Politician and Catholic Reformer', *English Historical Review*, 18 (1903), 24–51, 266–86, 439–69.

Vinay, V. 'La Riforma in Croazia e in Slovenia e il "Beneficio di Cristo" ', *Bolletino della Società di Studi Valdesi*, CXVI (1964), 19–32.

'Die Schrift "Il Beneficio di Giesu Christo" und ihre Verbreitung in Europa nach der neuen Forschung', *Archiv für Reformationgeschichte*, LVIII (1967), 29–72.

Wormald, B. H. G. 'The Historiography of the English Reformation', *Historical Studies: Papers read to the first conference of Irish Historians*, ed. T. W. Moody and T. D. Williams, I (London, 1958), 50–8.

Zeeveld, W. G. *The Foundations of Tudor Policy* (Cambridge, Mass., 1948).

Zimmermann, A. *Kardinal Pole, sein Leben und seine Schriften* (Regensburg, 1893).

Zonta, G. 'Francesco Negri l'eretico e la sua tragedia "Il libero arbitrio" ', *Giornale storico della letteratura italiana*, LXVII–LXVIII (1916), 263–324 and 108–60.

Index